Global Intellectual Property L

For Nicholas-Sejong and Oliver Kailash

Global Intellectual Property Law

Graham Dutfield

Professor of International Governance, School of Law, University of Leeds, UK

Uma Suthersanen

Reader in Intellectual Property Law and Policy, School of Law, Queen Mary, University of London, UK

Edward Elgar
Cheltenham, UK • Northampton, MA, USA

Published by
Edward Elgar Publishing Limited
The Lypiatts
15 Lansdown Road
Cheltenham
Glos GL50 2JA
UK

Edward Elgar Publishing, Inc.
William Pratt House
9 Dewey Court
Northampton
Massachusetts 01060
USA

A catalogue record for this book
is available from the British Library

Library of Congress Cataloguing in Publication Data

Dutfield, Graham.
    Global intellectual property law / by Graham Dutfield, Uma Suthersanen.
        p. cm.
    Includes bibliographical references and index.
    1. Intellectual property (International law) I. Suthersanen, Uma. II. Title.
    K1401.D88 2008
    346.04´8—dc22

                                                                2008023871

ISBN 978 1 84376 942 2 (cased)
ISBN 978 1 84720 364 9 (paperback)

Typeset by Cambrian Typesetters, Camberley, Surrey
Printed and bound in Great Britain by MPG Books Ltd, Bodmin, Cornwall

Contents

Preface

Intellectual property plays an increasingly vital role in global trade and economic development. Globalisation of trade means that intangible informational resources are now produced, exchanged and consumed anywhere and everywhere defying jurisdictional borders. Intellectual property has moved into the mainstream of national economic and developmental planning; in the recent past it has also emerged as a central element of multilateral trade relations.

The remits of intellectual property are being constantly pushed wider to include new subject matter. This is not surprising given the constant changes in socio-economic conditions, technology and market opportunities. Even the way intellectual property is conceived changes over time. Patents and copyright originated out of monopoly privileges granted by monarchs to traders, manufacturers and artisans. In time, they were seen as a form of personal property granted to inventors and authors. While to some extent they still are, it is probably more accurate to portray intellectual property rights as a class of intangible business asset that is usually held by companies performing the (admittedly important) roles in the modern economy of investor, employer, distributor and marketer. Individual creators are less and less frequently the ones owning and controlling the rights. These trends bring to the fore the issue of whether and to what extent intellectual property rights clash with current norms relating to human rights, economic governance, fairness and efficiency. Increasingly, then, intellectual property finds itself at the centre of debates on how human society and the resources upon which our well-being depends should best be organised to achieve just and effective outcomes. Thus, we see demands from indigenous peoples for proprietary protection of their ancestral knowledge, protests about the perceived approval of genetically engineered products through the aegis of patent laws, campaigns to improve access to life-saving drugs, criticisms of the alleged anti-development biases of current intellectual property rule-making, and calls for protecting one's dignity and persona through copyright and trade mark law.

This book on global intellectual property offers international and comparative perspectives on intellectual property law and policy. It examines the evolving impact of intellectual property on the international stage, especially in respect of trade, economics and culture. As such, it is by necessity *inter-disciplinary*. A focal point is the analysis of the philosophical, political and socio-economic parameters within which intellectual property producers and consumers operate. In our view, the complex, interactive and conflict-ridden nature of the globalisation process must inevitably force us to 're-learn' how to learn intellectual property law. Instead of the conventional formalistic learning method in which we must choose whether to focus on national, regional or international law, in this book we cover all three.

This book is our attempt, then, to make the study of global law and policy of intellectual property transcend disciplinary carbuncles such as territorially based case studies or statutes. In our view, no single jurisdiction, however important or influential it may be, can possibly be treated as representing all other jurisdictions or even any single one. While there is much similarity in intellectual property law, and the forces favouring harmonisation are very strong, divergent forces operate too as countries seek to translate (or mistranslate) international obligations in ways that further domestic economic interests. It is not a foregone conclusion that the harmonisers will win.

The present volume is the result of teaching in and research for the University of London's LLM programme on Global Policy and Economics of Intellectual Property Law which has been running successfully for several years. It comprises a comprehensive commentary on international intellectual property law primarily targeted at postgraduate-level students. The case selection is thematic rather than geographical, and is culled primarily from international and supranational jurisprudence (that is, the EU and the WTO), and where relevant, other national higher courts.

Graham Dutfield
Centre for International Governance, School of Law, University of Leeds

Uma Suthersanen
School of Law, Queen Mary, University of London

Acronyms

A2K	Access to Knowledge
AIPPI	Association Internationale pour la Protection de la Propriété Industrielle (International Association for the Protection of Industrial Property)
ALAI	Association Littéraire et Artistique Internationale
BIRPI	Bureaux Internationaux Réunis de la Protection de la Propriété Intellectuelle (International Bureaux)
CBD	Convention on Biological Diversity
CII	Computer-implemented invention
COP	Conference of the Parties to the Convention on Biological Diversity
CTM	Community Trade Mark
CTMR	Community Trade Marks Regulation
DIA	Development Impact Assessment
DMCA	Digital Millennium Copyright Act
DNA	Deoxyribonucleic acid
DRM	Digital rights management
ECJ	European Court of Justice
EPC	European Patent Convention
EPO	European Patent Office
FAO	Food and Agriculture Organization of the United Nations
FDA	Food and Drug Administration
FTA	Free trade agreement
GATT	General Agreement on Tariffs and Trade
GIs	Geographical indications
ICANN	Internet Corporation for Assigned Names and Numbers
ICCPR	International Covenant on Civil and Political Rights
ICESCR	International Covenant on Economic, Social and Cultural Rights
ICTSD	International Centre for Trade and Sustainable Development
IGC	Intergovernmental Committee on Intellectual Property and Genetic Resources, Traditional Knowledge and Folklore (of WIPO)
IPRs	Intellectual property rights
LDCs	Least-developed countries

MDGs	Millennium Development Goals
NGO	Non-governmental organization
OECD	Organisation of Economic Co-operation and Development
OHIM	Office for Harmonisation in the Internal Market
PLT	Patent Law Treaty
pma	*post mortem auctoris*
PVP	Plant variety protection
RNA	Ribonucleic acid
SME	Small and medium-sized enterprise
SPC	Supplementary protection certificate
TBA	Technical Board of Appeal (of the European Patent Office)
TK	Traditional knowledge
TPMs	Technological protection measures
TRIPS	Agreement on Trade-related Aspects of Intellectual Property Rights
UCC	Universal Copyright Convention
UDHR	Universal Declaration of Human Rights
UNCTAD	United Nations Conference on Trade and Development
UNDP	United Nations Development Programme
UNESCO	United Nations Educational, Scientific and Cultural Organization
UPOV	Union Internationale pour la Protection des Obtentions Végétales (International Union for the Protection of New Varieties of Plants)
USDA	United States Department of Agriculture
USPTO	United States Patent and Trademark Office
USTR	United States Trade Representative
WCT	WIPO Copyright Treaty
WHO	World Health Organization
WIPO	World Intellectual Property Organization
WPPT	WIPO Performers and Phonograms Treaty
WTO	World Trade Organization

PART I

The status quo and its origins

1. The globalisation of intellectual property

GLOBALISATION AND LAW

Globalisation is a process, or a series of processes, which create and consolidate a unified world economy, a single ecological system and a complex and dynamic network of communications that covers the world.[1] The world, thus, is interdependent and becoming ever more de-territorialized. Geographical, social and political boundaries definitely do not disappear but they are eroding.

In understanding globalisation processes, an important distinction to bear in mind is that between localised globalism and globalised localism, which shows that globalisation occurs in opposing directions often with great tensions between the two.[2] Localised globalism focuses on the recipients, who may be victims or beneficiaries depending on your standpoint. Globalised localism concentrates on the standard-setters, often situated in a small number of places. These are the ones who set the rules the rest of the world ends up following.

Let us look at these terms in more detail before proceeding. Globalised localism occurs when a local phenomenon is successfully globalised, for example, the English language, Coca-Cola, or EU or American copyright laws. Much usage of the concept of 'globalisation' concentrates on this phenomenon. Often, the entire process of international policy-making, negotiation, dialogue, rule-making, implementation and enforcement is driven by globalised localism.

Localised globalism refers to the situation when local conditions change and adapt to international and transnational influences. Examples include recognising increasingly international concerns about the environment, and changing local attitudes to deforestation or use of resources. The domestic implementation of the World Trade Organization's Agreement on Trade-related Aspects of Intellectual Property Rights (TRIPS) Agreement, for example, is an example of localised globalism whereby general principles recognised in a majority of countries force the remaining nations to change their laws or policies on intellectual property. A threat in this situation is that the local laws may be dispensed with and the local context completely disregarded.

This is all rather black and white. Perhaps a more correct term would be 'sustainable localised globalism' whereby some practical local structures, norms, traditions and practices are retained. This would better reflect what so often happens when international laws are interpreted in the light of local conditions. In the British colonial era, for instance, the Privy Council always stressed that British laws had to be adapted to the local conditions.

Notwithstanding this more nuanced interpretation of globalisation, developing countries implementing new multilateral or bilateral intellectual property agreements find their interpretative scope concerning rights, exceptions and limitations curtailed or limited to how the EU or the US interprets the treaties. We would argue that instead of automatically adopting the EU or US interpretations of certain international intellectual property provisions, it would be far better for countries to craft their rights, exceptions and limitations as they see fit, as long as their interpretations of these are consistent with their international obligations. The trouble is that the EU and US sometimes intervene and discourage them in various ways from doing so.

The complex way that intellectual property law is made, is subsequently 'traded' in the form, for example, of 'you "buy" our patent law and we'll buy more of your wine' types of transaction, and the contested nature of the rights granted requires us look at the law from all perspectives – local, regional, global and also holistic. One consequence of such a multi-faceted approach is that we are bound to encounter clashes between national, transnational, international, customary and social-economic rules as they relate to specific objects, works and ideas.

We may also find tensions between the rules, and even *within* them. For instance, an intellectual property right may be granted to a corporation in a symbol, but such legal protection may ignore the possible fact that a group of people has legitimate claims to the same symbol under non-international, customary law. Thus, to Rightholder A what the law is providing is an economic right. To Rightholder B, what she or he may seek to secure is a religious or cultural right, which may include the subsidiary right to prohibit any commercial activity relating to the symbol. Whose rights should take precedence? Traditional analyses of national intellectual property laws tend to dismiss such clashes as miscellaneous or esoteric concerns that are barely worth discussing. Nevertheless, as usage of the internet and the ensuing problems caused by file-sharing show, clashes of interests, rights and freedoms, including cross-cultural ones, are likely to become more serious. We should not be surprised that this is happening. In the wider world, tensions between private property, human rights, religion and mammon continually create sparks, some of which turn into conflagrations.

To make the situation even more tricky, current studies of the law tend to overlook the tensions inherent in the very basis of the legal entitlements provided under a given intellectual property right. This is particularly notice-able in the case of copyright. In some jurisdictions, copyright is mostly an economic right vested mainly in corporations. In others, copyright (or more accurately, author's rights) continues to be oriented around a set of moral rights vested in individual authors and artists. But in no country is the copy-right purely economic or purely moral in nature. Frequently the result is confusing and internally inconsistent law.

'A COMPETITION OF INTELLECT'?

The current conventional wisdom is that the world's most successful nations are those best at producing, acquiring, deploying and controlling valuable knowledge. Knowledge, especially new knowledge unavailable to one's rivals, is key to international competitiveness and therefore to national pros-perity. However clichéd such a view may be, the fact is that many policy-makers believe it to be true and are acting accordingly. As the United Kingdom government expresses it, for example, 'intellectual property is a critical component of our present and future success in the global economy'. Moreover, it asserts, the economic competitiveness of the UK as of its competitors 'is increasingly driven by knowledge-based industries, especially in manufacturing, science-based sectors and the creative industries'.[3]

But can intellectual property ever outpace tangible property as a funda-mental base of modern economies? According to some quite influential people it definitely can. Alan Greenspan, former Chairman of the Board of Governors of the US Federal Reserve, had this to say in his speech inaugurating the 2003 Financial Markets Conference of the Federal Reserve Bank of Atlanta:

> In recent decades . . . the fraction of the total output of our economy that is essen-tially conceptual rather than physical has been rising . . . Over the past half century, the increase in the value of raw materials has accounted for only a fraction of the overall growth of US gross domestic product. The rest of that growth reflects the embodiment of ideas in products and services that consumers value. This shift of emphasis from physical materials to ideas as the core of value creation appears to have accelerated in recent decades.

In a more populist tone, the *International Herald Tribune* recently claimed that whereas 'in another era, a nation's most valuable assets were its natural resources – coal, say, or amber waves of grain . . . in the information economy of the 21st century, the most priceless resource is often an idea, along with the right to profit from it'.[4]

Those who concur with such views, whether or not they accept the all too frequent hyperbole, tend to assume that knowledge-based economies are nowadays wealthier, almost by definition, than traditional or natural resource-based ones. This is of course basically true. Nonetheless, reality defies lazy platitudes. While Singapore is a prosperous and increasingly creative economy,[5] the similarly sized Qatar and Brunei are just plain rich. India, with Bollywood, its impressive and rapidly expanding software industry, and its sizeable and growing biotechnological capacity in relation to its GNP, is mired in poverty which may take generations to eliminate. Of course, India cannot become a rich oil-based economy when there is no oil to base its economy on. But most Indians work on the land, and the diffusion of state-of-the-art knowledge and technologies is only one part of the whole solution to the problem of how to eke a decent income from agriculture.

This kind of thinking is not so new as people might think. Policy-making inspired by such ideas goes back centuries. In the Middle Ages, Venetian glass-makers, whose techniques were acquired partly from Germany and Syria, were forbidden from plying their trade outside the city state or giving away their secrets. Transgressors could lose their lives. At the same time, foreign glass-makers were banned from operating there. It may not be entirely coincidental that Venice was the first place to pass legislation providing patents for inventions.

Venetian-style 'knowledge mercantilism'[6] has not been historically uncommon. But since the Industrial Revolution, knowledge economy rhetoric is often expressed in ways favouring more open trade. In this respect, some nineteenth-century voices manage to sound very twenty-first century. In 1852, Lyon Playfair, a politician and public intellectual of his day, warned that Britain needed to realise, as he thought its foreign competitors already did, that 'the competition of industry has become a competition of intellect'.[7] Later in life he noted that 'all countries of the world have been brought into a common market to compete for the margins of profit'.[8]

However, even if one accepts the economic and strategic importance of knowledge, it is not necessarily to be concluded that the more intellectual property you have and the stronger the rights are the better, or even that intellectual property is necessary at all. One may more safely conclude that intellectual property policy-making is a high stakes exercise and is consequently an inherently political activity.

RHETORIC, POWER AND THE VARIED INTERESTS OF NATIONS

It is generally assumed that wealth-creating knowledge of the kind that turns economies into knowledge-based ones, comes almost exclusively out of universities, corporate laboratories and film, music, art and design studios, and not out of such unlikely places as peasant farmers' fields and indigenous communities. Furthermore, that kind of economic transformation requires the availability of high US- or European-style standards of intellectual property protection and enforcement. Basically, rich countries have such standards, poor countries do not. Therefore, to be like rich countries, poor countries must adopt these standards; the 'magic of the marketplace' will presumably conjure up the rest.

Are such assumptions validated by reality? Statistics produced by international organizations like the UN Development Programme (UNDP), WIPO and the World Bank do indeed suggest that most developing countries are not only failing to be innovative but actually have to improve their innovation climate dramatically before they can be competitive in high technology fields, except perhaps as assemblers and exporters of high tech goods invented elsewhere. Admittedly, our usual indicators of innovation, such as R&D spending, education statistics and patent counts do not tell the whole story and may in fact be misleading. But there appears clearly to be a massive innovation gap between the rich and poor worlds that is not going to be bridged for a long time except by a few elite countries, like China, India and Brazil.

But is such a negative and pessimistic view about developing countries entirely accurate? Is there really a massive knowledge and innovation gap between the rich and poor worlds? Confusingly, the best answer to both questions is 'yes and no'. The 'yes' part is obvious. North America, Western Europe and East Asia have a massive lead over the rest of the world in virtually all of the usual social and economic indicators. But why is there a 'no' in the answer at all? Because there is a cultural bias in how we use terms like 'knowledge economy', 'information society', 'intelligent community' and 'creative industry'. The effect of this bias is to underestimate the presence and vital role of applied knowledge in all societies including those appearing to be the most backward and traditional.

Creativity and innovation are *not* the sole preserve of suited knowledge workers in glassy offices, unsuited bohemians in garrets, professional artists and musicians, or of laboratory scientists. If necessity really is the mother of invention, you would surely expect to see most innovation where the needs are greatest. And no needs are greater than those of desperately poor people getting themselves and their families through each day alive and well. Whether we look at health or agriculture, we find that peasant communities are often able to draw upon a huge body of knowledge passed on through many generations.[9] The same applies to hunters and gatherers. Local knowledge, technologies and traditional cultural expressions can be highly evolutionary, adaptive and even novel. In short, knowledge held within 'traditional' societies can be new as well as old. We should not be surprised by this. Traditional knowledge has always had adaptive elements because the ability to adapt is one of the keys to survival in precarious environments.

So can we just assume, as we tend to do, that the world's knowledge and innovation 'hotspots' are urban areas located almost exclusively in Europe, North America and East Asia? In fact, there are many other innovation hotspots, some in the most remote and isolated regions of the world. The problem is that few people recognise them as such, and few of those are in positions of real power or authority. Consequently, innumerable opportunities to harness local knowledge and innovation for trade and development are missed.[10]

Today's more positive view which informs the work of many development workers, seriously challenges the idea that knowledge wealth necessarily goes hand in hand with material wealth, and that innovation cannot be common where there is mass poverty. What they point out also is that knowledge and creative people may be far less scarce than are the institutions to help convert knowledge into wealth for local people and for the benefit of the wider economy.[11] Consequently, traditional knowledge and local innovations are being underutilised.

As to the notion that achieving national prosperity and international competitiveness requires countries to make available high US- or European-style standards of intellectual property protection and enforcement, there is very little evidence that this is the case. Naturally, transnational corporations like governments to believe this. Indeed, corporate lobbying has largely been responsible for the barely accountable extension of patents, copyright and trade marks to completely new kinds of subject matter in recent decades. Intellectual property law now encompasses such 'stuff' from the amazon.com 'one-click' shopping button to television programme schedules. We can patent microbes, plants and animals, even genes that have just been discovered and found to have some link to a disease. The binary code behind software programs is classed as a copyrightable work of literature. We can trademark the MGM lion's roar. Protection terms have been extended. The copyright term for authored works in Europe, the United States and many of their trade partners now continues for 70 years after the author's death.

But does every country in the world really need to adopt such standards, as they increasingly have to do, not so much because of TRIPS but as a result of new commitments arising from bilateral trade agreements? Arguably not. In fact such standards may make them worse off. The historical record strongly suggests that many of today's economic leader countries were themselves 'knowledge pirates' in the past, and benefited from being so.[12] As for the present, a case could be made for arguing that we in the developed world are not becoming knowledge-*based* economies as quickly as we are becoming knowledge-*protected* economies, or even – and this is a bit more worrying – knowledge-*overprotected* economies, in which dominant industries maintain their market power by tying up their knowledge in complex bundles of legal rights and instruments such as patents, copyrights, trade marks and restrictive contracts and licensing agreements. Such bundles of rights often cover just one product; a drug for example may be protected by a trade mark, multiple patents, trade secrets, safety and efficacy test data exclusivity, and copyright on the instructions.

It is far from clear that the creativity and innovation coming out of laboratories and studios is increasing at a rate anywhere near as fast as the rapidly growing size of corporate intellectual property portfolios. Worryingly, this heightened level of protection may not only be a bad thing for consumers in terms of higher prices, but it may actually stifle far more innovation than it promotes. And things may be getting worse. Every major company has to have an intellectual property management strategy, which usually entails the aggressive acquisition and enforcement of rights, because everybody else has one. Among the harmful consequences are increased prices, and a reduced access to knowledge that the generation of new knowledge encouraged by intellectual property rights is insufficient to compensate for.

Ironically, overly zealous enforcement of rights may be bad for business too. As a *Guardian* article rightly states: 'Microsoft's riches rest on copyright law. But they also depend on its constant violation . . . the fact that you can use most MS software for free has been an important factor in spreading the habit of using it and in killing competition'. And this is true – the mass-scale usage of an illegally reproduced product can sometimes make the lawful product a *de facto* standard in the marketplace as is the case with Microsoft.

Moreover, the author of this article points out a major dilemma for many consumers, which companies may need to take a flexible stance towards: 'in the US . . . it is illegal to copy your own CDs on to your own iPod. Obviously, this is a law that is broken all the time, or nobody there would ever buy an iPod. The 60GB model sells for $350; to fill it up with freshly downloaded content from the Apple store could easily cost another $25,000. In other words, rather like cigarettes, iPods should carry a financial health label stating that one either breaks the bank, or the law, in order to actually utilize the iPod to the maximum'.[13]

Another trend to mention here is that public interest and pro-competitive limitations and exceptions to the rights in many parts of the world are being narrowed. That is a serious concern for developing countries seeking to acquire expensive life-saving drugs. Other likely negative effects include undue constraints on the reproduction and distribution of educational materials in countries where such materials are scarce, expensive and desperately needed.

Of course, some would argue that copying is bad and that is the end of it. But others plausibly argue that a certain amount of copying and free-riding is necessary, if not beneficial, for competition in any economy, *and even for innovation*.[14] As for developing countries, imitation there as elsewhere is an essential stage in learning to innovate. Indeed, paradoxical as it might sound, imitation can be creative in itself. According to Kim and Nelson, 'imitation ranges from illegal duplicates of popular products to truly creative new products that are merely inspired by a pioneering brand'.[15] Distinct imitations may include 'knockoffs or clones, design copies, creative adaptations, technological leapfrogging, and adaptation to another industry'.[16] One should not take this argument too far, though. Copying CDs and misappropriation of trade marks provides no scope for learning at all. Moreover, if it is too easy to profit from uncreative imitation, there is unlikely to be much incentive to innovate.

However, while all developing countries have good reason to defend their right to tailor their intellectual property rules and policies to suit their specific needs and conditions, this does not make their interests identical. Lall's research found ample evidence that 'the need for IPRs varies with the level of development'. Based in part on the work of Maskus, he went on to say that:

> Many rich countries used weak IPR protection in their early stages of industrialisation to develop local technological bases, increasing protection as they approached the leaders. Econometric cross-section evidence suggests that there is an inverted-U shaped relationship between the strength of IPRs and income levels. The intensity of IPRs first falls with rising incomes, as countries move to slack IPRs to build local capabilities by copying, then rises as they engage in more innovative effort. The turning point is $7,750 per capita in 1985 prices . . ., a fairly high level of income for the developing world.[17]

It is one thing to say that relatively advanced developing countries prefer to weaken their intellectual property rights in order to advance their capacities to innovate through imitation-derived technological learning, and then strengthen them later when they are more innovative. It is quite another thing to assume that such a policy works just because many governments have favoured it. Nonetheless, intuitively it makes much sense and there is a wealth of historical experience to back it up.

For some people, the mobilisation efforts of corporate bodies, such as IBM in the arena of copyright protection of computer programs, and Pfizer in the arena of patent protection of pharmaceuticals, epitomise how global, avaricious and ambitious intellectual property-intensive companies are dictating intellectual property law and policy to the world. As Chapter 2 will show, when we realise how much corporate lobbying was behind the TRIPS Agreement and some other recent international intellectual property agreements, those concerned about the undue influence of large corporations have a point. From a historical perspective, when these corporations impose their preferred intellectual property rules on the world,[18] they echo the *lex mercatoria* spirit of the ancient guilds. Indeed, modern-day corporations as a grouping of economic actors with tremendous market power form a kind of globalised guild system. What we have, in a sense, is a curious throwback to the early-capitalist era of mercantilism.[19]

Historically, the mercantilist regarded the state as the appropriate instrument for promoting the well-being of his country and pursued national interests at all costs. Moreover, in his view the country was regarded as a unit; there were national interests to be promoted, quite irrespective of the interest of particular sections of individuals. In accordance with such an approach, the state harnessed and controlled resources, skills and products for the purposes and profit of the state.[20] This included the encouragement of commercial enterprises by the issue of patents of monopoly in respect of the introduction of new processes, the creation of privileged trading companies,[21] the foundation of colonies and plantations in order to secure supplies of material as well as a market for the finished commodities, and the establishment of manufactories financed and controlled by the state.[22] The mercantilist world was a dog-eat-dog world in which protectionism was the norm and trade advantages for a country were seen as trade disadvantages for its neighbours.

Indeed, such mercantilism, which sees trade as purely a zero-sum game, is reflected in the views of some quite prominent people today. For example, the very influential Bruce Lehman, erstwhile business lobbyist and head of the United States Patent and Trademark Office (USPTO), now claims in public that the US would have been better off pushing for strict environmental and labour standards in the Uruguay Round instead of insisting with so much determination on an intellectual property agreement.[23] The subtext here is that TRIPS was all about helping the US to sell more and buy less. If it isn't helping America to do this, then it is a failure. Consequently, other ways should be found to force American goods on foreigners while keeping out cheaper imports. Labour and environmental standard-setting may be the solution. Ironically, our modern guilds only pretend to care about America's balance of payments problems. If research, development and manufacturing can be done more cheaply on foreign soil but as well as in America, then they will be done on foreign soil. Can it be, then, that Lehman and like-minded people turned against TRIPS because in a sense it is actually working? Arguably, knowledge-based corporations can now relocate to India, China and Brazil with the confidence they lacked in the pre-TRIPS era when patent rights were unavailable, laden with limitations and exceptions, or were just ignored.

Realisation that intellectual property has wide-ranging repercussions is evidenced by the way intellectual property references more and more often find their way to the front pages of newspapers. Trade negotiators were largely unaware of these repercussions when the issue of intellectual property rights was linked with global trade during the Uruguay Round trade negotiations that culminated in the 1994 Agreement Establishing the World Trade Organization, annexed to which was the TRIPS Agreement. Far more attention was paid to the need to satisfy the pharmaceutical and entertainment industries than to ensure an intellectual property regime that was good for public health, education, food security and the interests of developing countries. According to Nobel laureate in economics, Joseph E. Stiglitz:

> I suspect that most of those who signed the agreement did not fully understand what they were doing. If they had, would they have willingly condemned thousands of AIDS sufferers to death because they might no longer be able to get affordable generic drugs? Had the question been posed in this way to parliaments around the world, I believe that TRIPS would have been soundly rejected.[24]

Stiglitz also notes that:

> Intellectual property is important, but the appropriate intellectual property regime for a developing country is different from that for an advanced industrial country. The TRIPS scheme failed to recognize this. In fact, intellectual property should never have been included in a trade agreement in the first place, at least partly because its regulation is demonstrably beyond the competency of trade negotiators.[25]

CREATIVITY AND THE EVOLVING INTELLECTUAL PROPERTY PARADIGM

What is intellectual property? In its purest sense, it is the only absolute possession in the world. As Chaffe stated, 'The man who brings out of nothingness some child of his thought has rights therein which cannot belong to any other sort of property'.[26] Law textbooks do not shy away from attempting to define intellectual property. One textbook defines intellectual property law as the 'branch of the law which protects some of the finer manifestations of human achievement'[27] Another states that intellectual property law 'regulates the creation, use and exploitation of mental or creative labour'.[28] For Spence, 'an intellectual property right is a right: (i) that can be treated as property; (ii) to control particular uses; (iii) of a specified type of intangible asset. In addition, intellectual property rights normally share the characteristics that they are: (i) only granted when the particular intangible asset can be attributed to an individual creator or identifiable group of creators, the creator(s) being presumptively entitled to the right; and (ii) enforced by both the civil and criminal law'.[29]

In its simplest form, intellectual property is a type of property regime whereby creators are granted a right, the nature of which is entirely dependent on the nature of the creation on the one hand, and the legal classification of the creation on the other. To be placed within one or other of the different classifications of 'intellectual property', one has to fulfil the relevant criteria (for example, novelty, originality or distinctiveness) and comply with certain formalities. Depending on these legal (and often artificial) classifications, the creation is accorded a bundle of rights, which vary considerably across the intellectual property spectrum in terms of scope and duration. Figure 1.1 presents a bird's-eye view of the entire intellectual property spectrum.[30]

Copyright, patents and trade marks are the accepted bastions of the intellectual property world, with their respective legal satellites that include utility models, unfair competition and passing off laws. Design law appears as an afterthought reflective of some elements of patent and copyright laws. A further consideration of the classifications and their subsidiary divisions gives rise to an increasingly complex array over sometimes overlapping rights for the benefit of creators, owners and traders. The WIPO Convention, for instance, adopts this classification perspective in defining intellectual property.[31]

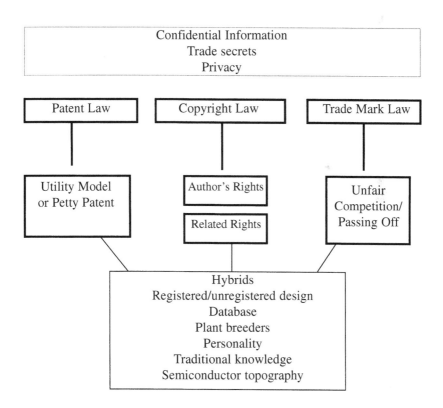

Figure 1.1   The intellectual property spectrum

(i) *Patent law*: This law grants protection of a limited duration to technological inventions and other types of functional subject matter. However,
creations which incorporate functional elements can sometimes also
constitute artistic works, industrial designs and even trade marks.

(ii) *Copyright law*: This law grants a less exclusive type of protection, with
a longer term of duration for literary, artistic and scientific creations, as
well as for related works such as performances, broadcasts and sound
recordings; a sub-category is design rights which protects the appearance of products, and often overlaps legally and conceptually with artistic works, which technically fall under copyright law.

(iii) *Trade mark law*: Marks which function as signs in the marketplace are
protected as trade marks. A sub-category is the common law action of
passing off, which is less generous in protection than the wider tort of
misappropriation or unfair competition. This area has the greatest potential for overlap not only with patents or copyright laws (especially in
relation to aesthetic and functional shapes), but also with other areas of
economic torts such as privacy, confidentiality, defamation, disparage-
ment of personality and trade, and fraud.[32]

Intellectual property is hardly a static conception, but is in a state of constant
evolution and reconsideration. The first English and Venetian laws were public
in nature, a means of harnessing foreign technologies, or of regulating and
censoring domestic printing. But by the nineteenth century, intellectual property had become classified as a type of private law, conferring private property
rights on the few. We now see a change as environmental, health and educational pressure groups clamour for a re-classification of intellectual property
rights as law with increasingly more influence in the public sphere than before.
Moreover, TRIPS has reinforced the public nature of intellectual property
rights in a way that WIPO had never done before, and indeed had been at pains
to avoid doing.

Along with this evolution, one sees old rights changing and new rights
being created all the time. Essentially, when it comes to extending intellectual
property to new types of creations, the options available to policy-makers are
to fit such products into existing intellectual property categories or to create
new intellectual property rights. In the words of Cornish,[33]

> Intellectual property may be extended to new subject matter either by accretion or
> by emulation. Accretion involves re-defining an existing right so as to encompass
> the novel material; emulation requires the creation of a new and distinct right by
> analogy drawn more or less eclectically from the types already known.

The accretion option was taken, for example, for photographs, films and
computer software, where the copyright system was stretched in ways that the

burgeoning industries concerned found to be satisfactory, albeit with some disagreement about how far and at what speed the stretching should be done. The accretion principle is untenable in the case of sound recordings and television broadcasts. In such instances, the preferred option is Cornish's emulation option. Utility models are another example of emulation. But, in the case of inventions, emulation is inherently risky in the sense that new rights are essentially experimental. Thus, accretion may be a safer option, and one could seek to protect sub-patentable inventions under design law.

Indeed, empirical research into the British, German and Australian utility models systems from a historical perspective indicates that the inception and subsequent development of second-tier patent protection was a response to perceived deficiencies in both patents and designs law. Existing design legislation did not, in the German and Australian experiences, protect functional innovations; whilst in the British case, design legislation was adapted to plug the gap found to exist in the protection of minor and incremental innovations and inventions. Moreover, a consideration of the actual subject matter of protection under the various European utility models laws reveals that the term 'utility model' often incorporates many of the elements that would ordinarily constitute a functional or technical design.[34] And indeed, the United Kingdom has introduced such a quasi design-utility model law with its unregistered design right which extends to protecting functional shapes.

The emulation option also leads us to the *sui generis* ('of its own kind') option. This strategy is sometimes chosen to enable innovators in certain fields of science, technology, culture or business to appropriate the outputs of their research in a more effective and balanced manner that, policy-makers believe, would have been difficult to achieve under existing regimes. Examples include plant variety protection, the European database right, and semiconductor chip design protection.

In respect of the latter, a modified copyright approach was adopted in the 1984 United States Semiconductor Chip Protection Act. This legislation is historically interesting as it re-introduced two elements which had increasingly fallen out of favour in the protection of scientific innovation: a non-registration system, and a criterion which was outside the accepted notions of originality, novelty or inventiveness. This legal formula was subsequently adopted by the United Kingdom in its 1988 unregistered design rights regime, but extended to all types of functional designs. The same formula was incorporated into the EU Unregistered Community Design Right protection (see Chapter 7).

Another type of industry-specific law is the US Vessel Hull Design Protection Act,[35] which is the result of a rather bizarre lobbying endeavour by the boat industry. Protection is granted to an original design of a vessel hull, vessel plug or vessel mould which makes the vessel attractive or distinctive in appearance to the purchasing or using public.[36] Originality, due to the industrial basis of the right, is even equated to prior art and is defined thus: 'the result of the designer's creative endeavour that provides a distinguishable variation over prior work, pertaining to similar articles which is more than merely trivial and has not been copied from another source'.[37]

Both laws reflect the 'no-registration/low threshold' formula which is a variation on the copyright, rather than industrial property, approach. Many policy-makers tend to equate copyright law with 'art' and 'music' whereas in reality, the copyright approach is extremely attractive to short-lived technologies and industries such as the toy, fashion and textile industries which are fast moving, quickly imitated and in need of immediate and automatic protection, without the encumbrance of application or registration costs. The lower thresholds (based on interpretations of terms like 'commonplace' and 'originality') are advantageous for industries which customarily rely on the prior state of the art and which represent incremental, rather than massive, design improvements. This lower threshold also allows industries to embark on market testing for their products without any loss of protection. Moreover, copyright laws gravitate towards the individual innovator, creator or designer and are thus friendlier to either the sole inventor or an SME-type inventor.

In this book we interpret the term 'creation' in a rather wide sense, defining the act of creativity as being the material realisation of an idea. In a rather simplistic sense, then, intellectual property law is the legal expression of people's recognised interests in valuable ideas, such interests being either economic or moral in nature, or both. These people are not necessarily the creators themselves.

Dealing with creations requires us to take into account subjective and objective considerations. On the subjective level, the work is the result of the creator's inherent and deep need or impulse to bring a work into realisation. All other extrinsic driving forces, such as payment, employment, the need to build a reputation in the scientific community or in the marketplace, remain subservient to the inherent need or impulse to create.

On the objective level, there are several factors which balance each other, and produce not only new types of products, but also different manifestations of similar products such as, for example, functional and aesthetic elements of light bulbs. This level *also* helps to explain why intellectual property demarcations are more aligned to objective considerations than to subjective ones. The objective considerations are:

a.   the 'objective' creative input of the creator such as creating a totally *novel* or *original* or *distinctive* creation, which is almost accidental rather than intentioned;
b.   market and societal constraints and/or demands.

In one sense, market constraints are equivalent to economic justifications of intellectual property, that is, certain products and/or markets need incentives to supply consumer demand. Examples of market-societal factors include:

a. perceived need by the market and society for the creation;
b. whether the creation satisfies the consuming market's cost-benefit analysis, that is, function, performance, reliability versus cost;
c. whether the creation appeals to sometimes competing societal needs or demands, which may, for example, be of aesthetic, ergonomic, environmental, religious, spiritual, moral character;
d. whether the creation satisfies the emotional and personal lifestyle needs of the consumers, for example, retail therapy, designer value and status of the creation (ranging from designer clothes to designer drugs); and
e. implications of the wider economic machinations.[38]

The importance of external market constraints has been alluded to by Franzosi in relation to patentable inventions.[39] Franzosi postulated that a patentable invention consists of a technical phase and a social phase. The technical phase consists of the invention which causes an active element of force to operate on a passive element or object to product a technical result, that is, the 'pure' act of reducing a discovery to a stable form. The social phase, on the other hand, is the application of the technical result to human needs to satisfy such needs and obtain a social result, that is, the creative impulse to solve a problem. This may take several more years to achieve. In his view, the social phase is the inspiration, the *raison d'être*, of the technical phase.

These theories, in turn, also intersect with Schumpeter's definition of 'innovation'[40] (that is, 'carrying out new combinations'), which comprises:

a. the introduction of a new good . . .
b. the introduction of a new method of production . . . which need by no means be founded upon a discovery scientifically new . . .
c. the opening of a new market . . .
d. the conquest of a new source of supply of raw materials . . .
e. the carrying out of the new organization of any industry . . .

Furthermore, Schumpeter notes that innovation does not occur purely within a natural or legal individual but tends to arise from social interaction which involves both creators and other actors. Schumpeter discusses economic leadership where ideas and creations, he says, 'are always present, abundantly accumulated by all sorts of people. Often they are also generally known and being discussed by scientific or literary writers'. However, society requires an 'economic leader' to amass all these things and to present it to society. In underlining the importance of other economic actors in bringing forth an invention, Schumpeter offers the secondary, and much narrower, basis of innovation as something which an economic leader must do in order to render an invention practical and acceptable to societal use.[41]

A correlated view is that most innovations, as opposed to ground-breaking and dramatic inventions, are routine and primarily devoted to product improvement or enhanced user-friendliness or searches for new uses for those products. Hence, much of creativity is dictated by market and societal needs and demands. There is, as we outlined above, synergy between the two types of inventive activity, and both types of activities are vital in enabling societal advance and growth.[42] Too many people focus on creation in the narrow sense of the word; that is, as something highly inventive, new, original or distinctive which is introduced on the market or into society.

In the final analysis, 'creativity', however defined, concerns the production and application of information in the conception, development and use of scientific, industrial and cultural goods, irrespective of whether the information or goods technically qualify as an invention, a literary work or a mark. Intellectual property is not always concerned with creativity, some forms of which fall outside the criteria of intellectual property protection.

That is the objective view. However, determining what is creative *and* protectable at the policy level is subject to constant revision and debate, and is an inherently political and commercial matter. It is rarely decided on the basis of genuine objectivity.

With this dynamic perspective, it seems inevitable that the intellectual property regime would outgrow its nineteenth-century boundaries to encompass all sorts of new, esoteric subject matter such as plant varieties and semiconductor topographies, often as it happens with low thresholds of creativity. As ever, but more than ever before, market trends and international business interests drive the political, legislative and judicial definitions of existing and potential intellectual property subject matter.

WHAT THIS BOOK IS (NOT) ABOUT

What are the rules governing freedom of expression and copyright? What rules *should* govern freedom of expression and copyright? Should intellectual property take precedence over public rights of access? Is intellectual property piracy the new terrorism? Are intellectual property rights human rights, or alternatively do they impinge on human rights? And are the powerful countries using intellectual property to keep poor countries poor? These are a few questions that seem pertinent in this young twenty-first century of ours. We hope this book provides a few of the answers to these questions and to many others that may form in the minds of the curious reader.

Above all, the book sets out to trace and explain the evolving remits of intellectual property, which are rapidly expanding to embrace new subject matter and (usually) increase the extent of protection. It does this by analysing intellectual property rules in various jurisdictions and in key international instruments like the TRIPS Agreement. We also look into the relationships between intellectual property law and science, education and culture, as well as more philosophical issues such as the commodification of persona, the commons, and of life itself. Most significantly of all, perhaps, the book examines the impact of intellectual property on the international stage, especially in respect of trade, development, economics, law, technology, human rights, and biological and cultural diversity.

A disclaimer is in order. This book is not a treatise on the general intellectual property law of any jurisdiction. There are some excellent books on the market which are. As for works specifically on the TRIPS Agreement, the *Resource Book on TRIPS and Development* produced by the UNCTAD-ICTSD Project on IPRs and Sustainable Development provides an extremely comprehensive analysis. The chapters are freely downloadable from the www.IPRsonline.org internet portal along with a wealth of other useful documents.

NOTES

1. Twining, W,. *Globalisation and Legal Theory*, Cambridge, UK: Cambridge University Press, 2000.
2. *Ibid.*
3. Gowers, A., *Review of Intellectual Property: A Call for Evidence,* HM Treasury, 2006.
4. Kanter, J., 'A New Battlefield: Ownership of Ideas', *International Herald Tribune*, 3 October 2005.
5. Chow, K.B., K.K. Leo and S. Leong, 'Singapore', in Suthersanen, U., G. Dutfield and K.B. Chow (eds), *Innovation without Patents: Harnessing the Creative Spirit in a Diverse World*, Cheltenham, UK and Northampton, MA, US: Edward Elgar, 2007, 73–118.
6. Stuart Macdonald coined the phrase 'information mercantilism'. See Macdonald, S., *Information for Innovation: Managing Change from an Information Perspective*, Oxford: Oxford University Press, 1998.
7. Dr Lyon Playfair, CB, FRS, 'Industrial Instruction on the Continent', London: George E. Eyre & William Spottiswoode, 1852, 3.
8. The Right Honourable Sir Lyon Playfair, KCB, MP, 'On Industrial Competition and Commercial Freedom. Being an Address Delivered at the National Liberal Club. April 24th, 1888', London: The Liberal and Radical Publishing Co., 6.
9. For examples, see Dutfield, G., *Africa and the Economy of Tradition*, Paris: Fondation pour l'Innovation Politique, 2005; Posey, D.A. (ed.), *Cultural and Spiritual Values of Biodiversity*, Nairobi and London: UNDP & IT Publications, 1999.
10. See Gupta, A.K., 'From Sink to Source: The Honey Bee Network Documents Indigenous Knowledge and Innovations in India', *Innovations: Technology, Governance, Globalization*, summer, 1(3), 49–66, 2006.

11. *Ibid.*
12. Ben-Atar, D.S., *Trade Secrets: Intellectual Piracy and the Origins of American Industrial Power*, New Haven and London: Yale University Press, 2004; Chang, H.-J., *Kicking away the Ladder: Development Strategy in Historical Perspective*, London: Anthem, 2002; Dutfield, G. and U. Suthersanen, 'Harmonisation or Differentiation in Intellectual Property Protection? The Lessons of History'. *Prometheus*, 23(2), 131–47, 2005.
13. Brown, A., 'Owning Ideas – The Boom in the Intellectual Property Market will not Reap Rewards for us All', *Guardian* 19 November 2005, http://www.guardian.co.uk/comment/story/0,3604,1646125,00.html
14. Dam, K.W., 'Some Economic Considerations in the Intellectual Property Protection of Software', *Journal of Legal Studies,* 24, 1995, at 321.
15. Kim, L. and R.R. Nelson, 'Introduction', in L. Kim and R.R. Nelson (eds), *Technology, Learning, and Innovation: Experiences of Newly Industrializing Economies*, Cambridge, UK: Cambridge University Press, 2000.
16. *Ibid.*, citing Schnaar, S., *Managing Imitation Strategy: How Later Entrants Seize Markets from Pioneers*, New York: Free Press, 1994.
17. Lall, S. (with the collaboration of M. Albaladejo), 'Indicators of the Relative Importance of IPRs in Developing Countries', Issues Paper no. 3, UNCTAD-ICTSD Project on Intellectual Property Rights and Sustainable Development, Geneva, 2003. (Citing Maskus, K.E., *Intellectual Property Rights in the Global Economy*, Washington, DC: Institute for International Economics, 2000, 95–6.)
18. The original 12 members of the Intellectual Property Committee in the 1980s, for instance, were Pfizer, IBM, Merck, General Electric, Du Pont, Warner Communications, Hewlett-Packard, Bristol Myers, General Motors, Johnson & Johnson, Rockwell International and Monsanto. Drahos, P., 'Global Property Rights in Information: The Story of TRIPS at the GATT', *Prometheus*, 13(1), 6–19, 1995. According to Sell, TRIPS is a case of 12 US corporations making public law for the world. Sell, S.K., *Private Power, Public Law: The Globalization of Intellectual Property Rights*, Cambridge, UK: Cambridge University Press, 2003, pp. 1, 96.
19. 'Mercantilism was the guiding principle of economic policy and the related theory in the age of absolute rulers in Europe', H. Kellenbenz (1965), cited in Braudel, F., *The Wheels of Commerce,* London: Collins, 1982, at 542. Braudel views the era of the mercantilist economy to have existed roughly between the thirteenth century and the eighteenth century. However, the term 'mercantilism' itself was first used by the French physiocrat Mirabeau in 1736, and subsequently by Adam Smith in the *Wealth of Nations* (1776). *The Blackwell Encyclopaedia of Political Thought* (D. Miller, J. Coleman, W. Connolly, A. Ryan, eds), London: Blackwell, 1991, 335. See also Mill, J.S., *Principles of Political Economy*, Book V, Chapter X, § 1, pp. 279 *et seq.*, London: Penguin, 1985.
20. Jardine notes that financial investment by way of patronage was often conferred on artists and craftsmen as a means of attaining social and political advantage. 'The valuable artefacts which they created (or obtained) for their patron were at the same time intrinsically costly commodities and potentially exploitable as the basis for a significant power-broking transaction.' Jardine, L., *Wordly Goods – A New History of the Renaissance*, London: Macmillan, 1996, 238–9.
21. The rise of the shopkeeper or merchant class brought new social distinctions within the shopkeeper trade as the cream of the trade sought to set itself above the rest by forming guilds. Thus, for instance, in Paris, the ordinance of 1625 formed six elite *corps* for drapers, grocers, moneychangers, goldsmiths, haberdashers and furriers; by the eighteenth century, their functions and status had been superseded by the French Chambers of Commerce. Braudel, *op. cit.*, 68, 81.
22. Machlup, F. and E. Penrose, 'The Patent Controversy in the 19th Century', *Journal of Economic History*, 1, 1950, at 2. The authors note that privileges accorded to inventors and craftsmen were 'merely one species in the large genus of privileges, charters, franchises, licenses and regulations issued by the Crown or by local governments within the mercantilist framework'. Other interventionist devices included the direct importation of foreign workers in order to establish a new industry, the fixation of prices and wages (partly in the

interests of production) and the enactment of Shipping Acts (such as the English Navigation Act 1651) to encourage shipping and the Navy, Braudel, *op. cit.*, 542; *The Blackwell Encyclopaedia of Political Thought*, 335.

23. For example at the 13th Fordham University conference on International Intellectual Property Law and Policy, New York, 31 March 2005.

24. *Ibid.*

25. Stiglitz, J.E., 'Intellectual-property Rights and Wrongs', available at http://www.dailytimes.com.pk/default.asp?page=story_16-8-2005_pg5_12.

26. Chaffe, Z., 'Reflections on the Law of Copyright: I and II'. *Columbia Law Review*, 45(4/5), 1945, in Berrings, R.C. (ed.), *Great American Law Reviews*, Birmingham: Legal Classics Library, 1984.

27. Cornish, W. and D. Llewelyn, *Intellectual Property: Patents, Copyright, Trade Marks and Allied Marks,* 5th ed., London: Sweet & Maxwell, 2003, 3. The authors add, though, that 'it also shields much that is trivial and ephemeral'.

28. Bently, L. and B. Sherman, *Intellectual Property Law* (2nd ed.), Oxford: Oxford University Press, 2004, 1.

29. Spence, M., *Intellectual Property,* Oxford: Oxford University Press, 2007, 12–13.

30. For an intriguing perspective on the intellectual property system, see M. Koktvedgaard, 'The Universe of Intellectual Property', *GRURInt*, 1996 at 296.

31. Article 2, para. viii, WIPO Convention (1967).

32. See Suthersanen, U., 'Breaking down the Intellectual Property Barriers', *Intellectual Property Quarterly* 267, 1998, 268 *et seq.*, discussing this problem of overlapping rights in relation to three-dimensional shapes.

33. Cornish, W.R., 'The International Relations of Intellectual Property', *Cambridge Law Journal*, 52(1), 46, 1993, at 54–5.

34. Suthersanen, U., G. Dutfield and K.B. Chow (eds), *Innovation without Patents: Harnessing the Creative Spirit in a Diverse World,* Cheltenham, UK and Northampton, MA, US: Edward Elgar, 2007.

35. Incorporated as 17 USC Chapter 12.

36. § 1201(a).

37. Excluded are staple, commonplace designs dictated solely by a utilitarian function of the article that embodies it.

38. Such as: adequate supply conditions (the nature of the relevant technology, ownership of raw materials, and the legal framework within which producers operate), viable demand conditions (the availability of and cross elasticity of demand for substitute products, the cyclical and seasonal character of the product, the marketing and purchase characteristics of the product sold, and the rate of growth and variability over time of demand). Suthersanen, at *op. cit.*, 280.

39. Franzosi, M., 'Patentable Inventions: Technical and Social Phases: Industrial Character and Utility', *European Intellectual Property Review*, 5, 1997, 251.

40. Schumpeter, J.A. (1983 [1934]), *The Theory of Economic Development: An Inquiry into Profits, Capital, Credit, Interest, and the Business Cycle*, New Brunswick, NJ: Transaction Publishers, 66.

41. *Ibid.,* 88–9.

42. Baumol, W., *The Free-Market Innovation Machine*, Princeton: Princeton University Press, 2002, at 22.

2. The international law and political economy of intellectual property

The commercial importance of intellectual property rights has grown considerably since the nineteenth century, but has really accelerated since the 1970s. A major explanation is the incessant and increasing pressure on businesses and national economies to be competitive. This puts a premium on creativity in terms of bringing new products and services to market, and of marketing existing products and services more effectively.

Intellectual property rule-making has become ever more responsive to this increased pressure, as well as to the willingness of national governments keen to enhance the competitiveness of their economies to effectively give transnational corporations what they want, at least most of the time. Consequently, since the 1960s and 1970s and up to the present, developed-country intellectual property regimes have undergone some quite profound changes. These changes are of three kinds.[1]

The first of these is the widening of protectable subject matter, including a tendency to reduce or eliminate exceptions. Examples of such accretion include the extension of copyright protection to computer programs as if they are literary works, the application of patent protection to cover computer programs, life forms, cells, proteins and genes, and the removal of exclusions on product patents for drugs. This has been achieved in various ways including legal reforms, rule changes, court decisions, and through the assumption (frequently propounded by legal practitioners, who are of course likely to have a vested interest), that the inclusion of such newly valuable products is fully consistent with existing practices and legal doctrines.

The second change is the creation of new rights. Examples of new systems created during the late twentieth century included plant variety protection (or plant breeders' rights) and rights to layout designs of integrated circuits. The third change was the progressive standardisation of the basic features of intellectual property rights. For instance, patent regulations increasingly provide 20-year protection terms, require prior art searches for novelty and examinations for inventive step (or non-obviousness), assign rights to the first applicant rather than the first inventor, and provide protection for inventions in a widening range of industries and technological fields.

These developments in intellectual property law, all of which began in

Europe or North America, are spreading to the rest of the world through agreements such as the World Trade Organization-administered Agreement on Trade-related Aspects of Intellectual Property Rights (TRIPS) and bilateral and regional free trade agreements, and at an accelerating pace. Consequently, national intellectual property, especially patent, regimes throughout the world are being increasingly held to standards of protection based on those of the most economically and politically influential countries.

Where did this internationalisation process start? Or to put it another way, what are the origins of international intellectual property rule-making? To answer, we must go back to the late nineteenth century.

THE PILLARS OF THE INTERNATIONAL INTELLECTUAL PROPERTY REGIME: THE PARIS AND BERNE CONVENTIONS

In the nineteenth century countries chose to further their economic interests by having quite distinct intellectual property laws, or even no laws. With no multilateral intellectual property agreements to establish common legal standards, this divergence was quite extreme compared to the present day. If this was the case, why would so many countries have come together to adopt international intellectual property treaties and create unions of participating countries, as they did from the 1880s?

In reality, there were common interests in what hitherto was an unprecedented era of international cooperation in commercial law which saw the creation of unions. These included the International Telecommunication Union in 1865 and the Universal Postal Union in 1874. There was much interest among businesses, authors, artists, designers and traders in acquiring patents, copyright, industrial designs and trade marks in those foreign countries where they sought to do business. And as international trade expanded, this interest increased resulting in the foundation of the Paris and Berne Unions for the protection of certain forms of intellectual property.

The Paris Union and the Convention for the Protection of Industrial Property

The Paris Convention for the Protection of Industrial Property was approved and opened for signature in 1883.[2] The term 'industrial property' was adopted in the Convention. According to Article 1:

> Industrial property shall be understood in the broadest sense and shall apply not only to industry and commerce proper, but likewise to agricultural and extractive

industries and to all manufactured or natural products, for example, wines, grain, tobacco leaf, fruit, cattle, minerals, mineral waters, beer, flowers, and flour.

Initially, the Paris Convention covered 'patents, industrial designs or models, trade-marks and trade names'. Since then the scope of industrial protection has been expanded in the Convention to embrace 'patents, utility models, industrial designs, trademarks, service marks, trade names, indications of source or appellations of origin, and the repression of unfair competition'. Nonetheless, it is probably best known for its provisions dealing with patents.

In the 1880s, there were five key areas of variation among patent systems. These were interpretations of novelty, the length of protection terms, the treatment of foreign applicants, the issue of whether or not patents needed to be 'worked' domestically, and exceptions to patentability. Let us look at each of these in turn.

Interpretations of novelty varied widely in nineteenth-century patent laws. In some countries, inventions could not be patented if there were prior knowledge, use or publication anywhere in the world. In most other countries, only unpublished foreign use or knowledge did not destroy novelty.[3] In Britain, on the other hand, only 'public manufacture, use or sale in England' invalidated patent applications for lack of novelty.[4]

There were no standard protection terms. The longest period of protection was provided by the USA, where patents were for 17 years from the date the patent was granted. France and Germany awarded patents for 15 years. British patents had a duration of 14 years from the filing date, but the protection term of foreign inventions previously patented abroad automatically ended upon the expiry of the foreign patent even if this was less than 14 years.

There were wide variations concerning regulation of local manufacture or use (that is, the 'working') of patented products or processes. In some countries (such as the USA),[5] patent holders were under no obligation to work the invention or even to commercialise it. In others, rival manufacturers could apply for a compulsory licence if the patent holder refused to work the invention or license it willingly. In some others (such as France), merely importing a patented product would lead to revocation of the patent.

In the USA and Great Britain no classes of inventions were explicitly excepted. Elsewhere exceptions were usually indicated in the statutes. The most common of these appeared to have been medicines and foods (as in France and Germany).

Because the differences between national laws were so great, there was little expectation that harmonising national laws through a single convention was achievable. But there was broad understanding that certain common principles and administrative procedures should be agreed upon.

As mentioned, an agreed text of the Convention was opened for signature at a conference in Paris in 1883. The Convention established the Paris Union for the Protection of Industrial Property, to consist of all member states, and whose International Bureau would be located in Switzerland. The founder members were Belgium, Brazil, France, Guatemala, Italy, Netherlands, Portugal, El Salvador, Serbia, Spain and Switzerland. Great Britain, Tunisia and Ecuador joined within a year. Ironically, while the USA and Germany were notable absentees, two founder members (Netherlands and Switzerland) were without a patent system. The USA did not join the Paris Union until 1887, and Germany not until 1903.

The most important patent-related matters dealt with in the Convention concerned national treatment, the right of priority, and rules relating to local manufacture. National treatment is the right of foreign citizens to be treated the same as nationals with respect to legal rights and remedies. National treatment was and continues to be one of the pillars of international intellectual property law.

An applicant for a patent in one member state was permitted a six-month period from the date of the first application (the priority date) to file for patents in other countries. During this period the applicant could prevent third parties from applying for a patent on the same invention. Moreover, subsequent applications during this period could not be invalidated on the grounds of prior registration, publication, or working by a third party. The USA and Germany, both of which granted patents only after examination, were unhappy with this provision. According to US practice, priority began from the date of publication of the patent, not of its filing. The German government felt that the priority period should be 12 months, since it often took at least that length of time for patents to be granted.[6] While such technical matters affected the decisions of these countries to delay joining the Union, strategic considerations are likely also to have been involved.

The Convention made no reference to compulsory licensing and stated that patents could not be revoked solely on the grounds of importation from a member state to the country where the patent was granted. However, members were otherwise free to require patents to be worked. This provision was a compromise that allowed importing as long as there was also local working.

On the other hand, the Convention made, and continues to make, no reference to three important areas of variation among national patent laws, indicating a lack of consensus. These were, first, the matter of whether national patent institutions had to examine patent applications or could serve merely as registration offices; second, the term of a patent; and third, exceptions from patentability on the basis of industrial or technological fields, or of morality concerns.

Since 1883, the Paris Convention has been revised six times, most recently in 1967, and its membership has expanded tremendously including many developing countries which joined in large numbers during the 1960s and

1970s. Apart from the extension of the priority date for patents to 12 months, the main substantive differences between the 1883 version and subsequent ones have been to do with working and compulsory licensing.

Under Article 19, members of the Paris Union are permitted 'to make separately between themselves special agreements for the protection of industrial property, in so far as these agreements do not contravene the provisions of this Convention'. Over the years, several such special agreements have been adopted, including: the Madrid Agreement for the Repression of False or Deceptive Indications of Source on Goods; the Madrid Agreement Concerning the International Registration of Marks; and the Lisbon Agreement for the Protection of Appellations of Origin and their International Registration.

The Berne Union and the Convention for the Protection of Literary and Artistic Works

In the area of copyright, the two countries with the most to gain from an international copyright convention in the late nineteenth century were Britain and France, not only because their output of literary and artistic works was so vast, but also because their authors were victims of large-scale copying in foreign countries that was permitted under national copyright regimes offering limited if any protection to foreigners. The latter problem was exacerbated by the reluctance on the part of many governments to give foreign authors and artists equal treatment under the law.

However, the nineteenth-century improvements in transport and communications made it far easier than ever for individuals in different countries to exchange ideas, organise themselves into societies and promote common demands across national boundaries. It should therefore not be surprising that, like the Paris Convention, the initiative to produce a multilateral treaty was taken by those who stood to benefit directly from enhanced international protection of literary and artistic works, in this case authors, publishers, lawyers and representatives of literary and publishers' societies.[7] By far the most important actor was the *Association Littéraire et Artistique Internationale* (ALAI), which was founded in 1878 by authors under the presidency of Victor Hugo to pursue their interests in a number of areas including 'the protection of the principles of literary property'.[8]

The first official call for the establishment of a universal law of copyright was made at the 1858 Brussels Conference on Literary and Artistic Property, which was attended by about 300 delegates including authors, lawyers, journalists, publishers and others.[9] Exactly 20 years later, two important events took place in Paris. The first was an international literary congress, which was attended by several famous authors and established the ALAI. Resolutions called, among other things, for countries to adopt national treatment with respect to their copyright laws, and to simplify procedures for acquiring the legal right. The second event was an international artistic conference which called for the creation of 'a general Union which would adopt a uniform law in relation to artistic property'. At ALAI's 1882 Congress, a German publisher proposed that a union of literary property between states be formed, which should accommodate 'the ideas and views of all interested parties: not only authors, but also publishers, booksellers, composers and music houses', and also that ALAI propose a meeting to negotiate the creation of such a union.[10]

Soon after, ALAI secured the support of the Swiss government to host a conference in Berne, which took place in September 1883. ALAI appointed a drafting commission, which during the conference prepared a draft convention of ten articles dealing with subjects such as beneficiaries of protection, works protected, translation rights, infringement and reciprocity provisions. The text of this document provided the basis for the Berne Convention for the Protection of Literary and Artistic Works, which was adopted at a diplomatic conference in 1886 attended by representatives of the following governments: Germany, Belgium, Spain, France, Haiti, Italy, Liberia, Switzerland, the UK and Tunisia. The USA and Japan were represented by observers.

The main tenets of the Berne Convention are national treatment, minimum levels of protection for the author, and the removal of any dependence on registration or other formalities in order to enjoy and exercise the rights provided. However, for authors to qualify for protection in a Berne Union country, the authors either qualify by nationality or by first publication. However, over the years, the provisions of the Berne Convention have become more substantial and detailed than the Paris Convention with respect to subject matter and the definition of the rights, including the limitations and exceptions.[11] Since 1886 the Convention has been amended six times to keep pace with the emergence of new technologies: Berlin (1908) incorporated photography, film, and sound recording; Rome (1928) added broadcasting; whilst Brussels (1948) added television.

The USA did not become a party to the Convention until 1989. Several reasons can be proffered. Apparently, the continental authors' rights orientation of the Convention, which appeared to prioritise the moral and material interests of authors over the economic interests of publishers and printers, was more than the USA felt it could accept, despite the fact that the Convention was acceptable to other common law countries such as the UK, Canada and Australia who were (and remain) similarly hostile to civil law concepts such as moral rights and authorial priorities.[12] A more pressing reason for not joining the Berne Convention was the desire to protect the US publishing industry and its 'manufacturing clause'.[13]

Often dissident or breakaway countries from the Berne Convention joined the Universal Copyright Convention (UCC), including the United States,

India, and many South American nations. The UCC, governed under the UNESCO mandate for education and scientific advancement, was an understandable haven for developing countries as it had the same provisions as the Berne Convention but with far fewer requirements, while recognising compulsory licences of translations.

Prior to the 1948 Brussels revision, there had been no serious impediments to seeking to expand authors' rights from the initial translation right to include public performance, cinematographic adaptation and moral rights. However, between 1948 and 1967, with the membership of the Berne Union increasingly comprising developing countries many of whom were also former colonial countries, there were objections to the introduction of further new 'Eurocentric' or 'old order' rights.[14] This was especially true of the attempt to introduce for the first time into international copyright law the fundamental right of reproduction in the 1967 Stockholm Convention. The counterproposal, led by a bloc of developing countries, was for provisions in the Berne Convention which would allow access to materials for educational purposes. The 'developing nations' argument of access to knowledge is not new. In the nineteenth century, for example, countries like Sweden, Japan, Ireland and Netherlands fought hard to limit the new international translation right as it was argued that the right to make free translation was of 'considerable value to less developed countries'.[15] Moreover the mechanism of compulsory licensing was not unknown, and the final version of the translation right allowed an author to enforce this right only if he had already licensed and authorised a translation of the work in that particular country.

Indeed, the translation right saga was, in some ways, responsible for the eventual settlement between the developed and developing nations in both the 1967 and 1971 revisions of the Berne Convention, when an extensive special regime was adopted through an Appendix which provided faculties for developing countries to apply special terms for reproduction and translation. The history of the first international right of translation is salutary in that the growing needs of developing countries politicised the Berne Union conferences in a manner not previously witnessed.

The Appendix to the 1971 Paris Act of the Convention provides – subject to just compensation to the right owner – 'for the possibility of granting non-exclusive and non-transferable compulsory licensing in respect of (i) translation for the purpose of teaching, scholarship or research, and (ii) reproduction for use in connection with systematic instructional activities, of works protected under the Convention'.[16] However, the Appendix's provisions are complicated, laden with restrictions and qualifications, and therefore difficult to put into practice. Consequently, it has only rarely been used.[17] Indeed, only eight developing countries are currently availing themselves of the two options. Another country has adopted option (ii) alone.

A major weakness of the Berne Convention was the limited nature of its application to authors and not owners of related rights such as performers, phonogram and film producers and broadcasters. These parties finally obtained an international rights regime under the 1961 Rome Convention for the Protection of Performers, Producers of Phonograms and Broadcasting Organisations.

As with the Paris Union, Berne Union members are permitted to make special agreements. The 1996 WIPO Copyright Treaty is one such agreement (see below).

THE WORLD INTELLECTUAL PROPERTY ORGANIZATION

Lying at the heart of the international intellectual property regime is the World Intellectual Property Organization (WIPO). The organisation was established by the 1967 Convention Establishing the World Intellectual Property Organization, and came into existence in 1970 when the Convention entered into force. In 1974, WIPO became a United Nations specialised agency. WIPO's two objectives as stated in Article 3 of the Convention are: (i) to promote the protection of intellectual property throughout the world through cooperation among states and, where appropriate, in collaboration with any other international organization; and (ii) to ensure administrative cooperation among the Unions. WIPO currently administers 24 multilateral agreements.

The organisation was not created *de novo*. Its origins lie in the 1893 merger of the secretariats (or 'international bureaux') of the Paris and Berne Unions. The merged organisation was known as the *Bureaux Internationaux Réunis de la Protection de la Propriété Intellectuelle* (BIRPI). The idea of transforming BIRPI into an international intellectual property organization arose at a 1962 meeting of the Permanent Bureau of the Paris Union and the Berne Union. The meeting recommended the setting up of a Committee of Governmental Experts in order to consider administrative and structural reforms to the Paris and Berne Union systems and prepare for a diplomatic conference. It is important to note that during this time, the decolonisation process, which had begun after the Second World War, was gathering pace and many new developing countries were becoming independent and seeking to join the United Nations and other international organisations. The United Nations itself was undergoing a period of transformation as it sought to accommodate a rapidly increasing membership with a wide range of interests and concerns. Which parts of the UN system should have jurisdiction over complex and politically contentious matters such as intellectual property was some way from being determined. In consequence, it was obvious that BIRPI could no longer remain

as a developed country 'club', and needed to have a more multilateral character that could attract developing countries including the newly independent
ones.

However, some developing nations had their own ideas about international
intellectual property norm-setting and were becoming assertive in expressing
them. This was cause for concern in some quarters. Indeed, the proposal to
establish a new organisation based on BIRPI was intended in part to ensure
that politicised organisations, including those known for accommodating the
specific concerns of the developing countries, would not be chosen as the
forum for negotiating intellectual property norms. According to Ladas, the
intent was 'to head off any attempt by outsiders, such as the United Nations
Economic and Social Council or the United Nations Conference on Trade and
Development, to deal with the subject of intellectual property and eventually
to form a Specialized Agency of the United Nations in this field'.[18]

A second meeting of the Committee took place in 1966 and was attended
by representatives from 39 nations of which nine were developing countries,
the rest being developed or European communist countries. The draft
Convention prepared by BIRPI on the basis of the views expressed by the
Committee at these two meeting was presented to a diplomatic conference in
1967 at Stockholm, where a final text was approved. The WIPO secretariat,
located in Geneva, Switzerland, is still known as the International Bureau.[19]

THE INTERNATIONAL INTELLECTUAL PROPERTY REGIME TODAY

In summary the international law of intellectual property in its present form
consists of three types of agreement.[20] These are multilateral treaties, regional
treaties or instruments, and bilateral treaties. Of these, the agreements that
affect the greatest number of countries are the TRIPS Agreement, and some of
the multilateral treaties administered by WIPO, especially the Paris and Berne
Conventions.

Multilateral Treaties

Most of these agreements are administered by WIPO, and are of three types:

1. *The standard-setting treaties*, which define agreed basic standards of
    protection for the different intellectual property rights, and also typically
    require national treatment. These include the Paris Convention, the Berne
    Convention, the 1961 Rome Convention for the Protection of Performers,
    Producers of Phonograms and Broadcasting Organizations,[21] the 1996

WIPO Copyright Treaty and WIPO Performances and Phonograms Treaty, and the 2006 Singapore Treaty on the Law of Trademarks. Important non-WIPO treaties of this kind include UNESCO's 1952 Universal Copyright Convention, the 1961 International Convention for the Protection of New Varieties of Plants (the UPOV[22] Convention), and the World Trade Organization-administered TRIPS Agreement.

2. *The global protection system treaties*, which facilitate filing or registering of rights in more than one country. These include the 1970 Patent Cooperation Treaty (PCT),[23] the 1891 Madrid Agreement Concerning the International Registration of Marks, and the 1958 Lisbon Agreement for the Protection of Appellations of Origin and their International Registration.

3. *The classification treaties*, which 'organize information concerning inventions, trademarks and industrial designs into indexed, manageable structures for easy retrieval'.[24] These include the 1957 Nice Agreement Concerning the International Classification of Goods and Services for the Purposes of the Registration of Marks, the 1968 Locarno Agreement Establishing an International Classification for Industrial Designs, and the 1971 Strasbourg Agreement Concerning the International Patent Classification.

Regional Treaties or Instruments

Examples of these kinds of agreement include the 1973 European Patent Convention, the 1998 European Community Directive on the Legal Protection of Biotechnological Inventions, the 1982 Harare Protocol on Patents and Industrial Designs within the Framework of the African Regional Industrial Property Organization, and the 2000 Andean Community Common Regime on Industrial Property. Some of these, such as Chapter 17 of the North American Free Trade Agreement, are components of trade agreements rather than stand-alone intellectual property treaties.

Regional agreements may appear to be far less important parts of the international intellectual property architecture than the multilateral agreements (and bilateral agreements less so still). Yet such instruments are extremely important. First, their membership may be quite large, covering 20 or more countries. Second, it is possible that novel provisions in such agreements could subsequently be globalised through their incorporation into new multilateral agreements.[25] Third, countries may be required to introduce provisions that go beyond what TRIPS requires such as extending patents to new kinds of subject matter and eliminating certain exceptions. Fourth, regional agreements might stipulate that contracting parties should accede to certain international conventions. The third and fourth points also apply to bilateral agreements.

Bilateral Agreements

Specifically, these include those bilateral agreements that deal with intellectual property as one of several trade issues covered. These agreements are discussed below.

THE AGREEMENT ON TRADE-RELATED ASPECTS OF INTELLECTUAL PROPERTY RIGHTS

Background

The 1994 Agreement on Trade-related Aspects of Intellectual Property Rights ('TRIPS' or 'the TRIPS Agreement'), one of the main outcomes of the Uruguay Round of the General Agreement on Tariffs and Trade (GATT), which is administered by the Geneva-based World Trade Organization (WTO), is of special importance in that it establishes enforceable global minimum (and high) standards of protection and enforcement for virtually all the most important intellectual property rights such as patents, copyrights and related rights, and trade marks in one single agreement.

The first attempt to frame intellectual property as an issue to be discussed in wider trade negotiations was made by a group of trademark-holding firms organized as the Anti-Counterfeiting Coalition, which unsuccessfully lobbied for the inclusion of an anti-counterfeiting code in the 1973–79 GATT Tokyo Round.

Following the lead set by the US trademark industries, the copyright, patent and semiconductor industries also decided during the early 1980s to frame the relative (and sometimes absolute) lack of effective intellectual property protection in overseas markets as a trade-related issue *and* a problem for the US economy that the government ought to respond to. So by the time the contracting parties of the GATT met in Punta del Este, Uruguay, in September 1986 to launch another trade round, US corporations had forged a broad cross-sectoral alliance and developed a coordinated strategy.

For those seeking high standards of intellectual property protection and enforcement throughout the world by way of the GATT, the strategy had three advantages. First, if successful the strategy would globalise these standards much more rapidly than could be achieved through the WIPO-administered conventions. This is first because it allowed for the possibility of including all the main intellectual property rights in a single agreement (which could also incorporate by reference provisions of the major WIPO conventions), and second, because once it was agreed that the Uruguay Round agreements had to be accepted as a package (that is, a 'single undertaking'), countries could not opt out of any one of them and be a member of the new World Trade Organization. Second, the GATT already had a dispute settlement mechanism, albeit a flawed one. WIPO has no enforcement or dispute settlement mechanisms except through the treaties that it administers, and these treaties do not provide much recourse for countries concerned about the non-compliance of other parties. Third, the broad agenda of the Uruguay Round provided opportunities for linkage-bargain diplomacy that WIPO, with its exclusive focus on intellectual property rights, did not allow. Hard bargaining by the US, Europe and Japan on intellectual property could thus be linked to concessions in such areas as textiles and agriculture, where exporting countries in the developing world were eager to achieve favourable settlements.[26]

In the event, the Punta del Este Declaration included 'trade-related aspects of intellectual property rights, including trade in counterfeit goods' as a subject for negotiations in the forthcoming trade round, which became known as 'the Uruguay Round'. In full, the Declaration's provisions on intellectual property are as follows:

> In order to reduce the distortions and impediments to international trade, and taking into account the need to promote effective and adequate protection of intellectual property rights, and to ensure that measures and procedures to enforce intellectual property rights do not themselves become barriers to legitimate trade, the negotiations shall aim to clarify GATT provisions and elaborate as appropriate new rules and disciplines.
>
> Negotiations shall aim to develop a multilateral framework of principles, rules and disciplines dealing with international trade in counterfeit goods, taking into account work already underway in GATT.
>
> These negotiations shall be without prejudice to other complementary initiatives that may be taken in the World Intellectual Property Organization and elsewhere to deal with these matters.

Eight years later, the outcome of these negotiations was the Agreement on Trade-related Aspects of Intellectual Property Rights (TRIPS). While the original purpose of an agreement on intellectual property rights at the Uruguay Round was to prevent the trade in 'counterfeit goods', the resulting agreement turned out to be much more ambitious than this.[27]

The insertion of 'trade-related' intellectual property rights into the Uruguay Round agenda and the subsequent adoption of an agreed text for an intellectual property agreement could not have been achieved without the effective lobbying activities in the USA of legal and policy activists and corporations, and a government and political establishment that, during the 1980s, was especially receptive to the diagnoses and prescriptions propounded by these individuals, firms and business associations.

According to Sell, TRIPS is a case of 12 US corporations making public law for the world.[28] Nonetheless, representatives of the USA, Europe and

Japan did not just sit down together and write the TRIPS Agreement themselves. Not only did divisions emerge between Europe and the US that
required compromises, but developing countries were much more involved in
the drafting than they are often given credit for. As Watal explains, they
achieved favourable language in ten of the 73 articles albeit with the necessary
support of a few developed countries.[29] The ten include those dealing with the
objectives and principles of TRIPS, limitations and exceptions to copyright,
exceptions to patents and compulsory licensing, and control of anti-
competitive practices in contractual licensing.

Objectives and Principles of TRIPS

The preamble affirms the desire of member states 'to take into account the
need to promote effective and adequate protection of intellectual property
rights', while 'recognizing the underlying public policy objectives of national
systems for the protection of intellectual property, including developmental
and technological objectives'.

Dealing with counterfeiting is clearly considered as important. Its main
importance lies in the fact that the trade in counterfeit goods is what makes
intellectual property most clearly trade-related. The preamble indicates that
members recognise 'the need for a multilateral framework of principles, rules
and disciplines dealing with international trade in counterfeit goods'.

And yet, the objectives as stated in Article 7 make no reference to the erad-
ication of counterfeiting. Rather, TRIPS is explicitly aimed at promoting
public policy objectives, the nature of such objectives presumably being left
to national governments, though technological development is given priority.

Article 8.1 allows member states implementing their intellectual property
regulations to 'adopt measures necessary to protect human health and nutrition, and to promote the public interest in sectors of vital importance to their
socio-economic and technological development'. These measures are not
obligatory but, again, they highlight the socio-economic welfare implications
of intellectual property rights. On the other hand, the proviso that such
measures be consistent with the provisions of TRIPS appears to narrow their
possible scope quite considerably.

It is worthwhile to mention Article 6, which states that 'for the purposes of
dispute settlement under this Agreement . . . nothing in this Agreement shall
be used to address the issue of the exhaustion of intellectual property rights'.
This is very significant in that it allows countries to adopt a regime of international exhaustion of rights. Accordingly, they cannot be challenged at the
WTO if their laws permit the importation of intellectual property-protected
goods legally placed on the market in a foreign country. Consider the example
of a patented medicine. For a developing country where the drug is too expen-

sive to be widely available to patients, the possibility exists for it to be purchased in a country where it is sold more cheaply and then imported, thereby undercutting the price of the same patented drug already on the domestic market. International exhaustion is unpopular with many international businesses since it makes it harder for them to separate national markets and set prices at levels intended to maximise their profits in each one.

National Treatment and Most-favoured Nation

By virtue of Article 3, members accept the principle of national treatment, that is, that each country must treat nationals of other members at least as well as it treats its own nationals. In other words, intellectual property protection and enforcement must be non-discriminatory as to the nationality of rights holders.

Article 4 upholds the principle of most-favoured nation. This means that any concession granted by one member to another must be accorded to all other members 'immediately and unconditionally'. So if country A agrees to take special measures to prevent the copying of the products of a company from country B, but turns a blind eye when the company is from country C, D or E, such inconsistency of treatment will violate this principle.

The Rights

Part II of TRIPS deals with the actual rights. These are very comprehensive, comprising the following:

1. Copyright and Related Rights
2. Trade marks
3. Geographical Indications
4. Industrial Designs
5. Patents
6. Layout Designs (Topographies) of Integrated Circuits
7. Protection of Undisclosed Information
8. Control of Anti-competitive Practices in Contractual Licences

To some extent the provisions are based on existing agreements. Thus WTO members are required to implement substantial parts of the Paris and Berne Conventions whether or not they are signatories to them. Nonetheless, while most developed countries were required only to make cosmetic changes to their intellectual property laws, most developing countries needed to reform their laws quite drastically. This is not surprising since the intellectual property standards provided in TRIPS tend to be modelled on the laws of the United States, Europe or are a hybrid mix of the rules of the two jurisdictions.

Transitional Arrangements

All countries had to apply Article 3, on national treatment, on most-favoured nation, and Article 5, concerning multilateral agreements on acquisition or maintenance of protection within one year of the entry into force of the WTO Agreement. But the developing countries and the former centrally planned socialist states were allowed a period of five years from the date of entry into force of the WTO Agreement to apply the full provisions of TRIPS, that is, 1 January 2000. The least-developed countries (LDCs), who are recognised as the poorest of the poor countries, were allowed until 1 January 2006 to apply TRIPS in full. This period has since been extended (see below).

National Enforcement and Administration Challenges

TRIPS places much emphasis on enforcement. With respect to the general enforcement obligations, procedures must be available that 'permit effective action against any act of infringement of intellectual property rights'.[30] They must be fair, equitable and not unnecessarily complicated, costly or time-consuming.[31] The judicial authorities must be granted the power to require infringers to pay damages adequate to compensate the right holder for the injury suffered due to the infringement.[32] Members are required to provide for criminal procedures and penalties 'at least in cases of wilful trademark counterfeiting or copyright piracy on a commercial scale'.[33] Remedies may include imprisonment and/or monetary fines. Such remedies may also be applied in other cases of intellectual property right infringement if done 'wilfully and on a commercial scale'. Members are not required to put in place a judicial system for enforcing rights separate from that for the enforcement of law in general.[34] Moreover, TRIPS creates no obligation to shift resources away from the enforcement of law in general towards the enforcement of rights. Nonetheless, poor countries may face a difficult dilemma when determining how to allocate the scarce resources they have.

The dynamic efficiencies of stronger and more effective intellectual property right systems may more than make up for the administrative and enforcement costs. Whether or not this turns out to be true, the costs must be borne before the benefits accrue and, for least-developed countries especially, these are likely to be particularly onerous. In addition, regulators and courts are likely to lack experience in dealing with intellectual property-related matters.

Institutional Arrangements: Final Provisions

Article 68 (Council for Trade-related Aspects of Intellectual Property Rights) sets out the role of the WTO Council for TRIPS. The Council is responsible for:

- monitoring the operation of TRIPS, and in particular members' compliance;
- affording members the opportunity to consult on matters relating to trade-related intellectual property rights;
- assisting members in the context of dispute settlement procedures; and
- carrying out other duties assigned to it by the members.

The Council is supposed to review the implementation of TRIPS at two-year intervals from January 2000. Article 71.1 states in addition that 'the Council may also undertake reviews in the light of any relevant new developments which might warrant modification or amendment of this Agreement'.

TRIPS-related Developments at the WTO

Developing country representatives continue to express concerns that TRIPS raises prices of drugs and educational materials in poor countries, legitimizes the 'biopiracy' of genetic resources and traditional knowledge, and blocks transfers of much-needed technologies. They have successfully resisted the further tightening of TRIPS rules and have put forward substantial counter-proposals relating to such matters as public health, the specific needs of least-developed countries, traditional knowledge and the compatibility between TRIPS and the provisions of the Convention on Biological Diversity (CBD) concerning benefit-sharing, protection of traditional knowledge and biotechnology transfer. And outside the WTO their improved negotiating strategies have delayed moves to harmonise international patent law and moderated some recent copyright treaties.

As for the developed countries and international businesses, who are constantly seeking ever higher levels of intellectual property protection and enforcement, TRIPS has to some extent been a disappointment. For one thing, the WTO system of trade governance currently does not make it easy to achieve radical revision of existing agreements or, for that matter, consensus on the need for new ones. For another, developing countries have tended not to implement TRIPS with much enthusiasm, and enforcement measures continue to be inadequate from the view of the intellectual property owners. Moreover, other forms of trade diplomacy seem to further their interests more effectively.

At the November 2001 Doha Ministerial Conference of the WTO, members agreed on the texts of three statements, all of which have provisions concerning intellectual property: (i) the Ministerial Declaration, (ii) the Decision on Implementation-related Issues and Concerns, and (iii) the Declaration on the TRIPS Agreement on Public Health (see Chapter 13).

The Ministerial Declaration covered a number of TRIPS-related matters including geographical indications (see Chapter 8), the relationship between

TRIPS and the Convention on Biological Diversity and the protection of traditional knowledge and folklore (see Chapter 14), and technology transfer.

Concerning the latter, the Declaration expressed agreement on the establishment of a Working Group to examine 'the relationship between trade and transfer of technology, and of any possible recommendations on steps that might be taken within the mandate of the WTO to increase flows of technology to developing countries'.

As to the specific needs of the LDCs, the Decision on Implementation-related Issues and Concerns reaffirmed the mandatory nature of Article 66.2 ('Developed country Members shall provide incentives to enterprises and institutions in their territories for the purpose of promoting and encouraging technology transfer to least-developed country Members in order to enable them to create a sound and viable technological base'). The TRIPS Council was directed to establish 'a mechanism for ensuring the monitoring and full implementation of the obligations in question'.

Pursuant to this, in February 2003, the Council for TRIPS adopted a decision requiring the developed country WTO members to 'submit annually reports on actions taken or planned in pursuance of their commitments under Article 66.2'.[35] Such reports must provide the following information: (a) an overview of the incentives regime put in place to fulfil the obligations of Article 66.2, including any specific legislative, policy and regulatory framework; (b) identification of the type of incentive and the government agency or other entity making it available; (c) eligible enterprises and other institutions in the territory of the Member providing the incentives; and (d) any information available on the functioning in practice of these incentives.

It is hard to see such pressure on developed countries to comply with Article 66.2 going very far. The real difficulty is that technologies tend to be privately owned and governments are limited in terms of how far they are able and willing to intervene so as to assure they are transferred to the LDCs.

In addition, the Doha Declaration on the TRIPS Agreement and Public Health allowed LDCs to delay implementation of patent protection for pharmaceutical products and legal protection of undisclosed test data submitted as a condition of approving the marketing of pharmaceuticals until 1 January 2016.

In November 2005, the TRIPS Council extended the deadline for fully implementing the rest of TRIPS by a further seven and a half years to 1 July 2013. Undoubtedly these are achievements for LDCs, even if some of them have already implemented some or all of TRIPS.

BEYOND TRIPS

Until recently, TRIPS seemed to be the most important element of the effort to pull up developing countries' intellectual property standards of protection and enforcement to the level of the developed countries and to modernise intellectual property protection so as to accommodate rapid advances in emerging fields like biotechnology and the digital technologies. But now, if recent trade deal-making and the views of people like Bruce Lehman are anything to go by (see Chapter 1), TRIPS may be outliving its purpose for those corporations that successfully lobbied for an intellectual property agreement in the Uruguay Round and the governments that took up their demands. Why? To recapitulate, first, because the WTO system of trade governance currently does not make it easy to achieve radical revision of existing agreements. Second, developing countries have tended not to implement TRIPS with much enthusiasm. Third, for the developed countries and transnational industry, other forms of trade diplomacy seem to further their interests more effectively.

What does transnational industry actually want? In the area of patents, the priority is global harmonisation pitched at a level such that TRIPS is the floor; the absolute minimum that is acceptable. WIPO has recently drafted a Substantive Patent Law Treaty that the organisation's Standing Committee on the Law of Patents is currently debating. Such a Treaty would intensify substantive patent law harmonisation in the interests of helping well-resourced companies to acquire geographically more extensive and secure protection of their inventions at minimised cost. Substantive harmonisation is more than just making the patent systems of countries more like each other in terms of enforcement standards and administrative rules and procedures. It means that the actual substance of the patent standards will be exactly the same to the extent, for example, of having identical definitions of novelty, inventive step and industrial application. Given the rich countries' interests in harmonisation, it is likely to result in common (and tightly drawn) rules governing exceptions to patent rights, and the erosion of freedoms to exclude from patentability types of subject matter or technological fields on public policy or national interest grounds. It is not surprising, then, that this initiative has met with considerable resistance from many developing countries with the consequence that negotiations are currently at a stalemate.

Harmonisation is important with copyright too, especially in such areas as term of protection and subject matter; for example, the developed countries are encouraging the developing countries to extend the term of copyright protection beyond that required by TRIPS to life of the author plus 70 years, as in Europe and the USA. But the situation is a little different. One reason is that the complex array of stakeholders[36] whose economic and moral interests are affected by copyright makes harmonisation much more difficult to achieve. Another is that rapid technological developments have made the transnational copyright industries determined to achieve an international regime that is sufficiently dynamic to respond speedily to the massive opportunities and vulnerabilities afforded by technological advances that: (a) provide new means for copyright owners to disseminate their works to the public; but that also (b) threaten to undermine the control over markets in these works by enabling copiers to flood markets with unauthorised versions of these works and by allowing potential consumers to copy them. Such 'dynamic responsiveness' cannot be achieved at the WTO; the WTO agreements have proved not to be susceptible to the substantial periodic revisions that would be necessary to satisfy industry.

The TRIPS approach to achieving ever higher intellectual property protection levels is being supplemented by an expanding menu of alternatives. These include new treaties, technical assistance, threats and intimidation, and 'forum management' including the use of WIPO and bilateral trade and investment agreements. Let us go through these in turn.

Since TRIPS entered into force a number of new multilateral treaties have been negotiated and adopted for this purpose. Most notable among these are the 1996 'Internet Treaties', that is, the WIPO Copyright Treaty (WCT) and the WIPO Performers and Phonograms Treaty (WPPT). In 2000, the Patent Law Treaty (PLT) was also adopted at a Diplomatic Conference. The PLT was intended to harmonise certain patent procedures but steered clear of matters relating to substantive patent law.

The provision of intellectual property technical assistance by international organisations, developed country governmental agencies, intellectual property offices and business and law associations has become quite controversial. Such assistance often seeks to promote standards of intellectual property protection higher than those required by TRIPS in order to protect the interests of providers and funders. Indeed, 'industry experts have played a prominent role in intellectual property-related technical assistance initiatives undertaken in the United States'.[37] Such assistance may involve training programmes, the dissemination of propaganda extolling the virtues of intellectual property and the harm caused by piracy, and even the drafting of legislation.

Sometimes rich countries are alleged to resort to intimidation and threats of trade sanctions against poor countries they accuse of condoning piracy or of having 'inadequate' intellectual property systems. The United States has been particularly aggressive in this regard. Indeed, its government is required to take a tough stance against 'offending' countries under the country's domestic trade law.

Forum management refers to a strategy sometimes referred to as forum shifting.[38] The former term is more accurate and better accommodates the sophistication of US trade and intellectual property strategy, which can involve both the opening up of new forums and the closing of old ones. Most countries seek to use it, but only the powerful nations can practise it well.

Weaker countries normally must unite to have a chance of being good forum managers.

The idea behind the forum management concept is that *where* negotiations take place can make a big difference to their outcome, and is therefore a strategic matter. Achieving goals relating to certain issues can involve the opening, closing and shifting of negotiating or jurisdictional forums. For example, in the 1980s the United States opened up the GATT as another forum to pursue its intellectual property-related interests. At the same time it kept the WIPO forum open to introduce 'TRIPS-plus' standards through new conventions such as the WIPO Copyright Treaty, and the Substantive Patent Law Treaty currently under negotiation. On the other hand, while the United States is seeking to confine traditional knowledge to WIPO's Intergovernmental Committee on Intellectual Property and Genetic Resources, Traditional Knowledge and Folklore (IGC), several developing countries have insisted that traditional knowledge also be covered by WIPO's Standing Committee on the Law of Patents, and in the TRIPS Council.

Perhaps the most significant new development in the field of intellectual property forum management is the proliferation of bilateral and regional negotiations on trade and investment that have led to many developing countries adopting heightened standards of intellectual property protection through the resulting agreements. These bilateral and regional agreements have proved to be a useful way to get individual, or sometimes groups of, developing countries to introduce so-called 'TRIPS plus' provisions that go beyond what TRIPS requires such as:

(i)   extending patents and copyright to new kinds of subject matter;
(ii)   eliminating or narrowing permitted exceptions including those still provided in US and European intellectual property laws;
(iii) extending protection terms;
(iv)   introducing new TRIPS-mandated intellectual property rules earlier than the transition periods allowed by TRIPS; and
(v)   ratifying new WIPO treaties containing TRIPS plus measures.

An early example of such a 'new generation' bilateral agreement is the 2000 Agreement between the United States of America and the Hashemite Kingdom of Jordan on the Establishment of a Free Trade Area, which requires patents to be available for any invention in all fields of technology without including the exceptions allowable from Article 27.3(b) of TRIPS, which permits WTO members to exclude plants, animals and essentially biological and macro-biological processes for the production of plants and animals from patentability. Jordan must also join UPOV. In addition, a supplementary memorandum of understanding requires Jordan to allow the patenting of business methods and computer-related inventions, neither of which is expressly required by TRIPS. While one must assume that the Jordanian government felt it was a good agreement for the country, such patents are highly controversial in the US and Europe. In addition, the US and the EU continue to pressure countries with 'inadequate' intellectual property right standards by threatening to remove trade concessions.

In addition, they appear sometimes to require, at least implicitly, that developing country parties drop certain intellectual property-related demands the same countries are making in multilateral forums such as the TRIPS Council.

The United States and the European Community both use the bilateralism strategy, but the USA has been the more aggressive. Nonetheless, the interest of the US, as an active and sophisticated intellectual property forum manager, in bilateralism and regionalism does not mean abandoning the multilateral approach. In this case forum management entails the proliferation of forums, keeping as many open at the same time as possible. According to the former United States Trade Representative, Robert Zoellick, US trade strategy is about not putting all of America's eggs in one basket:[39]

> When the Bush Administration set out to revitalize America's trade agenda almost three years ago, we outlined our plans clearly and openly: We would pursue a strategy of 'competitive liberalization' to advance free trade globally, regionally, and bilaterally ... At its most basic level, the competitive liberalization strategy simply means that America expands and strengthens its options. If free trade progress becomes stalled globally – where any one of 148 economies in the World Trade Organization has veto power – then we can move ahead regionally and bilaterally. If our hemispheric talks are progressing stage-by-stage, we can point to more ambitious possibilities through FTAs [free trade agreements] with individual countries and sub-regions. Having a strong bilateral or sub-regional option helps spur progress in the larger negotiations.

NOTES

1. Dutfield, G., *Intellectual Property Rights and the Life Science Industries: A Twentieth Century History*, Aldershot: Ashgate, 2003.
2. For history and background to the Paris Convention, see Anderfelt, U., *International Patent Legislation and Developing Countries*, The Hague: Martinus Nijhoff, 1971; Blakeney, M., 'Commentary', in A. Ilardi and M. Blakeney (eds), *International Encyclopaedia of Intellectual Property Treaties*, Oxford: Oxford University Press, 2004, 1–183; Penrose, E.T., *The Economics of the International Patent System*, Baltimore: Johns Hopkins University Press, 1951.
3. As with the United States today.
4. Ladas, S.P., *Patents, Trademarks, and Related Rights: National and International Protection. Volume 1*, Cambridge, MA: Harvard University Press, 1975, 26–7.
5. Interestingly, the patent regime currently in force in the United States *does* have certain provisions relating to local working. See Chapter 18 ('Patent rights in inventions made with federal assistance') of the United States Patent Code.

6. United Kingdom Board of Trade, *Report of the Committee Appointed by the Board of Trade to Inquire into the Working of the Patents Acts on Certain Specified Questions ('The Fry Committee')*, London: HMSO, 1901.

7. Ricketson, S., *The Berne Convention for the Protection of Literary and Artistic Works: 1886–1986*, London: Queen Mary College Centre for Commercial Law Studies, 1987, at 50.

8. *Ibid.*, 47.

9. *Ibid.*, 41–2.

10. *Ibid.*, 48–9.

11. Sterling, J.A.L., *World Copyright Law* (2nd ed.), London: Sweet & Maxwell, 2003, chapter 18.

12. The US publishing industry did manage to avail itself of the Berne Union protection and its qualification requirements by publishing in Canada; this attempt to take advantage of the first publication rules under the Convention was effectively stemmed by Article 6(1), Berne Convention.

13. From 1891 until 1986, US copyright law discriminated against foreign works in the notorious 'manufacturing clause', a protectionist measure intended to benefit American printers. Originally, this required all copyrighted literary works to be printed in the country. Although the clause was weakened over the years, when President Reagan vetoed a four-year extension in 1982 in the face of an unfavourable GATT panel ruling and complaints from Europe, Congress disregarded the ruling and overruled Reagan. The fact that the United States had by this time become by far the world's biggest exporter of copyrighted works suggests that its creative industries were not exactly held back by a copyright system that appears initially to have been inspired by infant-industry protectionism. Significantly, the world's leading producer of entertainment products did not sign the Berne Convention until 1989.

14. Masouyé, C., 'Décolonisation, Indépendence et Droit d'Auteur', 36, *Revue International de Droit D'auteur'*, 85, 1962; Olian, I.A., 'International Copyright and the Needs of Developing Countries: the Awakening at Stockholm and Paris', *Cornell International Law Journal*, 7, 81, 1974.

15. See Ricketson, *op cit.*, para. 8.26.

16. World Intellectual Property Organization, *Intellectual Property Reading Material*, Geneva: WIPO, 1998, 260–1.

17. Correa, C.M., *Intellectual Property Rights, the WTO and Developing Countries: The TRIPS Agreement and Policy Options*, London, New York and Penang: Zed Books and Third World Network, 2000.

18. Ladas, S., *Patents, Trademarks, and Related Rights: National and International Protection*, Cambridge, MA: Harvard University Press, 1975, at 92.

19. For a detailed discussion on WIPO, including how it operates and its legal and political role in the world, see May, C., *The World Intellectual Property Organization: Resurgence and the Development Agenda*, London: Routledge, 2007. Also, Musungu, F.S. and G. Dutfield, 'Multilateral Agreement and a TRIPS Plus World: The World Intellectual Property Organization', TRIPS Issues Paper no. 3, QUNO & QIAP, 2003.

20. UNCTAD-ICTSD, *Intellectual Property Rights: Implications for Development*, Geneva, 2003.

21. The Rome Convention is jointly administered by WIPO with the International Labour Organization and UNESCO.

22. The UPOV abbreviation is based on the French name of the organisation.

23. The purpose of the PCT, for example, is to facilitate patent applications in more than one country. By simplifying and cheapening the process, the treaty encourages patentees to secure protection over a broader geographical range. Instead of filing separately in all countries where protection is desired, applicants may file a single application in one language with a national patent office. When doing so they can designate all those signatory countries in which protection is also sought. After the examination of the patent, the application is transferred to one of nine International Search Authorities where a prior art search is conducted. After this it is then up to the patent offices of – or acting for – the designated countries to award the patent.

24. http://www.wipo.int/treaties/index.html.

25. For example, some of the language of the European Patent Convention and of Chapter 17 of the North American Free Trade Agreement was incorporated into TRIPS. Having made this point, the national laws of some influential countries may also be used as sources of text to be incorporated into multilateral agreements, although such countries are likely to be few in number (perhaps only the United States).

26. Ryan, M.P., *Knowledge Diplomacy: Global Competition and the Politics of Intellectual Property*, Washington, DC: Brookings Institution Press, 1998; Sell, S.K., *Power and Ideas: North-South Politics of Intellectual Property and Antitrust*, Suny Series in Global Politics, Albany: State University of New York Press, 1998.

27. In fact, it was agreed to delete the reference to counterfeit goods from the title of the agreement.

28. Sell, S.K., *Private Power, Public Law: The Globalization of Intellectual Property Rights*, Cambridge, UK: Cambridge University Press, 2003, 1, 96.

29. Watal, J., *Intellectual Property Rights in the WTO and Developing Countries*, New Delhi: Oxford University Press, 2001, 43.

30. Article 41.1.

31. Article 41.2.

32. Article 45.1.

33. Article 61.

34. Article 41.5.

35. World Trade Organization, 'Implementation of Article 66.2 of the TRIPS Agreement: Decision of the Council for TRIPS of 19 February 2003' [WTO document IP/C/28.]

36. These include authors, publishers, performers, film production companies, phonogram producers, internet service providers and broadcasters.

37. Matthews, D. and V. Muñoz-Tellez, 'Bilateral Technical Assistance and TRIPS: The United States, Japan and the European Communities in Comparative Perspective', *Journal of World Intellectual Property*, 9(6), 629–53, 2006, at 648. In the United States, much of the technical assistance is targeted at the enforcement of rights, which in many developing countries are mostly owned by foreigners. Some of it is provided through the US Agency for International Development and is classed as overseas aid.

38. See Braithwaite, J. and P. Drahos, *Global Business Regulation*, Cambridge, UK: Cambridge University Press, 2000.

39. Letter from Robert Zoellick to David Walker, Comptroller of the United States, December 2003: http://www.ustr.gov/releases/2003/12/2003-12-03-letter-gao.pdf

PART II

Principles of intellectual property

3. Legal, philosophical and economic justifications

In John Rawls's celebrated book, *A Theory of Justice,* we are offered a thought experiment that helps us to imagine what a just society should look like and how we might go about creating one.[1] According to Rawls's 'original position', we lack the most fundamental information about ourselves or our society. We may be geniuses or morons, young or old, male or female, ethnically in the majority or in the minority. We may be able-bodied or handicapped, rich people or paupers, talented or not. We do not even know what our conception of the good life to be, or anything of our psychological make-up. Neither do we know a thing about the kind of society in which we live. Behind this 'veil of ignorance', Rawls then invites us to consider what a just and fair society would look like. His belief is that in pursuing our own interests we would not be utilitarian. Neither, evidently, does he think we would strive for some kind of Pareto or Kaldor-Hicks optimality. Rather, we would opt for a set of principles – a hypothetical social contract[2] – that would promote a society that was fair to everyone – just in case.

Perhaps that is a useful way to think about intellectual property policy-making.[3] Given the wider range of stakeholders that range from the rich and powerful to the poor and underprivileged, what principles would we base our intellectual property regimes upon to ensure justice for all?

Of course, Rawls's thought experiment cannot help us when it comes to the nitty-gritty of intellectual property policy-making. But it can perhaps help us to come up with the right principles. After all, patents are often considered to be contracts between inventors and the state, and other intellectual property rights could likewise be understood this way. So why not take this contract idea further along the lines of Rawls?

Those opposing such a suggestion might argue, first, that utilitarianism and economic efficiency provide perfectly sound and practical starting points for designing intellectual property rules and defending them from critics. Besides, why should intellectual property rights have to give priority to fairness for all members of society when this may be at the expense of the creators and may also compromise economic efficiency?

However, as this book shows time and again, while intellectual property is increasingly conceived as being little more than a certain class of business assets held by companies, this is not all they are. Moreover, the human development impacts, both good and bad, of intellectual property rules surely make it irresponsible if not callous to treat economic efficiency as the primary criterion for 'good' intellectual property rules. Oddly, some critics of intellectual property hold to this view even as they decry the damage to social and cultural life wrought by intellectual property 'extremism'.[4] But we do not.

Legal, philosophical and economic arguments for protecting the creations, investments and business assets of authors, inventors, producers and traders go back to Roman times. Over time, intellectual property rhetoric has employed such terms as 'incentive', 'reward', 'natural rights', 'public interest', 'public goods', free-riding' and 'piracy'. While the justifications and rhetorics vary over time and whether the justifier or critic is a creator, investor, user or member of the public, some of them are very persistent.

Nowadays, patents are said to be an institutional means for investors and research corporations to be rewarded, or alternatively, incentivised, for investing in research and development, for deterring the pirating of their inventions by competitors, and for harnessing a nation's inventive spirit. Yet many individual inventors continue to speak, at least implicitly, in terms of natural rights. Copyright protection allows authors to claim their natural right to their creative attainments, and for upholding their fundamental right to enjoy their personal property. Yet corporations are more ambivalent about natural rights justifications as they are often about authors' moral rights, and tend to eschew individualism-based rhetoric although without abandoning it entirely whenever it suits them to revive it.[5] Trade marks are trickier but nevertheless attempts are still made to place trade mark justifications within a property framework.[6]

The variety of rationales and terms justifying 'intellectual property' as a classification of legal rights makes the concept very nebulous and ambivalent. Nonetheless, the highly successful deployment of the various justifying rhetorics has helped to ensure a tremendous expansion in the scope of intellectual property so that it now includes not only the traditional rights of patents, copyright, trade marks and designs, but also trade secrets, plant variety protection, database rights, geographical indications and rights to semiconductor chip topographies.[7]

This expansion is manifested in the lumping of rather disparate works under the same right in some areas, and the splitting of approaches in others so that we have not just property laws, but also the operation of tort-based rules and criminal sanctions with intellectual property having features of both private law and public law. Yet all of these somehow fit, albeit uneasily, under the umbrella of 'intellectual property' as if the term actually means something. In fact, it is not entirely clear to us that it actually does.

ECONOMIC RATIONALES

The conventional view is that economic well-being depends on achieving a workable competitive market economy. In setting out the conditions for such a market economy, classical thought is primarily concerned with allocative efficiency in terms of how effectively the allocation of resources satisfies the economic wants and desires of individuals in society, and generates the highest possible level of social well-being throughout the community as a whole.

Optimal efficiency in allocation, often understood as 'Pareto optimality' after the economist Vilfredo Pareto who conceptualised it this way, is reached when there can be no possible reallocations or changes so as to make one individual better off without making someone else worse off. At this point, one attains a Pareto efficient allocation of resources. Where a market is not Pareto-efficient, market failure is deemed to have occurred. In other words, market failure is a general term describing situations in which market outcomes are not Pareto efficient. Market failure is caused by a variety of factors, including the public goods phenomenon, the existence of market power to the extent of absence of perfect competition, and situations where externalities exist. It should further be noted that it is, in reality, impossible to generate a Pareto-optimal outcome since it is contingent on there being a purely competitive market, including the absence of externalities or public goods, the presence of private rights, and perfect enforcement of such rights.

Due to the restrictive application of the Pareto criterion, an alternative efficiency criterion is often used. This is the Kaldor-Hicks efficiency or the wealth maximisation criterion, which is named after Nicholas Kaldor and John Hicks. According to this, any change within an economy that favours *some individuals* at the expense of others will constitute an improvement, if the gains to the winners exceed the losses to the losers.[8] A simpler version of these theoretical positions is to note that they are but one means of stakeholder analysis (discussed below) whereby one identifies gainers and losers in a particular context, both in the short term and long term.

Public Goods and Free Riding

The attainment of Pareto efficiency is problematic when confronted with public goods. In an economic context, all intellectual subject matter is a public good.[9] Public goods are defined by two characteristics:

(a) non-excludability (that is, one cannot practically exclude people from using it);
(b) non-rivalrous consumption (that is, the use of the good by one does not limit or leave less for the other to use).

The problem with a public good is that if it is only regulated by the exigencies of market forces, where non-excludability and non-rivalry can flourish, the result is free-riding. As Demsetz observes:

> (what) converts a harmful or beneficial effect into an externality is that the cost of bringing the effect to bear on the decisions of one or more of the interacting persons is too high to make it worthwhile . . . 'Internalising' such effects refers to a process, usually a change in property rights, that enables these effects to bear (in greater degree) on all interacting persons . . . A primary function of property rights is that of guiding incentives to achieve a greater internalization of externalities.[10]

An assumption is that free-riders, who copy inventions and other creations, will manufacture and sell products and services at a lower cost than the actual creator. Is this necessarily harmful within a competitive market economy? Popular economics states that free-riding (that is, obtaining a benefit at no cost) is symptomatic of a privately supplied public good. Furthermore, free-riding leads to non-appropriability: the creator has difficulty in appropriating the value of the goods through its sale and dissemination. Due to the unavoidable presence of free-riders, dissemination of public goods is predicted to be lower than would be optimally efficient. Hence, the reluctance of private manufacturers to supply the relevant market adequately.[11]

If the market for those goods is then categorised as inefficient because consumer demand is not being satisfied, market failure is deemed to have occurred. To counteract this market failure and ensure a steady production of public goods, state intervention is justified and required. In the case of intellectual property, the state intervenes by creating and enforcing a system of property rights.

However, property rights need not be the only response to the public goods phenomenon. Alternative schemes for public goods include the following: (i) public ownership; (ii) a liability rules regime such as an unfair competition law; (iii) public subsidies; (iv) targeted taxation or state regulation; (v) tax credits to stimulate more relevant research such as in public health; (vi) sales taxes or levies on copying equipment or broadband services;[12] (vii) digital rights management and other technological means;[13] and (viii) prizes. At least one economic study has suggested that the more optimal model for societal well-being is a mixed reward-rights model.[14]

Nevertheless, property rights arguably remain one of the most efficient means by which to secure beneficial industrial progress at minimum public cost.[15] Such a view is consistent with J.S. Mill's concerning patents:

> The condemnation of monopolies ought not to extend to patents, by which the originator of an improved process is allowed to enjoy, for a limited period, the exclusive privilege of using his own improvement. This is not making the commodity

dear for his benefit, but merely postponing a part of the increased cheapness which the public owe to the inventor, in order to compensate and reward him for the service. That he ought to be both compensated and rewarded for it, will not be denied . . .[16]

STAKEHOLDER ANALYSIS

One means of viewing intellectual property policy-making is to utilise stakeholder analysis. The stakeholder process includes the identification of the key stakeholders within a particular policy area, in other words the different institutions and interests with a stake in the operation of the policy. The classical definition of stakeholder analysis is 'any group of individual who can affect or is affected by the achievement of the organization objectives' (see Table 2.1).[17] Stakeholders can be natural persons, groups or legal entities; nor are they limited to 'insiders' within the organisation. Indeed, modern stakeholder theories include any 'group or individual that can be influenced by, or can itself influence, the activities of the organisation'.[18] Some academics have pushed the concept of 'stakeholder' further to include anyone who has a stake or a vested interest in the organisation, including all living entities, as well as non-living entities such as the biosphere and water.[19]

A simple stakeholder-based rationale for intellectual property policy is that regulation of intellectual property products is necessary to create a balance between the competing interests of the main stakeholders in this game: the author-inventor, the producer-investor and the consumer (Table 2.2). There may be other stakeholders but these three lie at the heart of all the different justifications for patent and copyright laws. Trade marks are an entirely different species which is treated elsewhere in this book.

PHILOSOPHICAL RATIONALES

Deontological and Consequential Theories

Before we discuss some of the best-known philosophical justifications for intellectual property protection, we would remind the reader that this area of law and policy attracts many theoretical and empirical justifications, some of which are complementary, and others contradictory, and all of them *ex-post facto*. But most of them can also be approximated as being either deontological or consequential.

Deontological justifications for intellectual property (as opposed to consequentialist rationales) emphasise that rights are enforced with respect to

Table 2.1 A stakeholder map

Stakeholders	Needs	Examples of economic and philosophical rhetoric	Examples of jurisprudential rhetoric
Creator	Recognition, respect, remuneration	Personhood, ethics, capital reward	Hegel, moral rights, property rights, right to equitable remuneration (for example, employee-invention benefits)
Consumers (including future creators)	Access to and affordability of scientific and cultural technology	Public domain, public interest, access to medicines and education	Limitations and exceptions Experimental use freedom of expression
Producers	Enforceable and state-sponsored regime to protect investment/ capital	Market, fair competition	Property, tort or contract, presumptive contractual transfers

persons who are entitled to intellectual property as a matter of natural rights or as a matter of classical liberal or human rights or as a matter of duty. Kant's theoretical justification for author's rights, discussed below, is a prime example of a deontological theory which focuses on natural rights and duties rather than on the consequences of an action. To take another example, there are rules within intellectual property laws which recognise the moral rights of attribution and integrity of individual authors and inventors. These rules are based on the more general deontological view that such rights are manifestations of the duty of others to respect a creator's dignity, name and honour, and also arise from the natural principle of the inviolability of persons.[20]

Consequentialists, on the other hand, would argue that intellectual property protection is necessary because of the valuable and correct consequences it brings about in a society such as providing incentives or encouraging learning. This perspective accepts that intellectual property protection, irrespective of the form of protection (property, tort or criminal rules), is a necessary institutional strategy which is aimed at protecting and advancing the manifold interests of influential stakeholders. Consequentialists, therefore, would know that intellectual property law is necessary to reward authors, inventors, performers, producers, corporations and any other interest holder for their efforts.

Table 2.2   An institutional stakeholder map

Rights owners	Needs	Examples of economic and philosophical rhetoric	Examples of jurisprudential rhetoric
Single creator	Recognition, respect, remuneration	Personhood, ethics, capital reward	Hegel, moral rights, property rights, right to equitable remuneration
Corporate producers	Access to and affordability of works	Public domain, public interest, access to knowledge	Limitations and exceptions, freedom of expression
Others (for example, consumers, NGOs, collecting societies)	Enforceable and state-sponsored regime to protect investment/capital	Market, fair competition	Property, tort or contract, presumptive contractual transfers

Intellectual property law can also, from the more consequentialist view, be distorted to accommodate strange and unusual interests such as the *droit de suite* (or resale royalty right) which attaches to the physical subject matter (usually an original painting or manuscript), rather than to the intangible creation.

This category is a simplistic but powerful one as it has the ability to encompass rationales for intellectual property regulation based on positive rights, social contract, utilitarianism, public choice, and economics. Consequentialist thinking typically formed the basis of pre-modern intellectual property privileges in Venice and England, as well as modern statutory rights based on constitutions such as the US Constitution and the European Community Treaty. US patent and copyright laws are premised on the fact that the rights are conferred on authors and inventors to 'promote the progress of science and useful arts'.[21] The 2001 EC directive on copyright is justified on the basis that copyright laws 'protect and stimulate the development and marketing of new products and services and the creation and exploitation of their creative content';[22] more generally, copyright harmonisation within the European Union is justified on the grounds of fundamental principles of European law including 'intellectual property, and freedom of expression and the public interest'.[23]

Locke, Reward, and the Public Domain

It is clear that Locke's theory on property is most appropriate to the protection of investment-based intellectual property such as industrial property, inventions and inventions and sound recordings. Hegelian thought, discussed further below, lends itself more to the ethical and human rights considerations, and hence is useful for explaining, for example, why we have moral rights under copyright law.

The first justificatory strand is reflected in Locke's theory, which simply states that all resources given by God are part of the 'commons' other than one's own body. However, God has endowed every individual with a right to use (or expend labour on) such common resources. Where one has worked on such resources and 'mixed his labour', the resulting product of that labour will become that person's personal or private property.[24] The attraction of Lockean property lies in the central tenet that 'everyone has an inalienable right to his labour'. This basic tenet is then extrapolated by consequential reasoning to justify all sorts of extravagant rights for all sorts of persons. Not only does Lockean justification confer rights on the creator, but it also justifies rights for corporations, investors, and performers. Many industries would agree with this approach, and probably also with the more exaggerated version of the Lockean theory which was proposed by nineteenth-century property zealots who advocated for perpetual protection which arose from the permanent and inalienable natural right to man's work. [25]

Lockean theory has been criticised as being implausible seventeenth-century rhetoric being applied to modern intangible rights.[26] While the appropriation of physical matter from the commons does in some way diminish the opportunities for others to gain from the commons, it is argued that a creator, in the absence of prescriptive laws, does not diminish anything by using incorporeal elements from the commons.

Another view is that the Lockean doctrine is applicable only to subject matter of finite capacity, as in water or land, but not in instances of infinite resources such as intellectual property. As David Hume stated, 'property has no purpose where there is abundance' as property rights only arise out of the scarcity of objects.[27] There is no scarcity, surely, in intellectual property which can be consumed without the supply being exhausted. Intellectual property law artificially creates scarcity. From this perspective, technology is a strange creature which enables both scarcity and abundance.[28]

Lockean property, nevertheless, is not absolute. Conversely, these modern developments do suggest that although the Lockean concept of property may be dated, it is arguable that the Lockean proviso may be of more not less importance today due to the continuous encroachment of technology over intangible matter. His proviso is that the initial common resources or their equivalent should be either used or returned to the commons for others to exploit.[29] At least, the proviso offers two simple balancing factors: balancing the reward to the labourer-creator and the maintenance of the commons. Moreover, it is arguable that the Lockean proviso is so vague as to why subject matter should be excluded from protection that we can postulate several plausible policy rationales. Thus, one can argue that intellectual property subject matter must be made free for others for a variety of reasons:

- the raw materials and basic building blocks of creation must be left for future generations of creators; this would include discoveries, traditional or ancient knowledge, and creative works for which the relevant intellectual property rights have expired;
- intellectual property matter which has become *de facto* standards to which other creators or competitors require access;
- where intellectual property rights threaten the very existence and workings of the 'commons', that is, the competitive market system.

By employing Locke's concept of property as a justification for intellectual property, almost anyone or anything can constitute an inventor, author or an owner, as long as labour is expended.

Intellectual property is only held back by another Lockean tenet – a healthy public domain. Thus, it may be that older justifications for property rights such as Locke's theory are too basic and outdated; nevertheless, it is clear that since the beginning, there have been two key competing stakeholders: the labourer (inventor, author, investor, entrepreneur) and the 'commons' (which can be other labourers or competitors within the market or societal welfare sector such as health or education).

Hence, Locke's theory is useful in urging us to consider the need for the existence and maintenance of a 'public domain' (as opposed to several private domains) or an 'intellectual commons' (as opposed to intellectual property).[30]

Natural Rights, Personality and Reward

The second main philosophical justification for intellectual property rights emphasises that all creators should have their fair and equal share based on ethical grounds. During the eighteenth and nineteenth centuries, inventors and authors began to conceive of themselves as private personae, whereby works emanated from them rather than from the divine being. The Romantics stressed the individuality of creations. Immanuel Kant and Johann Gottlieb Fichte, for example, insisted that authors did not imitate nature, but rather 'spoke' original works derived from their inner personalities.[31]

The German copyright law, thus, derives not only from the Hegelian romantic notion that the authors' rights are for the protection of the authorial personality but also from the classic civil and political human rights regime. The ethos of the fundamental freedom of every person to personal development and human dignity is enshrined within the German and French copyright laws, for instance, in relation to their criteria of originality (that is, a work must constitute the personal intellectual creation of the author) and of moral rights (which allow an author to control the way his work is perceived by the public).[32]

From this perspective, the absence of law and rhetoric on the 'public domain' or 'intellectual commons' within many European civil law systems is understandable. These are noticeably less important than legalistic and administrative mechanisms such as a strong jurisprudential and political stance on collective management and copying levies.[33] The prime concern of this type of justification is to adopt rules which facilitate easy and mass usage of works, but still ensure that creators receive adequate and just remuneration for each type of exploitation and use. Thus, detailed mechanistic laws on collective management, levies and contractual arrangements allow all stakeholders from the author to a private user and his circle of friends and family to corporate producers (and even the state) to benefit from any exploitation of their works, whilst maintaining a strong deontological if somewhat impractical rhetoric based on natural rights and personal dignity which is so characteristic of continental European thinking.[34,35]

Kant and the Genesis of the Cult of Authorial Personality

Eighteenth-century German authors, under a patronage system and without a royalty or regular remuneration system, suffered severely from cross-border trading of pirated books. This was particularly acute within pre-unification Germany with its 300 odd independent states, each with its own regulatory system. The question as to whether unauthorised reproduction of books should be prohibited was answered in favour of the pirate booksellers as they produced cheaper editions, and the 'author' was an unstable concept.[36]

Kant, in his 1785 essay entitled 'On the Injustice of Counterfeiting Books', proposed to set out quite mathematically his thesis on why authors had rights to control the piracy of books.[37] He individualised the concept of the 'author' by rejecting the notion that authors were mere craftsmen. He instead internalised the source of inspiration within the author and rejected the notion that man's creation emanated from an extrinsic muse or inspiration, such as God. Moreover, this internal, author-centred inspiration was equated with 'original genius', that is, the work of the author, the product of the author and hence the property of the author. Kant also drew an important distinction as to how we perceive a book. Books can be mere commodities; but they are also, he pointed out, the manifestations of authorial personality and speech. A simplistic pictorial representation of the argument is shown on page 57:

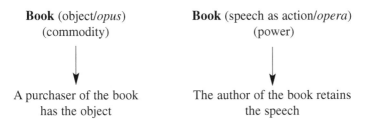

Book (object/*opus*)   **Book** (speech as action/*opera*)
(commodity)   (power)

A purchaser of the book   The author of the book retains
has the object   the speech

Hence, to counterfeit a book is to countermand the author's will. It must be noted that Kant does not really explore the notion of the 'will' which is taken to greater heights by his successor in intellectual property theory, Hegel. To Kant, the author retains the *opera* or speech. It is not a commodity to be sold and bought. The book as opus is merely the mute instrument which holds the book as *opera*.

Intriguingly, Kant's essay is partially economic in reasoning as he explains why the unlawfulness of the counterfeiter's action is economically detrimental to the publisher's business. He states that the counterfeiter, by his actions, seizes the business of another (that is, the publisher), who is authorised by the author himself to publish the work. The question then is: can the author confer the same permission on another?

If both the authorised publisher and the counterfeiter engage in publishing the author's book to the same public, then 'the labour of the one must render that of the other useless and be ruinous to both of them'. Hence, the contract of the author with an editor which reserves the right to allow yet another publisher to venture the publication of his work is impossible. Consequently, the author is not entitled to give the permission to any other publisher. Moreover, Kant reasons, the author has usually 'entirely and without reservation given up to the editor his right to the managing of his business with the public, or to dispose of it otherwise', and the counterfeiter 'does harm to the editor, to his rights, but not to the author'.

This is a remarkably consequentialist and market-based reasoning. The essay appears, at times, to be more concerned with the economic effects of having two competitors selling a perfect substitute product to the same consuming market. Moreover, the result is that harm is done to the editor, not the author. One should note, nevertheless, that in the prior passages of the essay, Kant emphasises that the publisher does not take up the 'speech' of the author. Rather, the publisher, as agent to the author, has a 'right to appropriate this profit to himself as the fruit of his property' where he is instructed to carry on the business on behalf of another (that is, the author). This agency rule is declared by Kant to be 'beyond a doubt in the elementary conceptions of natural right'. Thus, perhaps, Kant implicitly accepts that the author has natural rights in his work, since it must be the case that the editor himself by contract of agency gets a right to do business.

Hegel's Theory[38]

A powerful alternative to Lockean theory is the Hegelian theory of property based on the notion of personality. Hegel declared that property is the initial and final embodiment of freedom and individuality. Indeed, to fail to have a sphere of property in one's life is to fail to attain self-conscious knowledge of oneself as a free person.[39] To achieve a personality, and to be a person, an individual must control his external and internal environment and control his resources. Once again, control (as well as actualisation of one's will) is best achieved by a set of property rights.[40]

Much of Hegel's property theory relies on the notion that the 'will' is the core of an individual's existence and without the actualisation of the 'will', an individual does not gain the capacity to self-determine or concretise. Self actualisation of the 'will' is really an imposition of personality which in turn leads to propertisation. Personality is property as exemplified by life, limbs and liberty. As one commentator notes, Hegel's ultimate thesis is that

> private property involves the statement of an insight concerning the relation of persons, their wills and the world to which they lay claim, and the defence of that insight through an explanation of the institution of private property as we encounter it.[41]

Unlike Locke and Kant, Hegel does discuss, albeit briefly, intellectual property rights. First, he states that intellectual property is inalienable. Most property can be alienated, since the reason

> . . . I can alienate my property is that it is mine only in so far as I put my will into it. Hence I may abandon (*derelinquere*) as a *res nullius* anything that I have or yield it to the will of another and so into his possession, provided always that the thing in question is a thing external by nature.[42]

On the other hand, goods which constitute an individual's 'own private personality' and the 'universal essence of [his] self-consciousness' are inalienable and imprescriptible.[43] Does this apply to intellectual property? Hegel admits, as did Kant before him, that products of the mind can become 'things' which 'may then be produced by other people'.

> The result is that by taking possession of a thing of this kind, its new owner may make his own the thoughts communicated in it or the mechanical invention which it contains, and it is ability to do this which sometimes (i.e. in the case of books) constitutes the value of these things and the only purpose of possessing them. But

besides this, the new owner at the same time comes into possession of the universal methods of so expressing himself and producing numerous other things of the same sort.[44]

The crux of justifying intellectual property rights lies in paragraph 69, where he notes that:

Since the owner of such a product, in owning a copy of it, is in possession of the entire use and value of that copy *qua* a single thing, he has complete and free ownership of that copy *qua* a single thing, even if the author of the book or the inventor of the machine remains the owner of the universal ways and means of multiplying such books and machines, etc. *Qua* universal ways and means of expression, he has not necessarily alienated them, but may reserve them to himself as means of expression which belong to him.[45]

Thus, an author or inventor reserves the right of manufacture or reproduction, although his right to control the product of his mental property may be exhausted. Hegel remarks, in relation to paragraph 69, that the author's or inventor's right and power to reproduce 'has a special character, viz. it is that in virtue of which the thing is not merely a possession but a capital asset . . .'. Hegel admits that intellectual property is a purely negative right, and that the primary

. . . means of advancing the sciences and arts is to guarantee scientists and artists against theft and to enable them to benefit from the protection of their property, just as it was the primary and most important means of advancing trade and industry to guarantee it against highway robbery.[46]

Hegelian philosophy on intellectual property further allows for the public domain and for limitations and exceptions. He accepts, for example, that third parties other than the inventor or author can take possession of 'ideas' since the 'mode of expression' of such third parties will lead into a 'thing' which will have 'some special form of its own in every case' and can be further alienated. In other words, third parties are allowed to utilise intellectual property in order to create derivative works.

The result is that they may regard as their own property the capital asset accruing from their learning and may claim for themselves the right to reproduce their learning in books of their own.[47]

It is well worth nothing at length Hegel's final and very specific take on intellectual property as he manages to opine on all of the following: exceptions for teachers (including law professors), plagiarism, transformative use, minor modifications on inventions, and the perplexing case of factual anthologies:

Those engaged in the propagation of knowledge of all kinds, in particular those whose appointed task is teaching, have as their specific function and duty (above all in the case of the positive sciences, the doctrine of a church, the study of positive law, &c.) the *repetition of well-established thoughts*, taken up *ab extra* and all of them given expression already. The same is true of writings devised *for teaching purposes and the spread and propagation of the sciences.*

Now to what extent does the new form which turns up when something is expressed again and again *transform the available stock of knowledge,* and in particular the thoughts of others who still retain *external* property in those intellectual productions of theirs, into a private mental property of the individual reproducer and thereby give him or fail to give him the right to make them his external property as well? To what extent is such repetition of another's material in one's book a plagiarism? *There is no precise principle of determination available to answer these questions, and therefore they cannot be finally settled either in principle or by positive legislation. Hence plagiarism would have to be a matter of honour and be held in check by honour.*

Thus copyright legislation attains its end of securing the property rights of author and publisher only to a very restricted extent, though it does attain it within limits. The ease with which we may deliberately change something in the form of what we are expounding or *invent a trifling modification in a large body of knowledge or a comprehensive theory which is another's work,* and even the impossibility of sticking to the author's words in expounding something we have learnt, all lead of themselves (. . .) to an endless multiplicity of alterations which more or less superficially stamp someone else's property as our own. For instance, the hundreds and hundreds of compendia, selections, anthologies, &c., arithmetics, geometries, religious tracts, &c., show how every new idea in a review or annual or encyclopaedia, &c., can be forthwith repeated over and over again under the same or a different title, and yet may be claimed as something peculiarly the writer's own. *The result of this may easily be that the profit promised to the author, or the projector of the original undertaking, by his work or his original idea becomes negligible or reduced for both parties or lost to all concerned.*[48]

The highlighted concepts have, in turn, over the ensuing 150 years been used to justify many exceptions and the final statement on loss of profits can even be seen as the nascence of the three-step test, which can be found most recently in TRIPS, prohibiting all uses which 'conflict with a normal exploitation' of a work or patent.[49] Hegel is also prescient in predicting that the line between misappropriation and inspiration is thin, and difficult to draw. What is food for thought is whether future international law and policy should be based, as he suggests, more on *honour* rather than on positive legislation.

NOTES

1. Rawls, J., *A Theory of Justice*, Cambridge, MA: Harvard University Press, 1971.
2. One may compare this conception of the 'social contract' to that of Hobbes, whose original position was the terrifying anarchy of the 'state of nature', and that of Locke whose state of nature was far more benign, and who sought to show that the individual society member's consent to be governed could be withdrawn if that government became despotic.

3. We are not the first to think of this possibility. See Chander, A. and M. Sunder, 'Is Nozick Kicking Rawls's Ass? Intellectual Property and Social Justice', *UC Davis Law Review*, 40(3), 563–80, 2007.

4. For example, Lawrence Lessig, in his presentation at the TransAtlantic Consumer Dialogue-organised meeting on the Future of WIPO, held in Geneva in September 2004.

5. Thus we find recording industry lobbyists trying to get the sound-recording protection term extended by talking of impoverished elderly musicians subsisting on inadequate pensions.

6. Lunney, G., 'Trademark Monopolies', *Emory Law Journal*, 48, 367, 1999; Lemley, M., 'The Modern Lanham Act and the Death of Common Sense', *Yale Law Journal*, 108, 1687, 1999.

7. See Dreyfuss, R., D.L. Zimmerman and H. First (eds), *Expanding the Boundaries of Intellectual Property: Innovation Policy for the Knowledge Society*, Oxford: Oxford University Press, 2001.

8. Mercuro, N. and S. Medema, *Economics and the Law: From Posner to Post-Modernism* (2nd ed.), Princeton: Princeton University Press, 2006, chapter 1.

9. Landes, W.M. and R.A. Posner, *The Economic Structure of Intellectual Property Law*, Cambridge, MA and London: Belknap Press/Harvard University Press, 2003, at 13–16; cf. Arrow, K., 'Welfare Economics and Inventive Activity', in *The Rate and Direction of Inventive Activity*, Princeton: National Bureau of Economic Research, 1962, at 617–18.

10. Demsetz, H., 'Towards a Theory of Property Rights', *American Economic Review*, 57, 347–359, 1967, at 347, 348. Gordon similarly uses the externality notion to explain intellectual property but goes further to conclude that from this perspective, intellectual property is 'tort law turned upside down'. Gordon, W., 'Intellectual Property', in P. Cane and M. Tushnet (eds), *The Oxford Handbook of Legal Studies*, Oxford: Oxford University Press, 2003, at 622–3. For a criticism of the Demsetzian view that sees intellectual property, like real property, as existing to internalise negative externalities like free-riding, see Lemley, M., 'Property, Intellectual Property, and Free Riding', *Texas Law Review*, 83, 2031, 2005.

11. Landes and Posner *op. cit.*, at 22–3.

12. See Chapter 10.

13. See Chapter 10.

14. Shavell, S. and T. van Ypersele, 'Rewards versus Intellectual Property Rights', *Journal of Law and Economics*, 44(2), 525, 2001; and also Stiglitz, J., 'Give Prizes Not Patents', *New Scientist*, 16 September 2006, 21.

15. For a sceptical view of the role played by the intellectual property system in industrial progress, see, Vaver, D., 'Some Agnostic Thoughts on Intellectual Property', *Intellectual Property Journal*, 6, 125, 1991, at 126–7; Plant, A., 'Economic Theory Concerning Patents for Inventions', *Economica*, 1, 30, 1934, at 42–44; Machlup, F. and E. Penrose, 'The Patent Controversy in the 19th Century', *Journal of Economic History*, 1, 1950, at 21–2.

16. Mill, J.S., *Principles of Political Economy: With Some of their Applications to Social Philosophy*, 1848, Book V, Chapter X, § 5.

17. This is the seminal stakeholder definition in Freeman, R.E., *Strategic Management: A Stakeholder Approach*, Boston: Pitman, 1984 at 46. The earliest definition of stakeholder analysis, however, stems from an internal memo produced in 1963 by the Stanford Research Institute which defines stakeholders as: 'Those groups without whose support the organisation would *cease to exist*' (emphasis added) (in Freeman, at 31).

18. Friedman, A. and S. Miles, *Stakeholders: Theory and Practice*, Oxford: Oxford University Press, 2006, at 8–10.

19. *Ibid.*

20. Beitz, C.R., 'The Moral Rights of Creators of Artistic and Literary Works', *Journal of Political Philosophy*, 13(3), 330, 2005, at 337.

21. US Constitution, Article 1, § 8, cl. 8.

22. Recital 2, EC Directive 2001/29/EC of the European Parliament and of the Council of 22 May 2001; based on Articles 47(2), 55 and 95 of the EC Treaty.

23. Recital 3, EC Directive 2001/29/EC.

24. In: McPherson, C.B. (ed.), *John Locke Second Treatise of Government*, Indianapolis and Cambridge, UK: Hackett Publishing Company, 1980, Chapter V, Section 27.

25. Jobard, J.B.M., *Nouvelle économie sociale ou monoautopole industriel, artistique, commercial et littéraire*, Paris, 1844, at 5, 130, 239, cited by Machlup and Penrose, *op. cit.*, at 9.
26. For denunciations of the Lockean concept as applied to intellectual property, see Waldron, J., 'From Authors to Copies: Individual Rights and Social Values in Intellectual Property', *Chicago-Kent Law Review*, 68, 842, 1993, at 871, 879–80; and Kingston, W., *Innovation, Creativity and Law*, Deventer: Kluwer Academic Publishers, 1990, at 83.
27. Plant, *op. cit.*
28. Bethell, T., *The Noblest Triumph: Property and Prosperity Through the Ages*, New York: St. Martin's Press, 1998, at 263 et seq.
29. Locke, J., see note 24, paras 27, 31, 39.
30. See Elkin-Koren, N., 'Creative Commons: A Skeptical View of a Worthy Pursuit', in P.B. Hugenholtz and L. Guibault (eds), *The Future of the Public Domain*, The Hague: Kluwer Law International, 2006.
31. Woodmansee, M., *The Author, Art & the Market: Rereading the History of Aesthetics*, New York: Columbia University Press, 1994, at 53–4.
32. Hegel, G., *Philosophy of Right*, T.M. Knox translation, Oxford: Clarendon Press, 1967, at 68; Article 2(2), German Law on Copyright and Related Rights 1968 stating the creativity principle, and *Re Neo-Fascist Slant In Copyright Works*, Case 11 U 63/94, Oberlandesgericht (Regional Court of Appeal), (Frankfurt am Main), 6 December 1994, [1996] ECC 375, holding that copyright is part of the general inherent rights of a person and has a constitutional basis in Articles 1 and 2 of the German Constitution, which guarantee the basic human rights of human dignity and free development of personality. Claude Colombet, *Propriété littéraire et artistique et droits voisins*, Paris: Dalloz, 1997, at 12–14 (discussing the natural rights basis of French copyright law).
33. For a discussion on collective management, and the types of levies collected, see Suthersanen, U., 'Collectivism of Copyright: The Future of Rights Management in the European Union', in E. Barendt and A. Firth (eds), *Yearbook of Copyright and Media Law*, Vol. 5, Oxford: Oxford University Press, 2000, at 15–42.
34. Schricker, G., 'Efforts for a Better Law on Copyright Contracts in Germany – A Never Ending Story', *IIC*, 35(7), 850, 2004.
35. For a British perspective, see Suthersanen, U., 'Bleak House or Great Expectations: The Literary Author as a Stakeholder in Nineteenth-century International Copyright Politics', in Porsdam, H. (ed.), *Copyright and Other Fairy Tales*, Cheltenham, UK and Northampton, MA: Edward Elgar, 2006, 41–4. Indeed, this was a recurrent theme regarding authorial works, especially in the case of Coleridge – see Susan Eilenberg, *Strange Power of Speech: Wordsworth, Coleridge and Literary Possession*, New York and Oxford: Oxford University Press, 1992.
36. For an overview, see Woodmansee, *op. cit.*, Chapter 2.
37. Kant, I., 'On the Injustice of Counterfeiting Books', (1785), reprinted in Sterling, J.A.L., *World Copyright Law* (2nd ed.), London: Sweet & Maxwell, 2003, para. 80.13.
38. This section is based on Hegel's *Philosophy of Right* (translation by T.M. Knox), Oxford: Oxford University Press, 1967, First Part: Abstract Right, Sub-section 1 on Property.
39. Waldron, J., *The Right to Property*, Oxford: Clarendon Press, 1990, at 351 *et seq.*; Berry, C.J., 'Property and Possession: Two Replies to Locke: Hume and Hegel', in J.R. Pennock and J.W. Chapman (eds), *Property*, New York: New York University Press, 89–100, at 97.
40. Hegel, *op. cit.*, paras 42–3.
41. Knowles, D., *Hegel and the Philosophy of Right*, London: Routledge, 2002, at 112.
42. Hegel, *op. cit.*, para. 65.
43. *Ibid.*, para. 66.
44. *Ibid.*, para. 68.
45. *Ibid.*, para. 69.
46. *Ibid.*
47. *Ibid.*
48. *Ibid.*, with emphasis added.
49. Articles 13, 30, TRIPS.

4. Copyright

ORIGINS

The First Book Markets

Printing technology revolutionized the social and legal infrastructure of the book market. But it did not create the commercial book market. Commercial authors and booksellers have existed from time immemorial. An early example of a thriving monopolistic book trade and seller is the ubiquitous undertaker found in ancient Egyptian, Babylonian and Assyrian ceremonies, who simultaneously arranged funerals and sold copies of the best-selling papyrus known as the 'Book of the Dead'.[1] This document was the vital guide to dead souls during their voyage through the next life. Nevertheless, despite the presence of book traders and book monopolies, there was no recognisable 'author' until Ancient Greek times. Although clearly discernible and recognised as personalities, Greek writers such as Aristotle and Plato regarded themselves as teachers or philosophers rather than authors. Similarly, many Roman writers such as Tacitus and Cicero embraced the epithets of 'poet' or 'orator'; but, it was understood that these were men with private wealth whose lives would be devoted to other duties and pursuits such as advocacy, politics, public service or land management.[2]

The Ancient 'Author'

One view is that ancient authors had no real shares or interest in the profits of their works as what mattered most was fame and recognition.[3] Here then is the nascence of concepts such as the 'authorial persona', the moral right of attribution, and the acceptance that writers were rewarded in non-material terms. Indeed, the figure of the author was perhaps recognised, especially in high literature, primarily as a trade mark, rather than as a creator. The genre of the work, the type of audience it was intended for, its purpose and its symbolic value and its authority were all attributable to the name inscribed on the work. However, works of a vernacular nature were less inclined to be identified by the author save for a few great literary figures such as Petrarch.[4] Then as today, anonymity and pseudonymity were part of a game, where the eventual goal was to identify and attribute authorship. The emphasis on attribution and noto-riety explains the historical link between copyright law and unfair competi-tion, a link which has been given a modern flavour in recent US jurisprudence on the relationship between moral rights and the Lanham Act.[5] Indeed, misap-propriation rather than property laws figures more largely in the early history of protecting literary works. Many individual authors did condemn those who appropriated their works, calling them kidnappers or thieves. The Roman author Martial regarded his work as children and labelled the person misap-propriating his work as a kidnapper or *plagiarus* – an old Roman law label for the theft of slaves or children.[6] Further levels of protection were introduced by commercial enterprises such as publishers. The Roman commercial book trade in the first century AD comprised scribes making copies of texts for both indi-vidual customers and mass consumption, and was probably the basis of the world's first publishers' association. The cheap book prices were a reflection of the cheap slave labour and the absence of expensive typesetting or correc-tions or proofs. Indeed, book production from author to market could be accomplished within 24 hours.[7] With such efficiency and low costs, misap-propriation of texts between publishers was a threat.

It was to counter such a threat that the first Publishers' Association was formed by the leading Roman publishers in the second century AD 'for the better protection of their interests in literary property, and that each member bound himself not to interfere with the undertakings of his fellow members'.[8] This agreement is analogous to the mid-Victorian customary usages within the book industry when both British and American publishers developed a system of 'courtesy of the trade' whereby publishers would respect the first publish-ing house to announce the publication of an edition of a foreign work.[9] We should nevertheless note the contrary view that some Roman authors did despair as to their economic status, complaining that Roman patrons were stingy and did not highly value poetry and other higher forms of authorship – indeed, one Roman author points out that the only way poets could make ends meet was to sell pantomime scripts.[10]

Between the fall of the Roman Empire (at the beginning of the fifth century), and the twelfth century, the monopoly of storing, copying and producing books was enjoyed by the monasteries and other ecclesiastical establishments. It is often alleged that this period, the 'Monastic Age', gave rise to the first copyright decision *Finnian v. Columba* (c. 550 AD), where the Irish abbot Finnian accused another monk Columba from a rival monastery of surreptitiously making a copy of a Book of Psalms which Finnian had acquired previously in Rome. The dispute ends with the famous judgment of King Diarmid: 'To every cow her calf, to every book its copy'. Although subsequent research proves this charming tale of warring saints to be apoc-ryphal,[11] this tale does rightly set out an early legal precept adopted by the monasteries in relation to copying, that the owner of a manuscript was understood to possess the right to copy the work. This 'property' right was often commercially exploited, as the *Finnian* tale shows, by the monasteries who charged a fee for permission to copy one of their books.[12]

The twelfth century saw the start of the Secular Age when the book markets shifted from the monasteries to the main European cities, such as Paris and London, and to the university cities such as Bologna, Oxford and Cambridge.[13] The medieval book market expanded to comprise the following actors:

(i) *Stationers*: Stationers and the booksellers established themselves as the primary publishers and intermediaries between the author/scribe and the consumer. These publishers were also responsible for other services including the coordination of the manuscript production which included the illuminators, bookbinders and paper/vellum suppliers, book lending, and sale of paper/vellum, and other bookmaking accessories.

(ii) *Scholars*: Intellectual life outside the monasteries centred around the universities, scholars and students, leading to the further fuelling of the book market. Specifically, universities led to the increased dissemination of knowledge, and a growing demand by a new reading public – the university scholars and teachers. An increasing facet of the book trade was the assumption that both universities and stationers would censor manuscripts according to the political conditions.

(iii) *New markets*: The entry of all these market players created two types of sub-markets. The first one was the mass produced book market which made cheap and fast books due to the division of labour between the scribes and illuminators. The second market catered for those with luxurious tastes and produced books which were not so much literature as works of art in terms of illumination and decoration.[14]

(iv) *Creators/authors*: Finally, some mention must be made of the authors. Once divulged, it was impossible for authors to retain any rights in the work and thus authors relied on the very Roman system of patronage. Socio-economic changes in the authors' position meant that if the work became successful and was in demand, the author could turn publisher by hiring scribes to supply the market. One historian of medieval manuscripts notes this: 'From the economic viewpoint, the author's rights may be considered to be vested in that first edition, even if it only consisted of a single copy, since thereafter he had no rights in his work. Hence to some extent the patronage system allowed literary men to live by the pen; the price paid by the author was his obligation not to say anything displeasing to his patron, while at the same time trying to write to please a growing public.'[15]

Early Printing Technology and the Venetian Privileges

The genesis of early property rights in books was the highly lucrative privileges or letters patent regime, which created monopolies on the printing of certain works and which were the result of lobbying by individual booksellers or their guilds for either trade or legal mechanisms to protect their investments. In England and some of the European countries, the privileges regime soon developed into a censorship tool to control the new printing technology.[16] The Gutenberg Invention[17] (c. 1450–55 AD) heralded the making of a page of print from separate, movable, metallic types. However, the revolution relied on several factors.[18]

First, an emerging merchant and bourgeoisie social class contributed a reading public, a group of interested investors, and a new class of inventors. Second, the book trade infrastructure was ready to absorb the new printing press through the stationers and copyists. Third, the printing press was spurred by the increased use of paper, as opposed to vellum or other parchment material. Fourth, the printing and paper developments gave rise to new species of trades and activities such as playing cards, bill posters and advertising – which in turn led to a greater demand for print matter. Nevertheless, the Gutenberg invention travelled fast to Venice, London, Paris and Antwerp, and it spurred book production to hitherto unimagined volumes. One account is that the largest printing establishment of that era produced eight million books in Europe. The cost of books also went up with printed books costing three times more than a handwritten scribe copy would have. This may be surprising as mass-produced commodities should cost less; however, the increased charge reflected the luxury cost of the new technology.[19]

Acquisition of this new superior technology was the primary force behind the early Venetian intellectual property laws.[20] The 1469 privilege granted to Johannes of Speyer was akin to a modern-day patent grant as it gave him the exclusive right of exercising the trade of printing in Venice for five years, and the right to stop the operation of competing printing presses with fines and with the confiscation of tools and books.[21] However, other privileges resembled our modern concept of 'copyright' law and were limited to the right to print or deal in a particular book. Even then, it was clear that such copyright privileges could act as barriers to access to information and knowledge. The 1479 Episcopal privilege, for instance, was granted by the Bishop of Würzburg to three printers for the printing of the breviary book; the book was compulsorily required by all the clergy of the Bishop's diocese. Protection from competition (which certainly was a reasonable expectation from the printing centres such as Leipzig and Frankfurt) ensured a reasonable return 'for the outlay involved in printing these large and handsome books'.[22]

Early 'copyright' privileges gave not only printing rights but rights of importation into the territory.[23] However, none of these privileges was actually accorded to the author of the book until the Venetian privilege of 1486 which was granted to Marcus Antonius Sabellicus for his history of Venice.[24] After this, regular privileges for particular books were accorded either to authors on the basis that others may 'reap the fruits of his labours' (*ne alieni colligant fructus laborum et vigiliarum suarum*), or to publishers who wished protection for the trouble and expenses involved in printing and publishing the books. Nothing, however, came of these early authors' rights, and the first authors' laws emanated instead from England.[25]

First Modern Copyright Laws[26]

England

The introduction of the printing press into England in 1476 led to different regulatory and censorship mechanisms, though these mechanisms too can be traced to the commercial privileges system. Whatever the mode of control, it was inevitably recognised that some quasi-property rights existed over the printed literature. Moreover, as a consequence of the formation of the Stationers' Company in England in 1403, the regulation of privileges and printing became more established as this booksellers' guild comprised almost all the printers in England and began to wield more and more influence. The guild exercised a *de facto* monopoly system by constructing a private legal regime based on two factors:

(i)   mutual trust and respect of one another's claims, and
(ii) registration of the manuscript or 'copy' with the Company.

The trust-registration regime gave the bookseller or stationer an exclusive right *in* the copy – a right to print and sell the work. Since this private monopoly was enforceable only amongst guild members and not the general public, they sought and obtained a state imprimatur of this private system in 1557 when the Crown granted a royal charter to the Stationers' Company. Not only did it regulate the book trade (by providing the right of reproduction of stationers' 'copies', which allowed the guild to legally limit almost all printing to members of the company), but the charter also empowered the Company to search out and destroy unlawful books and/or stop non-guild stationers from printing registered works.[27] The issue of 'authorship' did not arise and most authors' remuneration was derived in the form of a sinecure or gratifications.[28] Although the records of the English Stationers' Company do show that authors were occasionally recorded as having retained printing rights in their own works, the circumstances reveal that the relationship was more of the usual publisher-guild nexus as the work would not have been financially attractive and the author was merely assuming the mantle of the risk-taker and would have had to underwrite the cost of printing.[29]

The English book monopoly came to an end in 1695 and was replaced, eventually and with much debate, by the Statute of Anne 1710.[30] A vital issue in these debates was whether and how the traditional concepts of property could be recast and moulded to incorporate the concept of incorporeal property rights, particularly in respect of books. Objections to incorporeal property ranged from the incapacity of literary property to be subsumed within definitional limits (the concept was considered too chimerical), to the difficulty of claiming that intellectual ideas were capable of occupancy, a fundamental requirement in traditional property law. The British legal copyright system finally latched onto the notion of 'labour' as being a quantifiable source for a literary property right, and to the criterion of registration or 'fixation' of works as being the identifier of this incorporeal right.[31]

One thing is clear – the Statute of Anne 1710 was the first modern copyright law which specifically granted a right of printing to authors of books for an initial 14-year period, and a further 14 years if the author managed to outlive this initial duration of protection.[32] Over the centuries, the law in Britain was slowly extended piecemeal to include engravings, fine arts, photographs, dramatic works, sculptures, and musical works. Rose suggests that the 1710 Statute of Anne not only stimulated the emergence of the 'modern proprietary author', but also the progression of copyright history from one of trade regulation and marketplace economics to the liberal culture of possessive individualism.[33] However, the converse can equally be claimed: that the natural rights theory was initially employed by the trade as a means to shift the law's apparent focus from publishers and booksellers to authors while continuing to promote the interests of the former. In any case, the natural rights theory, initially supported by the courts,[34] was ultimately rejected. The courts finally recast it as a statutory animal governed entirely by legislation.[35] Hence, the Statute of Anne made copyright the instrumental right that it is today, shaped entirely by the policy of the legislature and the courts.

France

The French authors' rights regime followed a similar trajectory to the British. Prior to the printing privileges era, there was no real regulation of the presses due to the fact that the trade of booksellers and publishers remained relatively new until the second half of the sixteenth century when the publishing houses, and hence competition, grew. Moreover, the high costs of materials and low prices for books made publishing a risky and long-term investment. Thus, the industry turned towards the state and obtained a private guarantee or a royal privilege from the monarch. The privilege covered one work and benefited one publisher, and forbade all other publishers to print or copy the work.

Furthermore, printers and publishers started forming guilds which exercised a corporate monopoly on who could have the right to print and publish books.

By the eighteenth century, the main Parisian book guild was a self-regulating corporation of printers and booksellers who by virtue of the royal privilege enjoyed an exclusive monopoly on the printing, production and distribution of books. The privilege was extended to authors who published and sold their own works. However a fossilisation of the guild system was inevitable, and a challenge for supremacy of the book trade was mounted by the provincial booksellers. The conflict arose due to the imbalance of privilege ownership: the Paris book trade was the largest corporate owner of printing privileges, whereas all the other traders had little privileges. The provincial traders argued for a wider publication policy, with less privileges, as this was essential to the spread of learning and hence in the public interest. The Paris guild, on the other hand, argued that the work was a creation of the author, and that the author had transferred property in the work to the publisher who had to absorb all the commercial risk. They argued, as the London booksellers had, that individual Parisian booksellers had acquired authors' rights in perpetuity, and that the renewal of printing privilege was a mere recognition of trade practice. It is interesting to note that on the eve of the French Revolution in 1777, Louis XVI issued six decrees dealing with the book trade. Of particular note are two privileges:

(a) one privilege for the publisher, granted in public interest, as a monopoly of limited duration to recoup investment;
(b) the other privilege for the author who, as creator of the work, obtained an exclusive right in perpetuity.

Nevertheless, with a growing reading public, a massive sub-publishing (and sometimes pirate) industry grew, especially in the border cities. Intriguingly, the sub-legal industry began to advocate the notion of the rights of the author as the originator of the work, and the first owner of the right in the work. The reason is understandable: the sub-legal publishing industry had to be able to argue that the natural right of the author trumped the guild printing privilege over a book, thereby allowing the author of a book to assign the right to publish to any publisher, including the non-French and provincial booksellers.

The book guilds and printing privileges came to an end with the Declaration of the Rights of Man and Citizen of 16 August 1789 which stated that all persons could write, speak and print freely. Moreover, the Declaration upheld the preservation of the natural and imprescriptible rights of man, which included the rights of liberty and property. With such clauses on property, freedom of the press and publication, legitimacy was conferred on the claims of the 'rights of authors'. Rapid commercialisation of the book publishing industry with the full abolition of the monarchy, and all its ancillary privilege systems, meant that the notion of an individual author as being the owner of a private property right in his work was commercially necessary.

A new author's era was ushered in with the Decree of 13/19 January 1791 granting the right of performance to an author of a dramatic work, and the Decree of 19/24 July 1793, granting the right of reproduction on authors, composers, painters, engravers and designers.[36] What sets apart French copyright law from British copyright law is the revolutionary and lyrical insistence on the supremacy and sacredness of the rights of the author. Indeed, the start of Le Chapelier's famous speech is worth repeating here: 'La plus sacrée, la plus légitime, la plus inattaquable et, si je puis parler ainsi, la plus personelle de toutes les propriétés, est l'ouvrage fruit de la penseé d'un écrivain'.[37] These two decrees governed French copyright law for the next 150 years, until the 1957 Copyright Law codified the pre-existing law.

Prussia

With Germany being a non-unified entity until 1871, early copyright history in this region is reflected in the conglomerate of different states and principalities, all with their individual state privileges and regulation. By the sixteenth century, there was rampant piracy of literary works from the establishment of the competing book industries in Leipzig and Frankfurt. This led to early philosophical writings and tribunal decisions on book piracy and authorship from luminaries such as Martin Luther and Albrecht Dürer. The early 1794 Prussian law regulated the publishing industry, but the regulations within it were based on an assumption of the existence of an author's right.[38]

The first real modern copyright law in this region was the Prussian Law of June 1837. Whereas the United Kingdom 1710 law was narrow in its coverage (only literary works), with no guidance on transfer of rights or limitations of rights, the Prussian law set out beneficiaries, the type of works to be protected, the conditions for transfer, duration of rights, and exceptions to the exercise of rights.[39]

The United States

The first American state copyright law, modelled after the British Statute of Anne, was passed in Connecticut in 1783;[40] this was soon followed by Massachusetts, Maryland, Georgia and New York, New Hampshire and Rhode Island. With the passing of the United States Constitution, which included an intellectual property clause,[41] Congress enacted the first federal copyright statute, the Copyright Act of 1790, which secured to authors, publishers, or their legal representatives two 14-year terms of copyright protection in books, pamphlets, maps and charts.[42]

TOWARDS THE MODERN ERA

It was now well accepted that authors deserve protection against all forms of misappropriation of their works. This belief became widespread in the nineteenth century, a century which saw a publishing boom, and perhaps not un-coincidentally, the genesis of international copyright law. The nineteenth century produced not only novels, but also large numbers of histories, geographies, biographies, religious works and political treatises. Between 1837 and 1901, approximately 50,000 novels were published in Britain alone.[43]

The Rhetoric of 'the Author'

What has changed significantly is the place of 'the author' in copyright discourse. Indeed, whereas the author takes a back seat in twenty-first century copyright debates, the nineteenth century saw authors, as their Greek and Roman predecessors had done, actively and effectively deploying the 'authorship' rhetoric to resolve issues affecting their moral and material interests.

The rhetoric served, first, to emphasise the noble art and profession of writing. Second, the rhetoric helped authors convince the public that copyright should be extended, and that authors had a right to earn a livelihood from their writings. One should note that by the end of the eighteenth century, copyright had yet to impact on authors' lives in terms of remuneration – most authors were paid a lump sum for their work as opposed to sales-based royalties and, moreover, authors were required to assign their copyrights to their publishers. Third, the authorship rhetoric solved the paradox of the nineteenth-century writing profession in that previously, imitation had been accepted as being part of the creative act whereas now, such acts were suddenly to be deemed as misattribution of authorship and plagiarism. Domestic protection was to no avail without international protection. Book piracy had affected the British and French book trades with cheaper reprints being published in Belgium, Ireland and the United States. These foreign editions soon infiltrated bookshops and circulating libraries.[44] New rights were needed and were effected by bilateral and international treaties with pirating nations.

Nineteenth-century American Policy on Piracy, Internationalism and Bilateralism

The 1790 Copyright Act limited copyright protection to 'a citizen or citizens of these United States, or resident therein' (section 5). As noted by some commentators, this provision constituted a piracy provision, which was the result of a developing country protecting its fledgling culture and industry whilst exploiting the works of developed countries such as France or the

UK.[45] The tendency to freely reprint foreign works was encouraged by the existence of tariffs on imported books that ranged as high as 25 per cent.[46]

Moreover, the lack of copyright protection for foreign authors was commonplace in the late eighteenth and early nineteenth centuries due to the absence of an international copyright agreement. This lack of copyright protection to foreign authors in the 1790 Act was particularly irksome to English authors – between 1800 and 1860, almost half of the bestsellers in the United States were pirated, mostly from English novels. Compared to a legitimate English edition, an American pirated edition cost approximately one-tenth of the total cost.[47] The European campaign to bring the United States into the nascent global copyright system is well documented, and it is interesting to appreciate the growth of copyright awareness amongst both British and American authors such as Charles Dickens, Gilbert and Sullivan, William Wordsworth, Henry Wadsworth Longfellow and Louisa May Alcott.[48] The concerted power of authors and public opinion did eventually culminate in a bilateral copyright agreement between the United Kingdom and the United States, though this did not come into being until 1891, five years after the Berne Convention.

The United States, however, was not to join the Berne Convention until 1989. It is noteworthy that the United States has, within the last hundred years, transformed itself from a copyright pirate nation to the global copyright sentry. It is well accepted that the United States has become the major copyright producer, exporter and lobbyist in the world. She takes an active part in setting international norms for intellectual property rights, and also seeks to encourage other countries to sign and ratify these norms.

New Technologies: Films, Sound Recordings, Performances and Broadcasts

Sound recording companies began demanding rights in the early twentieth century, especially with the advent of public radio broadcasting which broadcast both live music and recorded music. It was impossible to accommodate them within the Berne Convention (still the only copyright convention) as mechanical recordings just could not be considered to be 'authorial' works.[49] The Austrian 1936 law solved the legal dilemma by splitting the copyright regime into 'author's rights' (*Urheberrecht*) and 'related rights' (*Verwandte Schutzrechte*), with the latter covering rights of sound recording producers and broadcasters.

A similar problem arose in relation to film productions as opposed to cinematographic works (considered as creative authorial works), and again the Austrian double option was adopted in many European countries where the film director is considered the 'creative author'[50] (now with the full copyright term of life plus 70 years) whereas the film producer is given a reduced set of rights as protection for his financial investment in making and distributing the derivative product.[51] Of course, a slightly different approach is adopted in more pragmatic common law systems, where the film director is treated poorly, whilst the producer by some legal mechanism ends up either as the sole owner or joint owner of the full life plus 70 year copyright term in the film.

Performances were, and still are, difficult to categorise. The principal bar to treating performers as authors is that they do not *create* works, they merely *execute* them. The counter-argument is just as convincing: many performers do not mechanically execute the works but rather re-cast such works in their own individualistic manner. For example, performers routinely impose their own personality in *cadenzas* or jazz improvisations. The usual justifications for granting rights to authors (natural justice, economic incentives, and public interest arguments) seem to apply equally to performers. Moreover, the 1996 WIPO Performances and Phonograms Treaty confers moral rights on performances, thus taking performers a step closer towards the 'authorhood' status.[52] The phonogram producers (but not the film producers), performers and broadcasters finally got international recognition in the 1961 Rome Convention.[53]

Historically, there was reluctance within the United States to recognise related rights in performances and sound recordings. Instead, the US unfair competition law has been the basis of protection for these types of works, as well as rights (such as moral rights) until such time as Congress amended the federal copyright law. Today, the following beneficiaries receive protection under the US federal copyright law, albeit in an idiosyncratic fashion: phonogram producers and performers. For instance, performers only have performance rights in relation to digital rather than analogue recordings.[54] Works such as 'motion pictures and audiovisual works' are categorised as 'original works of authorship', and film producers acquire rights contractually and under the employment/commissioned works provision. Similarly, there are no broadcasting 'rights' as such under US copyright law, but copyright protection can be gained through recording the broadcast work (and hence claiming a performance right which will cover the act of broadcasting), and under the Communications Act.[55]

The Twenty-first Century Challenge: Digital Technology

The primary cry of the late twentieth century has been for a broader copyright regime due to the challenges posed by even newer technologies such as the reprographic, digital and compression technologies. The current problems did not arise from any single revolutionary invention but rather are due to the convergence of different technological developments: networked computers, digital file compression, increased computing power, the semiconductor chip leading to personal computing (not to mention affordable PCs), increased telephony coverage and, most importantly, higher communication speed.

Due to the perceived problems, in the last two decades of the twentieth century, the copyright law has been extended to cover computer programs (see Chapter 11),[56] electronic databases, uploading and downloading of copyright works over the internet and the distribution of works over the internet. The 1996 WIPO Copyright Treaty extended copyright law in a more perverse way by allowing copyright owners to place technological measures on CDs and on-line works which not only prevent the reproduction and dissemination of the copied work (the traditional prohibition under copyright law), but now also allow owners to prevent access to works.

The European response to the challenge has been hampered by the lack of harmonisation. This is despite the fact that copyright, as with other intellectual property rights, has been an EU matter for at least two decades.[57] In a 1988 Green Paper on copyright and the challenge of technology, the Commission examined the most urgent problems requiring immediate action at Community level with a view to adjusting to the emergence of new technologies. However, unlike the more harmonised position for trade marks, patent and design laws, harmonisation of copyright law within the EU is piecemeal as there are apparently too many cultural barriers to overcome. Thus, instead of one directive and regulation, there are seven directives. The usage of the directives as an instrument of harmonisation is deliberate as copyright is a particularly thorny matter apt to arouse the sensitivities of different member states. So far, the EU directives have harmonised the following aspects of copyright law: legal protection of computer programs and databases, rules on satellite broadcasting and cable transmission, introduction of rental, lending and resale royalty rights for the author, harmonisation of economic rights of authors and related rights owners, limited harmonisation of copyright exceptions, and the duration of protection. These various laws have effectively provided a TRIPS-plus level of copyright protection in the EU.

WHY COPYRIGHT?

Stakeholders and policy-makers from developed and developing countries face some fundamental questions about copyright law and policy such as:

1. Should copyright really subsist in telephone directories or lists?
2. Should copyright law be extended to protect traditional cultural expressions?
3. Is life plus 50 (or 70) years too long a term of protection for computer programs among other kinds of subject matter?

4. Why should the rights holder be remunerated when the lawful purchaser of a book or CD wishes to make a private copy of the work?

Perhaps we can glean some answers by examining briefly the justifications for copyright law and also looking at a well-known critique (see also Chapter 3). Early writers, such as Locke, Kant, Mill and Hegel offered a bifurcated perspective on the rationales for copyright: property rights should be granted either on the principle of rewarding or incentivising labour or on the more deontological and humanist principle of a person's right to personality and dignity. In later years, the arguments were couched in more Romantic rhetoric, with authors pursuing a more egotistical agenda and advocating authorial rights as being the natural and just result of either the author's persona or the author's labour. Nineteenth-century debates on copyright law began to adopt a more societal approach as lobbyists argued that author's rights benefited the common weal such as through the promotion and preservation of indigenous literature and arts. Mankind's fundamental freedoms included a right to be recognised and rewarded for moral and material interests resulting from any scientific, literary or artistic production.[58] In the mid-twentieth century, societal concerns soon encompassed economic goals as valued and pursued within a market-based economy. Copyright was now justified in economic terms. The result of this continuous stream of justifications has been to strengthen the proprietary component within copyright law over the public interest element. This strengthening, in turn, produces a steady proliferation of legal instruments which allow the author of a work (or the owner, in reality) to control exploitation of and access to the work.[59]

Although copyright law is often said to be a product of technology and commerce, it is decidedly also a product of historical and cultural norms. Different national laws offer different types of rights in relation to different types of works for different durations – and much of the divergence lies in the disparate historical and philosophical bases of copyright law. Nevertheless, this has a practical dimension as the world copyright system is roughly divided into the group of countries that adopt the common law or Anglo-American copyright system, and the group of countries that adopt the civil law or continental European legal traditions. Of course, within these two groups, there are idiosyncrasies such as Canada, which due to its Anglo-French legal traditions offers a truly third way by adopting principles from both sides of the divide.

The European civil law countries emphasise that copyright laws emanate from the need to protect the author or creator of the work. This emphasis is even reflected in the terminology employed by such countries – rather than 'copyright', the rights are referred to as author's right (*droit d'auteur* – French, *diritto d'autore* – Italian, *Urheberrecht* – German). Furthermore, the author's rights are divided into two distinct categories – economic rights and moral rights. Economic rights protect the author's ability to exploit his work in the market by allowing him to prohibit others from reproducing or performing or transmitting his work; whereas moral rights protect the author's personality and reputation. French copyright law, for example, sets no limits on the types of works protected as long as the work in question fulfils the criterion of individuality – in return, the law offers two broad rights to authors: the right of reproduction and the right of communication, and a very strong set of moral rights.

In contrast, British copyright law has limited and strictly defined categories of works and, in contrast to the French copyright law, offers strong economic rights whilst paying lip service to the notion of moral rights. This stems from the Anglo-American and common law traditions of emphasising the holder of the economic power, that is, the entrepreneur or the producer of the work, as opposed to the creator or the author of the work. This divergence is both academically and practically important as it has produced disparate consequences in respect of such basic matters as what types of works should be protected (for example, derivative works, non-original works and neighbouring works), the relationship between authorship and ownership of works (especially in relation to freelance authors, employees and contractual arrangements), moral rights, and defences.

Copyright has been controversial for quite some time. One of the most powerful critiques came from Sir Arnold Plant in the 1930s. Plant studied the early publishing history with the aim of demonstrating that the literary industry progressed without copyright institutions, and with authors being remunerated. Interestingly, we find that the arguments for both high prices and copyright protection by the music and film industry today are echoed by those of publishers in earlier centuries. This comment from 1878 has quite a contemporary feel: '. . . Four books out of five which are published do not pay their expenses . . . The most experienced person can do no more than guess whether a book by an unknown author will succeed or fail'.[60] Plant concluded that it is possible to envisage book production without copyright laws with authors or scholars willing to pay for publication of research.[61] An obvious counterargument to this, though, is that without adequate copyright protection, publishers would be reluctant to make the necessary investment.

On the other hand, it can be argued that in the context of internet publishing and enhanced technological protection tools, the publishing and media industry can use different business models coupled with normal e-commerce principles which rely on contract law to attract readership and consumption of works without copyright laws. It is not difficult to envisage exactly such a scenario in today's climate where costs of journals are spiralling upwards and where there is an unproven but important link between research quality and publication quantity. Moreover, open access publishing schemes, which have been so readily embraced by the learned publishing industry, indicate that the publishing world as rightly envisaged by Plant in the 1930s can and does survive without intellectual property laws as long as someone else foots the bill.

Open access publishing is not a new phenomenon as it has been the traditional basis of distributing free newspapers, television and radio broadcasts. These products can be viewed as open access products or services since intellectual property laws are not imposed on the consumer – instead, advertising, government and private financing schemes pay for the scheme. There are several notions of what constitutes 'open access'. One attempt offers this conciliatory definition:

> There is disagreement as to what constitutes an 'open access' journal . . . Regardless of definition, it is clear that open access publishing is in stark contrast to the traditional publishing model in two possible ways. 1) Access to articles published within these journals is free of charge to the public readership. 2) Copyright restrictions on authors may be removed, and authors retain rights rather than automatically transferring them to publishers.[62]

In the case of the open access publishing schemes, it is very often the scholar or an academic society which pays. However, it has proved a popular business model and there are now, according to the Directory of Open Access Journals, 3009 such journals.[63]

What all this does show is that when industries and creators eventually react to protect their investment and work, there is always some legal or regulatory mechanism at hand. The problem is that one size does not fit all. Authors who embrace the Creative Commons movement do not necessarily believe in the copyright system, on which the Commons movement frankly relies, but in their human right of dignity and personality, which includes a right to claim attribution. Producers would rely on any business model which prevented free-riding and captured all possible rents, even if such a model relied on patronage from societies/industries, contract law and digital rights management alone.

PRINCIPLES

Protectability

Copyright can be described as a property right, encompassing several distinct exclusive rights, which arise automatically upon creation of a particular class of works. This property right authorises the copyright owner (who may not necessarily be the creator or author) to do certain acts for a limited period of time. This ambiguous definition indicates the difficulty in drawing a full technical picture of copyright law from the global perspective. Pragmatically, and irrespective of jurisdiction, a person concerned with copyright protection of his work concentrates on five issues:

1. Does copyright subsist in the work?
2. Who owns the copyright in the work?
3. How long does copyright last for?
4. Has someone committed any infringing acts in relation to one's work?
5. What defences are available?

Eligible Subject Matter

The ambivalence and the open-ended nature of the Berne Convention on this matter is perhaps the reason why copyright subject matter has expanded over the last 200 years from literary and artistic works in the eighteenth century, to photographs in the nineteenth century, to cinematographic works at the turn of the century, thence to sound recordings and broadcasts and to computer programs in the mid-twentieth century, and finally to quasi-copyright/*sui generis* database protection in the latter part of the century (see Chapter 8).[64]

The Berne Convention, for instance, avoids this issue by expansively declaring that protection should be accorded to authors in their 'literary and artistic works' which is defined as including 'every production in the literary, scientific and artistic domain, whatever may be the mode or form of its expression'.[65] The provision then continues to offer an inclusive and open list of protectable subject matter including books, addresses, dramatic, musical works, films, photographs, works of applied art, translations, adaptations, and even collections of works such as encyclopaedias and anthologies which, 'by reason of the selection and arrangement of their contents, constitute intellectual creations'.[66] Nevertheless, it is ultimately up to individual countries to determine whether a work should be protected or not, and indeed, many countries do not even set out a definitive list of protectable subject matter. French copyright law, for example, offers an open list of protected subject matter including titles of works, and creations of the seasonal industries; but there is no need for a work to fall into any specific category, as protection is dependent solely on the criterion of originality. Indeed, some countries have gone beyond the Berne Convention to protect works created by legal authors (corporations or employers) and computer-generated works.[67] The TRIPS Agreement did nothing more than clarify that literary works included computer programs and certain types of databases. The Rome Convention 1961 sets out three further types of protectable subject matter: performances, phonogram productions (sound recordings) and broadcasts. However, the

Convention does not aim to offer a definitive nor exhaustive international list of neighbouring or related works. Consequently, some individual countries have an expansive list of neighbouring works so as to protect publishers or producers of non-creative photographs, new critical editions of public domain works, technical writings, databases and films.[68]

Exceptions

There are almost no statutory exceptions in either international or national laws, save for the 'no ideas' rule which is discussed below in relation to originality. The Berne Convention, for example, leaves it entirely in the hands of national legislation to exclude from copyright protection political speeches, legal proceedings, official legal, legislative and administrative texts.[69] Although the Convention protection will not extend to 'news of the day or to miscellaneous facts having the character of mere items of press information',[70] this merely clarifies that no reciprocal protection is expected should some national laws protect them.

Of course, national courts all over the world have, at some time or another either denied copyright protection or refused to extend it to a work that the court has found illegal, blasphemous, obscene or grossly immoral or fraudulent.[71] These are generally based on ancient manifestations of the public interest rule. One may argue that these old decisions reflect the prurient tastes of the nineteenth century and cannot seriously be considered today as being the basis for allowing courts to act as moralists in preventing copyright enforcement. An exception is where the work breaches prescribed law in some manner or where an original work comes into existence based on an infringement of another work. The British law, for example, recognises copyright in an infringing work, whereas United States copyright law specifically excludes protection to any part of a work in which pre-existing material has been used unlawfully.[72]

Criteria

There are three main conditions of protection. Is the work original? Related to this condition is the important distinction between ideas and expression. Second, does the work qualify for protection under national law? And finally, some countries provide that works (or some categories of them) will not be protected unless the work is fixed in some material form.

Originality
The notion of originality is fiendishly difficult to define, and yet is the universally enduring threshold that must be crossed in order for any work to be

granted protection for a term of at least 50 years *post mortem auctoris* (or 70 years *pma* in increasing numbers of jurisdictions including the EU, the US and Australia). Originality in most jurisdictions presumes some level or input of authorial personality, if only it be shown that the work was not copied, but 'originated' from the author. There is, however, no accepted standard as to what constitutes this authorial personality.

British, US, French and German copyright laws have historically employed a very low threshold of originality in order to extend the umbrella of copyright protection to works of cumulative creativity and low authorship values. The history of the Anglo-American copyright system clearly indicates that works of little creativity or personality could and still do obtain protection easily.

The EC software directive states that computer programs will be protected if 'they constitute original works in the sense that they are the result of their author's own intellectual creation. No other criteria, particularly of a qualitative or aesthetic nature, shall be applied to determine their eligibility for protection.'[73] This standard of originality was introduced in the computer program directive in order to counter the growing disparity of copyright protection of software between the different member states, especially Germany and the UK. German case law, by the mid-1980s, was refusing copyright protection to computer programs as it was requiring 'a significant amount of creativity with respect to selection, accumulation, arrangement and organisation' within programs before protection was accorded.[74] The 1991 EC software directive was the first directive on copyright law, and one of its primary aims was to specifically bar the application of the higher German threshold of creativity to software.[75] Chapter 11 discusses the issue of copyright (and patent) protection of software.

The question then arises as to whether this definition of originality is now the *de facto* concept of originality within EU copyright law. As a formula, the phrase is decidedly ambiguous. Moreover, the formula has not been adopted for *all* copyright subject matter but only in relation to photographs and databases.[76] This leaves a highly anomalous and unsatisfactory situation within the EU where there is a harmonised definition of originality for photographs, databases and computer programs, but one must revert to individual member states' jurisprudence on originality for all other types of subject matter.

Labour and 'sweat of the brow'

In the United Kingdom, early eighteenth- and nineteenth-century Chancery rulings readily accepted the rationale of copyright protection as protecting 'labour and investment'. This logically followed from the express premise in the Statute of Anne 1710 which saw copyright as a means to encourage 'Learned Men to Compose and Write useful Books'; moreover, early writings and cases on copyright law confirm this prevalence of reliance on and copying of pre-existing works.[77] The *de minimis* test, which is still adopted by British courts, demands that a work show 'skill, judgement and labour'.[78] This can be interpreted leniently enough to extend the copyright umbrella to works which evince little creativity or evidence of any kind of innovative jump above pre-existing works.

In the United States, a similarly low threshold of originality was applied, especially through the 'sweat of the brow' doctrine. This was subsequently raised by the US Supreme Court in the landmark decision of *Feist Publications, Inc v. Rural Telephone Service Co.*[79] In many instances, in both the UK and US, it appears that the law of copyright has been used as a substitute for a tort of misappropriation or unfair competition.[80] This is exactly the situation under French copyright law in relation to titles of works. The French Code states that the title of a work will be protected in a similar manner to the work itself if the title is 'original in character'; moreover, a protected title cannot be used to distinguish a work of the same kind, even if the entitled work is no longer protected, if such use is liable to create confusion. This sort of protection, going beyond the EU duration rule of 70 years *pma*, indicates unfair competition protection rather than copyright.[81]

Skill and judgement

British courts sometimes come close to framing the originality criterion as a test of the author's individuality and personality. Thus, in *Macmillan & Co Ltd v. Cooper*,[82] the House of Lords denied copyright protection to a condensed text of *Plutarch's Life of Alexander*, stating that it was necessary that the labour, skill and capital be expended sufficiently to impart to the product 'some quality or character which the raw material did not possess, and which differentiates the product from the raw material . . . It brings out clearly the distinction between the materials upon which one claiming copyright has worked and the product of the application of his skill, judgement, labour and leaning to those materials; which product, though it may be neither novel or ingenious, is the claimant's original work in that it is originated by him, emanates from him, and is not copied.' Similarly, disdain was shown by the House of Lords in *Cramp v. Smythson* for banal compilations showing no taste or judgement.[83] According to the court, a table of postal charges and measurements

> should be accurate so that there is no question of variation in what is stated . . . There is no room for taste or judgement . . . There was no feature of them which could be pointed out as novel or specially meritorious or ingenious from the point of view of the judgement or skill of the compiler. It was not suggested that there was any element of originality of skill in the order in which the tables were arranged.

Both these House of Lords decisions are important in that they highlight the logical tools (that is, skill and judgement) by which courts can deny protection to compilations and databases which largely comprise public domain or factual material. Canadian decisions also appear to still maintain the 'skill and judgement' approach in relation to originality in compilations.[84]

Creativity, individuality and personality

The French statute declares that all 'works of the mind, whatever their kind, form of expression, merit or purpose' will be protected.[85] There is no mention of originality but notwithstanding the silence of the statute, French jurisprudence decrees that a work must be original before copyright protection can be granted.[86] The fact that a work has not been copied is not vital, though it can go towards establishing the author's individuality or personality within a work. Instead, the underlying concern of the courts, when gauging whether a work is original or not, is to see whether the work reflects the 'stamp of the author's personality' (*l'empreinte de la personnalité d'auteur*),[87] irrespective of its genre, form of expression, merit or its purpose, but taking into account the level of freedom the author has to exercise his creative choices.[88] In relation to computer programs, the French Supreme Court determined the protectability of computer programs in a rather cryptic fashion by re-defining originality in terms of intellectual contribution or input (*l'apport intellectual*). The Court further suggested that protection could be refused if 'an automated or constraining logic' dictated how much such intellectual contribution was put into the work. In the aftermath of the EC software directive, however, most courts take originality of computer programs for granted.[89]

Under German copyright law, one has to show that the work is creative, and that there is evidence of authorial individuality or personality.[90] Historically, the high threshold of creativity has never been applied equally to all protectable categories of works but instead varies according to the nature of the subject matter under review. Therefore, the creativity level can be quite low for literary, musical and fine art works, but a high level is applied to works of applied art (or industrial designs).[91] Moreover, works which are incremental in nature tend to be shown special attention: tables, catalogues and forms. These works (called *kleine Münze* or small changes) tend to have little creative input but are nevertheless protected as it is argued that no other protection would otherwise be given to such non-creative but economically important works.[92] On the other hand, the courts are reluctant to grant protection to works of applied art on the basis that works of applied art can be protected under *sui generis* design law.

The idea–expression principle

The idea–expression principle is stated in various ways in various jurisdictions, and has since the late 1990s become a universally acknowledged principle, enshrined in the TRIPS Agreement and the WIPO Copyright

Agreement.[93] The TRIPS formulation of this principle is as follows: 'Copyright protection shall extend to expressions and not to ideas, procedures, methods of operation or mathematical concepts as such'.

The rule is elusive to understand, and almost impossible to apply in a rational and detached manner. An old pronouncement of this rule comes from Mr Justice Peterson who is quoted in respect of the adage: *what is worth copying, is worth promoting.* The judge's views on the idea–expression dichotomy are also worth noting:

> The word 'original' does not in this connection mean that the work must be the expression of original or inventive thought. Copyright Acts are not concerned with the originality of ideas, but with the expression of thought, and in the case of 'literary work', with the expression of thought in print or writing.[94]

A more recent House of Lords pronouncement of the test was given in *Designers Guild Ltd v. Russell Williams*,[95] where the court was reluctant to wholeheartedly embrace the idea–expression dichotomy. The court held that the 'idea–expression' principle supported two different propositions:

> The first is that a copyright work may express certain ideas which are not protected because they have no connection with the literary, dramatic, musical or artistic nature of the work. It is on this ground that, for example, a literary work which describes a system or invention does not entitle the author to claim protection for his system or invention as such. The same is true of an inventive concept expressed in an artistic work. However striking or original it may be, others are (in the absence of patent protection) free to express it in works of their own [cite omitted]. The other proposition is that certain ideas expressed by a copyright work may not be protected because, although they are ideas of a literary, dramatic or artistic nature, they are not original, or so commonplace as not to form a substantial part of the work.

The principle is equally accepted in the national laws of France, Germany and the United States. In France, it is an accepted tenet, in jurisprudence rather than statutory law, that mere ideas, methods, procedures or techniques are not protectable under copyright law, the rationale being that such subject matter belongs to the common heritage of mankind, a type of 'cultural fund, a space and memory which are open to everyone'.[96] The principle of not awarding protection to ideas or commonplace works is further accentuated by the fact that only intellectual creations are protectable subject matter. Despite this legal tenet, copyright protection was granted to the artist Cristo's work, which comprised of wrapping the Pont Neuf bridge in Paris using canvas and ropes; admittedly, the scope was limited in that the author could not oppose other types of works using the same style of wrapping.[97]

Registration and fixation

There are no further formalities required for copyright to subsist in a work such as registration or the affixation of a copyright notice or symbol – this is one matter which is governed by international copyright law. The Berne Convention leaves it to Union countries to determine whether or not fixation in 'some material form' should be a pre-requisite before protection is considered.[98] Difficulties can arise—an unfixed work from Country A, where protection is granted to unfixed works, may be refused protection in Country B, where protection is only granted to fixed works. This is irrespective of the national treatment principle: Article 5(2) emphasises that the 'extent of protection, as well as the means of redress afforded to the author to protect his rights, shall be governed exclusively by the laws of the country where protection is claimed'. Thus, protection is governed solely by the laws of the country where protection is claimed.

British copyright law states that copyright will not subsist in 'literary works' unless such works are 'recorded, in writing or otherwise'.[99] A person who gives an impromptu lecture or speech in UK will not gain any copyright protection unless and until the words are physically affixed – either by the author himself, by writing or tape recording or filming himself, or by someone else who makes a verbatim written record of the speech.[100] A similar provision exists in US copyright law.[101] In contrast, French copyright law contains no similar provision regarding fixation, and protection has been given to the laser light display which was considered as a 'visual creation' intended to reveal and highlight the lines and forms of the Eiffel Tower.[102]

Ownership

Initial authorship and ownership

International laws offer little assistance in relation to the issue of beneficiaries of protection. The preamble to the Berne Convention refers to the 'rights of authors in their literary and artistic works', whilst Article 2(6) lays down that protection under the Convention is to operate for the benefit of the 'author and his successors in title'; there is a presumption that the author of a literary or artistic work will be regarded as the person whose name appears on the work.[103] It is not clear whether the Convention limits authorship to natural persons or individuals or whether authorship can vest in a legal entity. Many common law countries, for example, vest authorship *ab initio* in employers who can be legal persons. Thus, the issue of authorship and ownership is something which is totally dependent on national laws (or regional laws[104]), with a distinct divergence between the civil law and common law approaches.

In most jurisdictions, whether common law or civil law, the ownership of copyright in a work *usually* vests initially in the author of the work, that is, the person who creates the work. Slightly different rules exist in all national laws in respect of employee works and films, and related rights. Where two or more authors contribute to a work, both authors will be entitled to joint ownership of the copyright. The general rule is that authorship is determined with reference to the person who expands skill or creativity in making the work, as opposed to the person who merely supplies suggestions or ideas. The British law does provide for an anomalous situation: in the case of a literary, dramatic, musical or artistic work which is *computer-generated* (and thus not created by a natural person), the author shall be taken to be the person by whom the arrangements necessary for the creation of the work are undertaken.

Employee authors

Again, this is an area of law which is not governed by international law. EU law does govern this area in relation to one type of work – computer programs. Due to intensive lobbying by large corporations during the passage of the computer program directive, all EU member states now provide an employee exception in relation to computer programs. The rule is that economic rights in the software and its documentation created by one or more employees in the execution of their duties or following instructions from the employer will vest in the employer. The position in relation to moral rights is still governed by the national laws – but most countries, including France, limit the moral rights of employee-authors of computer programs.[105]

Common law In most common law countries, such as the UK and US, important exceptions exist in respect of two situations. First, if the work is made by an employee in the course of his employment, his employer is the owner of any copyright in the work, unless an agreement exists between them which specifies otherwise. The criteria used to determine whether the creator is an employee or an independent contractor is largely judge-imposed. The test is usually whether the organization or the employer exercises control over the work of the employee. Factors which the courts look at include whether the author has responsibility for investing and managing the work, for purchasing his own equipment, and for hiring and firing assistants.[106]

A similar provision exists in US law where employee works are categorized as a 'work made for hire'. A work is made for hire when it is created by an employee within the scope of his employment. In such cases, the employer is considered the author and copyright vests in him. When determining whether a person is in fact an employee, the court takes into account, *inter alia*, of the following factors: the skill required to create the work; the source of the necessary instrumentalities and tools; the duration of the relationship between the parties; the method of payment, and provision of employee benefits and the tax treatment of the hired party.[107]

Civil law   Under the French Code, the right to ownership of a copyright work is given to the natural person who creates the work, irrespective of his status – an employee who creates a work during employment retains copyright in his work.[108] The employer may have the economic rights in the work transferred to him, but the contract of transfer should be in writing and should explicitly list the rights to be assigned to the employer. There is one instance where it is possible for an employer to be considered the 'author' of copyright in the work, and that is if the work qualifies as a collective work, that is, one where the contributions of all authors are merged into one work and it is impossible to attribute to each author a separate right as separate contributions cannot be identified, and the work was created on the initiative of a single principal.[109]

The German law is even stricter and makes no specific exceptions for employee works (save for the EU rule on computer programs). The author of a work is always the creator of a work, irrespective of whether he is self-employed, employed or engaged on a particular commission.[110] Copyright can derive only from natural persons and not a legal person, though the latter may acquire derivative exploitation rights. Sometimes, however, the courts, undoubtedly for reasons of business efficacy, have held that where an author has created a work in execution of his duties under a contract of employment, the employer may have an implied exclusive licence to use the work.[111]

Commissioned works

The position of the commissioned work in civil law countries is simple – the author is usually the owner of copyright in the work, with very rare exceptions such as commissioned advertising work under French copyright law.[112] Under UK law, where a work is commissioned, the ownership of copyright usually belongs to the creator of the work, but in certain circumstances, the court may find that the commissioner of a work has an implied licence to exploit the work in a limited manner, or that the commissioner of the work has an equitable title to the copyright in the work.[113]

Under US copyright law, the category of 'works made for hire' comprises not only employee works, but nine categories of specially commissioned works. Should a work fall within one of these categories, and if the parties have expressly agreed in writing that the work is to be considered a work made for hire, then the copyright will vest in the commissioner of the work. The nine categories whereby a commissioned author may 'lose' his copyright include economically important types of creations such as collective works, motion pictures or other audiovisual works, and compilations.[114]

Related rights

The *normal* rule in most jurisdictions is that performers, sound recording companies and broadcasters own the copyright in performances, sound recordings and broadcasts respectively.[115] The position in relation to films is a bit trickier. The Berne Convention states that 'ownership of copyright' in cinematographic works is a matter for the legislation in the country where protection is claimed.[116] Civil law *droit d'auteur* systems tend to view films as authorial works created, first and foremost, by directors. Many European countries also recognise other persons who have made creative contributions to the work. The French, for example, consider the following as authors of the film: the author of the scenario, the author of the adaptations, the author of the dialogue, the author of musical compositions, and the director. The German copyright law, on the other hand, does not have an automatic list of authors, but courts have recognised the director, cameraman and the film cutter as authors of a film.[117]

How then does the film industry work in practice in civil law systems, such as France and Germany? The answer is that there are two types of ownership within films: full copyright which is granted to creative contributors, and the related right (usually for a term of 50 years) granted to the film producer.[118] Moreover, several European laws (for example, French, German, Italian and Austrian) provide that economic rights are *presumed* to have been transferred to the producer.[119]

The common law approach is pragmatic and the general rule is that the film producer (or the risk taker) is the initial owner of the film. Due to EC law, the UK now also recognises the principal director as a joint owner of the copyright in the film, with the producer – unless, of course, the director is an employee of the producer, in which case, the latter takes it all. The same is true under US law: the producer is the initial owner of the copyright in the film since a film is categorised as a 'work made for hire' (see above).

Rights Conferred

Economic rights

International copyright law has seen the gradual but unceasing inflation of an owner's rights so that permission is now required for reproducing, adapting, communicating, distributing, renting and lending a work.[120] The 1996 WIPO Internet Treaties further widened the communication right to include a making available right, which has been incorporated into the national copyright laws of many countries including all the EU member states, Australia, Singapore and, implausibly, Iraq. Most of these rights are discussed in respect of digital technology in later chapters. The two oldest and most important economic rights are those of reproduction and communication.

(i) Right of reproduction This right, historically recognised in the first UK, Prussian and American copyright laws, is also recognised under the Berne

Convention,[121] the TRIPS Agreement and the WIPO Treaties. Copying means reproducing the work in any material form by any means. This vague and broad definition enables the rights holder, in many countries, to also control the acts of translation, adaptation and other types of alterations to the work.[122]

More current definitions also take into account that reproduction can include storing the work in any medium by electronic means, and also making transient copies of the work. Indeed, the 1996 WIPO Diplomatic Conference adopted an Agreed Statement which reads as follows:

> The reproduction right, as set out in Art.9 of the Berne Convention, and the exceptions permitted thereunder, fully apply in the digital environment, in particular to the use of works in digital form. It is understood that the storage of a protected work in digital form in an electronic medium constitutes a reproduction within the meaning of Art.9 of the Berne Convention.

The WIPO Treaties confirm that the reproduction right is available to all authors, performers and phonogram producers, whilst broadcasters are granted this right under both the Rome Convention and TRIPS.

(ii) Right of communication   This right, again recognised early on in French copyright law, is recognisable, in various guises, within the Berne Convention, the TRIPS Agreement and the WIPO Treaties. The WIPO Treaties confirm that the communication right is available to all authors, performers and phonogram producers, whilst broadcasters are granted a limited right to control the communication to the public of their television broadcast under the Rome Convention and TRIPS.

(iii) Right to control physical copies: distribution and importation   The WIPO Treaties provide authors, performers and phonogram producers with the exclusive right to authorise the making available to the public of originals and copies of works through sale or other transfer of ownership, that is, an exclusive right of distribution. Under the Berne Convention, it is only in respect of cinematographic works that such a right was ever granted explicitly.[123]

In relation to whether the international instruments accord a related right of importation, it is conceivable that a reading of Articles 44(1), 50(1)(a) and 51 of the TRIPS Agreement provides a specific right to prevent importation of 'pirated copyright goods'.[124]

(iv) Right to control physical copies: rental and droit de suite   The *droit de suite* (or resale royalty right) refers to the 'author's right to a share in the proceeds of subsequent sales of his original work – "original" meaning here the original form (physical copy) in which the work is embodied'.[125] The

Berne Convention provides for this right in relation to original works of art and original manuscripts, but makes it optional, and applicable only if the legislation in the country to which the author belongs so permits.[126]

TRIPS introduced for the first time internationally the rental right, albeit only in relation to computer programs, cinematographic works and sound recordings. Authors and phonogram producers now have the right to prohibit the commercial rental to the public of originals or copies of computer programs/films (authors) and sound recordings (producers).[127] The WIPO Treaties recognised and extended the rental right so that authors, performers and phonogram producers have this right in relation to phonograms or, in the case of performers, performances fixed in phonograms.[128]

(v) Technological 'rights' A new breed of laws was also introduced under the WIPO Internet Treaties which give protection to rights holders who use technological measures to protect their copyright works[129] and who use digital rights management systems[130] embedded in most digital versions of creative works today which allow owners to keep track of the distribution and usage of copyright works.

Moral rights
Historically, moral rights were recognised in both English and French jurisprudence as a set of rights to protect the author's reputation and the integrity of the work, as opposed to economic rights which allow the author to participate in the commercial exploitation of the work. One of the earliest judgments in this area comes, surprisingly, from England, where Lord Mansfield in *Millar v. Taylor*[131] defined the pre-Statute of Anne concept of copyright as thus:

> From what source, then is the common law drawn? . . . [The author] can reap no pecuniary profit if, the next moment after his work comes out, it may be pirated upon worse paper and in worse print, and in a cheaper volume . . . He is no more master of the use of his own name. He has no control over the correctness of his own work. He can not prevent additions. He can not retract errors. He can not amend; or cancel a faulty edition. Any one may print, pirate and perpetuate the imperfections, to the disgrace and against the will of the author; may propagate sentiments under his name, which he disapproves, repents and is ashamed of. He can exercise no discretion as to the manner in which, or the persons by whom his work shall be published.

In essence, moral rights are independent from economic rights, and have either the same term of protection as economic rights, or even longer terms. In France, moral rights are held in perpetuity. Most civil law countries also provide that moral rights are inalienable and cannot be transferred.[132] Indeed, moral rights may have little economic purpose other than rewarding and incentivising the author by non-pecuniary means. Yet, although most of the justifications for copyright law point to this factor, one of the poorest areas of development in international copyright law is in relation to moral rights, and rights for employees.[133] This is notable in the United States, which as the world's foremost exporter of copyright goods, has a remarkably poor record in relation to authors' moral rights.[134]

Internationally, the Berne Convention provides for two moral rights, that is:

- the right to claim authorship of the work, and
- the right to object to any mutilation or deformation or other modification of, or other derogatory action in relation to, the work which would be prejudicial to the author's honour or reputation.[135]

The WIPO Internet Treaties further substantiate these rights by adopting them, and by adding performers' rights of attribution and integrity in live and recorded aural performances.[136]

The TRIPS Agreement, whilst adopting all the main provisions of the Berne Convention, specifically excludes moral rights protection. Nevertheless, the state of moral rights in domestic US copyright law, and its claim to implementation of its obligations under Article 6*bis* Berne Convention, 'has not gone unquestioned'. Given 'the importance of the US role in the TRIPs Agreement negotiations, it is not surprising that such a potentially troublesome provision would have been set aside'.[137]

(i) Right of attribution   The paternity or attribution right allows the author to have his authorship (and sometimes his title) recognised 'in clear and unambiguous fashion'.[138] The attribution right is quite wide as it allows the author to choose whether to have the work published anonymously or pseudonymously. It also allows the author to prevent misattributions, misleading attributions (where the extent of the author's contribution is misrepresented), and false attributions (where the author's name is placed on a work he did not create, or on a mutilated version of his work).

(ii) Right of integrity   The right of integrity allows the author to object to all sorts of distortions, mutilations or modifications of the work including interpretations, additions, deletions, changes, imperfections which are a result of reproduction techniques, including poor or wrong colours in the case of artistic works.[139] Examples of instances where national courts have held that the integrity right has been infringed include unauthorised Christmas ribbon decorations tied to flying geese sculptures,[140] the enactment of the play *Waiting for Godot* by female actors, against the author's specific instructions that all roles be played only by males, the interruption by comments to the broadcast of a play (some comments were over five

minutes),[141] and juxtaposing songs within a compilation of recordings with an extreme right-wing presentation.[142]

(iii) Divulgation and retraction right[143]   This right is not specifically recognised under the international agreements, but is a specific right under French and German law. The right allows the author to decide when, where and in what form the work will be divulged to any other person. The divulgation right is also somewhat recognisable as the economic right of first distribution or first publication.

Comment

Arguably, these international rights which allow the copyright owner to control the distribution and commercial exploitation of the physical copy of the intangible creation go too far. The rental right, for example, purports to give authors the ability to control and charge for the hiring out of goods. This seems odd. Consider this analogy: I rent out my lawfully purchased Volkswagen car to my neighbour during the weekend, thus saving my neighbour the cost of purchasing and maintaining a car all year round. Yet, the dealer, importer, manufacturer and designer of the car have no entitlement to a cut from my (possibly) lucrative arrangement. Furthermore, the 'technological rights' appear to have transformed digital, intangible goods into physical, tangible goods.

It is not suggested that these rights of distribution, importation, rental and *droit de suite* are wrong, but rather that these rights should raise two concerns. First, there has to be a clearer balance between the rights of the author of the intangible work to control his physical manifestation of the product, and those of the owner of the physical goods themselves. The former rights appear to interfere with the latter. Second, such rights should make us more aware of how questionable, if not implausible, some of the justifications for 'intellectual' or 'intangible' property are.

Scope of Protection

It is usually an infringement to copy either the whole work or a 'substantial' part of the work, either directly or indirectly. Therefore, there is no need to prove that the whole work has been reproduced, as long as there has been reproduction of a substantial part of it. The question of whether a substantial amount of the work has been reproduced is dependent on several factors including: the quality and the quantity of what is taken, whether the copying relates to the idea or the expression of the idea, or whether the part which has been copied is commonplace or well-known or derived from some other source.

Moreover, infringement of copyright occurs when a defendant has taken a substantial amount of the plaintiff's work, irrespective of the fact that the defendant then expends further effort and skill in changing or altering the original work so as to give rise to another original work. In such a situation, the defendant may have created a fresh copyright work, but can still be held to have infringed the prior work. Thus, making a few changes to a work will not avoid infringement, unless those changes are *so substantial* that it can no longer be said that a substantial part of the original has been taken. Should a court be convinced that one has misappropriated a protected work so as to unfairly partake of the author's fruits of labour, the court will probably not hesitate to hold that an infringement of copyright has occurred.

Finally, the scope of copyright protection is dependent on the nature of the work. Lesser protection is available for historical or factual works as compared to fictional works, partly due to the fact that historical or factual works must necessarily rely on earlier sources or facts. Thus, the law will allow a wider use to be made of a historical work than of a novel, so that subsequent works of knowledge can be built upon existing works of knowledge. Having said this, it should be emphasised that this does not offer a *carte blanche* to subsequent users to copy substantial amounts from a historical or factual work.[144]

Defences

There is little guidance from international conventions in relation to defences. The Berne Convention does set out certain limitations, but in a narrow sense, rather than setting out broad principles. It provides for the possibility of using protected works in particular cases, without having to obtain the authorisation of the owner of the copyright and without having to pay any remuneration for such use including the following:[145]

- quotations of published works provided that their making is compatible with fair practice, and the extent does not exceed that justified by the purpose;
- use of literary or artistic works in publications, broadcasts or sound or visual recordings for teaching purposes, provided the use is compatible with fair practice;
- reproduction by the press, broadcasting or communication to the public by wire (cabling) of newspaper articles on current, economic, political or religious topics;
- reproduction for the purpose of reporting current events.

TRIPS does not give any further set of limitations beyond that already set out in the Berne Convention. Countries are free to introduce these and other limits into their national laws, for example, limits to the right of reproduction, but such limits have to be subject to the three-step test (see below).[146]

The two most discussed and analysed defences are the British-derived defence of 'fair dealing' and the US defence of 'fair use'.[147] 'Fair dealing' is available for the purposes of non-commercial research, private study, criticism or review, or reporting current events.[148] The notion is defined jurisprudentially, and a generous definition of it was set out by the UK Court of Appeal, in *Hubbard v. Vosper*,[149] which sets out the following guidelines:

- the defence is not confined to published works, but can apply to the publication of unpublished works;
- 'fair dealing' is a question of degree and must be a matter of impression, with the court looking to the number and extent of quotations and extracts;
- was the defendant's use of the work for comment, criticism or review as opposed to rival or competitive use?;
- if a defendant has the reasonable defences of fair dealing and public interest, they should not be restrained from publication by interlocutory injunction because such a defendant 'if he is right, is entitled to publish it: and the law will not intervene to suppress freedom of speech except when it is abused'.[150]

In contrast, the US concept of 'fair use' is codified in section 107 of the US Copyright Act, which states that

> . . . the fair use of a copyrighted work . . . for purposes such as criticism, comment, news reporting, teaching (including multiple copies for classroom use), scholarship, or research, is not an infringement of copyright. In determining whether the use made of a work in any particular case is a fair use the factors to be considered shall include –
> (1) the purpose and character of the use, including whether such use is of a commercial nature or is for nonprofit educational purposes;
> (2) the nature of the copyrighted work;
> (3) the amount and substantiality of the portion used in relation to the copyrighted work as a whole; and
> (4) the effect of the use upon the potential market for or value of the copyrighted work.
> The fact that a work is unpublished shall not itself bar a finding of fair use if such finding is made upon consideration of all the above factors.

The factors contained in section 107 are merely by way of example, and are not an exhaustive enumeration and other factors may prove to have a bearing upon the determination of fair use. Courts have held, however, that the fourth factor is probably the most important one, that is, market effect. The reasons being:

Economists . . .believe the fair use exception should come into play only in those situations in which the market fails or the price the copyright holder would ask is near zero . . . As the facts here demonstrate, there is a fully functioning market that encourages the creation and dissemination of memoirs of public figures. In the economists' view, permitting 'fair use' to displace normal copyright channels disrupts the copyright market without a commensurate public benefit.[151]

The three-step test

The three-step test comprises a triptych of constraints on the limitations and exceptions to rights under national copyright laws. It was first applied to the exclusive right of reproduction under Article 9(2) Berne Convention in 1967. Since then, it has been transplanted and extended into the TRIPS Agreement, the WIPO Copyright Treaty, the WIPO Performances and Phonograms Treaty and the European Union Copyright Directive.[152] It has also become a feature in both the European Union and United States bilateral and regional trade agreements currently in vogue. The most important version of the test is that in Article 13 of TRIPS, which reads:

Members shall confine limitations and exceptions to exclusive rights to certain special cases which do not conflict with a normal exploitation of the work and do not unreasonably prejudice the legitimate interests of the rights holder.

The test may prove to be extremely important if any nations attempt to reduce the scope of copyright law, because unless the WTO decides that their modifications comply with the test, such states are likely to face a legal challenge. Nevertheless, there is very little guidance on how this provision should be interpreted.

The test basically states that countries can introduce any limitation or exception to the economic rights granted under Berne, TRIPS and the WIPO Treaties as long as the limitation/exception complies with three conditions: it must be limited to certain special cases; it must not conflict with the normal exploitation of the work; and it must not unreasonably prejudice the legitimate interests of the author. All three steps have to be satisfied cumulatively. The test covers only those economic rights covered by the international treaties. It does not apply to optional rights such as the *droit de suite* or to non-TRIPS sanctioned moral rights.[153] Neither does the three-step test apply to extrinsic measures such as human rights or competition laws.

From the outset it is clear that it is difficult, if not impossible, to apply either the literal or the 'intention of the parties' approaches to this provision. What *do* phrases such as 'normal exploitation of the work' or 'unreasonable prejudice' actually mean?

To date, only one case has actually required an interpretation of the test.[154] This involved US copyright exemptions allowing restaurants, bars and shops to play radio and TV broadcasts without paying licensing fees. The WTO dispute settlement panel held the United States in breach of Article 13 TRIPS, and in doing so laid down several guidelines as to the interpretation of the three-step test.

First, the three requirements of the test are cumulative. In respect to the first condition, the phrase 'certain special cases' means that a limitation or exception in national legislation should be clearly defined and should be narrow in its scope and reach; there is no need, however, to identify explicitly each and every possible situation to which the exception could apply, provided that the scope of the exception is known and particularised. Here, the US exception did not qualify under the first condition as a substantial majority of eating and drinking establishments and close to half of retail establishments were covered by the exemption – this meant that the exemption did not qualify as a 'certain special case' in the meaning of the first condition of Article 13.

In respect of the second leg of the three-step test, the panel held that an exception or limitation to an exclusive right in domestic legislation rises to the level of a conflict with a normal exploitation of the work if uses that in principle are covered by that right but exempted under the exception or limitation enter into economic competition with the ways that right holders normally extract economic value from that right to the work and thereby deprive them of significant or tangible commercial gains.

The panel was reticent as to the exact scope of the third condition, but did address inconclusively an intriguing question: who can enforce the legitimate interests of right holders of various WTO members in panel proceedings within the WTO dispute settlement system? After all, if the US exemption is in breach of the three-step test in respect of EU rights holders, it must also be in breach of this provision in relation to other rights holders in other member countries. Basically, the panel held that there was no indication in the wording of Article 13 that the assessment of whether the prejudice caused to the legitimate interests of the right holder is of an unreasonable level should be limited to the right holders of the member that brings forth the complaint (that is, EU rights holders). Moreover, the panel noted that:

> . . . our assessment of whether the prejudice, caused by the exemptions contained in [the US exemption], to the legitimate interests of the right holder is of an unreasonable level is not limited to the right holders of the European Communities.

It is clear that Article 13 TRIPS (the three-step test) is a recognition that copyright is limited inherently by the public interest, and that exceptions and limitations must exist.[155] Can Article 13 allow for a more positive rights approach so that developing countries can implement clear exceptions which allow full access to educational and scientific information?

It should be noted that the discussion has focused on the TRIPS version of the three-step test. And the TRIPS Agreement does refer to the competing and complementary objects and purposes of the agreement under Articles 7 and 8. This is not so under the Berne Convention where it is very clear that the object and purpose of the Berne Convention is solely concerned with the protection of the rights of authors, without reference to other kinds of competing objects and purposes, such as education and research or the promotion of public access to information.[156]

Countries should learn how to apply the broad principles within international copyright law in a manner which suits their own constitutional, development and socio-economic needs. It is not suggested that the whole of the TRIPS Agreement or the WIPO Treaties be interpreted employing this approach. Nevertheless, one can only discern the meaning of certain phrases, provisions and principles, such as the 'three-step test', by looking at these provisions contextually within specific factual and political circumstances, rather than in an abstract fashion by looking at the intention of the parties to the treaty.

An interesting discussion on this topic is to be found in Ricketson's study on the three-step test.[157] His view is that the second step cannot be interpreted from a solely economic perspective as this would mean 'very little, if any, work left for the third step' to perform. Moreover, he acknowledges that the great bulk of uses that fall within the three-step test could, in a narrow and economic interpretation, be regarded as being within the scope of the normal exploitation of a work. Ricketson argues that the three-step test, especially at the second stage, must consider 'non-economic normative' factors. Moreover, Ricketson argues that because such factors would render the three-step test 'open-ended and uncertain', a balance, involving value judgements, would have to be struck by national legislation between the rights holders' interest and the needs of society and culture. Not only does he advocate a strong public interest ethos when applying the three-step test, he also advocates a teleological (evolutionary) approach by concluding that the three-step test is dynamic and should not become a

> 'grandfathering' clause that confers an immunity for all time on an exception under national law. By the same token, it is possible that new kinds of exceptions may arise that will fit within the second condition. It is not only economic issues that are relevant to the assessment required by the second step. 'Normative' issues of a non-economic kind also are relevant; that is, it must be determined whether the use in question is one that the copyright owner should control, or whether there is some other countervailing interest that would justify this not being so. In light of the other exceptions allowed under the Convention, such an interest would need to be one of some wider public importance, rather than one pertaining to private interests.

Duration

Since the inception of copyright in the eighteenth century, there has been a constant expansion of the duration of copyright protection. Take for example the UK, where the maximum term was 28 years under the 1710 Statute of Anne but which was extended to the term of the author's life in 1814,[158] and to seven years *post mortem auctoris* (*pma*) in 1842 in response to heavy lobbying by such writers as Dickens and Wordsworth.[159] Nevertheless, this was not the first system in the world to introduce the life of author formula into copyright law. The French Decree of 1791 held that the heirs or successors in title of the author should be proprietors of the works for five years after the death of the author, whilst the Prussian law of 1837 provided for protection for life plus 30 years.[160]

The Berne Convention adopted the international standard of life of the author plus 50 years *pma*, which was subsequently adopted in the 1994 TRIPS Agreement. Therefore, the *de jure* international standard for the term of protection of author's works is still life of the author plus 50 years. However, the Berne standard of life plus 50 *pma* has been pushed up to life plus 70 years *pma*. For example, in the EU, the general rule is that the term of protection for copyright is 70 years after the death of the author or 70 years after the work is lawfully made available to the public; whereas the term for protection for related rights is 50 years after the event which set the term running.[161] Consequently, we can expect to see an extended delay in works entering the public domain. Indeed, some works in circulation whose authors had died between 50 and 70 years ago moved in the opposite direction: from the public domain back into proprietary ownership.

This trend began its life as a result of EU copyright harmonisation, but it has now gathered momentum through the United States bilateral trade agreement drive. As a result of this, the copyright laws of Singapore, Australia, Chile and Morocco all adopt the longer life plus 70 years term.[162]

Where countries apply a term which is in excess of the Berne rule, Union countries are free to apply the comparison of terms test. The comparison of terms test is that the term of protection is governed by the law of the country where protection is claimed. The term of protection, however, cannot exceed the term fixed in the country of origin of the work (unless there are provisions stating otherwise in the country where protection is claimed). A Union country, of course, need not apply this test.

There are exceptions to this basic rule for certain categories of works:

- *cinematographic works*: Union countries have two options. They can either adopt the general term of life plus 50 years, or they may provide protection for 50 years after the work has been made available to the public, or, if not made available, then 50 years after the making of such a work (Article7(2)).

• *photographs and works of applied art*: For photographic works and works of applied art, the minimum term of protection is 25 years from the making of the work (Article 7(4)). The WIPO Copyright Treaty however obliges all signatories (including those belonging to the Berne Union) to provide the normal term of life plus 50 years for photographs.

• *moral rights*: The term of protection, insofar as moral rights are concerned, extends at least until the expiry of the economic rights (Article 6*bis*(2)).

Under the 1961 Rome Convention for the Protection of Performers, Producers of Phonograms and Broadcasting Organisations, it was provided that performers, phonogram producers and broadcasters should have protection for at least 20 years from when the fixation of the phonogram and performance was made (or from when the performance took place), or when the broadcast took place.[163] The TRIPS Agreement has extended the term of protection for phonograms and performances to 50 years.[164] The term of protection for broadcasters remains at 20 years, though under EU law, broadcasters can claim 50 years protection.

Regarding films, there is no international rule, but the EC directive on related rights has granted film producers certain economic rights for 50 years from first fixation or first publication or first communication to the public. Moreover, in respect of cinematographic works, the term of protection is 70 years after the death of the last of the following persons to survive, whether or not these persons are designated as co-authors:

(a) principal director;
(b) the author of the screenplay;
(c) the author of the dialogue; and
(d) the composer of music specifically created for use in the cinematographic and audiovisual work.

NOTES

1. Early 'books' comprised baked clay tablets which held Ancient Egyptian, Babylonian and Assyrian writings. The 'Book of the Dead' itself has been referred to, wrongly, as the oldest product of the human spirit. Champdor, A., *The Book of the Dead from the Ani, Hunefer and Anhai Papyri in the British Museum*, New York: Garrett Publications, 1966, 36–8; also Mumby, F.A., *Publishing and Bookselling: A History from the Earliest Times to the Present Day* (4th ed.), London: Jonathan Cape, 1956, at 15.
2. Fantham, E., *Roman Literary Culture: From Cicero to Apuleius*, Baltimore and London: Johns Hopkins University Press, 1996, at 193.

3. Stewart, S.M., *International Copyright and Neighbouring Rights* (2nd ed.), London: Butterworths Law, 1989, at 13.

4. Chartier, R., 'Figures of the Author', in B. Sherman and A. Strowel, *Of Authors and Origins*, Oxford: Clarendon Press, 1994, at 21.

5. See *Gilliam v. American Broadcasting Co.*, 538 F.2d 14 (2d Cir. 1976); *Dastar Corp. v. Twentieth Century Fox Film Corp.*, 539 US 23 (Supreme Court, 2003).

6. Dock, M.C., 'Genèse et Évolution de la Notion de Propriété Littéraire', [1974] *Revue Internationale Droit D'auteur* 127 at 135, citing Martial, Epigrams Book I, 52–3. Vitruvius's Preface acknowledges a similar sentiment: 'Our predecessors, wisely and with advantage, proceeded by written records, to hand down their ideas to after times, so that they should not perish . . . While, then, these men deserve our gratitude, on the other hand, we must censure those who plunder their works and appropriate them to themselves; writers who do not depend upon their own ideas, but in their envy boast of other men's goods whom they have robbed with violence, should not only receive censure but punishment for their impious manner of life.' Loewenstein, J., *Ben Jonson and Possessive Authorship*, Cambridge: Cambridge University Press, at 74 citing Vitruvius, VII, Preface, 1, 3 – *De Architectura*.

7. Mumby, *op. cit.*, at 17; Feather, J., *A History of British Publishing*, London and New York: Routledge, 1988, at 1.

8. Mumby *op. cit.*, at 22, citing Putnam, G.H., *Authors and their Public in Ancient Times: A Sketch of Literary Conditions and of the Relations with the Public of Literary Producers, From the Earliest Times to the Fall of the Roman Empire*, New York: G.P. Putnam's Sons, 1894.

9. Ricketson, S., 'The Birth of the Berne Union', *Colum.-VLA J.L. & Arts*, 11, 1986, at 13–14; Barnes, J.J., *Authors, Publishers and Politicians: The Quest for an Anglo-American Copyright Agreement 1815–1854,* London: Routledge, 1974, at 84.

10. Fantham, *op. cit.*, at 196.

11. There is no contemporary record of this judgment, and the earliest account of the story is 1532.

12. Rose, M., *Authors and Owners: The Invention of Copyright*, Cambridge, MA and London: Harvard University Press, 1993, at 7.

13. Thomas, M., 'Manuscripts', in L. Febvre and H.-J. Martin, *The Coming of the Book: The Impact of Printing 1450–1800*, London and New York: Verso, 1976, 19 *et seq*.

14. *Ibid.*, 27.

15. *Ibid.*, at 25.

16. Armstrong, E., *Before Copyright: The French Book-Privilege 1498–1526*, Cambridge, UK: Cambridge University Press, 1990, at 1. A privilege was a commercial monopoly either permanently or for a fixed period of time – usually accorded to the inventor or initiator of a new process, a new product or a new source of supply, which was capable of exploitation.

17. For disputes as to who actually invented the first press, see Febvre and Martin, *op. cit.*, 49–56.

18. For a comprehensive account, see Eisenstein, E., *The Printing Press as an Agent of Change*, Cambridge, UK: Cambridge University Press, 1980.

19. For example, 'Lutheranism was from the first the child of the printed book, and through this vehicle Luther was able to make exact, standardized and ineradicable impressions on the minds of Europe'. Eisenstein, E., *The Printing Revolution in Early Modern Europe*, Cambridge, UK: Cambridge University Press, 1979, 145.

20. Mandich, G., 'Venetian Patents (1450–1550)', *Journal of the Patent Office Society*, 30, 166, 1948.

21. The privilege was short-lived as Speyer died in 1470 shortly after obtaining the privilege, and by 1473, there were 134 presses operating in Venice, and Venice went on to become a great printing and publishing centre in Europe by the sixteenth century.

22. Armstrong, *op. cit.*, at 3.

23. The 1482 privilege granted by the Duke of Milan for six years gave a firm of publishers the right to print and import a single book, *ibid*.

24. Loewenstein argues that this was not an authorial privilege but rather a decree protecting a future printer who would gain exclusive rights to print the work. Thus, the decree secures the publication of the book but confers no rights, and instead 'protection gravitates to the manufacturer of a widely marketable object, not to the author'. See Joseph Loewenstein, *The Author's Due: Printing and the Prehistory of Copyright*, Chicago: University of Chicago Press, 2002, at 71.

25. However, by 1517, the privileges market grew so large that it paralysed the Venetian book trade and the Senate revoked all existing privileges not issued on its own authority – privileges would be granted for new works only and on a two-thirds Senate majority vote only. Armstrong, *op. cit.*, at 6–7.

26. For further information and documentation on the history of copyright see the website of the project: 'Primary Sources on Copyright (1450–1900)', http://www.copyrighthistory. org.

27. The Company stopped material which was considered to be seditious and heretical. Following the 1557 charter, there were three Star Chamber decrees in 1566, 1586 and 1637 and three Interregnum Ordinances which continued this relationship between the Company and the state. The final extension to the charter was the Licensing Act 1662 which remained in force until 1695. See Deazley, R., *On the Origin of the Right to Copy: Charting the Movement of Copyright Law in 18th Century Britain (1695–1775)*, Oxford: Hart Publishing, 2004, at 2; and Patterson, L.R., *Copyright in Historical Perspective*, Nashville: Vanderbilt University Press, 1968, at 6.

28. Chartier, R., 'Figures of the Author', in B. Sherman and A. Strowel, *Of Authors and Origins*, Oxford: Clarendon Press, 1994, at 16–17.

29. Patterson, *op. cit.*, at 66–7.

30. Officially 'An act for the encouragement of learning, by vesting the copies of printed books in the author's or purchaser of such copies, during the times therein mentioned'.

31. Sherman, B. and L. Bently, *The Making of Modern Intellectual Property Law: The British Experience, 1760–1911*, Cambridge, UK: Cambridge University Press, 1999, at 73, 142–57, 180.

32. 1709 Copyright Act (8 Anne, c. 19). Though it is difficult to accept that this was the first statute which gave recognition to the author. Instead the subsequent 1735 Engraving's Act (or Hogarth's Act) recognised the author; see Deazley, R., 'Re-reading Donaldson (1774) in the Twenty-first Century and Why it Matters', *European Intellectual Property Review*, 25(6), 270–9, 2003.

33. Rose, *op. cit.,* at 142. *Cf.* Deazley, 2004, *op. cit.,* at p. xxii.

34. *Millar v. Taylor* (1769) 4 Burr. 2303.

35. *Donaldson v. Beckett* (1774) 2 Bro. P.C. 129; (1994) 17 *Hansard Parl. Hist.* 953.

36. Article 1, 1793 Law. The term of protection was for ten years *pma*; For an English translation of the two French decrees, see Sterling, J.A.L., *World Copyright Law* (2nd ed.), London: Sweet and Maxwell, 2003, paras 80.07 and 80.08.

37. 'The most sacred, the most legitimate, the most unassailable, and if I may say, the most personal of all properties is the work, fruit of the thought of a writer…', at Sterling *op. cit.,* para. 80.07.

38. For a fascinating discussion on the evolution of authorship and copyright in Enlightenment Germany, see Woodmansee, M., 'The Genius and the Copyright: Economic and Legal Conditions of the Emergence of the "Author"'. *Eighteenth Century Studies*, 17(4), 425–48, 1984.

39. See Sterling, *op. cit.*, para. 80.09 for an English translation of the 1837 Prussian Law.

40. Entitled 'An Act for the Encouragement of Literature and Genius', the statute granted US authors and their heirs and assigns 'the sole liberty of printing, publishing and vending' to any new books, pamphlets, maps, or charts within the State of Connecticut for two renewable terms of 14 years.

41. 'To promote the progress of science and useful arts, by securing for limited times to authors and inventors the exclusive right to their respective writings and discoveries'. Article I § 8, cl. 8. See Walterscheid, E.C., *The Nature of the Intellectual Property Clause: A Study in Historical Perspective,* Buffalo and New York: William S. Hein, 2002.

42. The clause was derived from proposals introduced by James Madison and Charles Pinckney. James Madison offered the following commentary in *The Federalist*: 'The utility of [the copyright] power will scarcely be questioned. The copyright of authors has been solemnly adjudged, in Great Britain, to be a right of the common law. The right to useful inventions seems with equal reason to belong to the inventors. The public good fully coincides in both cases with the claims of individuals. The States cannot separately make effectual provision for either of the cases, and most of them have anticipated the decision of this point, by laws passed at the instance of Congress', *The Federalist*, No. 43, at 271–2 (James Madison) (C. Rossiter ed., 1961). See Patterson, *op. cit.*, at 203–12; Fenning, K., 'The Origin of the Patent and Copyright Clause of the Constitution', *Georgetown Law Journal*, 17, 109, 1929.

43. Webb, R.K., 'The Victorian Reading Public', in B. Ford (ed.), *From Dickens To Hardy*, Harmondsworth: Penguin, 1958, at 205; Sutherland, J., *Victorian Fiction: Writers, Publishers, Readers*, London: Palgrave Macmillan, 1995, 151–2.

44. Barnes, J.J., *Authors, Publishers and Politicians: The Quest for an Anglo-American Copyright Agreement 1815–1854*, London: Routledge, 1974, at 95.

45. Plowman, E.W. and L.C. Hamilton, *Copyright: Intellectual Property in the Information Age*, London: Routledge, 1980, at 16; Patterson, *op. cit.*, at 199 (noting the need to protect the new nation against the established trade in England).

46. Khan, B.Z., 'Does Copyright Piracy Pay? The Effects of U.S. International Copyright Laws on the Market for Books, 1790–1920', NBER Working Paper Series, Working Paper 10271, February 2004, http://www.nber.org/papers/w10271.

47. Ricketson, *op cit.*; Henn, H.G., 'The Quest for International Copyright Protection', *Cornell Law Quarterly*, 39, 43, 1953, at 43; Vaidhyanathan, S., *Copyrights and Copywrongs: The Rise of Intellectual Property and How it Threatens Creativity*, New York: New York University Press, 2001, at 50 (noting that a 'London reader who wanted a copy of Charles Dickens's A Christmas Carol would have to pay the equivalent of $2.50 in 1843 [while a]n American Dickens fan would have to pay only six cents per copy'); Stewart *op. cit.*, § 2.17, at 24–5.

48. Dutfield, G. and U. Suthersanen, 'Harmonisation or Differentiation in Intellectual Property Protection? The Lessons of History', *Prometheus*, 23(2), 131–47, 2005; Khan, *op. cit.*; Geller, P.E., 'Copyright History and the Future: What's Culture got to do with it?' *Journal of the Copyright Society of the USA*, 47, 2000, at 229; Barnes, *op. cit.*, at 95; Suthersanen, U., 'Bleak House or Great Expectations? The Literary Author as a Stakeholder in 19th Century International Copyright Politics', in H. Porsdam (ed.), *Copyright and Other Fairy Tales: Hans Christian Andersen and the Commodification of Creativity*, Cheltenham: Edward Elgar, 2006, 40–60.

49. Sterling *op. cit.*, at 18.

50. EC Term Directive, 93/98, [1993] OJ L290/9.

51. EC Rental Right and Lending Right Directive 92/100, [1992] OJ L346/61, Articles 94–5, German Author's Rights Law.

52. See Sterling, *op. cit.*, at 70.

53. Articles 10, 12, Rome Convention 1961. Although Marconi's first wireless telegraph signals went out around 1894, mass radio broadcasting began earnestly in the 1920s, with television broadcasting following soon after. The right of authors to control use of the underlying copyright works was solved earlier in the 1928 Rome revision of the Berne Convention (under Article 11*bis)*.

54. Digital Performance Right in Sound Recordings Act of 1995.

55. Sterling, *op. cit.*, at 211.

56. Despite an enormous debate as to whether software programmers were akin to literary writers, international pressure and the advent of the TRIPS Agreement decreed computer programs be considered as literary works. For an excellent critique of this debate, see Samuelson, P., R. Davis, M.D. Kapor and J.H. Reichman, 'A Manifesto Concerning the Legal Protection of Computer Programs', *Columbia Law Review*, 94, 2308, 1994.

57. EC Green Paper on Copyright and Challenges of the New Technology 1988.

58. This culminated, during the post-Second World War era, in copyright being included

internationally in human rights rhetoric, and being implicitly incorporated into the Universal Declaration of Human Rights and the 1966 International Covenant on Economic, Social and Cultural Rights. For a discussion on human rights within international copyright law, see Chapter 9 and Suthersanen, U., 'Towards an International Public Interest Rule? Human Rights and International Copyright Law', in J. Griffiths and U. Suthersanen (eds.) *Copyright and Free Speech*, Oxford: Oxford University Press, 2005, chapter 5.

59. Chapter 3 sets out in detail the theoretical rationales for intellectual property law.
60. *Edinburgh Review*, October 1878, which discussed the Report and Evidence of the Royal Commission on Copyright 876–8, cited in Plant, A., 'The Economic Aspects of Copyright in Books', *Economica*, 1, 167, 1934, at 167, 170–3.
61. Plant, *op. cit.*, at 1167, 170–3.
62. Warlick, S.E. and K.T.L. Vaughan, 'Factors Influencing Publication Choice: Why Faculty Choose Open Access', *Biomedical Digital Libraries*, 4, 1, 2007.
63. http://www.doaj.org/
64. Directive 96/9/EC of the European Parliament and of the Council of 11 March 1996 on the Legal Protection of Databases, 1996 OJ (L77) 20.
65. Articles 1, 2, Berne Convention for the Protection of Literary and Artistic Works (Paris Act, 1971).
66. Article 2(5), Berne Convention.
67. Section 9, UK Copyright, Designs and Patents Act 1988.
68. Sections 70 *et seq.*, German Authors' Rights and Related Rights Law, 9 September 1965.
69. German and US copyright laws, for instance, do not protect statutes, government reports and other primary material (section 5, German Law; section 105, US Law).
70. Articles 2*bis*, 2(8), Berne Convention respectively.
71. In UK, see *Murray v. Benbow* (1822) 1 Jac. 474 n. (where Lord Eldon refused to condemn and restrain pirated editions of *Cain* written by the famous poet Byron on the ground that the poem was 'intended to vilify and bring into discredit that portion of Scripture history to which it relates'). For an intriguing account of the conflict between religion and copyright, see Azmi, I., 'Authorship and Islam in Malaysia: Issues in Perspective', *IIC*, 28, 671, 1997.
72. Sterling, para. 6.33; section 103(a), US Copyright Act.
73. Article 1, Council Directive on the legal protection of computer programs (91/250/EEC, OJ 1991 L122/42).
74. *Inkassoprogramm*, BGH, 9 May 1985; (1986) 17 *IIC* 681.
75. Operating system – Betriebssystem, BGH 1991 GRUR 449; (1991) 22 *IIC* 723.
76. Article 3, Council Directive on the legal protection of databases (96/9/EC, OJ 1996 L77); Article 6, Council Directive harmonising the term of protection (93/98/EEC, OJ L290/9). W.R. Cornish pointed out, in an earlier edition of his work, that this was evidence of a 'campaign afoot within the E.C. to scotch the "debased" common law test of originality in favour of a threshold that all works be the author's "own personal creation" '.
77. 1710, 8 Anne, c.19; also Birrell, A., *Seven Lectures on the Law and History of Copyright in Books*, London: Cassell, 1899, pp.170–1; Sherman and Bently, *op. cit.*, 37–8.
78. *Ladbroke (Football) Ltd v. William Hill (Football) Ltd* [1964] 1 All ER 465, HL.
79. *Feist Publications, Inc v. Rural Telephone Service Co.* S.Ct 1282 (1991).
80. Dutfield, G. and U. Suthersanen, 'The Innovation Dilemma: Intellectual Property and the Historical Legacy of Cumulative Creativity', *Intellectual Property Quarterly*, 8(4), 379–421, 2004, at 392.
81. Article L.112-4, Intellectual Property Code 1992 (France); see also Sterling, para. 6.28.
82. (1923) 40 TLR 186 (PC).
83. *Cramp v. Smythson* (1944) AC 329 (House of Lords).
84. *CCH Canadian Ltd. v. Law Society of Upper Canada*, (2002) 18 CPR (4th) 161 (emphatically denying that the Anglo-Canadian standard of originality required creativity). See Sterling, *op. cit.*, at 317–21, for a summary of the Canadian position.
85. Articles L.112-1, L.112-2 and L.112-3 I.P. Code 1992 (France).
86. Early decisions and jurists rarely referred to the criterion of originality, and the concept appears to have been introduced into French copyright law under the influence of Henri Desbois in *Le droit d'auteur en France*, Paris: Dalloz, 1950.

87. CA Paris, 21.11.1994, (1995) RIDA 381; (1996) 170 RIDA 174, Cour de Cass., 29 May 1996.
88. Art.L.112-1, French Intellectual Property Code 1992; Dutfield and Suthersanen, 2004, *op. cit.*, at 392.
89. *Pachot*, Cass., 7 March 1986; (1986) 129 *Revue Internationale du Droit d'Auteur* 130; Article 1(3), Council Directive 91/250/EEC of 14 May 1991 on the legal protection of computer programs defines originality in computer programs.
90. Articles 2(2) and 11, German Law on Copyright and Neighbouring Rights 1965. See, for example, Schricker, G., 'Farewell to the "Level of Creativity" (Schopfungshohe) in German Copyright Law', 26 *IIC* 41, 1995; F. Grosheide, 'Paradigms in Copyright Law', in Sherman and Strowel, *op. cit.*, 224.
91. *Silberdistel, IIC* 140, Bundesgerichtshof (BGH), 1997.
92. As in the United States and United Kingdom, German copyright law does appear ready to bend and extend the umbrella of protection to works which are economically significant despite the philosophical barrier that is 'creativity'. Even legal headnotes in law reports, which must by their very nature rely very heavily on the court decision in question, manage to crawl into this *kleine Münze* category as long as one shows a modest degree of intellectual creativity. *Headnotes* (1993) 24 *IIC* 668, BGH; *Attorney's Brief* (1988) 19 *IIC* 854, BGH; see also Sterling, paras 7.09–7.10.
93. Article 9(2), TRIPS and Article 2, WCT.
94. *University of London Press v. University Tutorial Press* (1916) 2 Ch. 601 (in relation to copyright in examination papers); also note the more succinct restatement in *L.B. Plastics Ltd v. Swish Products Ltd.* (1979) RPC 551 (House of Lords) ('There can be no copyright in a mere idea', per Lord Wilberforce).
95. [2001] ECDR 10.
96. Edelman, B., 'The Law's Eye: Nature and Copyright', in Sherman and Strowel, *op. cit.*, at pp. 82–3.
97. TGI Paris, 10e Ch., 26 May 1987; in Lucas, A. and H.J. Lucas, *Traité de la Propriété littéraire et artistique*, Paris: Litec, 1994, at 222–4.
98. Article 2(1), Berne Convention.
99. Section 3(2), CDPA 1988 (UK).
100. *Ibid.*, section 3(3). The criterion is unnecessary in relation to certain types of works which must necessarily be fixed to come into existence, that is, artistic works, sound recordings and films.
101. Section 102(a), US Copyright Act 1976.
102. *Eiffel Tower*, Cass. Civ., I, 3 March 1992, discussed in Sterling, *op. cit.*, at para. 6.12.
103. Article 15(1), Berne Convention.
104. For example Article 1705(3), of the NAFTA.
105. Articles L.121-7, L.122-6, French Code.
106. *Market Investigations Ltd v. Minister of Social Security* [1968] 2 QB 173; *Stevenson Jordan v. Macdonald & Evans* (1951) 69 RPC 10.
107. Section 101(b)(1), US Copyright Act; *CCNV v. Reid*, 490 US 730.
108. Articles L.111-1, L.113-1, French Code.
109. Article L.113.5, French Code.
110. Article 7, German Law.
111. Article 43, German Law; see Sterling, *op. cit.*, at 201.
112. Article L132-31-132-33, French Code.
113. See *Ray v. Classic FM* (1998) FSR 622 where the court set out these general principles governing copyright ownership and client commissioner/service provider relationship.
114. Section 201(b), US Copyright Act. For the full list, see section 101(b)(2).
115. See Sterling, *op. cit.*, at 204–14.
116. Article 14*bis*, Berne Convention.
117. Sterling, *op. cit.*, at 194–5, for a detailed account of the different European systems.
118. See, for example, the EC Rental and Lending and Related Rights Directive 92/100, and the Information Society Directive 2001/29 where film producers are granted a 50-year term of protection.

119. Sterling, *op. cit.*, at 196–7.
120. Article 8, WCT; Articles 10 and 14, WPPT.
121. Article 9(1), Berne Convention,
122. Articles 12 (adaptation), 14(1) (cinematic reproduction), 8(1) (translation right),
123. Article. 14(1), Berne Convention.
124. For this interpretation, see Ricketson, S. and J. Ginsburg, *International Copyright and Neighbouring Rights: The Berne Convention and Beyond*, Oxford: Oxford University Press, at 688–90.
125. *Ibid.*, at 669 *et seq.*
126. Article 14*ter,* Berne Convention.
127. Articles 11, 14, TRIPS Agreement.
128. Article 7 WCT, Articles 9, 13, WPPT.
129. Article 11, WCT; Article 18 WPPT.
130. Article. 12, WCT; Article 19, WPPT.
131. (1769) 98 ER 201.
132. Sterling *op. cit.*, chapter 8 generally, for a detailed analysis of national provisions on moral rights.
133. For a UK analysis, with law reform proposals, of poor authorial protection, see Bently, L., *Between a Rock and a Hard Place: The Problems Facing Freelance Creators in the UK Media Marketplace*, London: Institute of Employment Rights, 2002.
134. The US federal copyright law does not confer moral rights on all authors, but merely on authors of works of visual art which is defined extremely narrowly to apply to: paintings, drawings, prints, sculptures or photographs, and only if such works exist in a single copy or in a limited edition of 200 copies that are signed and numbered by the author. Sections 101, 106A, US Copyright Act.
135. Article. 6*bis*, Berne Convention.
136. Article 5, WPPT.
137. Ricketson and Ginsburg, *op. cit.*, 616–17. This view is further substantiated by the strange language in relation to moral rights of section 3(b) of the United States Berne Convention Implementation Act 1988. This provision in effect declares that the adherence of the United States to the Berne Convention does not affect the US domestic law on moral rights.
138. Ricketson and Ginsburg, *op. cit.*, at 600.
139. It should be noted that the author has to show that there has been prejudice to his honour or reputation, and this can be either a subjective test (France) or objective test (Germany and UK).
140. *Snow v. Eaton Centre*, (1982) 70 CPR (2d) 105 (Ontario Supreme Court) (held infringement of the sculptor's integrity right as ribbons distorted the work).
141. *Godot* (France) and *Oppenheimer* (Germany) respectively, as reported in Sterling, *op. cit.*, 358.
142. *Neo-Fascist Slant in Copyright Works*, OLG Frankfurt-am-Main, 1994, December 6, [1996] ECC 375.
143. See generally Sterling, *op. cit.*, 340–3.
144. Suthersanen, U., 'Copyright in the Courts: The Da Vinci Code', *WIPO Magazine*, 9(3) 12–14, 2006.
145. Articles 10(1), 10(2), 10*bis*(1) and 10*bis*(2), Berne Convention.
146. In addition to this, all EU member states are limited by the list of defences set out in Article 5, Information Society Directive 2001/29.
147. See generally, Burrell, R. and A. Coleman, *Copyright Exceptions: The Digital Impact*, Cambridge, UK: Cambridge University Press, 2005.
148. Sections 29, 30 *et seq.*, CDPA 1988.
149. *Hubbard v. Vosper* [1972] 2 QB 84, at 94.
150. *Ibid.*, per Denning MR, at 97.
151. *Harper & Row, Publishers, Inc. v. National Enterprises*, 471 US 539 (S.Ct. 1985); and re-confirmed in *Steward v. Abend* 14 USPQ 2d 1614 (S.Ct. 1990) and *Campbell v. Acuff-Rose Music Inc*. 510 US 569; 114 *S.Ct.* 1164; 29 *USPQ* 2d 1961.
152. Article 9(2), Berne Convention; Article 13, TRIPS Agreement; Article 30, TRIPS Agreement; Article 10, WIPO Copyright Treaty.

153. Article 13, TRIPS Agreement; Article 10, WIPO Copyright Treaty.
154. Report on Section 110(5) of the United States Copyright Act, WT/DS160/5 (16 April 1999). For the decision, see Ficsor, M., 'How Much of What? The "Three-Step Test" and its Application in Two Recent WTO Dispute Settlement Cases'. *Revue Internationale du Droit d'auteur*, 192, 110–251, 2002.
155. Ricketson, S., 'US Accession to the Berne Convention: An Outsider's Appreciation. Part II', *Intellectual Property Journal*, 8, 87–119, 1994.
156. Article 1, Berne Convention.
157. See Ricketson, S., *The Three-step Test, Deemed Quantities, Libraries and Closed Exceptions – A Study of the Three-step Test in Article 9(2) of the Berne Convention, Article 13 of the TRIPS Agreement and Article 10 of the WIPO Copyright Treaty, with particular respect to its Application to the Quantitative Test in Subsection 40(3) of the Fair Dealing Provisions, Library and Educational Copying, the Library Provisions Generally and Proposals for an Open Fair Dealing Exception*, Sydney: Centre for Copyright Studies Ltd., 2002.
158. UK Copyright Act 1814.
159. UK 1842 Copyright Act (the Talfoud Act); Eilenberg, S., *Strange Power of Speech: Wordsworth, Coleridge and Literary Possession*, Oxford: Oxford University Press, 1992, chapter 8.
160. Sterling, *op. cit.*, para.11-02.
161. Council Directive 93/98/EEC of 29 October 1993 harmonising the term of protection of copyright and certain related rights. The directive is only applicable to economic rights, not moral rights, and the term of protection of moral rights varies considerably in different member states (for example, the duration of moral rights is life plus 70 years in Germany but perpetual in France).
162. For a discussion on this trend, see *Eldred v. Ashcroft*, 123 S.Ct. 769 (S.Ct, 2003).
163. Article 14, Rome Convention.
164. Article 14, TRIPS Agreement.

5. Patents and trade secrets

ORIGINS

Patents for inventions have their origins in Renaissance Italy. The Republic of Venice passed a patent law in 1474, whose underlying purpose was to attract men 'from divers parts' with the incentive of a ten-year monopoly right to their 'works and devices'.[1] The moral interest of inventors and the wider societal benefits were treated as complementary. Thus, in preventing others from building them and taking the inventor's honour away, it was believed that 'more men would then apply their genius, would discover, and would build devices of great utility to our commonwealth'.[2] The public interest was also upheld by a provision allowing for government use.

The next significant legislative development in patent law came in 1624 with the English Statute of Monopolies.[3] In reality, its primary purpose was to prohibit monopolies rather than to promote invention, and in passing the law the government hoped to encourage continental craftsmen to settle in the country.[4] Monopoly grants were declared illegal except 'the true and first inventor or inventors' of 'any manner of new manufactures within this realm' as long as 'they be not contrary to the law, nor mischievous to the state, by raising prices of commodities at home, or hurt of trade, or generally inconvenient'. Such inventors could acquire a patent or grant allowing up to 14 years' monopoly protection. Strict novelty was not required since courts interpreted the purpose of granting patents as being to introduce new trades to England whether or not they were 'novel' elsewhere in the world.[5] It is unlikely to be entirely coincidental that at this time England was less advanced technologically than near neighbours France and the Netherlands.[6] The Statute was amended several times but remained in force until 1977 when the UK patent system was overhauled to make it compatible with the 1973 European Patent Convention.

The original role of United States patent (and copyright) law was to implement Article 1 section 8 of the Constitution, which empowers Congress 'to promote the Progress of Science and useful Arts, by securing for limited Times to Authors and Inventors the exclusive Right to their respective Writings and Discoveries'. It was intended from the start that the patent system should be accessible to all classes of society and not just to the rich and well connected.[7]

Soon after independence, two patent laws were enacted, in 1790 and 1793. A third law, the 1836 Patent Act,[8] was arguably the first modern patent law. It required all applications to be examined by the government patent office for novelty and usefulness. Although this law did not discriminate between US and foreign inventors with respect to the examination or the extent of rights granted, foreign applicants had to pay much higher fees, especially if they were British. Such discrimination was abolished in 1861 for nationals of countries whose laws were non-discriminatory towards Americans.

Like Venetian patent law, the French Law on Useful Discoveries and on Means for Securing the Property therein to the Authors of 1791 treated as complementary the moral interest of inventors, albeit elevated to a human right, and the wider societal benefits of the law. The author's right to his *découverte industrielle* was deemed a property right, failure to recognise which would be to attack *les droits de l'homme*. However, the law's inherent instrumentalism considerably diluted the practical effect of the human right. First, right holders did not have to be inventors. As with the Statute of Monopolies, they could be importers of other people's inventions with or without their consent. Second, once a patent was awarded protected goods had to be made (or 'worked' in patent law parlance) domestically. If owners imported them instead the patent could be forfeited.[9] While the incorporation of author's rights into patent law did not endure, Paris Convention Article 4*ter* provides a related attribution right, stating that 'the inventor shall have the right to be mentioned as such in the patent'.

The German Patent Act (*Reichspatentgesetz*) of 1877 followed the US example by establishing an examination system. Elsewhere, registration systems – which granted patents without the need to convince a specialist that the documentation submitted with the application described a genuine invention – were the norm. Some European countries, though, managed without a patent law for much of the nineteenth century.

TOWARDS THE MODERN ERA

The modern system of patents for inventions has some fundamental characteristics that make it different from earlier patent systems. The first step in the modernisation of patents came with the adoption of the notion that patents represent a bargain in which inventors are granted limited monopoly rights by the government on behalf of society in exchange for the disclosure of technical information. Lord Mansfield was probably the first to formulate this view of patents as an information-for-monopoly transaction when he pronounced, in a 1778 case, that: 'the law relative to patents requires, as a price the individual should pay the people for his monopoly, that he should enrol, to the very best of his knowledge and judgment, the fullest and most sufficient description of all the particulars on which the effect depended, that he was at the time able to do'.[10]

In doing so he formulated the now conventional justification for patents that they are a bargain in which inventors are granted time-limited monopoly rights by the government on behalf of society in exchange for the disclosure of technical information that is presumed to advance scientific and technological development.

The second step came with the introduction of the requirement that patent applications be examined to ensure that the specification describes a genuine invention. The 1836 US 'Act to promote the progress of useful arts, and to repeal all acts and parts of acts heretofore made for that purpose' was itself quite innovative in that it required all applications to be examined by the patent office for novelty and usefulness. Gradually, other countries followed suit, the first being Germany through the 1877 *Reichspatentgesetz*. With such notable exceptions as the Netherlands (since 1995), most countries today have examination systems.

The third step came with the confirmation that the patentable bar should be kept low enough to capture the incremental inventions flooding out of the corporate research and development (R&D) facilities. In late nineteenth-century Germany, which had become dominant in the field of synthetic dyestuffs, the industry became concerned about whether or to what extent it should be considered inventive to apply known processes to make new dyes through fairly uncreative chemical 'tinkering'. The problem was not resolved until an 1889 Supreme Court case relating to the Congo red dye. The outcome was the fashioning by the Court of 'the new technical effect' doctrine, which softened the requirement of true inventiveness in certain cases where the result was a product with 'unexpected and valuable technical qualities'. The former, which one might refer to as the 'Aha! factor', continues in Europe to be relevant to considerations of non-obviousness and inventive step (see below). The latter has led to much uncertainty since an agreed definition of 'technical' continues to elude inventors, practitioners and jurists (see below). According to one account:

> The court argued that the process for making Congo red, lacking any inventiveness of its own, would as such not have been patentable. In this case, however, the application of the general method resulted in a dyestuff of undoubted technical and commercial value. Its unexpected and valuable technical qualities more than compensated for the lack of inventiveness of the process. In other words, the court said that, if the requirement of utility is particularly emphasized, it is no longer necessary to look at whether the requirement of inventiveness is also satisfied.[11]

The Court's decision had great long-term importance. First, it enabled the bigger firms to amass large patent holdings for inventions based on their organized large-scale research programmes. In consequence, it became economically more feasible for chemical firms to invest in organized large-scale in-house research and development. Second, it was a key stage in a gradual change in perception shared by industry, the patent office and the courts from one that treated invention as a solitary activity inspired – so it was often said – by individual genius, to one that considered it as a collective and almost routine corporate endeavour. In 1891 German patent law was reformed and incorporated the new technical effect doctrine, which is now part of modern European patent law.

In the post-Second World War period, the emergent American pharmaceutical industry seeing the possibility of making unprecedented profits from antibiotics screened through increasingly routine procedures faced similar uncertainty since it was questionable whether they could get patents for natural products discovered through what had become well-known procedures. Successful lobbying by the American pharmaceutical industry achieved the incorporation in the 1952 Patent Act of helpful language in order to ensure that antibiotics discovered through techniques of systematic screening could be patented. 'On behalf of their pharmaceutical industry clients, New York Patent Bar Association members drafted a Bill and were able to get it introduced in Congress, and this, supplemented by other Bills and pressures, brought about the changes they wanted'.[12] Essentially, the non-obviousness criterion was incorporated into patent law in a particular way that meant 'patentability shall not be negatived by the manner in which the invention was made'. Arguably, this phrase was intended to keep the innovation threshold low, and was successful.[13]

Overturning the flash of genius test in the US[14] and limiting the inventiveness threshold in Europe had a number of consequences. First, the collective and cumulative innovations of large firms could more securely be protected. Second, businesses could more easily surround their products with large portfolios of patents for inventions that were not markedly different from each other. Third, firms were better able to secure returns from investments in expensive research and development. As a result of these consequences, the larger ones were encouraged to create large in-house R&D structures.

ECONOMIC RATIONALES FOR THE PATENT SYSTEM

Over the years, states have granted patents for a variety of public policy purposes such as to encourage the immigration of craftsmen, to reward importers of foreign technologies, to reward inventors, to create incentives for further inventive activity, to encourage the dissemination of new knowledge, and to allow corporations to recoup their investments in research and development. From a public policy perspective, each of these justifications is as legitimate as the others depending on a country's economic circumstances among other factors. The way patents have been justified in different countries has always depended to some extent at least on the level of industrial development – and also to whom one speaks. Nonetheless, as with other forms of intellectual property (especially copyright), justice-based arguments for stronger and better enforced rights are also frequently deployed, and such claims can carry strong moral force. After all, many people would consider it just as immoral for somebody to copy an inventor's useful new gadget and claim it as his or her own as to similarly misappropriate somebody's new novel, song or painting.

Patents are tools for economic advancement that should contribute to the enrichment of society through (i) the widest possible availability of new and useful goods, services and technical information that derive from inventive activity, and (ii) the highest possible level of economic activity based on the production, circulation and further development of such goods, services and information. In pursuit of these aims, inventors are able to protect their inventions through a system of property rights – the patent system. Once these have been acquired, the owners seek to exploit them in the marketplace. The possibility of attaining commercial benefits, it is believed, encourages innovation. But, after a certain period of time, these legal rights are extinguished and the now unprotected inventions are freely available for others to use and improve upon.

One common way to interpret the modern patent system since the nineteenth century is as a regulatory response to the failure of the free market to achieve optimal resource allocation for invention. This is consistent with the public interest school of regulation, according to which one of the roles of the state is to resolve market failures. 'Patents are designed to create a market for knowledge by assigning propriety rights to innovators which enable them to overcome the problem of non-excludability while, at the same time, encouraging the maximum diffusion of knowledge by making it public'.[15] This explanation for patents assumes that knowledge is a public good. This notion was nicely articulated by Thomas Jefferson who wrote that the 'peculiar character' of an idea is that 'the moment it is divulged, it forces itself into the possession of everyone, and the receiver cannot dispossess himself of it', and also that 'no one possesses the less, because every other possesses the whole of it'. He then went on to explain that 'he who receives an idea from me, receives instruction himself without lessening mine; as he who lights his taper at mine receives light without darkening me'.[16]

Patents are temporary exclusionary rights that are alienable. As such, owners can exploit them in various possible ways. For example, patents themselves can be sold or licensed even before a product based on the invention has been developed. More advantageously, they can be converted into market monopolies if the invention so protected results in a commercial product and depending on certain factors such as the relationship between the invention and the product, which may actually be protected by more than one patent, and the extent to which substitute products exist on the market. The public goods explanation for patents posits that the possibility of acquiring such commercial advantages encourages both investment in invention and the research and development needed to turn inventions into marketable innovations.

But that is not all. Information about the invention as revealed in the patent and by the invention itself is, into the bargain, diffused throughout the economy. In this context, it is helpful to conceive of a patent as a contract between the holder and the government on behalf of the citizenry. The holder receives an exclusive right over his or her invention in exchange for the payment of fees and – which is much more important – for disclosing the invention to others. Without a patent, the inventor would have no incentive to disclose it. This would be a loss for society if such lack of protection left the inventor with no alternative but to keep it secret. Such an alternative is a feasible option in several technological fields including biotechnology. But it is also true that many kinds of product would upon examination readily betray the invention[17] that brought it into existence.

As for the creation of markets for knowledge, it might be useful here to explain why these are considered beneficial and how patents are thought to bring them into being. The explanation relates to the common situation that many patent holders are poorly placed to exploit their invention in the marketplace. Take the case of a creative but small company lacking the funds to develop and commercialise new products based upon its inventions. If such products are desirable for consumers, failure to commercialize would be a loss for society. But if the company owns a patent, a wealthier company may wish to license or buy the patent secure in the knowledge that the invention is legally protected. And if the invention were kept secret, how would bigger companies know about it? The disclosure of patent information makes it possible for prospective users to find inventions of interest and then to approach their owners.

One of the reasons why patents are so controversial is that the intellectual property incentive, as far as it actually works, functions by restricting use by others of the protected invention for a certain period. Yet follow-on innovation by others is more likely to happen if use is not restricted. Thus a balance between private control over the use of technical information and its diffusion needs to be struck. Where the line should be drawn is very difficult to determine but its ideal location is likely to vary widely from one country to another, and, one may argue, from one business sector to another. In countries where little inventive activity takes place, free access to technical information may well do more to foster technological capacity building than providing strong private rights over such information. In fact, technological capacity building may at certain stages of national development be best achieved by requiring foreign technology holders to transfer their technologies on generous terms rather than by trying to encourage domestic innovation by making strong legal rights available to all.[18] This suggests that developing countries should be careful not to make the rights too strong[19] until their economies are more advanced. Historical evidence indicates that several present-day developed countries, rightly or wrongly, took such a policy decision in the past.[20]

It is interesting to note that controversy surrounding the patent system is far from new. During the nineteenth century, patents came under attack. Ironically, free market economists and infant industry protectionists could be found on both sides of the debate. In 1869, Holland abolished its patent system for mixed reasons; both pro-free trade ideology and infant industry protectionism influenced the government's decision.[21] Britain came close to following its example. Indeed, *The Economist* confidently predicted its demise in a June 1869 editorial.

Views from the business sector as to the efficacy of patents were mixed. The inventor-industrialist Sir Henry Bessemer, who was granted about 120 patents between 1838 and 1883, was sufficiently positive about the law to claim that 'the security offered by patent law to persons who expend large sums of money . . . in pursuing novel invention, results in many new and important improvements in our manufactures'.[22] But other entrepreneurs of the era had much less confidence. The great Victorian engineer Isambard Kingdom Brunel actually refused to patent any of his inventions. As he expressed it, 'I believe the most useful and novel inventions and improvements of the present day are mere progressive steps in a highly wrought and highly advanced system, suggested by, and dependent on, other previous steps, their whole value and the means of their application probably dependent on the success of some or many other inventions, some old, some new . . . Without the hopes of exclusive privileges, I believe that a clever man would produce many more good ideas, and derive much more easily some benefit from them'.[23]

PRINCIPLES

Patents provide inventors with legal rights to prevent others from making, using, selling or importing their inventions for a fixed period, nowadays normally 20 years. Applicants for a patent must satisfy a national or regional[24] patent issuing authority that the invention described in the application is new, susceptible of industrial application, and that its creation involved an inventive step or would be unobvious to a typically skilled practitioner.

As legal documents, patents normally comprise two parts. The first is an abstract consisting of a title and a brief summary of the invention. The second is the specification. The specification is made up of (i) a description, which is likely to contain both text and diagrams or drawings, and (ii) one or more claims. In Europe, the description part of the specification tends first to explain the background to the invention, in doing so summarising the prior art. It then presents the problem to which the invention is addressed and the solution being offered. After this, it explains how to carry out the invention. This must all be done in a way that supports the validity of the claims and be sufficiently clear and descriptive for a person of normal skill in the relevant technical field to be able to repeat the invention. The claims set the boundaries for the monopoly right.

Two things should be clear from this brief survey of patent law economic history. First, patent systems were established ostensibly to fulfil public policy objectives relating to economic and technological progress. Second, these laws were bound to vary as a result of the different developmental opportunities and aspirations of countries, the perspectives of interest groups most able to influence legislatures, and 'path dependence'.[25] Having made those points, the rest of this chapter considers the basics of substantive patent law.

Protectability

The patent system recognises inventions of various forms. In Europe the following are possible:

- new things (products);
- new processes;
- new uses for old things;
- new advantages of old things used in an old way;
- selection patents.

Patents claiming new things are highly desirable for inventors since they cover any use of the product including those as yet undiscovered. When patents mainly protected mechanical devices for single applications there was no controversy about product patents. But once the question arose of whether chemical substances such as drugs and natural products could be patented, the situation changed. For example, a patented gene may turn out to perform many functions of which the initial discoverer who is the patent owner may be aware of only one. A new drug patented as a cure for cancer may later be found to cure heart disease. One may reasonably question, on grounds both of fairness and of public policy, whether the person who discovers one use of a product he has invented or made available to the public for the first time should continue to enjoy such a right to classes of product that can be highly versatile.

A patent protecting only a new process protects any product arising from it, but not the same product manufactured by a different process. While process patents tend to be less valuable than product patents, breakthrough process inventions can be highly lucrative. For example, the patent on recombinant DNA technique, invented by Stanley Cohen and Herbert Boyer, was patented by Stanford University and licensed widely, earning over $200 million in royalties between 1975 and 1997, when the patent expired.[26]

As it gets harder and more expensive for the pharmaceutical industry to discover new therapeutic substances, companies have increasingly directed research to finding new uses for old drugs. It is largely due to the demands of this industry that old substances for which a first or additional use has been discovered can be patented for such new use. For example, in the past, some synthetic dyes turned out to have anti-infective attributes.[27] As for additional uses, aspirin, sold initially as a painkiller and febrifuge, has turned out to have several unrelated medical applications.[28]

Second and further use patents have been more controversial than first use patents. In 1985, the European Patent Office (EPO) Enlarged Board of Appeal (EBA) affirmed the patentability of the former, but required that claims to them be drafted in a certain way known as the 'Swiss form of claims'. Accordingly, 'a European patent may be granted with claims directed to the use of a substance or composition for the manufacture of a medicament for a specified new and inventive therapeutic application'.[29] The word 'manufacture' serves the purpose of keeping the second use claim away from the ambit of the method of medical treatment exception (see below).

New (non-medical) advantage, or novelty of purpose, patents are also controversial. The patentability of new advantages was considered doubtful in Europe until the EBA's ruling in *Mobil/Friction reducing additive*.[30] Mobil's patent application relating to a friction-reducing additive in lubricating oil already used to inhibit rust formation claimed the use of the additive for reducing friction. According to Mobil, this particular useful advantage was previously unknown. The fact that the substance in question was being used in the same way as before did not, according to the EBA, render the advantage unpatentable.

Selection patents respond to a problem that is common in organic chemistry research. Frequently, a researcher will find that a particular useful effect will be shared by thousands of related compounds. Consequently, an inventor may disclose a very large number of chemicals, some of which may turn out to have other useful attributes. But by disclosing them already, the researcher will be precluded from filing subsequent claims on individual members of the group of chemicals already disclosed.

In an influential 1930 British patent case, I.G. Farbenindustrie argued that while its patent claimed a selection of substances that had been disclosed in an earlier patent, the selection shared certain beneficial and hitherto unknown properties. According to the court, such a patent may be valid if:

- the selection is based on some substantial advantage to be gained by the use of the selected members;
- all the selected members possess this advantage; and
- this advantage must be of a special character peculiar to the selected group.[31]

Scope of Protectable Subject Matter and Exceptions

In continental Europe, and in contrast to the USA and Great Britain, statutorily defined exceptions have been very common, although they have been reduced in recent years. The most common of these was medicines and foods. The first German patent law, for example, excluded 'inventions the realization of which are contrary to law or morals', and 'inventions of articles of food, drinks and medicine as well as of substances manufactured by a chemical process in so far as the inventions do not relate to a certain process for manufacturing such articles'.[32] This was largely because private (especially foreign) monopolies for such basic essentials were considered to conflict with the public interest. Such a view has deep roots in European society. With respect to drugs, protection may have been denied also so that the public would not be deceived into thinking that because an ineffective or dangerous drug had been patented, its use had been endorsed by the government.[33]

Excluding the patenting of drugs persisted until quite recently in several European countries. Pharmaceutical products became patentable in France only in 1960, in Ireland in 1964, in Germany in 1968, in Switzerland in 1977, in Italy and Sweden in 1978, and Spain in 1992. In Japan, they became patentable in 1976.

Interestingly, a few developing countries acted in the reverse direction. For example, in the late 1960s and early 1970s Brazil and India passed laws to exclude pharmaceuticals as such from patentability (as well as processes to manufacture them in Brazil's case). TRIPS compliance, though, has required these countries to change direction again. India finally allowed drugs to be patented, albeit with some continuing restrictions, in 2005.

Europe
Modern European patent law lays out the exclusions and exceptions in fairly

explicit form. Article 52(3), European Patent Convention (EPC)[34] ('patentable inventions') provides a list of subject matters that are not to be regarded as inventions, as such:

(a)   discoveries, scientific theories and mathematical methods;
(b)   aesthetic creations;
(c)   schemes, rules and methods for performing mental acts, playing games or doing business, and programs for computers;
(d)   presentations of information.

In addition, under Article 52(4), 'methods for treatment of the human or animal body by surgery or therapy and diagnostic methods practised on the human or animal body' are unpatentable on the grounds of not being susceptible of industrial application.

One view of Article 52(3) is that it does not read as a positive exclusion clause but rather as a negative definition of what constitutes an invention. It should be emphasised that these exclusions apply only to the extent to which a European patent application or European patent relates to such subject matter or activities 'as such'. One area in which this phrase has caused much consternation is computer programs.

On the one hand, the written law is clear and no patent protection can be granted to computer programs. The reason for the exclusion of programs for computers as such is that, like discoveries, scientific theories, mathematical methods and presentations of information, they are presumed to be not of a technical nature. The German legacy (see the Congo Red case discussed earlier) demands that patentability under European law requires a specific technical application *whatever that is*.

On the other hand, for the past 20 years the European Patent Office has interpreted the law so as to grant patent protection to computer-implemented inventions[35] as long as they are novel, inventive and make a technical contribution. Moreover, legal uncertainty on this matter is further caused by the divergent approaches of the national patent offices vis-à-vis the EPO as to what constitutes a 'computer-implemented invention' (CII). For instance, the UK patent regime is the most liberalised regime in relation to granting patents to CIIs compared to the German Patent Office which applies Article 52 strictly, and only issues patents for such inventions if the invention is part of a physical device.[36] A recent attempt by the European legislators to clarify and harmonise the issue came to naught in 2005 due to the impossibility of drawing a line between the two types of inventions.

Of course, part of the reason why there has been a real push to patent software is that the Americans do it. The difference between the US and EU position is partly due to the fact that the European patent system requires an invention to be of a technical character – and this is difficult to show where computer programs are concerned. US patent law merely requires that the invention uses a computer or software, and this is sufficient to make it technical, as long as useful, concrete and tangible results are provided. Chapter 11 discusses further the issue of patent (and copyright) protection of software so we will let the matter rest here.

As to exceptions, Article 53 ('exceptions to patentability') states that patents should not be granted in respect of:

(a) inventions the commercial exploitation of which would be contrary to '*ordre public*' or morality, provided that such exploitation shall not be deemed to be so contrary merely because it is prohibited by law or regulation in some or all of the Contracting States;

(b) plant or animal varieties or essentially biological processes for the production of plants or animals; this provision shall not apply to microbiological processes or the products thereof.

The true meaning and potential extent of the *ordre public*/morality exclusions are somewhat unclear. In French civil law, '*ordre public*' has a wider meaning than 'public order' and is more akin to 'public policy'.

The qualification to the Article 53(a) exception requires an explanation. Essentially, the fact that the publication or commercial exploitation of an invention is prohibited is insufficient in itself to render it unpatentable on *ordre public* or morality grounds. Take the example of a pharmaceutical. Although drugs can be patented upon their initial discovery, their sale is normally prohibited until such time as their developers are able to demonstrate to a state drug regulator that they are safe and effective. So this provision cannot be used to reject a drug patent application or delay its grant because its safety and effectiveness have yet to be proven. Nor can it be used to revoke a patent if it subsequently turns out that the drug is unsafe or ineffective.

On the other hand, to reject a patent application on *ordre public* or morality grounds for an invention whose publication or exploitation is not prohibited by law or regulation would not be permissible. So such prohibition appears to be a necessary but not sufficient condition for the refusal to grant a patent on these grounds.[37]

Europe's subject-matter exclusions have been a source of confusion and legal uncertainty, and nowhere more so than in the case of biotechnological inventions. This issue is dealt with elsewhere in this book. But suffice it to say that the European Commission has sought to resolve the problem through the 1998 Directive on the Legal Protection of Biotechnological Inventions. Software programs, of course, are another case in point of this confusion and uncertainty.

The United States

According to United States Patent Act section 101:

> Whoever invents or discovers any new and useful process, machine, manufacture, or composition of matter, or any new and useful improvement thereof, may obtain a patent therefor, subject to the conditions and requirements of this title.

In other words, a patentable invention may be a process, machine, manufacture or composition of matter. The process need not be new in the sense that a new use of a known process may be patentable.

Although it is well established that patents are not available for laws of nature, physical phenomena or abstract ideas, the United States has no statutory subject-matter exceptions to patentability. But this does not mean that the US patent system has readily accommodated discoveries arising from new technologies like biotechnology and information and communication technologies.

It is certainly true that the patenting of DNA sequences was deemed acceptable from the start by the PTO, but other types of subject matter presented real difficulties. In 1980, about the same year that DNA sequences were first being claimed, the US Supreme Court ruled by a narrow majority in *Diamond v. Chakrabarty* that a man-made oil-eating bacterium produced by Anand Chakrabarty, an employee of General Electric, could be classed as a 'composition of matter' or a 'manufacture', and therefore could be treated as a patentable invention. Initially, the PTO rejected the patent claims directed to the micro-organism itself on the basis that it was a product of nature. On appeal the Court of Customs and Patent Appeals overturned the patent rejection. According to the Supreme Court's majority opinion, the Congress had 'recognized that the relevant distinction was not between living and inanimate things, but between products of nature, whether living or not, and human-made inventions'. It also pointed out that Congress's intention at the time of the passage of the 1952 US Patent Act was for statutory subject matter to 'include anything under the sun that is made by man'. Consequently, Congress construed terms like 'manufacture' and 'composition of matter' broadly enough that life-form inventions could be patented without need for further legislation.

In 1985, the PTO Board of Patent Appeals and Interferences accepted (in *ex parte* Hibberd)[38] the patentability of plants, seeds and plant tissue cultures. Nonetheless, the decision did not permanently settle the question of whether or not plants are patentable. In December 2001, the Supreme Court finally confirmed the legality of patents on plants (see below).

In 1987, the PTO Board produced another ground-breaking ruling (in *ex parte* Allen) concerning a patent application on polyploid oysters.[39] Although the patent was rejected, the ruling established that multicellular organisms were patentable. A year later the first ever animal patent was granted for 'a transgenic nonhuman mammal' containing an activated oncogene sequence. The patent is commonly referred to as the oncomouse patent, since it describes a mouse into which a gene has been introduced which induces increased susceptibility to cancer.

As for software programs, the Supreme Court clarified in 1981 in *Diamond v. Diehr* that claims incorporating mathematic formulae were not automatically unpatentable, and in doing so opened the door to the patenting of software programs. The patent in question was on a process for curing synthetic rubber which involved the use of a mathematical formula and a programmed digital computer. The PTO had refused the patent on section 101 grounds, essentially that those steps in the process carried out by a computer under control of a stored program constituted non-statutory subject matter. But its decision was reversed by the Court of Customs and Patent Appeals.

The Supreme Court's majority opinion referred to a previous Court decision (*Gottschalk v. Benson*) which indicated that 'an algorithm, or mathematical formula, is like a law of nature, which cannot be the subject of a patent'. But the Court went on to explain that 'it is now commonplace that an *application* of a law of nature or mathematical formula to a known structure or process may well be deserving of patent protection'. Consequently, the Court held that where

> a claim containing a mathematical formula implements or applies that formula in a structure or process which, when considered as a whole, is performing a function which the patent laws were designed to protect (e.g., transforming or reducing an article to a different state or thing), then the claim satisfies the requirements of §101.[40]

As to methods of doing business, these were considered unpatentable for many years on the basis of a series of court decisions going back to 1908. However, in assessing the validity of a software-related invention the Court of Appeals for the Federal Circuit repudiated this judicially created exception for business methods.[41] In doing so, the Court argued that these earlier decisions forming the basis for the exception had not in fact established the inherent unpatentability of business methods under section 101. Rather, they had denied the validity of patents for such reasons as that they were merely mathematical algorithms and were therefore abstract ideas, or that the 'inventions' in question lacked novelty. In sum, according to the Court, a business claim should be treated by the PTO in the same way as any other process claim.

Criteria

As we saw, applicants for a patent must satisfy a national or regional patent

issuing authority that the invention described in the application is new, susceptible of industrial application (or 'useful' in the United States), and that its
creation involved an inventive step or would be unobvious to a skilled practitioner.

Novelty

The European Patent Convention considers an invention 'to be new if it does
not form part of the state of the art' on the priority date, which is 'held to
comprise everything made available to the public by means of a written or oral
description, by use, or in any other way, before the date of filing of the
European patent application'.[42] This indicates that inventions which are
publicly available may form the state of the art whether or not they have been
described in writing or even orally. The European Patent Office Technical
Board of Appeal has ruled that 'the concept of novelty must not be given such
a narrow interpretation that only what has already been described in the same
terms is prejudicial to it . . . There are many ways of describing a substance'.[43]
Furthermore, the TBA subsequently found that it may not necessarily be the
case that for novelty to be destroyed, 'all the technical characteristics
combined in the claimed invention need to have been communicated to the
public or laid open for public inspection'.[44] According to Bently and Sherman,
'it has long been recognised that the information disclosed by a product is not
limited to the information that is immediately apparent from looking at the
product. Importantly, the information available to the public also includes
information that a skilled person would be able to derive from the product if
they analysed or examined it'.[45] However, to demonstrate lack of novelty, a
person skilled in the art would have to be able to discover the composition or
the internal structure of the product and reproduce it without 'undue burden'.[46]

How foreign prior art may be used in determining the novelty of an invention varies from one legal jurisdiction to another. In some countries inventions
cannot be patented if prior knowledge, use or publication exists anywhere in
the world. This is the case for Europe. Elsewhere, only unpublished foreign
use or knowledge cannot be taken into account in prior art searches. But in a
few countries, only domestically held knowledge, use or manufacture is
accepted. These different conceptions of novelty may respectively be referred
to as absolute novelty, mixed novelty and local novelty.[47]

In contrast to Europe, the law in the United States is that undocumented
knowledge held only in foreign countries does not form the state of the relevant art (that is, mixed novelty).[48] Although an applicant is not allowed to
receive a patent if 'he did not himself invent the subject matter sought to be
patented',[49] there are concerns that this loophole sometimes allows people to
copy such undocumented foreign knowledge and claim they have come up
with a new invention.

The notorious patent on the use of turmeric powder for wound healing[50] granted to the University of Mississippi Medical Center may be an example of this.[51] The patent provoked considerable anger in India because such use of turmeric was common knowledge there. Yet the Indian government agency that challenged the patent had to do more than persuade the US Patent and Trademark Office that this was true. It had to provide published documentation. Because it was able to do so the patent was revoked.[52] Yet the patent should never have been granted in the first place.

Inventive step

Article 56 of the EPC states that 'an invention shall be considered as involving an inventive step if, having regard to the state of the art, it is not obvious to a person skilled in the art'. But drawing the line between the obvious and non-obvious may be no easy matter. To do this in an objective manner, the EPO has adopted what is called 'the problem and solution approach', which seeks to answer whether the solution offered in the patent would have been obvious to a person skilled in the art on the priority date.[53] In the case in which the approach was initially adopted, the Technical Board of Appeal accepted, in the light of fresh experimental evidence presented by the appellants, the 'surprising' nature of the improvement described in the patent application, which is to say the existence of that aforementioned 'Aha! factor'.[54]

The UK approach is slightly different in that the evaluation of obviousness is based on a four-step test, first laid out in 1985 by the Court of Appeal. These are to:

(i)   identify the inventive concept embodied in the patent;
(ii) assume the mantle of the normally skilled but unimaginative addressee in the art at the priority date and to impute what was common general knowledge in the art in question;
(iii) identify what, if any, differences exist between the matter cited as being 'known and used' and the alleged invention; and
(iv) ask whether, viewed without any knowledge of the alleged invention, those differences constitute steps which would have been obvious to the skilled man or whether they require any degree of invention.[55]

In the United States, section 103 of the Patent Act provides for non-obviousness as follows:

A patent may not be obtained though the invention is not identically disclosed or described as set forth in section 102 of this title, if the differences between the subject matter sought to be patented and the prior art are such that the subject matter as a whole would have been obvious at the time the invention was made to a person having ordinary skill in the art to which said subject matter pertains. Patentability shall not be negatived by the manner in which the invention was made.

Arguably, the seminal case in that country is *Graham v. John Deere*, in which the Supreme Court expressed its opinion concerning the meaning of section 103. Accordingly, the obviousness or non-obviousness of an invention should be assessed by:

- determining the scope and content of the prior art;
- ascertaining the differences between the prior art and the claims at issue; and
- resolving the level of ordinary skill in the pertinent art resolved.

The Court went on to indicate that secondary considerations could be used to clarify the circumstances surrounding the origin of the subject matter sought to be patented, and which might serve as confirmations of non-obviousness. Such considerations could include commercial success, long felt but unsolved needs, and failure of others to come up with the same invention.[56]

Since then higher courts have applied a non-obviousness test commonly referred to as teaching, suggestion or motivation to combine the prior art, or 'TSM' for short. The test has been criticised for lowering the bar to an excessive degree, such that what would be obvious according to the *Graham* assessment could be found non-obvious and undeserving of a patent monopoly. However, the April 2007 Supreme Court decision in *KSR International v. Teleflex* appears to have raised the obviousness bar again. For those concerned about the poor quality of many issued US patents, this is a welcome decision, though it has not been universally praised.

Industrial application

Industrial application is a relatively undemanding criterion. Article 57 EPC states that 'an invention shall be considered as susceptible of industrial application if it can be made or used in any kind of industry, including agriculture'. In effect, an invention lacking a practical application is unlikely to be patentable. If it has one, then it will probably pass the industrial applicability test.

In the United States, the operative term is 'useful'.[57] Although usefulness appears to be a less demanding requirement, it is possible for a claimed invention to pass the test of industrial applicability in Europe but to fail the usefulness test in the USA. 'One can imagine a product or a process giving an answer to a technical problem, or involving steps of technical nature, but without any utility: such an invention, patentable according to the European system, shall not be patentable according to the American system'.[58]

However, in the last few years, the EPO and the UK Intellectual Property Office have apparently shifted towards the standards of the United States by accepting the 'sufficiently specific, substantial and credible' utility test fashioned by the USPTO in 2001 to deal with gene patent applications.[59] So perhaps we are now in the midst of a process of convergence based on utility rather than industrial applicability.

Ownership

In Europe, a patent belongs to the inventor (or the co-inventors) or his successor in title.[60] In Europe, as elsewhere, the inventor is often an employee, in which case the right to the patent depends on the law of the State in which the inventor is employed. In the UK and Germany, for instance, if an invention is made in the course of the employee's normal duties, the national patent laws vest *ab initio* ownership in the employer, whilst giving employee-inventors a right to claim compensation should the invention be a success or of outstanding benefit to the employer.[61] This area is becoming of increasing importance, due of course to the proliferation of university inventions.[62]

In the world of business, patents are bought, assigned, mortgaged, licensed, cross-licensed and pooled. Patent licensing is very important for small firms which may, as mentioned earlier, be poorly placed to exploit their invention in the marketplace. As for large firms, some of them can amass huge revenues not just from generating new patent-protected products, but from licensing patents to other firms interested in exploiting the inventions in the marketplace. It is the alienable nature of patents that enables them to function as currency in knowledge transactions.

Scope of Protection

The claims set the boundaries for the monopoly right. The scope of the claims should be no broader than the information disclosed in the description. In the patent law of the United States and the UK, the claims define the scope of the invention by placing 'fence posts' around it. In order to place the fence posts as far apart as possible, patent drafters will try to anticipate all conceivable embodiments and variants of the invention so that others will be unable to 'invent around' the patent. In some other jurisdictions, the claims are meant to provide 'sign posts' for the invention so that the inventive step is defined and patent examiners can more clearly identify what is new about the invention. The European Patent Convention reflects a compromise between fence post and sign post claiming.[63]

Rights Conferred

Article 28 of the TRIPS Agreement presents the rights conferred in a succinct manner and in doing so reflects common practice nationally. Accordingly, in the case of a product patent, third parties cannot without the owner's consent make, use, offer the product for sale, sell, or import it for those purposes. As regards a process patent, third parties cannot use the process or use, offer for sale or sell the product obtained directly by that process or import it for those purposes. This language is very similar to section 154 of the US Patent Act.

The European Patent Convention, however, does not lay out the rights conferred. These are left to the national jurisdictions. However, the Community Patent Convention, which has still not been implemented, defines the rights in a detailed manner.[64] Some countries have drawn upon the language of the EPC in their national laws. One such country is the United Kingdom, where the rights conferred are presented in the context of what it means to infringe a patent. Section 60 of the UK Patents Act 1977, states that the following acts done without the patent owner's consent are infringing:

(a) where the invention is a product, he makes, disposes of, offers to dispose of, uses or imports the product or keeps it whether for disposal or otherwise;

(b) where the invention is a process, he uses the process or he offers it for use in the United Kingdom when he knows, or it is obvious to a reasonable person in the circumstances, that its use there without the consent of the proprietor would be an infringement of the patent;

(c) where the invention is a process, he disposes of, offers to dispose of, uses or imports any product obtained directly by means of that process or keeps any such product whether for disposal or otherwise.

In addition to these, a person also infringes a patent if without the owner's consent he:

supplies or offers to supply in the United Kingdom a person other than a licensee or other person entitled to work the invention with any of the means, relating to an essential element of the invention, for putting the invention into effect when he knows, or it is obvious to a reasonable person in the circumstances, that those means are suitable for putting, and are intended to put, the invention into effect in the United Kingdom.

Defences and Public Interest Provisions

As we saw earlier, patents may be considered as tools for economic advancement that should contribute to the enrichment of society. In reality, though, balancing the interests of inventors, users of other people's inventions and society as a whole in the design of patent systems is extremely difficult.

Among the safeguards commonly made available to ensure that patent rights do not overprotect at the expense of users and the public are defences to infringement, such as private use and experimental use, and compulsory licensing and government use provisions. Outside patent law, competition law may also come into play.

The Private and Experimental Use Defences

European countries tend to provide defences to infringement in their statutes in the form of limitations to the rights conferred. The most important ones are: (i) private and non-commercial use, and (ii) experimental use. These tend to conform to the Community Patent Convention.[65] For example, the UK Patent Patents Act 1977 provides a list of defences to infringement.[66] The general defences to an act that would otherwise constitute infringement as laid out in section 60(5) include if it is done privately and for purposes which are not commercial, and if it is done for experimental purposes relating to the subject matter of the invention. It should be noted that the two defences are separate. Recent court decisions in Europe have tended to interpret the experimental use exception quite broadly. In consequence, the exception is able to cover commercial as well as non-commercial acts. As Cornish explains in his survey of recent European court decisions, 'even if the concern initiating the trials is a commercial organisation, the exception may apply if the immediate purpose is to discover more about the properties of the invention. The courts will no longer insist that that motivation must be "solely" or "exclusively" to gain more scientific knowledge'.[67] This approach seems sensible and much better accommodates the present reality that universities and businesses increasingly collaborate, that it is difficult to separate out pure and applied science, and that it is far from obvious where to draw the line between commercial and non-commercial research.

In the USA, the scope of the common law experimental use exemption attracted critical attention as a result of the judgment in *Madey v. Duke University*.[68] The judgment gave rise to concerns that the US may have gone too far in interpreting the exemption into a state of virtual non-existence, and that in doing so it may well hinder universities from conducting the basic research upon which subsequent commercially oriented research so often depends, and which the private sector cannot be relied upon to carry out all by itself.[69] In the opinion of the Court of Appeals for the Federal Circuit, despite a university's non-profit status, its apparently non-commercial projects 'unmistakably further the institution's legitimate business objectives'. As long as such projects are 'not solely for amusement, to satisfy idle curiosity, or for strictly philosophical inquiry', then they do not qualify for the experimental use defence.

There may be wider implications too for the United States. An article in *Science* at the time noted the prediction expressed by some that Congress may respond to the Court's decision by imposing its wish 'to have the final word on the right balance between patent holders and the needs of academic researchers', concluding with a warning: '. . . that is, if all the scientists haven't moved to China'.[70] This is probably an exaggerated concern, but it does suggest, based as it was on the views of scientists interviewed by the article's author, that not only may an excessively narrow research exemption hinder follow on innovation, but it may also stop basic research in its tracks.

The TRIPS Agreement makes no reference to private or experimental use. Instead it incorporates a modified form of the Berne Convention's three-step test (see Chapter 4). Accordingly, Article 30 permits WTO members to provide limited exceptions to the rights conferred provided that:

(1) such exceptions do not unreasonably conflict with a normal exploitation of the patent; and
(2) do not unreasonably prejudice the legitimate interests of the patent owner,
(3) taking account of the legitimate interests of third parties.

Compulsory licensing and government use

Compulsory licensing and government use measures, which allow third parties or the government to use a patented invention for a royalty or fee, are provided in some countries' laws, though not necessarily in their patent laws, for such purposes as:

* to deal with a situation in which a patent owner is unwilling to work his invention;
* to satisfy an unmet demand from the public for a patented product;
* to introduce price-reducing competition for important but expensive products, for example, some drugs;
* to deal with a situation in which refusal to license a patent, or the imposition of unreasonable terms, is preventing the exploitation of another invention which is of technical or economic importance;
* to prevent abuses of patent rights including by breaking up competition-inhibiting monopolies and cartels;
* to prevent the creation of *potential* competition-inhibiting monopolies and cartels.

In international law, compulsory licensing provisions arose as a compromise between those countries that preferred to have patents revoked in cases of non-working and other nations that were less keen to interfere with the freedom of patent owners to set up manufacturing facilities where they pleased. Conflict arose between two groups of countries. The first group consisted mainly of the most advanced industrialized countries who considered it unreasonable and unrealistic to require patent holders to set up manufacturing facilities in every domestic market. The second group was made up mostly of less industrially advanced countries seeking to protect their emerging industries. Supporters of the latter position increased in number during the 1960s. This was because many newly independent countries joined the Paris Union, and these tended to be much less interested in using intellectual property rights to generate their own technologies than in acquiring useful technologies from foreigners.

The original 1883 Paris Convention text stated that 'the patentee shall remain bound to work his patent in conformity with the laws of the country into which he introduces the patented objects'. But subsequent revisions strengthened the rights of patent holders in this respect, principally by providing for compulsory licensing as a sanction for non-working, albeit without completely excluding the possibility of revocation. According to the current text of the convention, 'a compulsory licence may not be applied for on the ground of failure to work or insufficient working before the expiration of a period of four years from the date of filing . . . or three years from the date of the grant of the patent, whichever period expires last'. Such a licence must be non-exclusive and non-transferable, and an application for one 'shall be refused if the patentee justified his inaction by legitimate reasons'.

Compulsory licensing provisions are very common. 'About one hundred countries recognised some form of non-voluntary licensing in their patent laws by the early 1990s'.[71] National patent laws in Europe tend to provide for compulsory licensing and government use. Despite this, the grant of compulsory licences has generally been quite rare. One exception is Canada which, between 1969 and 1992, granted 613 licences for the manufacture or importation of medicines.[72] Probably the main reason has been that procedures for granting such licences tend to be cumbersome and time-consuming.

In the United States, on the other hand, while the patent law contains no reference to compulsory licensing, for much of the twentieth century American courts had few qualms about using compulsory licensing in response to abuses by patentees including antitrust violations. The Federal Trade Commission has also issued compulsory licensees when regulating corporate mergers and acquisitions.[73] In addition, government use measures have been invoked on occasions, usually for national defence purposes, but also to reduce drug prices and in pursuit of environment protection and economic development. It is rather ironic, then, that today the United States actively discourages other countries from resorting to compulsory licensing.

The TRIPS Agreement provides some detailed provisions concerning compulsory licensing. In light of recent public health crises in many developing countries these have proved extremely controversial. They are discussed elsewhere in this volume.

Duration

European Patent Convention Article 63 establishes a patent term of 20 years from the filing date. This is repeated in the TRIPS Agreement and is now the global standard. Why 20 years and not, say, 15 or 25 years, and for all industrial sectors? This is an example of political convenience trumping economic logic. When governments undertake to harmonise regulatory standards it may be politically difficult for any of them to accept levels less favourable to powerful interest groups than the present ones. This is especially the case when, as in intellectual property rights, the economic stakes are so high for private industry. The progressive strengthening of domestic intellectual property standards results from the lobbying pressure of interest groups which stand to gain the most economically. Governments will usually find it more politically palatable to raise intellectual property standards than to lower them, since opponents are unlikely to be so well-organised or resourced. Since the minimum patent term in Europe – as apparently elsewhere – was 20 years, it was expedient to choose this term rather than a lower one.

As for the decision to make patent terms equal for all industries, economic rationality also had nothing to do with it. After all, product life cycles within different industrial sectors can vary tremendously. For example, semiconductor products now have an average life cycle of only 12–16 months,[74] which is likely to be a shorter period than the time it takes for a patent to be granted. In the pharmaceutical sector the situation is very different. Aspirin, for example, recently celebrated its centenary, while many other health products may be marketable for several decades. But interest group politics may not provide the complete explanation either. As one commentator sees it, a standardised term 'would preserve the notion that intellectual property was indeed an area of real framework law which applied across the economies of member states and did not constitute a form of sector-specific "industrial" policy which it would be if many sectoral-based periods of protection were possible'.[75] In a similar vein, Merges argued in a submission to a US Senate Committee that the *raison d'être* of the patent system would be undermined if the rights granted varied according to specific industries:

> Patents issue every day for devices ranging from the proverbial mousetrap to super-conductors and man-made organisms . . . In the eyes of the patent system . . . all inventors are created equal . . . Indeed, it is this equal treatment which distinguishes a true patent *system* from a series of *ad hoc* awards to inventors.[76]

In some jurisdictions the 20-year term can under certain circumstances be extended for pharmaceutical products. In the US, the 1984 Drug Price Competition and Patent Term Restoration Act (usually referred to as 'the Hatch-Waxman Act') allows patent term extensions of up to five years to compensate for the restriction on the effective protection term because of the time needed to acquire the Food and Drug Administration's marketing approval. In exchange, generic firms only need to file a so-called Abbreviated New Drug Application (ANDA) with the Food and Drug Administration (FDA) for their equivalent drugs, rather than go through extensive clinical trials to demonstrate the safety and efficacy of their version of the soon to go off-patent medicine. Second, the legislation incorporated the so-called 'Bolar exemption', which meant that certain acts performed before the expiry date of the patent that would normally infringe it are allowed as long as they are related to seeking FDA approval and do not constitute commercial use. The Bolar exemption was named after a court case involving Hoffman LaRoche and a generic producer called Bolar,[77] and has been incorporated into the patent laws of several countries.[78] In the European Community, for example, the rules provide that generic companies may use the original producer's data to obtain their own regulatory approval after eight years even if the patent is still in force. But the generic version cannot be marketed until ten years after the date of the original product's first marketing, or longer since this must be after the expiry of any patents.[79]

The World Trade Organization has determined that Bolar exemptions, or regulatory review exceptions to be more formal, do not conflict with the TRIPS Agreement. However, a stockpiling exception is not allowable.[80] Thus, the regulatory review exception as provided in the following subsection of Canada's Patent Act was deemed by a dispute settlement panel as not conflict-ing with TRIPS:

> It is not an infringement of a patent for any person to make, construct, use or sell the patented invention solely for uses reasonably related to the development and submission of information required under any law of Canada, a province or a coun-try other than Canada that regulates the manufacture, construction, use or sale of any product.

On the other hand, this subsection, which provided for a so-called stockpiling exception, was held to be in conflict with TRIPS:

> It is not an infringement of a patent for any person who makes, constructs, uses or sells a patented invention in accordance with subsection (1) to make, construct or use the invention, during the applicable period provided for by the regulations, for the manufacture and storage of articles intended for sale after the date on which the term of the patent expires.

In 1992, the European Council adopted a Regulation requiring European Union countries to provide monopoly rights for medicinal products beyond the life of the basic patents protecting them, to make up for the time taken to secure marketing authorization.[81] These rights are known as supplementary protection certificates (SPCs). Applications by a patent holder for an SPC must be made to the national patent offices within six months of receiving marketing authorisation for the drug in question in that country. The maximum possible extension period is, as in the USA, five years.

TRADE SECRETS AND CONFIDENTIAL INFORMATION

The inclusion of undisclosed information in TRIPS was strongly opposed by developing countries that did not consider confidential information to be a form of intellectual property. However, Switzerland and the United States, who were concerned to safeguard trade secrets internationally, successfully persuaded other governments to accept their proposal for such protection. Because no previous convention provides for protection of undisclosed information, the strategy adopted by the two countries was to argue that such protection is a necessary measure for countries to fulfil their obligations to suppress unfair competition as required by Article 2 of TRIPS, which requires members to comply with various parts of the Paris Convention including the provisions dealing with unfair competition.

Members must enable natural and legal persons to prevent 'information lawfully within their control from being disclosed to, acquired by, or used by others without their consent in a manner contrary to honest commercial practices'. Acts contrary to honest commercial practices that are mentioned include breach of contract and breach of confidence. To be protected, information must be secret (that is, not generally known among or readily accessible to persons within the circles that normally deal with the kind of information in question); have commercial value because it is secret; and have been subject to reasonable steps to keep it secret. Members are also required to prevent disclosure of data that pharmaceutical and agrochemical producers must submit to the government as conditions for approval of the marketing of new products (see Chapter 13).

It can be argued that trade secrets do not serve the public interest as well as patents. This is because, while society may benefit from availability of the product or technology associated with a trade secret, this kind of intellectual property right keeps technical information that would be disclosed in a patent application outside the public domain. Nevertheless, effective trade secrecy protection is widely considered to be essential for encouraging technology transfer.[82] It is also important for the seed industry, since it is commonly used to protect the inbred parent lines of hybrids, since if these are accessed by competitors, the same hybrids could easily be developed by these rivals.

NOTES

1. Kaufer, E., *The Economics of the Patent System*, Chur: Harwood Academic Publishers, 1980, at 5–6.
2. Patent Law of Venice, translated by F.D. Prager in his own translation of an article by G. Mandich. Prager, F.D., 'Venetian Patents 1450–1550', *Journal of the Patent Office Society*, 30(3), 176–7, 1948.
3. Officially, 'An Act concerning Monopolies and Dispensations with penall Lawes and the Forfeyture thereof'.
4. MacLeod, C., 'The Paradoxes of Patenting: Invention and its Diffusion in 18th and 19th Century Britain, France, and North America', *Technology and Culture*, 32(4), 885–911, 1991, at 891.
5. A 1602 court case (*Darcy v. Allin*) determined that 'the introducer of a new trade into the realm, or of any engine tending to the furtherance of a trade, is the inventor'. Quoted in Webster, T., *Reports and Notes of Cases on Letters Patent for Inventions*, London: Thomas Blenkarn, 1844, at 756. A 1691 patent dispute (*Edgeberry v. Stephens*) clarified that

   > if the invention be new in England, a patent may be granted though the thing was practised beyond the sea before; for the statute speaks of new manufactures within this realm; so that if they be new here, it is within the statute; for the Act intended to encourage new devices useful to the kingdom, and where learned by travel or study, it is the same thing.

6. Cornish, W.R., *Intellectual Property: Patents, Copyright, Trade Marks and Allied Rights* (4th ed.), London: Sweet and Maxwell, 1999, at 111.
7. Khan, B.Z., 'Intellectual Property and Economic Development: Lessons from American and European History', London: Commission on Intellectual Property Rights, 2002.
8. Officially titled 'An act to promote the progress of useful arts, and to repeal all acts and parts of acts heretofore made for that purpose'.
9. Kronstein, H. and I. Till, 'A Reevaluation of the International Patent Convention', *Law and Contemporary Problems* 12, 765–81, 1947, at 772.
10. *Liardet v. Johnson*, [1778] 1 WPC 52 at 54.
11. Belt, H. van den, and A. Rip, 'The Nelson-Winter-Dosi Model and Synthetic Dye Chemistry', in W.E. Bijker, T.P. Hughes and T. Pinch (eds), *The Social Construction of Technological Systems*, Cambridge, MA: MIT Press, 1989, at 154.
12. Kingston, W., 'Removing some Harm from the World Trade Organisation', *Oxford Development Studies*, 32(2), 309–20, 2004, at 310.
13. It should be mentioned that this was not the view of the Supreme Court, which in 1966 considered that the 1952 Act did not change 'the general level of innovation necessary to sustain patentability'. At the same time, though, the Court admitted that the intention of 'the last sentence of § 103' was 'to abolish the test . . . announced in the controversial phrase "flash of creative genius" '. *Graham v. John Deere*, 148 USPQ (BNA) 459 (1966).
14. In a controversial 1941 judgment (*Cuno Engineering Corporation v. Automatic Devices Corporation* (1941) 314 US 84), the US Supreme Court denied the patentability of a mechanical device on the grounds that the inventor's skill had not 'reached the level of inventive genius which the Constitution authorizes Congress to award'.
15. Geroski, P., 'Markets for Technology: Knowledge, Innovation and Appropriability', in P. Stoneman (ed.) *Handbook of the Economics of Innovation and Technological Change*, Oxford and Malden: Blackwell, 90–131, 1995, at 97; also, Arrow, K.J., 'Economic Welfare and the Allocation of Resources in Invention', in NBER, *The Rate and Direction of Innovative Activity*, Princeton: Princeton University Press, 1962.

16. Letter to Isaac McPherson written on 13 August 1813, and reprinted in A.A. Lipscomb and A.E. Burgh (eds), *The Writings of Thomas Jefferson*, Washington, DC: Thomas Jefferson Memorial Association, 1903.

17. In this context the word 'invention' refers to the act of bringing a new thing into existence rather than to the thing itself.

18. This point applies to those developing countries that have attained a reasonable capacity to adopt and benefit from such technologies. Countries with very limited capacity have far less to gain from free access to technologies.

19. Here 'strong' refers to the extent of enforceability of the rights and to indicate the absence – or at least relative lack – of exceptions to patentability by subject matter or technological field.

20. Chang, H.-J., *Kicking away the Ladder: Development Strategy in Historical Perspective*, London: Anthem, 2002; Dutfield, G. and U. Suthersanen, 'Harmonisation or Differentiation in Intellectual Property Protection? The Lessons of History', *Prometheus*, 23(2), 131–47, 2005.

21. Cullis, R., 'Technological Roulette: A Study of the Influence of Intrinsic, Serendipitous and Institutional Factors on Innovation in the Electrical, Electronic and Communications Engineering Industries', PhD thesis. University of London, 2004, at 183–4.

22. Quoted in Mokyr, J., *The Lever of Riches: Technological Creativity and Economic Progress*, New York: Oxford University Press, 1990, at 248.

23. Quoted in Buchanan, A., *Brunel: The Life and Times of Isambard Kingdom Brunel*, London and New York: Hambledon and London, 2002, at 177.

24. Such regional authorities include the European Patent Office, the Eurasian Patent Office and the Office of the African Regional Industrial Property Organization.

25. Path dependence refers to a situation in which apparent anomalies result from decisions made in the past intended to fulfil objectives or solve problems that have become irrelevant. Once the feature in question becomes established it can persist when no longer necessary (or even when sub-optimal from an economic efficiency perspective) and exert a strong influence on the evolutionary trajectory of a given institution, technology, law, or economic system.

26. McKelvey, M., *Evolutionary Innovations: The Business of Biotechnology*, Oxford: Oxford University Press, 1996, at p. xix. The initial patent application was filed in 1974, but was overridden by subsequent applications. The definitive patent (no. 4,237224) was filed in 1979 and awarded in 1980. The title of the patent was 'Process for producing biologically functional molecular chimeras'.

27. Of these, perhaps the most important was Prontosil Red. In 1932, Gerhard Domagk discovered that the substance, which became the first sulphonamide drug, inhibited streptococcal infections. The active part of the chemical, sulphanilamide, though, did not have dyeing qualities. Lesch, J.E., *The First Miracle Drugs: How the Sulfa Drugs Transformed Medicine,* New York: Oxford University Press.

28. Jeffreys, D., *Aspirin: The Story of a Wonder Drug*, London: Bloomsbury, 2004.

29. Eisai, G5/83 [1985] OJEPO 64.

30. *Mobil/Friction reducing additive*, G2/88 [1990] EPOR 73.

31. IG Farbenindustrie's patents (1930) 47 RPC 289.

32. Section 1, Patent Law. Dated 25 May 1877. *Reichs-Gesetzblatt* (Imperial Law Journal) No. 23, 501.

33. Lewers, A.M., 'Composition of Matter', *Journal of the Patent Office Society*, 4(11), 530–53, 1922, at 530.

34. European Patent Convention 2000 (EPC 2000) as adopted by decision of the Administrative Council of 28 June 2001.

35. See for example, T208/84 *Vicom*, T26/86 *Koch*, T115/85 *IBM*, T935/97 *IBM* and T1173/97 *IBM*.

36. An example is a recently granted Adidas patent on a new shoe with a computer chip that enables the shoe to respond to different surfaces.

37. For further discussion, see Carvalho, N.P. de, *The TRIPS Regime of Patent Rights*, London, The Hague, New York: Kluwer Law International, 2002, at 170–5.

38. 227 USPQ (BNA) 443 (Bd. Pat. App. & Int. 1985).
39. 2 USPQ 2d (BNA) 1425 (Bd. Pat. App. & Int. 1987).
40. 450 US 175, 209 USPQ 1.
41. *State Street Bank & Trust Co v. Signature Financial Group, Inc.*, 47 USPQ 2d 1596, 1604 (Fed. Cir. 1998) 149 F.3d 1368.
42. Article 54.
43. Decision of EPO Technical Board of Appeal, Case No. T 12/81 – 3.3.1 (9 February 1982). Two decisions of the Boards of Appeal of the EPO 35, 39–40 (Carl Heymanns Verlag 1982).
44. Thomson/Electron tube – Decision of EPO Technical Board of Appeal, Case No. T 953/90 – 3.4.1 (12 May 1992). 13 EPOR 415.
45. Bently, L. and B. Sherman, *Intellectual Property Law* (2nd ed.), Oxford: Oxford University Press, 2004, at 419–420.
46. 'Where it is possible for the skilled person to discover the composition or the internal structure of the product and to reproduce it without undue burden, then both the product and its composition or internal structure becomes state of the art'. Availability to the public – Decision of the Enlarged Board of Appeal, G01/92 (18 December 1992). 8 EPOR 241.
47. See Grubb, P.W., *Patents for Chemicals, Pharmaceuticals and Biotechnology*, Oxford: Clarendon Press, 1999, at 54. Today, mixed novelty operates in Australia, China, Republic of Korea and the United States. Local novelty operates in Egypt, Fiji, New Zealand and Panama. Ozawa, M., *Study on Protection of Traditional Knowledge and Intellectual Property: From an Era of Preservation to the Utilization of Genetic Resources and Traditional Knowledge*, Tokyo: Institute of Intellectual Property, 2002, at 46, Appendix A.
48. A person shall be entitled to a patent unless –
    (a) the invention was known or used by others in this country, or patented or described in a printed publication in this or a foreign country, before the invention thereof by the applicant for patent, or
    (b) the invention was patented or described in a printed publication in this or a foreign country or in public use or on sale in this country, more than one year prior to the date of the application for patent in the United States . . . 35 USC §102.
49. See 35 USC § 102(f).
50. US Patent No. 5,401,504 (issued 28 March 1995) (use of turmeric in wound healing).
51. It is worth emphasising the words 'may be'. Many patents are granted that should not be and the problem seems largely due to the failure of the system to more efficiently enable examiners to identify novelty-destroying prior art published even in the US.
52. Ganguli, P., *Intellectual Property Rights: Unleashing the Knowledge Economy*, New Delhi: Tata McGraw Hill, 2001, at 156.
53. Szabo, G.S.A., 'The Problem and Solution Approach in the European Patent Office', 26 IIC 457, 1995.
54. *Bayer/Carbonless Copying* T1/80 [1979–85] B EPOR 250.
55. *Windsurfing v. Tabur Marine* [1985] RPC 59, at 73–4. See Griffiths, A., 'Windsurfing and the Inventive Step', *Intellectual Property Quarterly*, 160, 1999.
56. *Graham v. John Deere*, 148 USPQ (BNA) 459, 1966.
57. 35 USC 101 Inventions patentable.
58. Gallochat, A., 'The Criteria for Patentability: Where are the Boundaries?' Prepared for the WIPO Conference on the International Patent System, Geneva, 25–7 March 2002.
59. USPTO, 'Utility Examination Guidelines', Federal Register 66(4); 1092–99, 2001; *ICOS Corp/Novel/V28 seven transmembrane receptor* [2002] 6 OJEPO 293; *Aeomica Inc* BL O/286/05. Thambisethy, S., 'Legal Transplants in Patent Law: Why Utility is the New Industrial Applicability'. LSE Law, Society & Economy Working Paper 6, 2008; D. Matthews pers. com, Apr. 2008.
60. Articles 60–61, 71–4, European Patent Convention.
61. See UK Patents Act 1977, sections 7, 39–43; Pakuscher, E., 'Rewards for Employee Inventors in the Federal Republic of Germany – Part 1', *European Intellectual Property Review*, 11, 318, 1981.
62. Cornish, W.R., 'Rights in University Inventions', *European Intellectual Property Review*, 13, 1992; for the US perspective, see S. Cherensky, 'A Penny for their Thoughts System',

Prepared for the WIPO Conference on the International Patent System, Geneva, 25–7 March 2002; Sagar, R. and A. Nagarsheth, *Ownership of Employee Inventions and Remuneration: A Comparative Overview*, London: Intellectual Property Institute, 2006.

63.   Cornish, W. and D. Llewelyn, *Intellectual Property: Patents, Copyright, Trade Marks and Allied Marks* (5th ed.), London: Sweet & Maxwell, 2003, at 166.

64.   CPC, Articles 25 and 26.

65.   CPC, Article 27.

66.   Section 60(5).

67.   Cornish, W.R., 'Experimental Use of Patented Inventions in European Community States', 29 *IIC* 735, 1998, at 753.

68.   *Madey v. Duke University*, 64 USPQ 2d 1737 (Fed. Cir. 2002).

69.   For examples of how basic research carried out in universities, hospitals and government research agencies contributed to major biomedical revolutions, see Dutfield, G., *Intellectual Property Rights and the Life Science Industries: A Twentieth Century History*, Aldershot: Ashgate. 2003.

70.   Malakoff, D., 'Universities Ask Supreme Court to Reverse Patent Ruling', *Science*, 299, 26, 2003.

71.   Reichman, J. and C. Hasenzahl, 'Non-voluntary Licensing of Patented Inventions: Historical Perspective, Legal Framework under TRIPS, and an Overview of the Practice in Canada and the United States of America', Issues Paper 5. UNCTAD-ICTSD Project on IPRs and Sustainable Development, 2002, at 12.

72.   *Ibid.,* at 4.

73.   *Ibid.,* at 19.

74.   Hall, B.H., and R.M. Ham, 'The Determinants of Patenting in the US Semiconductor Industry, 1980–1994', Presented at the NBER Patent System and Innovation Conference, Santa Barbara, California, January 1999.

75.   Doern, G.B., *Global Change and Intellectual Property Agencies*, London and New York: Pinter, 1999, at 46.

76.   Merges, R.P., 'Contracting into Liability Rules: Intellectual Property Rights and Collective Rights Organizations', *California Law Review*, 84(5), 1293–1386, 1996, at 1315.

77.   *Roche Products Inc. v. Bolar Pharmaceutical Co., Inc.*, 221 USPQ 937 (Fed. Cir 1984).

78.   See Correa, C.M., 'Protecting Test Data for Pharmaceutical and Agrochemical Products under Free Trade Agreement', in P. Roffe, G. Tansey and D. Vivas-Eugui, *Negotiating Health: Intellectual Property and Access to Medicines,* London: Earthscan, 81–96; Pugatch, M.P., 'Intellectual Property, Data Exclusivity, Innovation and Market Access', in Roffe *et al., op. cit.*, 97–132.

79.   Directive 2004/27/EC of the European Parliament and of the Council of 31 March 2004 amending Directive 2001/83/EC on the Community code relating to medicinal products for human use.

80.   WTO, 'Canada – Patent Protection of Pharmaceutical Products. Complaint by the European Communities and their Member States. Report of the Panel' [WTO document WT/DS114/R, 2000].

81.   Council Regulation (EEC) No. 1768/92 of 18 June 1992 concerning the creation of a supplementary protection certificate for medicinal products. A similar regulation was passed in 1996 for plant protection products (Regulation (EC) No. 1610/96 of the European Parliament and of the Council of 23 July 1996 concerning the creation of a supplementary protection certificate for plant protection products).

82.   Barton, J.H., 'New Trends in Technology Transfer', ICTSD-UNCTAD Issue Paper No. 18, Geneva: ICTSD-UNCTAD, 2007.

6. Trade marks

ORIGINS

Origins of Marks and Symbols

There is very early evidence of the usage of marks and devices to distinguish goods of one trader from another. Branding, for instance, has been in use to mark slaves, animals and goods since the early Minoan, Egyptian, Mesopotamian, Etruscan and Chinese civilisations.[1]

From medieval times, marks were used by various guilds to police the quality of the goods produced by guild members, and to protect members from competitors. After the demise of guilds, marks were still used by traders and manufacturers, especially with the growing numbers of shop-merchants and specialised goods shops which sprang up in the Industrial Revolution.

The Industrial Revolution, which began in the latter part of the eighteenth century, brought about several economic and social changes. One of the most important changes to make an impact on the evolution of trade marks was the emergence of a large consumer class in the newly formed industrial cities. This new class was armed with spending power, and a social ambition to emulate the upper classes.[2] A wide range of new consumer goods was introduced to meet this rapidly growing demand. Increasingly, retailing and advertising techniques were modernised and intensified to increase sales. There had been advertising of some sort since the seventeenth century. However, with the removal of official restrictions on printing in 1695, the eighteenth century saw the number of individual advertisements printed in the newspapers running into millions; supplemented by a proliferation of shop signs, handbills and trade cards.[3] 'Over time, as consumers started to realise that some marks indicated a particular manufacturer, and in turn goods of a certain standard, the nature of the mark changed from being a source of liability to become an indicator of quality.'[4]

Early Protection of Trade Marks

In Europe, courts began to recognise the legal effect of 'marks' by the sixteenth century, and held that if another trader were allowed to use the same sign, this would allow a fraud to be committed on the public. This basis for protection was eventually to become, under the British Courts of Chancery, the basis of the action for 'passing off' to protect a trader who had developed a reputation or goodwill in a particular sign or symbol.[5] An early decision described it thus:

> A man is not to sell his goods under the pretence that they are the goods of another man; he cannot be permitted to practise such a deception, nor to use the means which contribute to that end. He cannot therefore be allowed to use names, marks, letters or other indicia, by which he may induce purchasers to believe that the goods which he is selling are the manufacture of another person.[6]

By the late nineteenth century, Britain had introduced a system of registration of marks,[7] especially as there was already judicial recognition of the 'trade mark' and its value. Lord Westbury, for instance, in a pre-registration decision described a trade mark as '. . . a brand which has reputation and currency in the market as a well-known sign of quality; and that, as such, the trade mark is a valuable property . . . and may be properly sold with the works'.[8] The notion that a manufacturer who places on his goods a particular mark can prevent others from using the same mark to sell similar goods similarly appeared for the first time in American jurisprudence in the middle of the nineteenth century.[9]

INTERNATIONAL TRADE MARK LAW IN THE MODERN ERA

Phillips notes astutely that:

> Trade mark law and practice as we know it today more or less started afresh in the mid-1990s, with the establishment of the internationally accepted TRIPs norms, the implementation of the Community trade mark and Madrid Protocol systems, and the introduction of Federal anti-dilution laws in the United States.[10]

The Paris Convention for the Protection of Industrial Property (see Chapter 2) provides international protection for industrial property including trade mark rights. In relation to trade marks, service marks, trade names and well-known marks, the Convention extends its rules on national treatment and priority rules. This is also extended to the protection of marketers against unfair competition and the protection of flags and armorial bearings.

All countries which are party to TRIPS have national registration systems for trade marks. The procedural aspects of applying for registration vary from country to country, and below we set out the salient points under the European Community registration system and the international Madrid/Protocol system.

European Community Registration

The Community Trade Mark Regulation establishes a unitary right that has equal effect throughout the territory of the European Union. The Community Trade Mark (CTM) can be registered, transferred, surrendered or revoked only for the whole Community. Registration is made with a single application to the Office for Harmonisation in the Internal Market (OHIM). It is still possible, of course, to obtain national trade mark registration in individual EU member states, but all national trade mark offices and courts are bound by community laws, and they take into account the decisions of OHIM and the European courts.

Applications can be filed in any official language but must indicate a second language from the five Office languages, namely English, French, German, Italian and Spanish. The Office examines each application according to certain formalities, entitlement and absolute grounds. The application is published for opposition or observation purposes, and oppositions must be filed within three months following the publication. The decisions of the Office are subject to an appeal before the Board of Appeal, and from there, to the European Court of Justice. For infringement proceedings, jurisdiction is based on the member state of the defendant's domicile or establishment, or the plaintiff's domicile or establishment; and if there is no such state, then jurisdiction is awarded to the Spanish Community Trade Mark Courts. Being a unitary right, decisions on infringement etc. are enforceable throughout the Community without further proceedings.

International Registration

The oldest international filing system is the Madrid Agreement for International Registration. The Agreement is an arrangement between some of the members of the International Union aiming to facilitate protection in multiple jurisdictions by providing for a common route for obtaining and administering a registration in multiple jurisdictions. 'International Registration' does not result in a common or unitary right but only in a bundle of rights arising from registration in each national jurisdiction (rather like the Patent Cooperation Treaty). Despite its age, not many countries are parties to the Agreement, including the USA, Japan and the UK.

The Protocol to the Madrid Agreement, established in 1989, is similar but independent from the Madrid Agreement. The scope of the Protocol is to provide an alternative and more attractive way of routing an application to many destinations. The Protocol is administered by WIPO. International registration will still only provide a bundle of national registrations which are subject to national laws. However, international registration under the Protocol is based either on application or registration in the country of origin, and the applicant must indicate the countries where a territorial extension of the basic registration is being sought. Application is then transferred to the Bureau (that is, WIPO) and following examination and publication, it is communicated to the designated territories. There is a provision which makes the mark vulnerable to a central attack for a period of five years. However, the owner of the fallen registration has the right to file for an independent registration of the mark in the other territorial offices within a three-month period following cancellation of the international registration and with the priority of the original registration.

RATIONALES FOR THE TRADE MARK SYSTEM

Indicator of Origin

The accepted and traditional role of a trade mark is to act as an 'indicator of origin'. Phillips further notes that trade marks can function in two distinct ways: to identify the *actual physical origin* of the goods/services, and to guarantee the *identity of the origin* of the goods/services. The first type relates to the ancient function of trade marks, that is, to designate that goods come from a particular manufacturer. This function, that is, the use of the trade mark to indicate the actual source of the product, has not been accepted by the European Court as the proper justification of a trade mark.

Instead, the European Court has opted for the second function as being the sole justification for trade mark protection, that is, 'to guarantee the trade mark as an indication of origin'.[11] The European Court of Justice confirmed and expanded this view:

> Moreover, according to the case-law of the Court, the essential function of a trade mark is to guarantee the identity of the origin of the marked product to the consumer or end-user by enabling him, without any possibility of confusion, to distinguish the product or service from others which have another origin, and for the trade mark to be able to fulfil its essential role in the system of undistorted competition . . . it must offer a guarantee that all the goods or services bearing it have originated under the control of a single undertaking which is responsible for their quality.[12]

Goodwill and Quality of Goods

The more American perspective of the role of the trade mark is that a trade mark 'is merely one of the visible mediums by which the good will is identified, bought and sold, and known to the public'.[13] Indeed, some have argued that a trade mark is more than a mere symbol of goodwill but rather it is 'an agency for actual creation and perpetuation of goodwill'.[14] Thus, consumers purchase a trade-marked product because it guarantees quality. According to perhaps the most oft-cited American trade mark historian, Schechter, the role of the mark is then to 'identify a product as satisfactory and thereby to stimulate further purchases by the consuming public'.[15]

Social Function or Lifestyle Indicator

Trade marks serve not only to identify and differentiate products in the marketplace, but also to differentiate their purchasers or wearers. Trade marks have become 'fashion statements'.[16] One of the basic functions of a trade mark is to act as a sign, a conveyor of information.[17] Trade marks can convey a variety of messages and information to the consumer, and to the public. 'Fashion trade marks do much more than simply indicate the origin or quality of manufactured products. They enable consumers to buy goods which speak to the world and declare: "this is the sort of person I am" '.[18]

Indeed, modern business itself has cynically utilised this ability of a trade mark to be a conveyor and purveyor of lifestyle messages, and have transformed them into sales rhetoric. Nike for example owes its enormous success not only to the performance of its shoes but to its apparent allegiance to 'young' values and the firm has done much to enhance this creed, which includes embracing politically correct language in relation to its manufacturing methods. The same applies, uncynically one hopes, to trade marks such as Fair Trade and Cafédirect which constantly emphasise 'fair' trading practices. The packaging of both brands of coffee positively glow with philanthropic maxims including the following: 'A better deal for coffee growers'; 'Guarantees a better deal for Third World Producers'; 'All Cafédirect growers are always paid a good minimum price to cover the cost of production however low the international market falls'.

Marketplace and Competition Function

A primary economic role of the trade mark is to enable competitors to guard against unfair trading or competition. Consumers rely on trade mark law to protect the distinctive power of the mark so that it can convey information in a more efficient manner. Trade mark owners rely on trade mark law to prevent other competitors misappropriating or tarnishing their business goodwill, which may lead to the dilution of the mark. The market as a whole relies on the law to regulate the use of trade marks so as to protect against confusion in the marketplace which would severely compromise consumer choice.

The traditional 'indicator of origin' function sets down merely one parameter of trade mark law. If one investigates European trade mark law, for instance, one can find that the trade mark directive is replete with provisions which operate to protect the marketplace, including the rights of other market traders vis-à-vis a trade mark owner, rather than being solely concerned with protecting the trade mark owner against diminution of goodwill caused by confusion. After all, trade mark theory constantly emphasises that protection is necessary to correct the market failure which may result if one allows others to misappropriate distinctive signs.[19]

Another succinct restatement of the function of the trade mark system is proffered by Phillips. He states that the function in every developed economy is to establish an equilibrium of creative tension between the following interests: trade marks owners, competitors and other non-competing market players, and finally consumers of both the trade-marked goods, and other consumers.[20]

PRINCIPLES

There are many advantages to gaining trade mark protection including the fact that the term of protection is theoretically infinite and the criterion of protection can be perceived to be less onerous than that under copyright, patent and some of the *sui generis* laws. This chapter concentrates on European trade mark law for two reasons. First, the legislation is analogous to the TRIPS Agreement in certain core definitions (subject matter and scope of protection). Second, this regional jurisdiction has seen an incredible amount of jurisprudence emanating from the European Court of Justice in the last ten years and reveals a complex and fluctuating area of policy and law.[21] Where relevant and deemed interesting, reference is also made to US trademark[22] law.

Protectable Subject Matter

Trade mark law, as governed by the EC Trade Mark Regulation and Directive, adopts an expansive notion of trade mark:

> any sign capable of being represented graphically, particularly words, including personal names, designs, letters, numerals, the shape of goods or of their packaging, provided that such signs are capable of distinguishing the goods or services of one undertaking from those of other undertakings.[23]

A similarly wide definition is available under Article 15, TRIPS Agreement:

> Any sign, or any combination of signs, capable of distinguishing the goods or services of one undertaking from those of other undertakings, shall be capable of constituting a trademark. Such signs, in particular words including personal names,

letters, numerals, figurative elements and combinations of colours as well as any combination of such signs, shall be eligible for registration as trademarks. Where signs are not inherently capable of distinguishing the relevant goods or services, Members may make registrability depend on distinctiveness acquired through use. Members may require, as a condition of registration, that signs be visually perceptible.

From both definitions, it is clear that trade mark protection is not limited to names or visual signs or even three-dimensional shapes, but also includes any sensory marks which are perceptible to the human senses such as olfactory and aural signs. Examples of protected trade marks include the three-dimensional shape of the Coca-Cola bottle, the colour combinations used on drugs and pills, the sound of the roar of the lion for MGM in the United States, the advertising jingles, and the smell of a fabric conditioner or washing powder.

Criteria of Protection and Excluded Subject Matter

Graphic representation
There is one main criterion to trade mark protection: the mark must be distinctive. But before we turn to discuss the elusive notion of distinctiveness, it should be noted that some laws, such as the EU trade mark regime, require the fixation or graphic representation of the trade mark. This visibility/fixation criterion is not compulsory under the TRIPS Agreement.[24]

Under EU trade mark law, the sign must be capable of being represented graphically. This is rather similar to the fixation criterion as required in some countries. The requirement is not onerous, especially for smell trade marks where the law does not require proprietors to write down the complex and usually secret chemical formula; rather, what is required is some point of fixation. Thus, in one tribunal decision, it was held that the description of the mark as 'the smell of fresh cut grass' in relation to tennis balls was an adequate representation of the mark.[25]

In relation to sound marks, the graphic representation of sounds must be made either by musical notation (with stave, clef, notes and rests), or by a sonogram with a timescale and a frequency scale.[26]

Distinctiveness
The sign must be capable of distinguishing goods and services; that is, the mark must have 'distinctive character'. Under EU trade mark law, the distinctiveness of a mark depends, to a certain extent, on what is excluded.

First, there are *absolute legal bars,* meaning legal thresholds which exclude marks inherently not distinctive, and those that cannot be protected on public interest grounds. In most cases, a trade mark can overcome the absolute bar if its owner shows that the mark has acquired distinctiveness through actual use.

A simple yet classic example is the word 'Apple': 'apple' used on a box containing apples would have a descriptive meaning, and would not be allowed as a trade mark; 'Apple' printed on a computer has acquired a distinctive and trade mark meaning, and denotes the source of the computer.[27] Second, EC trade mark law sets out *relative legal bars* which are thresholds that exclude inherently distinctive trade marks which nevertheless cannot be protected because they conflict with an earlier mark or sign which belongs to another trader.

In brief, the absolute legal bars exclude five categories of trade marks, which we will look at in turn:

- marks which are devoid of any distinctive character;
- marks which are descriptive;
- marks which are generic;
- marks which comprise certain types of shapes;
- marks which are refused on general grounds of morality and public policy.[28]

Devoid of distinctive character   The first absolute bar under the European law is that a trade mark must not be 'devoid of *any* distinctive character'.[29] The European Court of Justice has interpreted it to mean that all trade marks 'must be capable of identifying the product as originating from a particular undertaking and thus distinguishing it from other undertakings'.[30] A more wordy explanation was offered by the British court in relation to the same provision:[31]

> What does devoid of any distinctive character mean? I think the phrase requires consideration of the mark on its own, assuming no use. Is it the sort of word (or other sign) which cannot do the job of distinguishing without first educating the public that it is a trade mark? A meaningless word or a word inappropriate for the goods concerned ('North Pole' for bananas) can clearly do. But a common laudatory word such as 'Treat' is, absent use and recognition as a trade mark in itself (. . .) devoid of any inherently distinctive character.

Single letters, numbers, and colours *per se* without any unusual or fanciful features would be devoid of any distinctive character, since they are considered to be in the public domain and form part of the store of signs available to all traders.[32] As one court has stated, a sign is devoid if it is 'commonly used in trade in connection with the presentation of goods or services or in respect of which they could be used in that way', as such a sign will not enable consumers to distinguish the goods or services.[33] Another example is the mark AD2000 which was rejected on the ground that it was devoid of any distinctive character. It was held that although an idiosyncratic combination of letters and figures might well possess a distinctive character, the term 'AD2000' was not an idiosyncratic combination as most people when seeing or hearing the mark would think of the year. In the court's view, a sign possessed distinctive character when it was endowed either by 'nature' or 'nurture' with the capacity to communicate the fact that the goods are those of a particular undertaking.[34]

Descriptive marks   The second absolute legal bar to registration is in respect to trade marks which consist exclusively of signs or indications which may serve in trade to designate the kind, quality, quantity, intended purpose, value, geographical origin, time of production of the goods or of rendering of the service, or other characteristics of the goods or service (descriptive marks).[35] The policy rationale is clear: other traders need to access such words in order to describe their own goods and services, unless there is convincing evidence that the market has attached a secondary meaning to the word. Examples of descriptive terms which would be denied protection, unless there is evidence of acquired distinctiveness, include:

- terms indicating kind, quality or quantity of the goods or services such as 'best', 'good', or 'extra' or 'pint' or 'kilo' or 'Frootloops' for cereal preparations containing fruits;
- terms which inform of the intended purpose of the product such as 'Get Thin' for weight loss products;
- terms indicating value such as 'Bargain' or 'Super';
- terms indicating geographical origin of the product or service such as 'Argentine Beef' for butchers;[36]
- terms indicating the time of production of goods or rendering of services such as '24-hour online'.

A key decision in this area from the European Court of Justice is the *Windsurfing Chiemsee* decision.[37] The key issue was whether a local company, called Windsurfing Chiemsee, based at a location close to Chiemsee, the largest lake in Bavaria, could be allowed to claim the word 'Chiemsee', which was used on its clothing, and which was part of its registered graphic trade mark. The defendants sold similar goods in a town situated near the shores of the Chiemsee lake, and its goods also bore the designation 'Chiemsee', but it was depicted in a different graphic form from that of the trade marks which identified Windsurfing Chiemsee's products. The defendants contended that the word 'Chiemsee' was an indication which designates geographical origin and must consequently remain available to all traders operating in that region, and should not be capable of protection. The Court of Justice held that the underlying purpose of the trade mark law was to ensure that geographical names remained available for use by all:

> . . . it is in the public interest that they remain available, not least because they may be an indication of the quality and other characteristics of the categories of goods concerned, and may also, in various ways influence consumer tastes by, for instance, associating the goods with a place that may give rise to a favourable response.[38]

There were, the Court held, two exceptions to this rule:

- where a geographical name had, through use, become associated with a particular product, and in assessing the extent of distinctive character, the authorities should evaluate all available evidence and were entitled to resort to a national opinion poll in cases of difficulty;
- where there was currently no association in the minds of the average consumer with the name in question, and in assessing this, one could take into account the extent of familiarity with the name among the appropriate class of persons, characteristics of the place identified by the name, and the nature of the goods.

This area of law is in a state of confusion which, according to some writers, is the result of a series of European Court of Justice (ECJ) decisions.[39] The subsequent ECJ case was *Procter & Gamble Co. v. OHIM (Baby Dry)*[40] where the Court of Justice held that the term 'Baby Dry' was registrable and not descriptive of the essential characteristics of goods in question which were disposable nappies. Despite the fact that the words 'Baby Dry' were partly descriptive of one of the essential characteristics of the goods (that is, nappies keep a baby dry), the Court of Justice upheld the registration of 'Baby Dry' as a trade mark for nappies because of the 'unusual syntactical juxtaposition' of the words Baby and Dry, adding that it was not a normal way for English speakers to refer to nappies. In a subsequent decision, *OHIM v. Wrigley (Doublemint)*,[41] the ECJ held that 'Doublemint' was a purely descriptive mark. Confusingly, the Court held that although 'Double' and 'Mint' in combination gave rise to a variety of possible meanings, the resultant word was descriptive. The Court referred to the public interest basis of the provision, citing the *Windsurfing* decision as stating the authoritative position, and failed to mention the *Baby Dry* decision.[42]

Generic marks The third absolute bar denies registration to trade marks which consist exclusively of signs or indications which have become customary in the current language or in the *bona fide* and established practices of trade.[43] Examples include '4 Star ****' for brandy or hotels, or the picture of grapes for wine. The reasoning is that such generic marks do not allow the 'relevant public to repeat the experience of a purchase, if it proves to be positive, or to avoid it, if it proves to be negative, on the occasion of a subsequent acquisition of the goods or services concerned'.[44]

Examples include words that other traders might legitimately wish to use for their products such as *aspirin, cornflakes, escalator, linoleum, yo-yo,* which have all been held to be generic and not registrable under either European or United States laws.

Shape marks   Under Article 7(1)(e), European Community Trade Mark Regulation (CTMR), a sign will not be registered as a trade mark if it consists *exclusively* of:

(a)   the shape which results from the nature of the goods themselves;
(b)   the shape of goods which is necessary to obtain a technical result (for example, the head of a screwdriver; the shape of a ball; the shape of a wheel);
(c)   the shape which gives substantial value to the goods (for example, an elaborate bottle for perfume).

Article 7(1)(e), CTMR acts as a bastion of control for shape marks. What is its *raison d'être*? One simple explanation is that the legislature constructed this provision so as to minimise areas of cumulative protection between patent, design and trade mark laws, and part of the role of this clause is to prevent trade mark proprietors obtaining permanent monopolies in functional engineering designs and shapes. However, in *Philips v. Remington,*[45] the European Court of Justice held that the rationale of this exclusion is to prevent anti-competitive protection in relation to 'technical solutions' or 'functional characteristics of a product'. The shape exclusion in European trade mark law is intended to

> . . . prevent the protection conferred by the trade mark right from being extended, beyond signs which serve to distinguish a product or service from those offered by competitors, so as to form an obstacle preventing competitors from freely offering for sale products incorporating such technical solutions or functional characteristics in competition with the proprietor of the trade mark.

In the decision of *Dyson,* the applicant attempted to register the transparent bin of its vacuum cleaner for vacuum cleaners.[46] The decision should clearly have come within the shape exclusions under Article 7(1)(e), CTMR. Instead, the Court of Justice pointedly ignored this ground, and instead held that the mark (that is, the shape of the transparent part of the cleaner) was not a sign. The Court held that should trade mark registration be accorded to this 'mark', it would cover all types of shapes of transparent collecting bins.

Moral and public policy bars   Finally, marks can be refused protection due to general public interest reasons namely:

- the mark is contrary to public policy or accepted principles of morality, or
- the mark is of such a nature as to deceive the public (for instance as to nature, quality or geographical origin of goods), or
- the mark comprises a specially protected emblem, or
- their use is prohibited, or
- if the application for trade mark is filed in bad faith.[47]

Thus, the word 'Orwoola' for woollen goods may be excluded on the specific ground that it is descriptive, and also on the more public interest ground that the mark would be deceptive if the goods were not 100 per cent wool. Another example is 'Eurolamb' which was refused registration on the ground that it was deceptive if the meat originated outside Europe, and descriptive should the meat actually come from Europe. Similarly, if the meat was not lamb, then 'Lamb' was deceptive, and if it was, the term was descriptive![48]

Relative grounds for refusal

As mentioned above, registration will also be refused to distinctive trade marks which nevertheless conflict with earlier trade marks or with any other rights which exist in the sign. Protection will be refused if the mark for which registration is sought

- is identical to an earlier registered mark, in relation to identical goods, or
- is identical or similar to an earlier registered mark, in relation to identical or similar goods, *and* if there is confusion including a likelihood of association;
- is identical or similar to a registered famous mark, in respect of either similar *or* dissimilar goods, *and* if unfair advantage is taken of or is detrimental to the distinctive character or repute of the famous mark (anti-dilution).[49]

The relative grounds for refusal mirror the provisions dealing with trade mark infringement, and thus Article 8, CTMR is analogous to Article 9, CTMR on infringement. Thus most of the discussion in the next section is applicable here.

Scope of Protection and Duration

Article 16(1), TRIPS Agreement states the following in relation to the scope of trade mark protection:

The owner of a registered trademark shall have the exclusive right to prevent all third parties not having the owner's consent from *using* in the course of trade *identical or similar* signs for goods or services which are *identical or similar* to those in respect of which the trademark is registered where such use would result in a *likelihood of confusion*. In case of the use of an identical sign for identical goods or services, a likelihood of confusion shall be presumed. The rights described above shall not prejudice any existing prior rights, nor shall they affect the possibility of Members making rights available on the basis of use. (Emphasis added)

As is clear from the italicised terms in the paragraphs above, the TRIPS provision is analogous to the scope of protection offered under the CTMR where the trade mark proprietor has the right to prohibit anyone who in the course of trade uses:

- a sign which is *identical* with an earlier trade mark in relation to goods or services which are identical with those for which it is registered (*double identity*);
- a sign which is identical with or *similar* to an earlier trade mark and is used in relation to goods or services similar to those for which the earlier mark is registered, and there exists a *likelihood of confusion* on the part of the public (*confusing similarities*).

As we can see, there are three important elements:

(1) unauthorised use
(2) of an identical/similar mark on identical/similar goods,[50] and
(3) a likelihood of confusion

The following discussion focuses on European case law in order to give a bird's eye view of the law, and a flavour of the increasing complexity in this area.

Before going further, though, it should briefly be noted that the term of protection for trade marks is very dependent on individual countries. Under the TRIPS Agreement, the minimum term of protection is a term of no less than seven years, with the registration being renewable indefinitely.

Use in the course of a trade

Trade mark infringement occurs when there has been unauthorised use of a sign. What does 'use' actually signify? There are no guidelines within the TRIPS Agreement though the European legislation does offer a non-exhaustive list of activities that can constitute unauthorised use:

- affixing it to goods or to their packaging;

- offering the goods, or putting them on the market or stocking them for these purposes under that sign, or offering or supplying services under the sign;
- importing or exporting the goods under that sign; and
- using the sign on business papers and in advertising.[51]

Other types of unauthorised uses which would probably constitute infringement of the mark include use of a mark on a website, applying to register another's trade mark, and even invisible use such as use of the mark in a metatag.[52]

A trade mark is only infringed if there is unauthorised use 'in the course of trade'. In *Arsenal v. Reed*,[53] the famous football club, said to be quite popular in certain parts of North London, owned several trade marks including 'Arsenal' and 'Arsenal Gunners' in respect of articles of clothing and sportswear. Mr Matthew Reed sold several items of clothing, including scarves, bearing these marks, with a disclaimer that certain products were not official merchandise of the club. One argument was that these marks were badges of support, loyalty and affiliation, and did not indicate the trade origin of the merchandise; hence, it could be said that Reed's use of the signs was non-trade mark use.[54] The Court of Justice rejected this view and instead held that the use of Arsenal's marks by Reed was such as to create the impression that there was a 'clear possibility' that some consumers would draw a link, in the course of trade, between the goods concerned and the trade mark proprietor. This was so despite the disclaimers on Reed's stall that the goods were not all Arsenal official merchandise.

The case was remanded back to the UK courts. The first instance judge, despite the clear line given by the Court of Justice, chose nonetheless to find Reed not guilty of trade mark infringement on the grounds of non-trade mark use, holding that only trade mark use can constitute an infringing 'use' of a trade mark. On appeal to the UK Court of Appeal, it was held that this was an erroneous application of the European Court of Justice's guidelines, and that registration of a trade mark gave the proprietor a property right, and not merely a right to stop 'trade mark use'. As long as the unauthorised 'use' jeopardised the essential function of the trade mark (that is, as a guarantee of origin of the merchandise), such use would constitute unlawful use.[55]

Double identity

In *British Sugar v. Robertson*,[56] the claimant had registered the mark 'Treat' for dessert sauces and syrups, whereas the defendant made and sold a toffee flavoured spread called 'Robertson's Toffee Treat'. The primary issue was whether the Robertson product was a dessert sauce/syrup, and hence identical to the claimant's goods, or was it a spread? It was held that the 'Toffee Treat' was not a dessert sauce or syrup, but it was a 'jam', as it was packed in jam jars and supermarkets regarded it as a spread rather than as a dessert. The Court suggested several factors which would be useful in gauging whether products were identical: the respective *uses* and *users* of the respective goods or services; the physical nature of the goods or acts of services; the respective trade channels through which the goods or services reach the market; and the extent to which the respective goods or services are competitive.

Confusing similarities

In *Sabel v. Puma*,[57] Puma were registered proprietors of two pictorial trade marks depicting large cats in various bounding and leaping positions. The mark was registered for leather goods and articles of clothing. Subsequently, Sabel applied to register their mark which depicted a bounding cheetah, with the word 'Sabel' for leather and imitation leather products, and clothing. The European Court of Justice was asked to determine the scope of trade mark protection, especially in relation to the test for determining the likelihood of confusion. Specifically, would the mere association which the public might make between the two marks, through the idea of a 'bounding feline', justify refusing protection to the 'Sabel' mark for products similar to those on the list of articles covered by Puma's priority mark?

The Court of Justice held that the test for trade mark protection is whether there is a 'likelihood of confusion' which includes the 'likelihood of association'; the two notions are not alternatives but rather complementary concepts. To find trade mark infringement, some degree of confusion on the part of the public is essential. Moreover, likelihood of confusion should be appreciated globally, taking into account all the factors relevant to the case, such as visual, aural and conceptual similarity of marks. The Court further noted that the ordinary consumer *normally* perceives the mark as a whole, and does not necessarily analyse each element of the mark, adding that the more distinctive and strong a mark was, the greater the likelihood of confusion.

This approach was further approved by the Court of Justice in *Canon Kabushiki Kaisha v. Metro-Goldwyn Meyer*[58] which involved two near-identical marks in relation to similar goods in Germany. Canon was the proprietor of the 'Canon' trade mark in relation to video recorders and cameras, whereas the defendant wanted to register 'Cannon' for video film cassettes. The German Supreme Court noted that the two marks were phonetically equivalent, and that the first registrant, Canon, had a strong market reputation. However, the German Court also noted that, paradoxically, the strong similarity may not result in actual consumer confusion as the German public did not view both sets of goods as deriving from a common source.

The Court of Justice disagreed, holding that despite a lesser degree of similarity between the goods of the two parties, where the marks are very similar, and where the earlier mark and its reputation is distinctive, the first mark should prevail. Taking a 'global' account of the mark meant that marks with highly distinctive character, either *per se* or because of their market reputation, enjoyed a broader scope of protection than marks with less distinctive character. Here, the important issue is whether the public believes that the goods come from the same undertaking or from economically linked undertakings, irrespective of the fact that the public is not confused as to the place of production of goods.

In reality, however, the decisions appear rather quixotic. Note the following examples: 'Bud' and 'Budmen' (similar marks); 'Giorgio Aire' and 'Miss Giorgi' (dissimilar); 'Mystery' and 'Mixery' (similar); 'Viagra' and 'Viagrene' (similar), 'Asterix' and 'Starix' (dissimilar); 'Oxbridge' and 'Bridge' (similar).[59] As Bently and Sherman accurately state: 'these counter-examples are a useful reminder that the rulings are fact-specific, so previous decisions are helpful only to provide a sense of the standards being applied; they have virtually no value as precedents'.[60]

Well-known marks

Article 6*bis*, Paris Convention sets out the following:

> (1) The countries of the Union undertake . . . to refuse or to cancel the registration, and to prohibit the use, of a trademark which constitutes a reproduction, an imitation, or a translation, liable to create confusion, of a mark considered by the competent authority of the country of registration or use to be *well known* in that country as being already the mark of a person entitled to the benefits of this Convention and used for identical or similar goods. These provisions shall also apply when the essential part of the mark constitutes a reproduction of any such well-known mark or an imitation liable to create confusion therewith. (Emphasis added)

Articles 16(2), and 16(3), TRIPS Agreement augment this scope of protection for well-known marks:

> (2) Article 6*bis* of the Paris Convention (1967) shall apply, *mutatis mutandis*, to services. In determining whether a trademark is *well-known*, Members shall take account of the knowledge of the trademark in the relevant sector of the public, including knowledge in the Member concerned which has been obtained as a result of the promotion of the trademark.

> (3) Article 6*bis* of the Paris Convention (1967) shall apply, *mutatis mutandis*, to goods or services which are *not similar* to those in respect of which a trademark is registered, provided that use of that trademark in relation to those goods or services would indicate a connection between those goods or services and the owner of the registered trademark and provided that the interests of the owner of the registered trademark are likely to be *damaged* by such use. (Emphasis added)

Basically, this TRIPS provision supplements the protection for well-known marks required by Article 6*bis* of the Paris Convention, and emphasises that the provisions must be applied also to services. Second, it is required that knowledge in the relevant sector of the public acquired not only as a result of the *use* of the mark but also by other means, including as a result of its promotion, be taken into account. Furthermore, the protection of registered well-known marks must extend to goods or services which are not similar to those in respect of which the trade mark has been registered, provided that its use would indicate a connection between the parties.

Similarly, the European Community Trade Mark Regulation states that the trade mark proprietor has a right to prevent unauthorised use in the course of trade,

> (c) any sign which is identical with or similar to the Community trade mark in relation to goods or services which are not similar to those for which the Community trade mark is registered, where the latter *has a reputation* in the Community and where use of that sign without due cause *takes unfair advantage of, or is detrimental to*, the distinctive character or the repute of the Community trade mark. (Emphasis added).

Under European jurisprudence, it must be shown that the mark acquires reputation in the European Community. In *General Motors Corporation v. Yplon*,[61] the European Court of Justice had to determine the notion of reputation in relation to the word mark 'Chevy' for motor vehicles which the defendants were using in respect of detergents and cleaning products. The defendants were based in Belgium and claimed that the mark 'Chevy' had no reputation in the Benelux region.

The Court held that a mark would have a reputation where it was known by a significant part of the public concerned by the products covered by the trade mark. This 'public' could be, depending on the product or service marketed, either the public at large, or a more specialised group of public (for example, traders in a specific sector). The national courts should, in order to determine the reputation of the mark, take into consideration relevant facts such as: market share held, intensity, geographical extent, duration of use, and the size of investment made by the undertaking promoting it. Moreover, the reputation should exist in a substantial part of the Member State, or region.[62]

The US trade mark law, as we see below, protects *famous* trade marks.

Limitations and Defences

Article 17, TRIPS Agreement sets out the 'trade mark' version of the three-step test:

Members may provide limited exceptions to the rights conferred by a trademark, such as fair use of descriptive terms, provided that such exceptions take account of the legitimate interests of the owner of the trademark and of third parties.

Article 12 of the European Community Trade Mark Regulation offers more specific lines of defences. The provision states:

A Community trade mark shall not entitle the proprietor to prohibit a third party from using in the course of trade:
(a) his own name or address;
(b) indications concerning the kind, quality, quantity, intended purpose, value, geographical origin, the time of production of the goods or of rendering of the service, or other characteristics of the goods or service;
(c) the trade mark where it is necessary to indicate the intended purpose of a product or service, in particular as accessories or spare parts,
provided he uses them in accordance with honest practices in industrial or commercial matters.

The US trade mark law has a case-made fair use doctrine whereby an unauthorised use of another's trade mark will not infringe it if three conditions are fulfilled, namely:

(1) the trade mark proprietor's product or service must be one which is not readily identifiable by the defendant if he does not make use of the trade mark;
(2) only so much of the trade mark may be used as is reasonably necessary to identify the product or service; and
(3) the user must do nothing that would, in conjunction with the mark, suggest sponsorship or endorsement by the trade mark holder.[63]

UNITED STATES TRADE MARK LAW

The general principles under US trade mark law are analogous to EC trade mark law as discussed above; however, there are important differences. This section discusses briefly the most salient divergences between the two jurisdictions.

Trade marks are protected either under the federal statute, namely the Lanham Act (15 USC sections 1051–1127), under states' statutory law, and common laws. Indeed, there is no need for registration to obtain rights in the mark as long as legitimate use has been made of the mark. Owning a federal trade mark registration does have some advantages including the legal presumption of the registrant's ownership of the mark, the right to use the mark nationwide in relation to the goods and/or services listed in the registration, and the ability to bring an action concerning the mark in federal court.

Under the Lanham Act, a trade mark consists of 'any word, name, symbol, or device, or any combination thereof . . . [used] to identify and distinguish . . . goods . . . [or] services'.[64] This definition includes all sorts of marks consisting of words, logos, and product designs and configurations, trade dress, sound marks, and even scents – as long as these marks act as an indicator of source.

The US federal law protects trade marks that are distinctive and *famous*. Section 43, Lanham Act sets out the rule as follows:

(c) The owner of a *famous* mark shall be entitled, subject to the principles of equity and upon such terms as the court deems reasonable, to an injunction against another person's commercial use in commerce of a mark or trade name, if such use begins after the mark has become *famous* and causes *dilution* of the distinctive quality of the mark, and to obtain such other relief as is provided in this subsection. In determining whether a mark is distinctive and famous, a court may consider factors such as, but not limited to –

(A) the degree of inherent or acquired distinctiveness of the mark;
(B) the duration and extent of use of the mark in connection with the goods or services with which the mark is used;
(C) the duration and extent of advertising and publicity of the mark;
(D) the geographical extent of the trading area in which the mark is used;
(E) the channels of trade for the goods or services with which the mark is used;
(F) the degree of recognition of the mark in the trading areas and channels of trade used by the mark's owner and the person against whom the injunction is sought;
(G) the nature and extent of use of the same or similar marks by third parties; and . . .[65]

Thus, US trade mark law protects not only against the misappropriation of famous marks, but also against any act which dilutes the distinctiveness of the mark. Dilution itself is defined in the Act as the 'lessening of the capacity of a famous mark to identify and distinguish goods or services, regardless of the presence or absence of (1) competition between the owner of the famous mark and other parties, or (2) likelihood of confusion, mistake or deception'.[66]

Thus, unlike traditional trade mark principles, where the likelihood of confusion among consumers must be shown, dilution recognises injury to a trade mark proprietor in cases where there is no such confusion, for example, if someone started selling 'Kodak' bicycles or 'Coca-Cola' pianos, it would injure the distinctiveness of the 'Kodak' and 'Coca-Cola' trade marks by blurring[67] its distinctiveness even if there were no evidence that any consumers actually thought the bicycles or pianos came from the film or drinks corporations. All a trade mark proprietor need do is show that the defendant's mark is *likely* to cause dilution of the famous mark. Moreover, the law allows a trade mark proprietor to sue by way of a 'dilution by tarnishment' cause of action, which is defined as 'association arising from the similarity between a mark or trade name and a famous mark that harms the reputation of the famous mark'.[68]

THE COMMON LAW ACTION OF PASSING OFF

A passing off action allows a trader to prevent another trader from passing their goods off as if they were the first traders. A nineteenth-century English definition of this form of action states that:

> A man is not to sell his goods under the pretence that they are the goods of another man; he cannot be permitted to practise such a deception, nor to use the means which contribute to that end. He cannot therefore be allowed to use names, marks, letters, or other indicia, by which he may induce purchasers to believe, that the goods which he is selling are the manufacture of another person.[69]

It is a common law action, rather than one based on statute law, and hence is moulded by case law.[70] It is to be distinguished from unfair competition law as exists under civil law jurisdictions, and as set out in Article *6bis*, Paris Convention (see below).

Briefly, the law today is employed to stop any misrepresentation in the course of trade to prospective customers calculated to injure the business goodwill of another trader and that causes actual damage. There are two valid definitions of what constitutes passing off. In the early classic formulation set out in the *Advocaat* case,[71] Lord Diplock held that five characteristics must be present in order to create a valid cause of action for passing off:

(i)   a misrepresentation,
(ii)   made by a trader in the course of trade,
(iii)   to prospective customers of his or ultimate consumers of goods or services supplied by him,
(iv)   which is calculated to injure the business or goodwill of another trader (in the sense that this is a reasonably foreseeable consequence), and
(iv)   which causes actual damage to the business or goodwill of the trader by whom the action is brought or (in a *quia timet* action) will probably do so.

A later re-formulation of this classic test was offered by Lord Oliver in the *Jif Lemon* decision[72] where he stated that in order to succeed in an action for passing-off, a claimant must show that

(i)   the claimant had goodwill,

(ii)   a misrepresentation had been made by the defendant, that would be likely to deceive the public, and

(iii) the misrepresentation would be likely to damage the claimant.

It should be emphasised that the action for passing off is not concerned with copying or slavish imitation (as under unfair competition law) and these acts *per se* are not considered unlawful outside the recognised intellectual property laws. This was forcefully stated in the *Roho* decision:

> There is no tort of copying. There is no tort of taking a man's market or customers. Neither the market nor the customers are the plaintiff's to own. There is no tort of making use of another's goodwill as such. There is no tort of competition.[73]

This sentiment is echoed in other judgements emanating both from the High Court in England and Wales, and also from other common law jurisdictions.[74] Rather, the law on passing off emphasises the notions of confusion to and deception of consumers. In the *Jif Lemon*[75] case, the plaintiff was held to have established a trading reputation in lemon juice sold in plastic containers which looked like life-sized lemons. The defendant sold lemon juice in similarly shaped lemon containers, and although the two containers bore dissimilar marks ('Jif' as opposed to 'RealLemon'), the court held that passing off had been established. The House of Lords proceeded to offer a re-formulation of the test of passing off:

> First, he must establish a goodwill or reputation attached to the goods or services which he supplies in the mind of the purchasing public by association with the identifying 'get-up' (whether it consists simply of a brand name or a trade description, or the individual features of labelling or packaging) under which his particular goods or services are offered to the public, such that the get-up is recognised by the public as distinctive specifically of the plaintiff's goods or services. Secondly, he must demonstrate a misrepresentation by the defendant to the public (whether or not intentional) leading or likely to lead the public to believe that goods or services offered by him are the goods or services of the plaintiff . . . Thirdly, he must demonstrate that he suffers, or in a *quia timet* action, that he is likely to suffer damage by reason of the erroneous belief engendered by the defendant's misrepresentation that the source of the defendant's goods or services is the same as the source of those offered by the plaintiff.[76]

With these principles in mind, it is clear that different considerations arise in the action for passing off – the element of confusion is insufficient, and it must be shown that the plaintiff has a sufficient trading reputation which will lead consumers, acquiring the defendant's products, into thinking that they are securing the goods of the plaintiff. Moreover, the product or its get-up or packaging must have some distinguishing feature upon which his trading reputation is founded.[77]

TRADE MARKS AND UNFAIR COMPETITION

Rationale

Unfair competition is a broad concept, and its relationship to intellectual property goes far beyond its relevance to trade mark law and passing off. Nonetheless, since trade marks play a huge role in marketing goods and services, we will deal briefly with unfair competition here.

One view as to the function of unfair competition law is that it acts as a corollary to competition law. While competition law protects the institution of competition as the chosen order of the marketplace, unfair competition theory regulates the behaviour of the various competitors with regard to their behaviour in the marketplace. This is in tandem with the view that unfair competition law relates to the conduct of an imitator, rather than what is imitated.[78]

The second view holds that unfair competition should not be ethics-based but rather should determine whether or not the result of the competitor's behaviour hinders or stifles the competitive process of differentiation and imitation. This view upholds the sanctity of consumer welfare as the prime consideration, as opposed to upholding moral standards within the marketplace. From this perspective, imitation products on the market may reflect the dishonest business practices of the imitator, but should also be regarded as being economically beneficial to the consumer in bringing the price of the product down and in forcing standardisation of the product.[79]

Definitions

Most WTO member states do have a general unfair competition law which is based on fault or wrongdoing, as set out in Article 10*bis* of the Paris Convention. Any infringement of an intellectual property right invariably involves fault or wrongdoing on the part of the imitator. The difficulty lies in that in addition to regulating the conduct of the imitator in order to maintain a fair marketplace, unfair competition laws can also indirectly serve as a means of conferring proprietary rights. In this manner, rather than market regulatory mechanisms, the law is seen as an important supplement to intellectual property protection.

In this way, one can understand the reasoning behind the classification of unfair competition under Article 1(2), Paris Convention as part of the industrial property regime. Article 10*bis*, Paris Convention goes further and defines the concept of 'unfair competition' as 'any act of competition contrary to honest practices in industrial or commercial matters'.[80]

According to the Paris Convention, acts of confusion, of denigration and of misleading indications are specifically prohibited:[81]

- all acts of such a nature as to create confusion by any means whatever with the establishment, the goods, or the industrial or commercial activities, of a competitor;
- false allegations in the course of trade of such a nature as to discredit the establishment, the goods, or the industrial or commercial activities, of a competitor;
- indications or allegations the use of which in the course of trade is liable to mislead the public as to the nature, the manufacturing process, the characteristics, the suitability for their purpose, or the quantity, of the goods.

The TRIPS Agreement incorporates the substantive provisions of the Paris Convention by reference and explicitly mentions Article 10*bis* in the sections dealing with geographical indications and undisclosed information.[82] Specifically, WTO members must provide legal means to prevent any use of geographical indications that would constitute unfair competition. Also, members must ensure effective protection against unfair competition with respect to undisclosed information.

Confusion

The prohibition of acts which create confusion with distinctive signs, products or services of the competitor is the basis of this classical rule against unfair competition. One can even find this rule under the common law action for passing off. The prohibition of confusion may supplement existing laws for the protection of distinctive signs. However, national laws of many countries do differ in one important feature: the nexus between unfair competition law and trade mark protection. The question arises of whether these two laws co-exist in a cumulative, supplementary, or mutually exclusive manner.

Slavish Imitation

In principle, products that are not, or are no longer, protected by intellectual property rights may be freely copied and imitated. Unfair competition law should not extend the boundaries of intellectual property legislation. However, the circumstances in which such copying is done may amount to unfair competition. Many European countries, for instance, prohibit the slavish copying of goods if such reproduction leads to a deception of consumers as to the origin of the product. These cases can be addressed under the topic of causing confusion (see above). Furthermore, systematic copying or copying made possible by a breach of confidentiality is also considered not to be 'fair' market behaviour.

Different opinions exist, however, whether and to what extent elements such as confusion, slavish imitation or parasitic behaviour should be taken into account. Under French law, for example, the law adopts three different stances simultaneously.[83] A first view is that copying an item in the public domain cannot amount to fault and it is not a civil wrong to reproduce an unprotected object even if damage is caused. A further element such as confusion is required. The second contrary notion is that the slavish reproduction of a product in the public domain is wrong if this is done with a view to creating a confusion in the public concerning the origin of products sold, and indeed, the mere fact of slavish imitation demonstrates an intention to cause confusion, and a fault should be inferred. The final position is that the taking of fruits of another's industry and investment is unjust enrichment and therefore, unfair competition law should be invoked on the basis of parasitic competition '*concurrence parasitaire*'.[84]

The second and third approaches pose a serious problem. This is that unfair competition law can usurp patent, copyright and trade mark laws by either conferring or extending protection of inventions, works and marks.

NOTES

1. Shao, K., 'Look at my Sign – Trademarks in China from Antiquity to the Early Modern Times', 87 *Journal of the Patent and Trademark Office Society,* 87, 654, 2005; Schechter, F., *The Historical Foundations of the Law Relating to Trade Marks*, New York: Columbia University Press, 1925, at 38–77.
2. This was especially true of Londoners. George, M.D., *London Life in the Eighteenth Century*, London: Penguin, 1925, chapter 4; Gilboy, E.W., 'Demand as a Factor in the Industrial Revolution', in A.H. Cole (ed.), *Facts and Factors in Economic History: Articles by Former Students of Edwin Francis Gay*, Cambridge, MA: Harvard University Press, 1932, at 620–40.
3. Styles, J., 'Manufacturing, Consumption and Design', in J. Brewer and R. Porter (eds), *Consumption and the World of Goods*, London: Routledge, 1993, at 540.
4. Bently, L. and B. Sherman, *Intellectual Property Law* (2nd ed.), Oxford, Oxford University Press, 2004, at 694.
5. Bently and Sherman, *op. cit.*, at 695. *Blanchard v. Hill*, (1742) 2 Atk. 485 (which was probably one of the earliest recorded trade mark infringement actions brought before an equity court).
6. *Perry v. Trefitt*, (1842) 6 Beav. 66; 49 ER 749.
7. Trade Mark Registration Act 1875 which gave the registered proprietor the right to the exclusive use of the mark in respect of the specified goods.
8. *Hall v. Barrows*, (1863) 4 De GJ & S 150, 12 WR 322.
9. *Thomson v. Winchester* (though the court did not use the word 'trademark', relying instead on the general tort of fraud), 36 Mass. (19 Pick.) 214 (Sup. Ct. 1873).
10. Phillips, J., *Trade Mark Law: A Practical Anatomy*, Oxford: Oxford University Press, 2003, at 14. The relevant instruments Phillips refers to are Directive 89/104/EEC on trade marks, 21 December 1988; Community Regulation EC No. 40/94 on the Community Trade Mark, 20 December 1993; and the Protocol relating to the Madrid Agreement concerning International Registration of Marks 1989. For discussion on anti-dilution laws in the US and elsewhere, see Simon, I., 'The Actual Dilution Requirement in the United States, United

Kingdom and European Union: A Comparative Analysis', *Boston University Journal of Science and Technology Law*, 12(2), 271, 2006.

11. Recital 7, Council Directive 89/104; and Hag II, (1990) CMLR 571, at 608 (ECJ).

12. *Philips Electronics NV v. Remington Consumer Products*, [2002] 2 CMLR 1329 (ECJ), para. 30; see also Case C-349/95, *Loendersloot*, [1997] ECR I-6227, paras 22 and 24; and Case C-39/97, *Canon*, [1998] ECR I-5507, para. 28; and *Arsenal Football Club plc v. Matthew Reed*, Case C-206/01 [2003] ETMR 227 (ECJ).

13. *Coca-Cola Bottling Co. v. Coca-Cola Co.*, 269 F. 796 (D. Del. 1920).

14. Schechter, F., 'The Rational Basis of Trade Mark Protection', *Harvard Law Review*, 40, 813, 1927, at 818; Norman, H., 'Schechter's *The Rational Basis of Trade Mark Protection* Revisited', in N. Dawson and A. Firth (eds), *Trade Marks Retrospective*, London: Sweet & Maxwell, 2000, at 192.

15. Schechter, 1927, *op. cit.*

16. Phillips, *op. cit.*, at 27.

17. See Kitchin, D, D. Llewelyn, J. Mellor, R. Meade and T. Moody-Stuart (eds), *Kerly's Law of Trade Marks and Trade Names* (13th ed.), London: Sweet & Maxwell, 2001, para. 2-06.

18. Phillips, *op. cit.*, at 27.

19. Suthersanen, U., 'The European Court of Justice in Philips v Remington – Trade Marks and Market Freedom', *Intellectual Property Quarterly*, 7, 257–83, 2003; Landes, W.M. and R.A. Posner, *The Economic Structure of Intellectual Property Law*, Cambridge, MA: Belknap Press/Harvard University Press, 2003, chapter 7. For a slightly esoteric justificatory basis for trade mark law, see Maniatis, S.M., 'Trade Mark Rights: A Justification Based on Property', *Intellectual Property Quarterly*, 6, 123–71, 2002.

20. Phillips, *op. cit.*, at p. 32.

21. Maniatis, S., *Trade Marks in Europe: A Practical Jurisprudence,* London: Sweet & Maxwell, 2007.

22. Note that the term used in the United States is 'trademark', while in the UK and Europe we use 'trade mark'. TRIPS and the relevant WIPO treaties follow the US in this regard.

23. Article 2, First Council Directive of 21 December 1988, to Approximate the Laws of the Member States Relating to Trade Marks (89/104/EEC), 11 February 1989; Article 4, Council Regulation (EC) No. 40/94 of 20 December 1993 on the Community Trade Mark, OJ, No. 11, of 14 January 1994 [hereinafter referred to as CTMR].

24. Article 15, TRIPS Agreement.

25. *Vennootschap Onder Firma Senta Aromatic Marketing's Application*, [1999] ETMR 429 (Office for Harmonisation in the Internal Market (Second Board of Appeal)).

26. See for example *Metro Goldwyn-Mayer Lion Corp's Application*, Case R-781/1999–4, [2004] ETMR 24 (roar of a lion) or *Shield Mark*, [2004] ETMR 33 (first nine notes of Für Elise)

27. Lastowka, G., 'The Trademark Function of Authorship', *Boston University Law Review*, 85, 1171–241, 2005.

28. Article 7(1)(a)–(d), CTMR.

29. See generally, Phillips, *op. cit.*, at 86–98.

30. *Linde AG, Winward Industries, Rado Watch Co. Ltd.* Joined Cases C-53/01, C-54/01, C-55/01, [2003] ETMR 963, at para. 47.

31. *British Sugar Plc v. James Robertson & Sons Ltd.* [1996] RPC 281.

32. *Ty-Nant Spring Water Ltd.'s Trade Mark Application* [1999] ETMR 974, OHIM, Third BoA.

33. *Rewe-Zentral v. OHIM (Lite)*, T-79/00, [2002] ECR II-705.

34. *Allied Domecq plc's Application: AD2000 Trade Mark*, (1997) RPC 168.

35. Article 7(1)(c), CTMR.

36. Of course, it is open to countries to provide, by way of derogation from this provision, that signs or indications which serve to designate the geographical origin of the goods may constitute collective marks – this is discussed elsewhere.

37. *Windsurfing Chiemsee Produktions und Vertriebs GmbH v. Boots und Segelzubehor Walter Huber* (C108/97); and *v. Attenberger*, (C109/97), [1999] ETMR 585.

38. *Ibid.,* at para. 35.

39. Bently and Sherman, *op. cit.*, at 803; also Davis, J., 'The Need to Leave Free for Others to Use and the Trade Mark Common', in J. Phillips and I. Simon (eds), *Trade Mark Use*, Oxford: Oxford University Press, 2005, at 30–45.
40. Case C-383/99 P, (2002) ETMR (3) 22.
41. Case C-191/01P, OJ C304, 13.12.2003, p. 2, (2003) ETMR (88) 1068.
42. For further discussion on this rather confusing area, see Phillips, *op. cit.*, at 78–84, and Bently and Sherman, *op. cit.*, at 807–10.
43. Article 7(1)(d), CTMR.
44. *Best Buy Concepts v. OHIM* [2004] ETMR 19 (Court of First Instance). For further discussion, see Phillips, *op. cit.*, at 76–8, and 169–87.
45. *Philips Electronics NV v. Remington Consumer Products*, [1998] RPC 283 (EWHC); [1999] RPC 809 (EWCA); [2002] CMLR 1329 (AGO and ECJ). (*Cf. Ide Line AG v. Philips Electronics NV*, (1997) ETMR 377 (Swedish District Ct.). See also U. Suthersanen, 'The European Court of Justice in Philips v Remington – Trade Marks and Market Freedom', [2003] *Intellectual Property Quarterly*, 3, 257.
46. *Dyson Ltd v. Registrar of Trade Marks*, Case C-321/03, OJ C56, 10.03.2007, p. 2.
47. Article 7(1)(f) and (g), CTMR.
48. *BOCM Pauls Ltd and Scottish Agricultural College's application*, [1997] ETMR 420; Phillips, *op. cit.*, 67–73.
49. Article 8, CTMR.
50. It should be noted that trade mark registration for a mark is often conferred in relation to one or several classes of goods, and trade mark protection does not confer protection against unauthorised use of the mark for all types of goods, or in all areas of commerce. Even in the case of well-known marks, where the protection is wide, evidence of confusion and damage is necessary. In normal cases, trade mark protection is limited by the class of goods for which the mark is applied. The classification system, in most countries, follows the Nice Classification which currently contains 45 classes. See the 1952 Nice Agreement Concerning the International Classification of Goods and Services for the Purposes of the Registration of Marks of 15 June 1957, and Phillips, *op. cit.*, at 45–6.
51. Article 9(2), CTMR.
52. See generally Phillips, *op. cit.*, at chapters 7 and 17.
53. *Arsenal Football Club plc v. Matthew Reed* Case C-206/01, [2002] ETMR 227 (ECJ).
54. This was the holding of the first instance court – *Arsenal Football Club plc v. Matthew Reed*, [2001] ETMR 77.
55. *Arsenal Football Club plc v. Matthew Reed*, [2002] EWHC 2695 (Ch.); [2003] EWCA 696. See Sumroy, R. and C. Badger, 'Infringing "Use in the Course of Trade": Trade Mark Use and the Essential Function of a Trade Mark', in J. Phillips & I. Simon (eds), *Trade Mark Use*, Oxford: Oxford University Press, 2005, at 163–80.
56. (1996) RPC 281.
57. *Sabel BV v. Puma AG, Rudolf Dassler Sport*, Case C-251/95 (1997) ECR I-6191, I-6224.
58. Case C-39/97 [1999] (1999) ETMR 1.
59. *Laboratoires RTB, SL v OHIM* , T-156/01; *Mystery Drinks GmbH v. OHIM*, T – 99/01 [2004] ETMR (18) 217; *Jose Alejando SL v. OHIM*, T-129/01; *Pfizer v. Eurofood Link (UK)*, [2000] ETMR 187; *Les Editions Albert Rene v. OHIM*, T-311/01; *Dunsford-Wesley v. Manufacturas Antonio Gassol SA*, R310/2000-4. All these examples are set out in Bently and Sherman, *op. cit.*, at 856.
60. Bently and Sherman *op. cit.*, at 857.
61. Case C-375/97, [1999] 3 CMLR 427.
62. For a further discussion, see Bently and Sherman, *op. cit.*, at 867–77.
63. Phillips, *op. cit.*, at 222.
64. Lanham Act, section 1127.
65. Lanham Act, section 43 (15 USC, section 1125). Note that the Act further stipulates that some uses will constitute 'fair use' of the mark, including using the famous mark in comparative advertising, in a non-commercial manner and in news reporting and commentary, Lanham Act, section 43(c)(4).
66. Lanham Act, section 45 (15 USC, section 1127). The law on dilution was recently amended

by the Trademark Dilution Revision Act which came into force on 6 October 2006, and is codified in 15 USC, section 1125(c).

67. 'Blurring' is a legal concept, and is defined as an 'association arising from the similarity between [an accused mark] and a famous mark that impairs the distinctiveness of the famous mark', and directs courts to consider all relevant factors in determining a likelihood of dilution by blurring, including (1) the degree of similarity between the marks; (2) the degree of inherent or acquired distinctiveness of the famous mark; (3) the extent to which the famous mark is used exclusively; (4) the degree of recognition of the famous mark; (5) whether the defendant intended to create an association with the famous mark; and (6) any actual association between the accused mark and the famous mark.

68. For a further study on this, see Whittaker, K.R., 'Trademark Dilution in A Global Age', *University of Pennsylvania Journal of International Economic Law*, 27, 907, 2006; Simon, I., 'Dilution in the United States and European Union (and Beyond) Compared, Part I: International Obligations and Basic Definitions', *Oxford Journal of Intellectual Property Law and Practice*, 1, 406–12, 2006 and 'Part II: Testing for Blurring', *Oxford Journal of Intellectual Property Law and Practice*, 1, 649–59, 2006.

69. *Perry v. Trefitt* (1842) 6 Beav. 66, at p. 73.

70. The ability to bring a common law action for passing off, in addition to an action based on registered trade marks, is specifically preserved under some statutes – see, for example, section 2(2), 1994 Trade Marks Act (UK).

71. *Erven Warnink BV v. J Townsend & Sons (Hull) Ltd.* (1979) AC 731; [1979] FSR 397.

72. *Reckitt & Colman v. Borden (Jif Case)*, (1990) 1 All ER 873; [1990] RPC 340.

73. *Hodgkinson & Corby Ltd. and Roho Inc. v. Wards Mobility Services Ltd.*, (1995) FSR 169; Suthersanen, U., 'Case Comment', *Journal of Business Law*, 197, 1995.

74. *Cadbury Schweppes v. Pub Squash*, [1981] RPC 429 (Privy Council); *Moorgate Tobacco v. Phillip Morris*, [1985] RPC 219 (Australian High Court). See also Bently and Sherman *op. cit.*, at 761–5.

75. *Reckitt & Colman v. Borden* (1990) RPC 340, HL.

76. *Ibid.*, at 499.

77. *Edge v. Nicolls,* (1911) AC 693, HL.

78. Suthersanen, U., *Design Law in Europe,* London: Sweet & Maxwell, 2000, at 402.

79. *Ibid.*

80. Article 10*bis* (2), Paris Convention.

81. Article 10*bis* (3), Paris Convention.

82. Articles 22–4, 39, TRIPS Agreement.

83. Suthersanen, *op. cit.*, 2000, at 403–6.

84. Kamperman Sanders views *concurrence parasitaire* as a synthesis of traditional French law on unfair competition and unjust enrichment, Kamperman Sanders, A., *Unfair Competition Law: The Protection of Intellectual and Industrial Creativity*, Oxford: Clarendon Press, 1997, at 29.

7. Designs

ORIGINS[1]

Designs stand at the junction of art and industry, manifesting themselves in many different product markets. For example, the nature of protection can vary as between the cultural artistic market and a consumer-orientated general products market. Accordingly, as the conventional wisdom has it, protection for designs is possible under all intellectual property regimes, with the emphasis on copyright, *sui generis* design laws and unfair competition.

A more expansive view is that the notion of design, and hence the nature of its protection, is a result of the socio-economic framework which sustains it. This is clear from the historical interplay between the concept of 'design' and economic factors. The various rationales for design protection indicate that a major impetus in introducing intellectual property protection for design is the belief that design plays a role in promoting and maintaining competition within a market economy. The historical study of the development of the design phenomenon underlines such rationales.

The history of design ostensibly starts with the first cave paintings, and goes from Stone Age pottery, through Medieval and Renaissance design art to the present day. However, at some point, the notion of 'design' changed from fine art to industrial art. Why did this occur? One reason is the changes in market conditions in Europe in the seventeenth century. From that point onwards, history shows that designers were always led by market and consumer considerations.

The notion of 'industrial design' was alien in the medieval world where art and industry were unified in concept and in practice. Why is this? Pevsner notes that one major factor which contributed to this was the social and economic stratification of the classes which ensured that the realm of arts and industry were in the hands of the artist-craftsmen. In Medieval pre-industrial society there were cultured and leisurely patrons served by a class of equally cultured and guild-trained craftsmen.[2] Braudel offers further market-based reasons as to why no demarcation between art and industry was necessary. First, there was a lack of tooling and production capabilities to make goods on a mass scale.[3] Second, the income level of the general population could not support a large consumer product industry in the medieval market system.

Third, the absence of a large consumer market was also bolstered by the hand-icraft production system. Each finished article was made individually, leading to high costs per unit product – the main clientele came from the church, the court and the merchant ranks.[4] Furthermore, from the mid-fifteenth century onwards, it was an established rule that the possession of collectible *objets d'art* was an indication of individual worth in society. There was no real pressure on the European sixteenth- and seventeenth- century craftsmen to adopt a consumer-orientated approach.[5]

However, it would not be accurate to portray the pre-Industrial Revolution era as one where the artist-craftsmen were totally inured to market forces. The gentle erosion of the secure and protected domain of the artist-craftsmen had begun during the seventeenth century. There was an expansion of trade routes and commercial opportunities that led to a slow growth in output amongst the craft trade. Jardine traces the concept of consumer choice and product diversity to the steady flow of goods from the Ottoman Empire to Europe. A pattern began to emerge whereby the general craftsman shifted his skills towards specialisation as a measure to secure a competitive edge.[6]

Unlike the pre-industrial era, where supply of goods was slow and inelastic, the last half of the eighteenth century to the nineteenth century saw a greater response to market demands. Several factors contributed to the growing importance of design.

First, growth in both supply and demand created competitive pressures that led to demands for product innovation, notably in the application of some characteristic feature or aspect of skill to distinguish a product and attract the interest of customers.[7] Second, the furious pace of inventions and innovations enabled new manufacturing techniques, with greater production units at lower costs, thus encouraging and catering for a growing consumer market.

Another influential factor was the massive organisational changes which occurred in the production process, heralding the arrival of the mass manufacturer. Although the factory system had existed in some form or other prior to the nineteenth century, it primarily functioned as a source of luxury goods.[8] Now, the previous manufacturing process whereby goods were made from start to finish by a single craftsman was to evolve into a process whereby goods were being produced in a series of stages by different specialists. This phenomenon was already noted at the turn of the eighteenth century. Adam Smith observed that one factor which accounted for the increase in the quantity of work was the invention of a 'great number of machines which facilitate and abridge labour, and enable one man to do the work of many'.[9]

The addition of the designing stages in the manufacturing process gave rise to the profession of designers or 'art-workers' who 'translated the ideas of fine artists into mass production'.[10] Foremost of their tasks was to determine the commercial viability and desirability of consumer products. A slightly related aspect is the initial stirrings of standardisation of goods such as the sizing of ready-made clothing, shoes and hats.[11]

As a result of mercantile economic policies, the early intellectual property laws were effectively a system of incentives to introduce and support new industries. In relation to design protection within Europe, the first *sui generis* design statute enacted was the English 1787 Act in respect of textile designs.[12] One of the chief products on sale to the British public, and for which the demand grew ever greater, was cotton textiles, especially flowered fabrics which were either painted or printed. Annual production of printed textiles in the United Kingdom increased from one million pieces to sixteen million pieces.[13] The demand for such fabrics was further realised with the contemporaneous inventions of new methods of textile spinning and weaving, leading to the enrichment and empowerment of the cotton mills owners.

With the rise of the cotton industry, and its new role as a source of public income, the policy by the late eighteenth century was to protect it at all costs against foreign competition, especially in relation to French imports into the United Kingdom. The legislative programme for the protection of the cotton industry included the prevention of exportation of new machinery to foreign countries,[14] and the prohibition of the export of sketches, models or specifications.[15]

It also included the world's first modern design legislation, 'An Act for the encouragement of the arts of Designing and Printing of Linens, Cottons, Calicoes and Muslin'.[16] The Act vested in designers, printers and proprietors of new and original patterns the sole right and liberty of printing and reprinting them for the duration of two months from the date of first publication. This right was given on condition that the name of the printer or proprietor was marked on each piece. An infringer who knowingly printed, worked or copied or published or exposed for sale such an original pattern without the consent of the proprietor in writing was liable to a special action on the case, damages and costs.

That copyright law was the chosen vehicle for protection may be due to two factors. First, the textile design industry had early associations with subject matter such as engravings and prints, the latter having been brought under the aegis of copyright law. Second, there appears to have been no distinction between the terms 'copyright' and 'patent'. As Sherman points out, the word 'copyright' prior to the 1850s 'referred to the form or style of right protected and, as such, meant something very different from what it means today. Moreover, the term "copyright" was not limited to works we now see as part of the copyright law (such as literary or dramatic works) but extended to include inventions and ornamental as well as non-ornamental designs'.[17]

By the nineteenth century, the importance of product design was clear – it directly enabled producers and manufacturers to satisfy a number of consumer and market demands. New retailing outlets emerged to make demanded goods available to the public. This was paralleled by the growth in the advertising industry, which signalled the intense competition which had arisen between manufacturers as each tried to gain a foothold in the product market.

Advertising literature began to exhort the design as a means of selling the product, as it still does. The traditional ornament and decoration which were used as an expression of the craftsman's skill in working precious and delicate materials were ignored. There was a change of emphasis in the design of products from artistic exclusivity to commercial acceptability.[18] At times, considerable effort was expended to make simple articles look more intricate, and therefore more expensive. The era was one of indiscriminate application of ornament, widening the gulf between art, style and function.

The association of design with industrial production, mass manufacture and mass consumerism ultimately led to a distinctly hostile attitude towards design, not only legislatively but also from the perspective of the 'art' consumer. The image of the manufacturer, armed with an arsenal of materials and machines, and turning out thousands of cheap articles at the same time and at the same cost, was firmly established. The prevailing social *and* legal attitude was that a shift had occurred in the design of products: from the high cost, high quality product of the artist-craftsman to the low cost, and often, low quality, industrial design product of the industrial manufacturer.[19] Mass-produced articles of general use were seen as a debasement of art. The solution proposed by some was to reject the industrial element in this process. Similarly, the Romantic view of art as transcendent and of the artist as a superior being evolved.

A demarcation, not necessarily accurate, was made between the artist's work, which was a product of high creativity, immune to and cushioned from the exigencies of the market and from the public, and the industrially manufactured work, which was seen as a product made for and ultimately aimed at mass consumption.[20] This demarcation, unfortunately, exists to this day in the TRIPS Agreement, as legislatures still struggle to classify design under either copyright law (high creativity) or industrial property law (machine-made production).

RATIONALISING DESIGN LAW

The historical development of the concept of 'design' from its origins of 'art' and 'craft' has today come full circle. The traditional view is that the discipline of design arose from the field of arts and crafts. The difference between a seventeenth-century pattern-maker and a modern industrial designer is less one of the nature of their respective creative activities than of the economic, technological and social constraints within which the activity is performed. At one point in the design circle lies the value- and emotion-laden sentiments of beauty, aesthetics and pleasure; at another point in this circle, design leads and is led by competitive market needs and conditions. Reichman ascribes this characteristic of design to 'compete in both the specialised market for artistic works and the general products market' as a result of the two-market conundrum. According to Reichman, 'this "two-market conundrum" facilitates extension of the generous modalities of copyright law into the general product market for which it was not designed'.[21]

One rather romantic view of why designs need protecting is offered by Govaere:

> Like patent and copyright, design rights have a reward and incentive function, but the objective is different. The objective of granting an exclusive right in an industrial design can be defined as providing the possibility of obtaining a return for investment made, and progress achieved, in the field of aesthetics in order to stimulate overall research and development of the aesthetic features of technical or functional products.[22]

Unfortunately, Govaere's perception of design rights as the promoter of aesthetic features does not align with that of legislatures and courts who have continuously sought to deny artistic copyright protection to industrial designs.

Under United States law, the rationale for *sui generis* design patent protection is clear from the first Supreme Court decision in this area. In *Gorham Mfg. Co. v. White*,[23] the Court held that:

> The acts of Congress which authorize the granting of patents for designs were plainly intended to give encouragement to the decorative arts. They contemplate not so much utility as appearance, and that, not an abstract impression or picture, but an aspect given to those objects mentioned in the acts . . . [T]he thing invented or produced, for which a patent is given, is that which gives a peculiar or distinctive appearance to the manufacture, or article to which it may be applied, or to which it gives form. The law manifestly contemplated that giving certain new and original appearances to a manufactured article may enhance its saleable value, may enlarge the demand for it, and may be a meritorious service to the public . . . The appearance may be the result of peculiarity of configuration, or of ornament alone, or of both conjointly; but in whatever way produced, it is the new thing, or product, which the patent law regards . . . We do not say that in determining whether two designs are substantially the same, differences in the lines, the configuration, or the modes by which the aspects they exhibit are not to be considered; but we think the controlling consideration is the resultant effect.[24]

The European Union design law was premised on similar ideas which acknowledge design to be a 'marketing tool of ever-increasing importance' and a 'significant aspect of modern culture'. In defining the need for an effective regime of protection within the Community, the European Commission similarly trumpeted the importance of the influence of good design on the competitiveness of the economy.[25] Indeed, poor design has been shown to constitute a handicap in today's world market.[26]

NATURE OF PROTECTION: COPYRIGHT OR DESIGN LAW?

The ambiguity of 'design' results in overlap with other intellectual property laws, such as copyright, unfair competition, utility model and trademark laws. The issue has been avoided within the Berne and Paris Conventions as both agreements accept design as being appropriate subject matter for copyright and industrial property protection. The key provision under the Berne Convention is Article 2(7), which basically leaves it to Berne Union (and now WTO members) to decide whether works of applied art and industrial design should qualify for protection under copyright law, and if so, the conditions of protection. Nevertheless, irrespective of the mode of protection, some sort of protection to works of applied art and industrial designs must be provided where there is no *sui generis* design law. This corresponds to a similar obligation under the Paris Convention. This problem is not alleviated by the ambivalent attitude of the TRIPS Agreement to designs. The TRIPS Agreement has simultaneously adopted both the Paris and Berne positions and obliges members to provide for a minimum standard of protection without specifying the nature of protection.[27]

The common elements present in the copyright approach to design protection are:[28]

- copyright is accorded automatically; thus, there are no formalities nor registration procedures;
- an anti-copying right is proffered, as opposed to an exclusive right;
- the main criterion of protection is originality, which is easier to fulfil than that of novelty;
- the duration of protection is much longer than under the registered approach: most countries offer at least 50 years *pma*.

Under the *sui generis* approach, one option is to offer protection under a liability-based regime (for example, unfair competition law). The other option is a property-based regime. Registered *sui generis* design rights are property-based, while unregistered *sui generis* design rights are liability-based.[29] The registration-based *sui generis* design laws in the world are fashioned upon patent law. The common denominator in this approach is that protection is accorded upon registration or deposit of the design. Furthermore, the following features regularly appear in most *sui generis* systems:[30]

- where protection is granted upon registration, publication usually follows registration though some countries provide for secret or deferred publication;
- upon registration, most countries confer an exclusive right; the proprietor of the design right is thus given the right to sue any person who produces an identical or similar design for infringement, even if the latter design arises from an independent creation;
- the usual criterion for protection is novelty, though the standard of novelty required varies from country to country ranging from domestic novelty to universal novelty;
- a short duration of protection is usually conferred (for example, the European Community Registered Design Right confers a maximum 25-year term of protection).

The European Union legislators declared a third way by advocating a shift of focus from outdated notions of decoration and ornamentation to a focus on design as a marketing tool for products. However, even with this 'revolutionary' new design law, European law still struggles with the question of whether designs should be cumulatively protected under other intellectual property rights, especially copyright law. Moreover, having decided to adopt both the patent and copyright approaches, the current EU Community design law offers the design owner a two-tier system of rights. The proprietor will be entitled to quasi-copyright protection under the Community unregistered design right automatically upon the first marketing of his/her design; alternatively, the design holder can opt for stronger, exclusive protection under the Community registered design right. The criteria of protection for both the unregistered and registered design rights will be the same: novelty and individual character. The final position within the European Union can only be described as complex as a designer will have the following options:

- Community registered design right; or
- Community unregistered design right;
- National registered design right;
- National unregistered design right (only available in the United Kingdom);
- National copyright (subject to various criteria, varying according to each member state).

There is, of course, always the possibility of claiming protection for the shape of a product through trade mark, unfair competition and even patent or utility models laws.

PRINCIPLES

Protectable Subject Matter

The hybrid nature of a design makes it difficult to categorise definitively either as an industrial work or as an artistic work. Part of this problem lies in the ambiguity of the term 'design' which can be applied to almost any product or work. Yet, in traditional legal terms, the concept of industrial design concentrates on the appearance of a product. Thus, a design connotes an element or characteristic completely separate from the object it enhances or to which it is applied. It is something often added to an object, having no relation to its overall form or function, sometimes by an artist not even remotely connected with its design. Examples of such behaviour are plentiful: antique coffee mills or porcelain statues made into lamps, ashtrays with varied ornamentation and animals.

Where the TRIPS Agreement is concerned, no attempt is made to define what constitutes industrial designs, albeit textile designs are specifically mentioned; hence, the notion of 'industrial design' as employed in the TRIPS Agreement can refer to all types of aesthetic, useful and functional designs including subject matter protected as 'works of applied art' or 'works of artistic craftsmanship' under copyright law, or even as utility models. In relation to textile designs, members must protect textile designs either through design or copyright laws.[31] Importantly, there is no guidance as to the relationship between works of applied art (specifically referred to in Article 12 TRIPS) and industrial designs. Moreover, 'industrial design' can be taken to include indigenous and folkloric ornamentation, icons and symbols.

The EU design law defines 'design' as follows: 'the appearance of the whole or a part of a product resulting from the features of, in particular, the lines, contours, colours, shape, texture and/or materials of the product itself and/or its ornamentation'.[32]

This definition of design, anchored in the appearance of the whole or part of the product, will apparently include any element which can be perceived by the human senses such as the weight or flexibility of a product or the tactile impressions given, for example, by textiles.[33] There is no specific indication that the design must be visible to the naked eye. However, the design of internal mechanisms (such as the 'under the bonnet' parts of motor vehicles) will normally only qualify as designs if they pass a visibility test. Moreover, the European Union design law does not require any qualitative requirement of artistry or aestheticism, and a design need not have an 'aesthetic quality' to qualify for protection.[34]

Criteria

Article 25(1), TRIPS Agreement, provides that protection should be given to 'independently created industrial designs that are new or original'. It adds that, if countries wish to, this can be determined with reference to whether the designs differ significantly from known designs or combinations of known design features. One commentator suggests that this is probably meant to exclude copied or imitated designs, in part to assuage those members who had argued unsuccessfully for criteria of new *and* original.[35] WTO members are left with the option of implementing the criterion of either novelty or originality. Members are even allowed to adopt more criteria of protection as is apparently the case under the current US design patent regime and arguably also under the European Community design right. Members are also offered the opportunity of anchoring their chosen criterion of protection (that is, originality or novelty) in a prior art base constituting 'known designs or combinations of known design features'.[36] This may allow a member to opt for an originality requirement which adopts an objective standard, rather than a copyright law standard, as the standard of originality under copyright law is not normally objective, but subjective: any product which is the result of independent human intellect and creativity is offered protection, even if it resembles another product.

Novelty[37]

The EU design law grants protection to designs which fulfil the twin criteria of novelty and individual character. A design shall be considered new if no identical design has been made available to the public before the date of filing of the application for registration or, if priority is claimed, the date of priority. The test envisages an objective comparison between the design under consideration and antecedent designs in prior art. The law does not offer any guidelines as to the assessment of novelty, but merely requires, by implication, that a design for which registration is applied must differ in material details. Factors taken into consideration include: the degree of the designer's freedom in developing the design; the application of a known design to a new product or medium or the fact that the design is a novel arrangement or configuration of known design features. Note however that the European design law embraces 'relative novelty', as opposed to an absolute or universal degree of novelty, that is to say, disclosures will not be taken into account if these events could not 'reasonably have become known in the normal course of business to the circles specialised in the sector concerned, operating within the Community'.

An important consideration is the grace period of 12 months preceding the filing date or the priority date, within which designs could be tested in the market without endangering the novelty of the design. The grace period is in respect of *any* disclosure of the design made by the designer, his successor in title or any third party.[38] The grace period is also available in relation to any disclosure of the design which is the result of abusive conduct. During this period, the design proprietor will be able to claim the Community unregistered design right.

Individual Character[39]

A design shall be considered to have individual character if the overall impression it produces on the informed user differs from the overall impression produced on such a user by any design which has been made available to the public before the date of filing of the application for registration or, if priority is claimed, the date of priority. In assessing individual character, the degree of freedom of the designer in developing the design shall be taken into consideration.

Several issues arise. First, the test reinforces the notion that the design must be considered in its entirety. Irrespective of the number of detailed differences which exist between the design under review and the prior design, if the overall impression is one of similarity, the subsequent design will not have individual character. Second, the assessment must take into account the designer's freedom in developing the design.

It is difficult to see how the test of individual character can be carried out unless the informed user relates his impression of the design to a relevant product or trade environment; in other words, the user must be informed as to a particular design as employed within a specific product market. The criterion of individual character is gauged by the hypothetical informed user. The early commentaries suggest that, in line with the 'design is a marketing tool' theory, the informed user will normally, though not necessarily, be the end consumer or purchaser of the product.[40]

US design patent regime: new, original, non-obvious and ornamental[41]
In the United States, protection is available under patent law for 'any new, original and ornamental design for an article of manufacture'. Furthermore, in order for a design to qualify for design patent protection, it must present an aesthetically pleasing appearance that is not dictated by function, and it must satisfy the general criteria of patentability: full novelty and non-obviousness.[42] In brief, the law does not give protection to 'new designs' or 'original designs', but rather to designs which fulfil both criteria and requires candidates to fulfil a higher threshold of protection by requiring non-obviousness as well, a term more identified with the patent criterion of inventive step.

Exceptions – the Functionality Dilemma

There are no compulsory provisions as to excluded subject matter or limitations/exceptions to protection under the TRIPS Agreement, though Articles

25(1) and 26(2) offer members an optional mandate. The difference between the two provisions is the following: designs under Article 25.1 do not qualify for design protection in the first place, whereas under Article 26.2, works would normally be protectable, but are excluded for some exceptional reasons.

Under Article 25(1), WTO members may exclude designs which are 'dictated essentially by technical or functional considerations'. Since this is optional, members may also choose the alternative of granting *sui generis* protection to both aesthetic and functional designs as is the case, for example, under the United Kingdom unregistered design right system which protects certain types of functional designs.[43] Should members wish to tailor the protection of designs to meet the conditions and demands of domestic firms, they can do this too. Thus, the European Union's design laws have adopted a specific 'interconnections' exclusion clause, whilst the British/Hong Kong copyright laws limit copyright protection of functional design drawings and works of applied art.[44] Another example of a member limiting its copyright protection of industrial designs is US copyright law.[45]

Under the EU law, design protection will not be granted to the following subject matter:[46]

(a) features of appearance of a product which are solely dictated by its technical function;

(b) 'interconnection' features, i.e. features of appearance of a product which must necessarily be reproduced in their exact form and dimensions in order to permit the designed product to be mechanically connected to or placed in, around or against another product so that either product may perform its function;

(c) designs which are contrary to public policy or to accepted principles of morality.

In relation to (a), protection is denied to features where a certain technical function is dictated *solely* by those features. It will be rare, though possible, for a whole design as such to be denied protection. It is clear that the provision excludes those features which have no alternative physical manifestations by which to achieve the product's technical function. There is no reference in the legislation to the exclusion of abstract subject matter such as ideas, principles of construction, etc. However, the absence of such a clause may be ameliorated by the provision within the Design Directive which obliges the court to consider the degree of freedom of the designer in developing his design when assessing individual character and scope of protection.

Exclusion (b) relates to whether the design in question incorporates any interconnecting features. An interconnecting feature is any feature of the designed product which will enable that product (Product A) to be 'mechanically connected or placed in, around or against' another product (Product B).

The exclusion will probably not apply to the whole design of the product but only to those features which actually physically interface with another product. This interconnection exclusion does not apply to features within a modular system.[47] This has been taken to refer to designs destined for modular systems, and which by their nature must fit together or be capable of assembly. Examples of this include modular toy systems such as Lego bricks or modular furniture systems.

Exclusion (c) is the most peculiar provision of the lot, as it takes a moral stance and denies protection to such designs as are contrary to public policy or to accepted principles of morality. The rule emanates from a reluctantly accepted international policy in intellectual property law of not according protection where public morality is offended or if the protection is against public policy.[48] Arguments for including such a clause within an intellectual property regime range from environmental[49] to socio-political. Nevertheless, it is hard to see why it should apply to designs. No guidance is offered in any of the official commentaries on the Regulation or Directive as to the standards of public policy or morality to be applied.

Scope and Duration of Protection

In Europe the design proprietor can opt for a registered national or Community design right, in which case he will have an exclusive right to use it. 'Use' is defined to cover, in particular, the making, offering, putting on the market, importing, exporting or using of a product in which the design is incorporated or to which it is applied, or stocking such a product for those purposes.[50] The duration of protection will be for an initial period of five years, which is renewable for four further periods of five years, up to a maximum of 25 years.

If, on the other hand, the proprietor opts for the unregistered Community design right, a right against copying is conferred.[51] Moreover, the anti-copying right is limited in that it will not be effective where use is deemed to result from 'copying the protected design if it results from an independent work of creation by a designer who may be reasonably thought not to be familiar with the design made available to the public by the holder'.

The unregistered Community design right arises automatically and lasts for a period of three years only from the date on which the design was first made available to the public within the Community.[52] However, the scope of protection for both types of rights is identical: it will include any design which does not produce on the informed user a different overall impression.[53]

The design right will not extend to acts done privately and for non-commercial purposes; acts done for experimental purposes; and acts of reproduction for the purpose of citation or teaching, which comply with fair trade practice and do not prejudice the normal exploitation of the design.[54]

In TRIPS the minimum term of protection is ten years. The TRIPS Agreement does not specify whether this term is to be computed from the date of filing (if any) or the date of issue. This provision is taken to refer only to situations where *sui generis* design law is the only means of protection. If a WTO member opts for copyright protection of industrial designs, the duration of protection must be governed by Article 7 of the Berne Convention. The general rule for copyright is that the duration of protection must be 50 years *pma*. The exceptions to this general rule include works of applied art – members remain free to provide for a shorter duration of protection, as long as a minimum term of 25 years from the making of the work is granted.[55]

CONCERNS WITHIN DESIGN LAW

Why are we protecting design? The answer appears to be because the design is an important attribute of intra- and inter-industry competition in many countries. Thus, design protection plays a role in relation to competition, encouragement and innovation. A basic rationale for the protection of design is to reward the designer's creativity and to provide incentives for future contributions; however, a balance must be maintained between such reward and the long-term goal of promoting competition within a market-based economy. The balancing act is difficult and no more so than in design law.

A trite and Hohfeldian re-statement of the legal dilemma would be to state the following axioms:

- conferring property rights on one set of persons (for example, creators) will correspond to the harm suffered by another set of persons (for example, competitors);
- intellectual property rights benefit society in promulgating the production of more intellectual property goods;
- however, an over-strong right can be harmful to society;
- to avoid market failure, these property rights must be controlled;
- the role of the legislator and the courts is to steer a course between these two extremes.

Unfortunately, the relationship that design law has with market considerations has proved insoluble – this is clearly indicated by the weirdly wonderful spare parts saga in the EU, discussed elsewhere.[56] And as history once again shows, design as a profession is influenced largely by the dynamic market conditions which cause the constant metamorphosis of the artist into a designer, into an industrialist and back into an artist. Indeed, many today advocate that design is the art of our age, with the current trend being to use industrial objects as a reflection of the cultural identity of society today as is evidenced by the London Victoria and Albert Museum's collection of Dr Martens shoes or the New York Metropolitan Museum of Modern Art's collection of Hilti chairs, typewriters, electric toasters, lamps, meat slicers and electric razors.

An apt finale to this discussion is the opinion of Lord Reid in the infamous *George Hensher Ltd. v. Restawile Upholstery (Lancs) Ltd.* decision whereby five separate judgments were handed down by the House of Lords as to what constituted a work of 'artistic craftsmanship':

> I think that by common usage it is proper for a person to say that in his opinion a thing has an artistic character if he gets pleasure or satisfaction or it may be uplift from contemplating it . . . if unsophisticated people get pleasure from seeing something which they admire I do not see why we must say that it is not artistic because those who profess to be art experts think differently. After all there are great differences of opinion among those who can properly be called experts . . . If any substantial section of the public genuinely admires and values a thing for its appearance and gets pleasure or satisfaction, whether emotional or intellectual, from looking at it, I would accept that it is artistic although many others may think it meaningless or common or vulgar'.[57]

NOTES

1. Much of this section is based on Suthersanen, U., *Design Law in Europe*, London: Sweet & Maxwell, 2000. On design history and its relationship with industrialisation and consumerism, see Braudel, F., *Civilization and Capitalism 15th–18th Century, Volume 1 (The Structures of Everyday Life), Volume 2 (The Wheels of Commerce), Volume 3 (The Perspective of the World)*, London: Collins, 1981, 1982, 1984; Pevsner, N., *The Pioneers of Modern Design – From William Morris to Walter Gropius*, London: Penguin, 1960; Ashworth, W., *A Short History of International Economy Since 1850*, London: Longman, 1987; Mantoux, P., *The Industrial Revolution in the Eighteenth Century – The Outline of the Beginnings of the Modern Factory System in England*, London: Methuen University Paperbacks, 1964 (re-publication of the original 1928 edition); Jardine, L., *Wordly Goods – A New History of the Renaissance*, London: Macmillan, 1996; and Heskett, J. *Industrial Design*, London: Thames & Hudson, 1980.
2. Pevsner, *op. cit.*, at 45.
3. Braudel, *The Structures of Everyday Life,* at 303.
4. Ashworth, *op. cit.,* at 5; Mantoux, *op. cit.*, at 30–31; Jardine, *op. cit.*, at 72.
5. Heskett, J., 'Industrial Design', in H. Conway (ed.), *Design History*, London: Routledge, 1992, at 118.
6. Heskett, 1980, *op. cit.*, at 11.
7. For a similar situation arising in the twentieth century, see Wang, S.Z., 'Chinese Modern Design: A Retrospective', in D. Doordan (ed.), *Design History – An Anthology*, Cambridge, MA: MIT Press, 1995. The author notes that the rising income levels of the Chinese people have resulted in them rejecting poorly designed, old-fashioned products; instead, there is a tendency to seek better-quality and better-looking products, at 237–8.
8. Braudel, *The Wheels of Commerce*, at 298–302; and Gilboy, E.W., 'Demand as a Factor in the Industrial Revolution', in A.H. Cole (ed.), *Facts and Factors in Economic History: Articles by Former Students of Edwin Francis Gous*, Cambridge, MA: Harvard University Press, 1932, at 620–40.

9. Smith, A., *An Inquiry into the Nature and Causes of the Wealth of Nations*, London: Henry Growde, 1904, 9.
10. Sparkes, P., *An Introduction to Design & Culture in the Twentieth Century*, London: Allen & Unwin, 1987, 4.
11. Styles, J., 'Manufacturing, Consumption and Design', in J. Brewer and R. Porter *Consumption and the World of Goods*, London: Routledge, 1993, at 527–53.
12. Mantoux, *op. cit.,* Part II, chapters 1 and 2.
13. Forty, A., *Objects of Desire – Design and Society since 1750*, London: Thames and Hudson, 1968, 47.
14. 14 Geo. III, c. 71. The 1774 Act making it an offence to export 'tools or utensils used in manufacturing cotton or cotton and linen mixed'.
15. 1781 Act (21 Geo. III, c. 37). This was subsequently extended by the 1785 Act to metal trades (25 Geo. III, c. 67).
16. 1787, 27 Geo. 3, c .38.
17. Sherman, B., 'Remembering and Forgetting the Birth of Modern Copyright Law', *Intellectual Property Journal*, 10(1), 5, 1996. See Edmunds, L., *The Law of Copyright in Designs*, London: Sweet & Maxwell, 1895, at 1. The notion of a 'patent' was similarly obfuscated; thus, at the end of the seventeenth century, the stationers' companies in London had two types of copyright: the stationer's copyright which was a private copyright for a particular work; and the printing patent which was generally perceived to be a govermental copyright awarding the general privilege to print a certain class of works, usually for life. See Patterson, L.R., *Copyright in Historical Perspective*, Nashville, TN: Vanderbilt University Press, chapter 5.
18. Heskett, *op. cit.,* at 12.
19. This view was particularly espoused by John Ruskin and William Morris who epitomised and encouraged the view that products of machine were not to be placed on the same pedestal as creative and craftsman-like art, emphasising the importance of the 'artist craftsman' over the capitalist industrial designer. Pevsner, *op. cit.,* at 25; Hobsbawm, E.J., *The Age of Capital, 1848–75*, London: Abacus, 1988, 324 *et seq*; Forty, *op. cit.,* at 58–61.
20. Hobsbawm, *op. cit.,* chapter 15.
21. Reichmann, J., 'Legal Hybrids between Patent and Copyright Paradigms', *Columbia Law Review*, 94, 2432, at 2461.
22. Govaere, I., *The Use and Abuse of Intellectual Property Rights in EC Law*, London: Sweet & Maxwell, 1996, 26–7.
23. 81 US (14 Wall.) 511 (S. Ct., 1872).
24. *Ibid.*, at 524–5.
25. European Commission, *Green Paper on the Legal Protection of Industrial Design*, Brussels, June 1991 (III/F/5131/91-EN), p. 2.
26. Ullman, D., *The Mechanical Design Process*, New York: McGraw-Hill, 1992, at 3 ('. . . it has been estimated that 85 percent of the problems with new products – not working as they should, taking too long to bring to market, costing too much – is the result of poor design process'). Others confirming this view include Ughanwa, D. and M. Baker, *The Role of Design in International Competitiveness*, London: Routledge, 1989, 245–7.
27. Article 25, TRIPS Agreement.
28. Suthersanen, *op. cit.,* at 103–12.
29. A WTO member is also free to adopt both ways of *sui generis* protection, as illustrated by the Japanese example: in addition to its registered design law, Japan now confers a three-year term of protection on unregistered designs, based on liability principles. See UNCTAD, *The TRIPS Agreement and Developing Countries*, Geneva, 1996, para. 251.
30. Suthersanen, *op. cit.,* at 103–12.
31. Article 25(2), TRIPS Agreement.
32. Article 1(a), European Parliament and Council Directive 98/71/EC of 13 October 1998 on the legal protection of designs.
33. See early draft of Article 3(a), Preliminary Draft, *Green Paper on Designs*.
34. Recital 14, Directive.
35. Gervais, D., *The TRIPS Agreement: Drafting History and Analysis*, London: Sweet & Maxwell, 1998, para. 2.125.

36. Article 25(1), TRIPS.
37. Articles 3–5, Directive 98/71/EC on the legal protection of designs; Articles 4–6, Council Regulation EC No. 6/2002 of 12 December 2001 on Community designs.
38. Article 6 (2) Directive.
39. Articles 3–5, Directive 98/71/EC on the legal protection of designs; Articles 4–6, Council Regulation EC No. 6/2002 of 12 December 2001 on Community designs.
40. Para. 5.5.6.2, *Green Paper on Designs*.
41. For a comparison of the EU and US design approaches, see Suthersanen, U., 'Harmonising Design Law in a Free Trade Area: Jurisprudential Lessons from the European Union and the United States', in C. Antons and C. Heath (eds), *Intellectual Property Harmonisation within ASEAN and APEC*, Max Planck Institute Series on Asian Intellectual Property Law, Vol. 10, The Hague: Kluwer Law International, 2004, 57–92.
42. §§ 102, 103, 171, US Patents Act
43. Sections 213 *et seq.*, United Kingdom Copyright, Designs and Patents Act 1988.
44. For example, sections 51 and 52, United Kingdom Copyright, Designs and Patents Act 1988.
45. Designs potentially fall under the category of 'pictorial, graphic and sculptural works', which include 'works of artistic craftsmanship' insofar as their form but not their mechanical or utilitarian aspects are concerned, and designs of 'a useful article' if such design incorporates pictorial, graphic, or sculptural features that can be identified separately from, and are capable of existing independently of, the utilitarian aspects of the article. See also the definition of 'useful article', section 101, US Copyright Act.
46. Articles 7–8, Design Directive; Articles 8–9, Design Regulation.
47. Article 7(3), Directive; Article 8(3), Regulation.
48. Article 27(2) of TRIPS Agreement; Article 53(a) European Patent Convention; Article 3(1)(f) EC Trademark Directive of 21 December 1988 (89/104/EEC); Article 6 quinquies Marks, B3 of the Paris Convention for the Protection of Industrial Property of 20 March 1883 (1979 Stockholm version).
49. For the potential width of the morality/*ordre public* clause, see *Plant Genetic Systems,* T356/93 (1995) EPOR 357, in relation to Article 53 European Patent Convention.
50. Article 12, Directive; Article 19, Regulation.
51. Article 19(2), Regulation.
52. Article 11, Regulation.
53. Article 9, Directive; Article 10, Regulation.
54. Article 13, Directive; Article 22, Regulation.
55. Article 7(4) of the Berne Convention.
56. For a full account of this, see MacQueen, H.L., *Copyright, Competition and Industrial Design*, Edinburgh: Edinburgh University Press, 1995, at 94.
57. (1975) RPC 31, at 54.

8. Other intellectual property rights

UTILITY MODELS AND PETTY PATENTS

Justifications for Second-tier Patents

The theoretical rationale for utility models derives from the fact that most social welfare-enhancing inventions are cumulative in nature and that many of them are sub-patentable in the sense that the novelty and inventive step requirements are too high for the patent system to accommodate them.

Although utility model laws confer exclusive property rights, the underlying rationale is usually to accede to industries' call for an anti-copying right or a misappropriation tort. Indeed, the main practical justification derives from the fact that many inventions are vulnerable to unfair copying, and that in many cases the sub-patentable ones are the most vulnerable of all. If one accepts the 'unfair copying' argument favouring intellectual property protection, it follows that any subject matter evincing some sort of intellectual or capital investment, and which is open to imitation and copying, should arguably be considered a worthy intellectual property good and requiring protection.

However, whilst some industries tend to be very enthusiastic about low cost, fast protection regimes (such as a no-examination utility model system or a no-registration property right), other industries are highly suspicious of such systems, especially when they are viewed as curtailing industries' right to innovate on the basis of low-level access to a large public domain and 'creative imitation', a term adopted here in recognition that imitation is often not only an essential stage in learning to innovate but can even be creative in itself. So one really needs to know to what extent copying is a problem in the different industries, and whether such inventions are better left in the public domain and open to imitation and free-riding.

There is a view that utility models are especially good for developing countries seeking to advance technological capacity through local incremental innovation. It is sometimes claimed, too, that utility models systems are particularly advantageous for small and medium-sized enterprises (SMEs). For one thing, it is quite likely that SMEs have a large presence in those industries where minor innovation is the norm and unfair copying is rife. Indeed, it is often argued that a cheap and rapid second-tier patent regime would improve the legal environment for SMEs, especially those which are engaged in an ongoing process of innovation and adaptation. This is the case particularly in relation to those product sectors which are concerned, not so much with revolutionary technological breakthroughs, but more so with incremental or improvement innovation. For example, one reason for the proposed European Commission Directive on the protection of inventions by utility model is the perceived need for a rapid and cheap protective regime for such minor innovations in the following industries: toy manufacturing, clock and watch making, optics, microtechnology and micromechanics.[1] For another, it may even be that more innovations, of both the breakthrough and incremental varieties, emanate from SMEs than from larger multinational conglomerates. Another reason why utility models may be good for SMEs is that the cost factor may inhibit them from using the patent system as much as they would desire. The second-tier patent regime is viewed as the ideal solution as it is a system geared towards the needs of SMEs.

On the other hand, there are fundamental concerns about utility models as a policy solution to the question of what, if anything, should be done about sub-patentable inventions. First, the fact that the utility models regime represents a lowering of thresholds without an appropriate examination system in place may result in legal uncertainty and excessive litigation. Indeed, there is a reasonable concern that larger market players may use utility models as a means of circumventing the more stringent criteria under the patent system and overuse the system in ways that make it hard for SMEs to compete. Certainly, the lack of substantive examination prior to grant can give rise to uncertainty for third parties when conducting infringement searches to ascertain what valid rights exist in a particular field of technology, which may act as an additional barrier to competitors. It can also lead to abusive behaviour.

Definition and Protectability

The term 'utility model' is a generic term which refers to subject matter that lies between that protectable under patent law and *sui generis* design law.[2] The term is not an accepted or clearly defined legal concept within the international intellectual property paradigm, although it is bandied about by legislators and jurists usually to refer to a second-tier patent system offering a cheap, no-examination protection regime for technical inventions which would not usually fulfil the strict patentability criteria.

Utility models are referred to in Australia as 'innovation patents', in Malaysia as 'utility innovations', in France as 'utility certificates', and in Belgium as 'short-term patents'. Some systems define utility models as incorporeal subject matter such as technical concepts or inventions or devices;

while others anchor their definitions in three-dimensional forms. Yet others offer a utility model type of protection which, in actuality, is tantamount to patent protection without examination and for a shorter duration.

As far as one can perceive, there are three traits common to all the national 'utility model' laws from a global perspective, which are:

1.   All utility model laws confer exclusive rights on the proprietor of the right (as opposed to an anti-copying right).
2.   Novelty is a criterion in all utility model systems, though the standard of novelty varies widely.
3.   Registration is a requirement but usually there is no substantive examination of applications.

The major points of divergence can be summarised thus:[3]

(i) Subject matter under protection   Some utility models laws protect only the three-dimensional form while others extend the umbrella of protection to cover technical inventions and processes. A majority of utility model laws simply adopt the domestic patent law definition of protectable subject matter.

(ii) Granting procedure   Many systems adopt a simple registration procedure with cursory examination, while a few implement a detailed examination process. In practice, some examining offices offer an optional detailed search facility with the payment of supplementary fees. Other jurisdictions expressly call for a detailed search on validity to be carried out on the commencement of civil proceedings.

(iii) Substantive criteria   Herein lies the greatest disparity between the utility model systems. While all major utility model systems adopt the criterion of novelty, the level of novelty required ranges from universal novelty, to relative novelty, to domestic novelty. A second criterion is usually, though not always, imposed in the form of inventiveness or usefulness. Again, the standard employed for the level of inventiveness varies greatly.

There is also a significant propensity within current utility models laws to link the definition of the utility model to an element of industrial application. A final element of divergence is the duration of protection which varies from six years to 15 years.

International Conventions and Multilateral Agreements

On the international front, utility models are recognised under the 1883 Paris Convention for the Protection of Industrial Property as industrial property.

However the Convention is silent on its definition and scope, and merely confirms that the international principles of national treatment and the right of priority are accorded to utility models.[4] Thus, Article 1(2) states: 'The protection of industrial property has as its object patents, utility models, industrial designs, trade marks, service marks, trade names, indications of source or appellations of origin, and the repression of unfair competition'.[5]

The ambiguity of the term 'utility model' is also reflected in the cross-referencing and interdependency of priority periods between utility models, industrial designs and patents. Thus, a period of priority can be secured for an application for industrial design based on the filing date of a utility model; and a period of priority can be secured for a utility model application by virtue of a right of priority based on a patent application (and vice versa).[6]

TRIPS fails explicitly to mention second-tier or utility model protection, thus leaving WTO members free to formulate or reject second-tier protection regimes as they see fit. It is arguable that by reference to Article 2(1), TRIPS Agreement, the relevant provisions of the Paris Convention provisions (including Article 1(2)) are extended to all WTO countries. But this still does not require WTO members or signatories to the Convention to provide utility model laws.

Furthermore, national utility model systems tend to adopt the International Patent Classification (IPC) as provided by the 1971 Strasbourg Agreement for the International Patent Classification, which facilitates the retrieval of patent documents in order to conduct effective novelty searches and determine the state of the art. Indeed, Article 1 states that the IPC covers not just 'patents for invention', but also 'inventors' certificates, utility models and utility certificates'.

The facilitated means of securing international protection that the Patent Cooperation Treaty provides for patents covers utility models as well. By virtue of Article 2, the PCT clarifies that ' "application" means an application for the protection of an invention; references to an "application" shall be construed as references to applications for patents for inventions, inventors' certificates, utility certificates, utility models, patents or certificates of addition, inventors' certificates of addition, and utility certificates of addition'. International applications may, thus, be for second-tier patents as well as standard ones.

PLANT VARIETIES

Background

Breeding as a science
For almost all of human history, farming and crop improvement were carried

out by the same people and in the same places: by farmers on the farm. The separation of the two activities is very recent, starting in the nineteenth century. In some parts of the developing world, though, it has hardly begun.

From neolithic times, farmers have set aside some of their harvested seeds for replanting. They selected such seeds, whether consciously or unintentionally, on the basis that the plants producing them possessed desirable traits such as high yields, disease resistance, or drought or frost tolerance. Over the generations, this practice resulted in ever increasing quantities of locally adapted varieties known as 'landraces', 'folk varieties' or 'farmers' varieties'.

This situation changed in North America and Europe from the late nineteenth century as the profession of farming became separated from seed production and the emerging seed producers started to select from the existing materials to increase their share in the market. This commercial crop improvement remained merely empirical and experimental but with a growing scientific basis in mathematics applied to selection methods. Very soon after the 1900 rediscovery of Mendel's insights into the laws of heredity, scientists sought to apply genetics to crop improvement. This led to the directed development of 'pure lines' of self-pollinating crops. Pure lines are uniform, breed true to type and contain consistent and identifiable traits that can be transferred to other plants. According to Pistorius and van Wijk, 'while Mendelian breeding allowed for a controlled mixing of genetic characteristics, pure line breeding offered a practical method to 'fix' them in succeeding generations'.[7]

Breeding new plant varieties is actually a very laborious and time-consuming process. It takes about seven to ten years to get from the first cross to the marketable variety. The first task is to determine the objectives of the breeding programme. One obvious goal is to produce varieties with higher yields, but there are many other possible objectives such as the development of varieties with added or improved characteristics such as pest resistance, disease resistance or drought tolerance, compatibility with inputs such as fertilisers and pesticides, and improved consumption or food-processing characteristics. A major challenge for breeders is to respond on the one side to the requirements of varying farming conditions, and on the other hand to the need to develop varieties that can be sold widely. Furthermore they increasingly have to respond to the ever-changing demands of conglomerate seed and chemical companies, food-processing companies, and supermarket chains.

The basic conventional technique is known as 'crossing and selecting', which involves crossing two or more parent lines or varieties with desirable traits to produce multiple offspring. Of these, the best plants are selected and allowed to breed again. Again, the best ones are selected for breeding and the process is repeated a number of times. After eight to 12 generations, an improved variety is produced that breeds true and is ready to be planted by farmers.

But breeding is rarely this simple. For one thing, a new variety may be derived from 50 or more parental lines. For another, a variety used in the breeding programme may be the source of only one desirable trait and many undesirable ones. So how does the breeder incorporate this single trait into his or her new variety while excluding the others? To explain in the simplest terms, let us call plants from the parent line or new variety into which the single trait is to be introduced 'Group A'. We shall then call members of the 'donor' plants (which could well be a wild or semi-domesticated relative) 'Group B'. These Group B plants, then, are the source of just one desirable trait out of many unwanted ones, for which as little as one allele (a DNA sequence that codes for a gene) may be responsible. For the breeder to transfer this allele without the undesirable traits, he must first cross Group A and Group B plants and then 'back-cross' those offspring containing the trait with plants from Group A. This is repeated through the generations, selecting plants that retain the trait and back-crossing them with Group A plants. In time, the proportion of genes from Group B plants contained in the offspring goes down in conventional selection systems from 50–50 in the first generation to a negligible figure.

These approaches generally work well with crops like wheat, rice and sorghum that self-fertilise. These tend to be genetically stable and consequently breed true. But as with humans and animals, inbreeding can be deleterious for cross-pollinators such as maize, pearl millet and cruciferous crops like cabbages and oilseed rape. This is not such a problem for plants that can reproduce asexually, such as vines, apple trees and potatoes, where the genetics are fixed through this reproduction system: once a new variety has been bred, it can be multiplied through vegetative forms of propagation, whether cuttings, grafts or tubers. But for cross-fertilising seed crops, the breeder must find another approach.

Maize breeders in the early twentieth century came up with a solution by applying the rediscovered principles of Mendelian genetics. George Shull, a breeder working at a US government research centre, managed to induce the characteristic of (what he called) 'heterosis' in the corn plants resulting from his cross-breeding of inbred lines. This phenomenon, commonly referred to as 'hybrid vigour', is manifested in heightened yields. But because they are hybrids, the offspring cannot breed true and the maximum yield enhancements thus last only for a single generation. The additional advantage that hybrid varieties provide a uniform crop compared to the open pollinated populations became apparent with large-scale agricultural mechanisation. So while farmers stand to benefit from seeds providing this hybrid vigour, they need to buy seeds at the beginning of every planting season to enjoy equally productive future harvests. If farmers replant the seeds from hybrid crops, the resulting plants tend to be 'segregated', reflecting the characteristics of the grandparents. This necessity to buy seed was and continues to be a boon for the seed companies that could correct a major risk factor in seed production, namely that seed markets are generally anti-cyclic, that is, after a good harvest – when the seed producer has good stocks – farmers save their seed and the demand for seed is high when seed production conditions have been poor. Hybrids create a stable seed market.

Unfortunately for breeders (and presumably for farmers), hybridisation does not work for some of the most economically important crops such as wheat. This of course presents problems for breeders. Plants are self-reproducing. With no law to prevent it, there is nothing to stop farmers from replanting harvested seed, or even multiplying seed for the purpose of selling it in competition with the breeder (assuming this would be more profitable for them than selling harvested produce). This is of course where intellectual property rights come in.

Apart from these techniques, other techniques like tissue and cell culture development have been used for several decades. These enable scientists to regenerate large numbers of plants that are genetically identical and free from disease. These techniques do not replace conventional breeding but can improve its efficiency. More recently molecular biology introduced new opportunities in breeding, either to make conventional breeding more efficient and effective (marker-assisted selection) or by moving foreign genes into the breeding materials (genetic engineering) not just from other plant species, but from completely different forms of life. For example, scientists have succeeded in inducing insect resistance in crops like corn and cotton by inserting genes from a soil microbe called *Bacillus thuringiensis* that is toxic for certain insects. These techniques include direct gene transfer into tissue cultures using bacteria or viruses as carriers of the foreign DNA, and such devices as high-velocity 'gene guns' which shoot DNA-containing 'bullets' into cell nuclei. The new science of genomics is being used to identify useful genes and the plants which contain them.

The emergence of the modern seed industry

During the nineteenth-century westward expansion of the USA, the government sought to encourage settlement. One way to do this was to entrust the farmers themselves with the selection, breeding and multiplication of seed. To this effect, the Patent Office, first, and then the US Department of Agriculture (USDA), provided farmers with free seed packets for them to experiment on. At the time the seed industry was small and insignificant. Farmers used these seeds and those introduced by the immigrants arriving in the USA to breed varieties adapted to suit their own needs and the local ecological conditions. The number of such varieties increased enormously. Later these farmer-bred and selected crop varieties formed the basis of the public and private sector breeding programmes.

Fowler argues that the separation of farming from breeding, the undermining of the customary practice of seed saving in the case of hybridised crops, and the commodification of the seed cannot be explained by advances in plant breeding science and technology alone.[8] When scientifically bred seeds came onto the market, subsistence agriculture had largely been replaced by commercial farming anyway. Mechanized harvesting and the consolidation of landholdings had made seed selection non-viable compared to the greater convenience of purchasing mechanically cleaned seed from dealers. And, since most farmers were no longer improving seeds themselves, the attraction of selecting and replanting was declining even before scientifically bred varieties were becoming widely available.

In 1890, 596 firms were involved in commercial seed production. Having formed a business association called the American Seed Trade Association (ASTA) a few years earlier, they were becoming active in defending their interests. One of ASTA's early campaigns was to stop the government from providing farmers with seeds. This failed for lack of support from the public and Congress, many of whose members sent seed packets to constituents. However, during the first two decades of the twentieth century, the government increasingly sent seeds only of the most common varieties to farmers, while passing on the more exotic germplasm to the government experiment stations and colleges. A later campaign by ASTA from the First World War onwards was to oppose the saving of seed by the farmers.

Shortly after the First World War, the Secretary of Agriculture decided that the USDA would henceforth support research aimed at the development of hybrids and ending farmer participation in breeding programmes. The implications of the emergence of corn hybrids for private sector breeding cannot be underestimated. Several of the world's major twentieth-century seed companies first came to prominence through their successful breeding of hybrid corn varieties. Many of these old seed companies are now owned by companies like Monsanto, Syngenta, Dupont and Delta & Pine Land, which was itself bought by Monsanto in 2006.

Contrary to the US situation, virtually all the cultivable land in nineteenth-century Europe had been farmed for a very long time. Most of those major crops whose origins were exotic, like wheat, rye, maize, potatoes and tomatoes, had become well-established and integrated into local farming systems for centuries or even millennia. Although some such crops were vulnerable to devastating diseases due to widespread genetic uniformity (most notoriously potatoes), European farmers developed a huge range of varieties over the centuries to suit local conditions. European governments generally did not find it necessary to encourage farmers to breed new varieties themselves as in the US case.

Introducing new species and formal experimental breeding were carried out first by wealthy landowners, and from the early twentieth century by the small family seed firms. These firms descended from farmers that made it their main business to provide seed for other farmers and who then started breeding programmes to better meet the requirements of their customers. As in the USA, public research institutions and universities were also carrying out breeding work which benefited the emerging private plant breeding sector.

The UPOV Convention

The UPOV Convention was adopted in Paris in 1961 and entered into force in 1968. It was revised slightly in 1972 and more substantially in 1978 and 1991. The 1978 Act entered into force in 1981, and the 1991 Act in 1998. All members, with the exception of Belgium, are parties to either the 1978 or the 1991 Acts. New members are required to accept UPOV 1991.

The Convention established an organisation called the *Union Internationale pour la Protection des Obtentions Végétales* (UPOV). The official English translation is International Union for the Protection of New Varieties of Plants. UPOV has a close association with WIPO to the extent that the latter organisation's director-general is also secretary-general of UPOV.[9]

The existence of UPOV can be attributed to a number of associations, of which the most important was probably the *Association Internationale des Selectionneurs pour la Protection des Obtentions Végétales* (International Association of Plant Breeders) (ASSINSEL). ASSINSEL's members decided at their 1956 Congress to call for an international conference to consider the possibility of developing a new international instrument for protecting plant varieties. ASSINSEL requested the French government to organise what became the International Conference for the Protection of New Varieties of Plants. The Conference, which convened in May 1957 in Paris, established the basic principles of plant breeders' rights that were later incorporated into the UPOV Convention. Only European governments were invited to participate or attend as observers.

A Committee of Experts was set up charged with the following tasks: (a) studying the legal problems arising out of the protection of the breeder's right as defined by the Conference; (b) giving as precise formulations as might be appropriate of the basic technical and economic principles laid down by the Conference; and (c) preparing the first draft of an international convention for submission to a later session of the Conference itself. The Committee met twice before appointing a Drafting Group to develop a legal text. One of the important issues the Committee had to decide upon was whether the convention would be incorporated into the general framework of the Paris Convention, or whether a separate convention was necessary. It decided in favour of the latter but recommended that the new office administering the convention should work closely with the *Bureaux Internationaux Réunis de la Protection de la Propriété Intellectuelle* (BIRPI), the forerunner to WIPO.

The second meeting of the International Conference for the Protection of New Varieties of Plants took place in November 1961, with 12 European countries being invited, as were BIRPI, the FAO, the European Economic Community, the Organisation of Economic Co-operation and Development (OECD), and other business associations including the *Communauté Internationale des Obtenteurs de Plantes Ornementales de Reproduction Asexuée* (CIOPORA), and the *Fédération Internationale du Commerce des Semences* (FIS). Since then ASSINSEL, FIS and the new International Seed Federation (comprising the merged ASSINSEL and FIS) along with CIOPORA and the International Chamber of Commerce have played key roles in shaping the evolution of the UPOV Convention through its various revisions.

UPOV and Substantive Plant Variety Protection Law

Compared to some other important international agreements on intellectual property, such as TRIPS and the Paris Convention on the Protection of Industrial Property, the UPOV Convention's provisions are extremely detailed and specific. In order to join the Union, countries are supposed to have plant variety protection (PVP) regimes already in place and these are normally scrutinised by UPOV to see that they are in harmony with the Convention's provisions.

The most substantial revisions took place in 1978 and 1991 and these are discussed and compared below. But first it is important to note that the French word *'obtention'* in the name of the Union and the Convention is significant since it indicates that rights can be acquired not just by those who breed new varieties in the classic sense of creating new varieties by crossing and selecting sexually reproducing plants, but also by those who improve plants based on the discovery and selection of mutants or variants found in a population of cultivated plants. Thus, UPOV 1991 clarifies that a breeder is the person 'who bred, or discovered and developed, a variety'. In doing so, this latest revision is consistent with the original intent of the Convention to protect varieties that may not be attributable entirely to the application of scientific breeding. At the same time, it represents a divergence from patent law which professes not to allow mere discoveries to be protected.

To be eligible for protection under the UPOV system, plant varieties must be new, distinct, stable and uniform. To be new, the variety needs not necessarily to be so in the absolute sense, but not to have been offered for sale or marketed, with the agreement of the breeder or his successor in title, in the source country, or for longer than a limited number of years in any other country. To be distinct, the variety must be distinguishable by one or more characteristics from any other variety whose existence is a matter of common knowledge anywhere in the world, implicitly including among traditional farming communities. Compared to UPOV 1978, the requirement in the most recent version has been relaxed somewhat. It does this by dropping the phrase 'by one or more important characteristics' after the word 'distinguishable'. To be considered as stable, the variety must remain true to its description after repeated reproduction or propagation. In order for a variety to be stable it must have a certain level of uniformity which avoids change in the variety through genetic drift. This requirement also shows the specific nature of the UPOV system since the uniformity requirement cannot practically be the same for species with different ways of reproduction; self-fertilising species can be much more uniform than cross-fertilising crops. Uniformity requirements are made relative instead, that is, a new variety should be uniform when compared to the varieties of the same species. This means that when the plant breeding techniques were refined, the uniformity requirement gradually increased, placing it beyond the reach of farmer-breeders who may select in landraces to develop new varieties. Unlike patents, there is no disclosure requirement. Instead, applicants are required to submit evidence that the variety meets the protection requirements (for example, in the USA) or to submit the plant material for which protection is sought to the responsible governmental authority for testing to ensure that the above eligibility requirements have been met.

What is a 'plant variety', and how may it be distinguished, for the purposes of intellectual property protection, from a 'plant'. This is very important given the increased application of genetic engineering to crop research and the fact that in some jurisdictions, plants are patentable but plant varieties are only protectable under national PVP systems.

The original 1961 version of the UPOV Convention defined 'plant variety' as including 'any cultivar, clone, line, stock or hybrid which is capable of cultivation'. The 1991 revision contains a more detailed definition, according to which a plant variety is:

> a plant grouping within a single botanical taxon of the lowest known rank, which grouping, irrespective of whether the conditions for the grant of a breeder's right are fully met, can be:
> – defined by the expression of the characteristics resulting from a given genotype or combination of genotypes,
> – distinguished from any other plant grouping by the expression of at least one of the said characteristics, and
> – considered as a unit with regard to its suitability for being propagated unchanged. (Article 1(vi), UPOV 1991)

UPOV 1978, which several countries are still contracting parties to, defines the scope of protection as the breeder's right to authorise the following acts: 'the production for purposes of commercial marketing; the offering for sale; and the marketing of the reproductive or vegetative propagating material, as such, of the variety'. The 1991 version extends the scope of the breeders' rights in two ways. First, it increases the number of acts for which prior authorisation of the breeder is required. These include 'production or reproduction; conditioning for the purpose of propagation; offering for sale; selling or other marketing; exporting; importing; stocking for the above purposes'. Second, such acts are not just in respect of the reproductive or vegetative propagating material, but also encompass harvested material obtained through the use of propagating material, and so-called *essentially derived varieties*.

However, the right of breeders both to use protected varieties as an initial source of variation for the creation of new varieties and to market these varieties without authorisation from the original breeder (the 'breeders' exemption') is upheld in both versions. This represents a major difference with patent law, which normally has a very narrow research exemption. At this point it is worth mentioning that many plant breeders are concerned about the effects of patents on free access to plant genetic resources including varieties bred by others.

One difference between UPOV 1978 and UPOV 1991 is that the latter extends rights to varieties which are essentially derived from the protected variety. So the breeder of PVP-protected variety A has the right to demand that the breeder of variety B secure his or her authorisation to commercialise B if it was essentially derived from A. The main idea here is that breeders should not be able to acquire protection too easily for minor modifications of extant varieties produced perhaps through cosmetic breeding or genetic engineering, or free-ride without doing any breeding of their own, problems that the increased application of biotechnology in this field appeared likely to exacerbate.

Beyond resolving these particular issues, but related to them, the provision was also intended to ensure that patent rights and PVP rights operate in a harmonious fashion in jurisdictions where plants and their parts, seeds and genes are patentable and access to these could be blocked by patent holders. Such a practice would undermine one of the main justifications for PVP protection, which is that breeders should be able to secure returns on their investments but without preventing competitors from being able freely to access breeding material. It should be noted here that the PVP-issuing office will not itself determine whether a variety is essentially derived from an earlier one. This will be left to the courts. So far, only one court, in the Netherlands, has been called upon to make such a determination and it found in favour of the defendant.[10] According to the court, the general rule is that distinguishable varieties are normally independent, the essentially derived variety (EDV) provision being an exception to this rule that ought to be construed narrowly. Given that one of the two varieties at issue differed in several ways in shape and form from the variety from which they were allegedly essentially derived, the exception was not applicable. As for the other variety, no convincing case had in any case been made that it was an EDV, besides which the Community Plant Variety Office made no mention of its similarity to the already registered original variety nor did it find any grounds to investigate such a possibility.

In the EU, the 1998 EC Directive on the Legal Protection of Biotechnological Inventions seeks to make PVP and patents operate more harmoniously by providing that where the acquisition or exploitation of a PVP right is impossible without infringing a patent, or vice versa, a compulsory licence may be applied for. If issued, the licensor party will be entitled to cross-license the licensee's patent or PVP right. Subsequent legislation in Germany and France restores the breeder's exemption in that it explicitly allows breeders to use genetic materials that include patented components for further breeding. When the new variety contains the patented component, however, consent has to be sought for the marketing of that new variety; when the patented component is 'bred out' of the material, the patent holder has no rights in the new variety.

There is no reference in the 1978 version to the right of farmers to re-sow seed harvested from protected varieties for their own use (often referred to as 'farmers' privilege'). The Convention establishes minimum standards such that the breeder's prior authorisation is required for at least the three acts mentioned above. Thus, countries that are members of the 1978 Convention are free to uphold farmers' privilege or eliminate it. All UPOV member countries implemented the exemption for 'private and non-commercial use' under the UPOV Act of 1978 so as to include the re-sowing and in some cases the local exchange or sales of seed. However, this was not the case in ornamental crops in the Netherlands, where a stronger protection was deemed necessary. In the USA this was interpreted very widely, resulting in practice in sales of farm-saved seed being allowable to a level where it would contribute less than 50 per cent of total farm income, thus resulting in large quantities of seed being 'brown bagged' to the detriment of the commercial interests of the breeder.

The 1991 version is more specific about this. Whereas the scope of the breeder's right includes production or reproduction and conditioning for the purpose of propagation,[11] governments can use their discretion in deciding whether to uphold the farmers' privilege which includes only the use of saved seed on the same farm (and thus excludes any type of exchange or sale of such seed). According to Article 15, the breeder's right in relation to a variety may be restricted 'in order to permit farmers to use for propagating purposes, on their own holdings, the product of the harvest which they have obtained by planting . . . the protected variety'. Even though the Act states that the legitimate interest of the breeder explicitly has to be taken into account, the seed industry generally dislikes the farmers' privilege. The EC Regulation 2100/94 on Community Plant Variety Rights, which was adopted in 1994, restricts farmers' privilege to certain crops, and breeders must be remunerated through the payment of royalties unless they are small farmers, in which case they are exempted. Interestingly, the European Community's patent rules also require that farmers' privilege be provided and defined under the same terms as the above Regulation. The United States' PVP rules are less strict in this regard: seed saving must be restricted to the amount necessary for on-farm replanting and it is not clear how the legitimate interest of the breeder is implemented since royalty payments on farm-saved seed are not required.

UPOV 1991 extends protection from at least 15 years to a minimum of 20 years. This later version is silent on the matter of double (that is, both patent and PVP) protection. Allowing double protection without any restriction was to ensure that the intellectual property practices of the USA and Japan, which allowed such double protection, would be fully compliant with UPOV. Nonetheless, most countries expressly forbid the patenting of plant varieties, including all European countries, where it has caused some legal uncertainty.

Until the late 1990s, the overwhelming majority of UPOV members were developed countries, reflecting the fact that in many developing countries, especially in Africa, private sector involvement in plant breeding and seed supply is quite limited. Moreover, as just mentioned, in many of these countries small-scale farming communities are responsible for much of the plant breeding and seed distribution, as they have been for centuries. Consequently, until recently there would have been few domestic beneficiaries of a PVP system apart from the public institutes for agricultural research.

However, many developing countries are now joining UPOV. In many if not most, cases, this is not because of any strong domestic demand for PVP, but because of their obligations under Article 27.3(b) of TRIPS or trade agreements. The UPOV system is the only *sui generis* system for plant varieties that exists in international law and is currently being actively promoted worldwide by the organisation itself, as well as by the USA and the European Community through bilateral free trade agreements that tend to require developing country parties to join UPOV.

GEOGRAPHICAL INDICATIONS

Origins

Geographical indications (GIs) are unusual for two reasons. First, they have an extremely short history. Unlike the other intellectual property rights covered in TRIPS and in previous multilateral treaties, the term is completely new, first seeing the light of day during the Uruguay Round in proposals made by the European Community and by Switzerland. This is true despite the fact that related terms like indications of source and appellations of origin are included in the 1891 Madrid Agreement on the Repression of False or Deceptive Indications of Source in Goods, and in the 1958 Lisbon Agreement for the Protection of Appellations of Origin and their International Protection.[12]

Indeed, it was only in July 1992 that the European Community adopted a Regulation on the Protection of Geographical Indications and Designations of Origin for Agricultural Products and Foodstuffs.[13] Under this Regulation, the European Commission maintains a register of protected designations of origin and protected geographical indications. As we will see, the Regulation has proved to be controversial.

This second unusual feature of geographical indications is that, unlike patents, copyright or trade marks, they are not themselves a discrete and universally accepted category of intellectual property right. Different countries may well protect them under specific geographical indications laws, as in the European Union. But they may alternatively be protected under an appellations of origin regime, trade mark law, consumer protection law, or under the common law tort of passing off.

Perhaps the longest established geographical indications regime is the French appellations of origin system for products considered to be distinctively local due to a combination of traditional know-how and highly localised natural conditions. The appellations of origin system evolved in response to problems of illegal labelling and overproduction. A government agency validates *Appellation d'Origine Contrôlée*, so that producers of wines, cheeses, and other foodstuffs, whose goods are renowned for their distinctive qualities and geographic origins, are protected from those who would undermine or exploit their good reputation by making similar, but false, claims. For example, wines from the Champagne region of France are protected in this way.[14]

In countries like the United States and the United Kingdom, geographical indications tend to be protected under trade mark law. In the United States, Idaho potatoes and Florida oranges, for example, are protected as certification marks. Two well-known British ones are Stilton cheese and Harris Tweed.

Stilton is a popular British cheese that is made by hand using a recipe that is at least 300 years old.[15] The cheese is named after a small town in the East Midlands located on the old Great North Road from London to the North. In the old days, horses for the stagecoaches would be changed there. At the Bell Inn, travellers would be served a local cheese that became commonly known as Stilton. In 1727, Daniel Defoe, the author of *Robinson Crusoe* and *Tour through England and Wales*, mentioned passing through Stilton, 'a town famous for cheese'.

Stilton cheese has been protected by certification trade marks since 1966, and has been a European 'Protected Designation of Origin' (PDO) since 1996, which ensures protection throughout the European Union and obviates the need to apply for trade mark protection in every member country.

The owner of the marks is the Stilton Cheesemakers' Association, which was founded in 1936 to look after the interests of the producers and to ensure that standards are maintained at licensed dairies. Six of the eight dairies are members of the Association, the other two being licensees of the trade marks and the PDO. The marks are the word 'Stilton' and the logo of the Association which includes a cylindrical block of cheese with a slice missing and a crown on top.

In order to use the name 'Stilton', a cheese must

- be made only in the three counties from local milk which is pasteurized before use. These counties are Leicestershire, Derbyshire and Nottinghamshire;
- be made only in a traditional cylindrical shape;
- be allowed to form its own crust or coat;
- be un-pressed;
- have delicate blue veins radiating from the centre;
- have a taste profile typical of Stilton.

Clearly, the cheese market is a highly competitive one. Since the prestige of British cheese, excellent as much of it is, is not especially high in Europe or elsewhere, marketing such a product is a serious challenge. In this respect, the Association has been successful. Stilton is not only popular in the UK but is exported to about 40 countries.

Harris Tweed is a cloth made in the Scottish islands of Lewis, Harris, Uist and Barra, which together form a large part of an area known as the Outer Hebrides.[16] It is handwoven and made from wool that is spun and dyed in the Outer Hebrides. This area of Scotland has been known for producing fine quality cloth for several centuries. While mechanisation during the Industrial Revolution transformed production in other areas, the Outer Hebrides continued to make cloth entirely by hand, and it remains to a large extent a cottage industry.

From the mid-nineteenth century, this cloth became popular throughout the UK. At the time, the methods used were as follows:

> The raw material, wool, was produced locally and part of it would have been used in its natural uncoloured state, the rest was dyed. In the 19th century vegetable dyes were used. Following dyeing, the wool was mixed, the shade being regulated by the amount of coloured wool added; then it was oiled and teased; the latter process involves pulling the wool apart to open out the fibres. The next part of the prepara-

tion, carding, results in the fibres of the wool being drawn out preparatory to spin-ning. This was a very lengthy process followed by spinning carried out on a famil-iar spinning-wheel by women. Until the turn of the century a very early type of handloom was used for weaving with a manually operated shuttle. The final process is finished where the tweed is washed and given a raised compact finish. Those involved in this process were often accompanied by songs in Gaelic. (Harris Tweed Authority Website)

Around the beginning of the twentieth century, a degree of modernisation took place and production increased in consequence. Following a meeting of producers in 1906, the Harris Tweed Association was established three years later to apply for a trade mark that would help the producers compete in a market in which industrial spinning mills able to mass-produce cloth were threatening to force out the small producers. The Harris Tweed mark, which was granted in 1909, comprises the words 'Harris Tweed' with an orb and a Maltese cross and has since become very well known. The official definition of Harris Tweed then was 'a tweed, hand-spun, hand-woven and dyed by the crofters and cottars in the Outer Hebrides'.

In 1934, the trade mark definition was changed to the following: 'Harris Tweed means a tweed made from pure virgin wool produced in Scotland, spun, dyed and finished in Outer Hebrides and hand-woven by the islanders at their own homes in the Islands of Lewis, Harris, Uist, Barra and their several purtenances and all known as the Outer Hebrides'. This of course allows for increased production while ensuring that it was still at least to some extent a tradition-bound cottage industry, albeit less so than before.

Production reached a peak of 7.6 million yards in 1966, but subsequently began to contract as Harris Tweed became less fashionable. Moreover, the British textiles industry, once the world's largest, was about to begin shrink-ing in the face of competition from lower cost producers overseas. In order to be more competitive, it was felt necessary to retrain weavers, introduce tougher standards and better meet new demands, including for softer, lighter cloth.

In 1993, the UK government came to the producers' aid by passing legisla-tion, the Harris Tweed Act. The law set up the Harris Tweed Authority, a statu-tory body, in place of the Harris Tweed Association. Under the Act, Harris Tweed has a new definition as follows:

> Harris Tweed means a tweed which has been hand woven by the islanders at their homes in the Outer Hebrides, finished in the islands of Harris, Lewis, North Uist, Benbecula, South Uist and Barra and their several purtenances (The Outer Hebrides) and made from pure virgin wool dyed and spun in the Outer Hebrides.

Unlike Stilton, the future of Harris Tweed is less secure, hence the need felt by the government to take legislative action. Stilton, on the other hand, has not needed to resort to state intervention. This point highlights the fact that GIs and certification trade marks for traditional goods are useless without good standards of quality control and marketing, and up-to-date information on markets including foreign ones if the products are to be exported. But even then, success is far from guaranteed.

The United States and Australia, both as it happens important wine producers, have argued that trade marks are in fact sufficient to protect geographical indications. Indeed, the popular view in the United States is that there is nothing wrong with selling locally made products using words like Champagne and Chablis.

One point of consistency with trade marks, though, is that when a once local product becomes generic it can no longer be protected. This has been the fate of certain products named after places such as Cheddar cheese and Dijon mustard, which can now be produced anywhere. One would suppose that once a product becomes generic there is no going back. However, with political will, some supposedly generic products can be 're-localised'. This has been the case for sherry, a fortified wine named by linguistically challenged English people after a district of Spain called Jerez.[17] 'Cyprus sherry', sold under that name since the 1930s, has thus been renamed 'Cyprus fortified wine'. The naming of South African wines sold in that country as sherry and port must be phased out under the terms of the 2000 European Union and South Africa Free Trade Agreement. In 2005, the European Court of Justice ruled it illegal for any cheese produced outside Greece to be called feta, despite the fact that in Denmark, Germany and France locally made cheeses with the word 'feta' in the name had been sold for several decades. Feta is not in fact the name of a place but is just the Greek word for 'slice'.

Geographical Indications at the World Trade Organization

Geographical indications are defined in the TRIPS Agreement as 'indications which identify a good as originating in the territory of a Member, or a region or locality in that territory, where a given quality, reputation, or other characteristic of the good is essentially attributable to its geographical origin'.

WTO members are required to permit legal action enabling traders to prevent: (a) the designation or presentation of a good (such as a trademark) that suggests, in a manner that misleads the public, that the good in question originates in a geographical area other than the true place of origin; and (b) any use which constitutes unfair competition. Article 23 deals solely with wines and spirits, which are subject to additional protection. This evidences how far the European wine and spirit-exporting countries were willing to go to pursue their economic interests with respect to such goods.

In November 2001, the WTO members attending the Doha Ministerial Conference agreed by virtue of Ministerial Declaration paragraph 18, 'to negotiate the establishment of a multilateral system of notification and registration of geographical indications for wines and spirits by the Fifth Session of the Ministerial Conference'. With respect to the possible extension of the enhanced protection of geographical indications to products other than wines and spirits, the Ministerial Declaration acknowledged that issues related to this matter would be addressed in the Council for TRIPS, an indication of the lack of consensus.

Several WTO members do not consider a special GIs regime of the kind existing in the European Union to be necessary. A few of them have other concerns too, such as the possibility that an existing trade mark with a similar or identical name to a GI will have diminished protection, and also that the register established under the 1992 Regulation is discriminatory.

A WTO dispute concerned the EC Regulation on geographical indications. Australia and the United States initiated a complaint against the European Community for its methods of protecting GIs, which it was alleged was incompatible with the TRIPS Agreement. One aspect of this dispute is that the Regulation was allowed under Article 17. Much discussion ensued as to whether Article 17 allowed members to provide 'limited exceptions' such as 'fair use of descriptive terms', provided that such exceptions take account of the interests of the trade mark owner and third parties.

Australia and the US argued that the 'fair use' example suggested that exceptions were to be confined to those circumstances where third parties needed to use the mark, such as for denominative purposes, but not to indicate commercial trade origin. Under US domestic law as set out above, the 'fair use' defence which permits the good faith use of a mark to describe the geographical origin of goods is not available if the use is 'as a mark'.[18] European jurisprudence, on the other hand, has held that a defendant's use of a geographical indication that also denoted trade origin and was confusingly similar to an earlier registered trade mark could fall within the defence allowing for use in accordance with 'honest practices' of indications of the geographical origin of goods, with the emphasis being on the 'honesty' of the trader.

The Dispute Panel did not fully accept the position of Australia and the US, and adopted a formalistic interpretation of the TRIPS Agreement, holding that the EC Regulation was a permissible exception under Article 17 of TRIPS. However, the Panel did concur with the complainants' view that the Regulation violated the national treatment provision in TRIPS by discriminating against foreign nationals seeking to have their GIs registered in Europe.[19]

A Pro-development Intellectual Property Right?

Despite the fact they are in TRIPS largely at the instigation of the European Commission and certain EU member states, GIs have for several years been promoted as a concession to developing countries that they ought to take advantage of. Supposedly, they provide the means by which developing countries can use intellectual property to protect categories of local rural knowledge that they possess in abundance. In particular, the European Union and the Swiss government are very keen to promote GIs worldwide by arguing that this part of TRIPS can potentially provide substantial gains for developing countries. This seems plausible when one considers that GIs are especially appropriate for the produce of small-scale producers and cultivators, and, it should be underlined here, not just for foods and beverages but also for handicrafts and other hand-made items.[20]

GIs appear superficially to be a subject that developing countries should be able to adopt a unified stance on. Indeed, generally speaking developing countries consider the additional protection extended only to wines and spirits to typify the lack of balance in TRIPS. But after that, the consensus starts to break down.

Many developing countries are rich in traditional knowledge having applications in agriculture, food production and small-scale manufacturing. So GIs would appear to have real potential in terms of developing and exploiting lucrative markets for natural products including those manufactured by resource-poor farming communities. Such countries tend to favour the extension of the additional protection to cover all products, not just beverages. Are they right to be so pro-GI with respect to products they wish to export? Possibly so, but caution should be exercised. At present the potential of geographical indications for developing countries is somewhat speculative because this type of intellectual property right has been used only in a few countries outside Europe. Moreover, many GIs have quite small markets, and a relatively small number are traded internationally.

Other developing countries do not have an abundance of traditional knowledge and are key exporters of products that compete with well-established GI-protected goods coming from Europe. For those countries, GIs may be considered a threat and not an opportunity. Indeed, some such countries are understandably concerned that the present enthusiasm for GIs among Europeans is really about protectionism. For example, New World developing country wine producer countries like Chile and Argentina and also South Africa are competitors with Europe, and tend to be unhappy about the privileged status of wines and spirits because this serves the interests of their Old World competitors. Many of the place names in these countries originated in Europe. Some developed countries, such as Australia, feel the same way.

In short, there is no 'developing country position' on GIs and it is unlikely there will be one. But since the interests and negotiating positions of developed countries also differ sharply, these negotiations on GIs could end up in stalemate anyway.[21]

DATABASES

Origins and Justifications

Historical concepts of 'database'
In its widest sense, a database is a point of reference in which information is stored and from which it is sourced. Legalistically and sociologically, the notion of a 'database' is not entirely new. One of the earliest examples is the ancient Hindu text, the Rig-Veda, which is primarily an organised collection of over 1,000 Sanskrit hymns. This 'database' was certainly the product of considerable investment, having been produced between 1500 and 900 BC. The earliest forms of anthologies or stories from the Middle Ages also functioned as a sort of database of information. Early manuscripts were organised into discrete pieces (quires or *peciae*), with the manuscript owners licensing each piece at a time so that several copyists were making copies from the same manuscript simultaneously, having paid a licence fee which was determined per user or per part of manuscript. Thus, the European book production and copying practices in the fourteenth and fifteenth centuries were administered in a manner similar to today's practice of allowing several licensed users to access parts of a complete collection simultaneously.[22]

A slightly later example of recognition that compilations of materials represented a 'symbol' of storage, preservation, verification and availability for the user is the publication of Shakespeare's First Folio in 1623. This compilation, comprising all of Shakespeare's plays, offered a means of preserving them from total destruction. It also constituted a value-added product in that not only did it make available previously unprinted plays, but it also presented hitherto published plays in a new, verified and edited version, distinguishing them from the pre-existing adulterated copies which were then in circulation. This process of compiling, verifying and publishing the First Folio was beyond the means of any individual, so a syndicate of five publishers was specially formed to provide the considerable financial investment required.[23]

The concern for legally protecting such collections is not new. An early example of rights extending to compilations is provided by Article 8 of the 1837 Prussian Law[24] which provided for educational and research institutions to enjoy a 30-year right over new editions of their works, including 'works which in one or several volumes constitute a single edition and thereby can be regarded as belonging together' or 'collections of articles and studies of different aspects of academic research' – the duration for these works was computed from the time of completion or publication with ownership vested in the corporate body as producer of the compilation.

The best-known illustration of legal protection of databases under copyright law is Article 2(5), Berne Convention,[25] whereby protection is conferred on 'collections of literary or artistic works such as encyclopaedias and anthologies which, by reason of the selection and arrangement of their contents, constitute intellectual creations', where the separate database copyright subsists independently of the copyright in each of the works forming the collection.

From these historical antecedents we can state that the 'database' was already recognised as being a compilation (or collection) of materials which offered the user the convenience of accessing from one point all the materials or items contained within the database, as opposed to the user independently searching and recovering the discrete items or materials.

The demand and supply of databases has increased exponentially over the last decade, with greater digital storage technology, a rise in computing power, and the increase in consumer access to and consumption of electronic goods. The fact of interactivity has ennobled traditional databases with another dimension of usage and value to the consumer. Today, we understand the term database to cover a myriad of products, including anthologies of e-books, directories, share price indices, on-line information services, and indeed the whole internet can be perceived conceptually as a database. Even genetically coded information can constitute a 'database'.[26]

Not surprisingly, the increase in value of these information products has led to the view that an increase in protection is necessary to protect the investment. It is not disputed that intellectual property rights are created or strengthened in order to construct or assist in maintaining a healthy economic infrastructure; nor is there much argument against introducing remedies to curtail the misappropriation of another person's investment. Ostensibly, both the EU and the US approaches underline the aim of their database regimes as being to provide incentives for the protection of the investment required in producing and marketing value-added products for the economic well-being of the two regions and to curtail the activities of the parasitical free-rider.[27]

Can Databases be Protected by Copyright Law?

An equally established notion was the availability of intellectual property laws, primarily copyright law, as a means of protecting such compilations. Yet within the last decade, there have been moves towards an independent and separate regime of database protection.

The EU position

The EC Database Directive harmonises the position of database copyright in European Member States' copyright laws.[28] In order to qualify for copyright protection, the database must constitute the 'author's own intellectual creation by reason of its selection or arrangement'.[29] The author of the database will then be granted a set of exclusive rights in respect of the *expression* of the database.[30]

The situation prior to the enactment of the Directive varied greatly between member states. Some members, such as Ireland, the UK, the Netherlands and the Nordic countries, offered greater protection to non-creative compilations than others. In the Netherlands, for instance, it was possible to obtain protection for comprehensive and non-selective compilations, not under copyright law but rather under the '*geschriftenbescherming*' rule which confers a limited term of protection on non-original writings.[31] On the other hand, the Scandinavian countries provided a limited term of protection to producers of non-original compilations under the 'catalogue' rule.[32] Besides these quasi-copyright rules, unfair competition law was another favoured option for protecting compilations. Indeed, under UK copyright law, courts sometimes protected compilations of information due to *mala fide* on the part of the defendant in availing himself of the fruits of another person's labour.[33] In any event, even if copyright protection could be obtained for databases, the scope of protection only extended to the expression of the database, that is, its selection and arrangement, and to its contents.[34]

The United States position

The various unsuccessful attempts to introduce *sui generis* database protection into the United States have been viewed as nothing more than an attempt to redress a perceived lacuna in copyright law, especially in the context of comprehensive databases. It is clear that the Supreme Court's ruling in *Feist*[35] caused consternation. The US copyright law defines compilations as works formed by the 'collection and assembling of preexisting materials or of data that are selected, coordinated, or arranged in such a way that the resulting work as a whole constitutes an original work of authorship'.[36]

It was not always clear, before the 1991 *Feist* decision, whether US copyright law protected factual compilations or not. Some US courts applied a 'sweat of the brow' theory which protected factual databases, as long as investment and labour could be shown; other courts only protected factual compilations which contained sufficient creativity in their 'selection, coordination or arrangement'. Moreover, despite the divergent stances between the courts, most courts appeared to be protecting directories.[37]

The Supreme Court in *Feist* denied copyright protection to a telephone book alphabetically listing names and phone numbers. The decision, in retrospect, was unsurprising factually; why *should* telephone directories be protected under copyright law? However, the reasoning of the Court was far-reaching. It had always been implicit in previous decisions protecting directories and other compilations that courts had conferred copyright protection partly due to a desire to prevent the copier from competing unfairly with the compiler by appropriating the fruits of the compiler's efforts. In other words, as national European courts had done, the US courts had substituted unfair competition law with copyright protection.

The *Feist* decision noted that since facts are not copyrightable and compilations of facts generally are, originality of a factual work resides in the *selection, coordination, or arrangement of facts*, with the scope of protection concomitantly limited to that original selection, coordination, or arrangement. More interesting was the anchoring of this reasoning in the US Constitution. The Court held that copyright advances the progress of science and art, and that 'originality is a constitutional requirement'. Thus, in the copyright context, 'original . . . means only that the work was independently created by the author (as opposed to copied from other works), and that it possesses at least some minimal degree of creativity'.[38] Therefore facts standing alone (which are merely discovered and not created), and unoriginal compilations of facts, cannot be protected by copyright.

Rationale for *Sui Generis* Database Protection

The main reason for a *sui generis* database right is the inability of legislators, especially in the EU and in the US, to extend the remits of copyright law to protect factual, comprehensive, labour-intensive databases. A second reason why countries have started to investigate *sui generis* database rights is the on-going wider US–EU–WIPO negotiations for an international treaty on databases.[39] A final reason for the US and international proposals for a database right is that the European database right is only available to EU residents or corporations. The right can be extended to non-EU citizens on the basis of reciprocity, if other countries grant equivalent protection to databases made by EU citizens or corporations.[40] The US has limited pressure it can bring to bear on the EU;[41] the discrimination appears to be permitted under Articles 3 (national treatment) and 4 (most-favoured-nation treatment) of TRIPS, since the *sui generis* regime is not within the remit of the Agreement. In any event, the official US response to this is that 'consistent with US trade policy, it is desirable to secure for US companies the benefit of the EU Database Directive and laws in other countries protecting database products'.[42]

Property or Tort?

The European Database Directive adopts a positive rights model and grants a property right for an initial period of 15 years to a database maker who has invested substantially. There is no clear policy reason why the property route was opted for other than that it was easier than creating an EU-wide unfair competition right in relation to databases.[43] Nevertheless, the *sui generis* database right does have similarities to a cause of action in misappropriation in that the aim of the property right is to 'safeguard the position of makers of databases against misappropriation of the results of the financial and professional investment . . . against certain acts by a user or competitor'.[44]

On the other hand, the United States lawmakers and lobbyists were faced with the constitutional dilemma of creating a property right for database proprietors in light of the Constitution[45] and the stance of the Supreme Court in *Feist*. It would have been difficult to argue that a positive property right in compilations which did not pass the basic criterion of 'modicum of creativity' demanded under the *Feist* doctrine would nevertheless satisfy the constitutional remits of intellectual property legislation.[46] Consequently, all subsequent bills have taken the form of a misappropriation type model granting negative rights based on the constitutional commerce clause.[47]

Salient Features of the EU Database Right

What is a database?
A database is defined as a 'collection of independent works, data or other materials which are arranged in a systematic or methodical way, and are individually accessible by electronic or other means'. The definition is wide enough to encapsulate many forms of collections, and many guidelines are enumerated within the explanatory recitals of the Directive. Thus, for example, the definition will cover all literary, musical or artistic collections of works or collections of other material such as texts, sounds, images, numbers, facts and data; but a recording, or an audiovisual, cinematographic, literary or musical work (that is, a book or a symphony) *per se* will not be considered to be a database. Moreover, compilations of recordings of performances on a CD will not be considered a database because these do not 'represent a substantial enough investment to be eligible under the *sui generis* right'.

The substantial investment requirement
The database right is conferred on the maker of a database which shows that there has been

- qualitatively and/or quantitatively

- a 'substantial investment' in either the
- obtaining, verification or presentation
- of the contents.

The recitals further explain that the notion of 'investment' can consist in the deployment of financial resources or the expending of time, effort and energy. The expenditure of investment need not be related solely to the production or creation of a database; instead, a database maker who expends considerable time and effort in verifying or maintaining the database contents is equally eligible for protection. As to the question of substantiality of investment, this can only be decided by the courts on a fact-to-fact basis.

Nature and scope of protection
The rights holder can exercise the twin rights of extraction and re-utilisation in relation to the 'whole or a substantial' part of the database. The law defines 'extraction' as the 'permanent or temporary transfer of all or a substantial part of the contents of a database to another medium by any means or in any form'.[48] Re-utilisation is defined as 'making available to the public all or a substantial part of the contents of a database by the distribution of copies, by renting, by on-line or other forms of transmission'.[49] It should be noted that the doctrine of exhaustion is not applicable to the re-utilisation right in relation to on-line database services or products.[50]

Unlike copyright law, there is no provision which limits the right to the 'expression' or 'arrangement or selection or organisation' of the database. In this, the prohibition against extraction moves dangerously close to the creation of an intellectual property right in information *qua* information, a factor that is substantiated when one realises the tightness of the exceptions under the Directive. Nevertheless, it is clear from the law that the rights cannot in any way constitute an extension of copyright protection to mere facts or data; nor should such rights give rise to the creation of a new right in the works, data or materials themselves.[51]

Another concern is that the definitions of extraction and re-utilisation are so wide as to include all sorts of activities including the downloading and printing of contents or the loading and running of electronic or on-line databases. In respect of the latter situation, it further appears that on-line screen displays which result in a temporary transfer of the whole or a substantial part of the database contents is sufficient to trigger the 'extraction' right:[52] this act can ordinarily occur when one is, for example, reviewing or accessing a data CD since a computer, in order to access a CD-ROM, may have to reproduce the data onto its RAM. However, some comfort can be found in the European Court of Justice's pronouncement in the *Fixture Marketing* cases where the terms 'extraction' and 're-utilisation' were defined to refer to any unauthorised act of appropriation and distribution to the public, and the fact that the terms do *not* imply direct access to the databases.

The repeated and systematic extraction and/or re-utilisation of insubstantial parts of the contents of the database implying acts which conflict with a normal exploitation of that database or which unreasonably prejudice the legitimate interests of the maker of the database shall not be permitted. The law specifically states that the right to prevent unauthorised extraction and/or re-utilisation relates to all acts by the user which go beyond his legitimate rights and thereby harm the investment. The two rights thus extend not only to 'the manufacture of a parasitical competing product' but also to any user who 'causes significant detriment, evaluated qualitatively or quantitatively, to the investment'.[53] The European Court of Justice has also found that repeated or systematic extraction or re-utilisation of an insubstantial part of the database can only be regarded as an infringement if the cumulative effect is to reconstitute and/or make available to the public the whole or a substantial part of the contents, thereby seriously prejudicing the maker's investment.

Duration

With such powerful rights, the issue of the duration of such rights has been a matter of some controversy. The proprietor initially obtains a 15-year term from the year following the completion of the database; if, however, the database is first made available to the public within this initial term, protection will be extended to run 15 years from the year following the date on which the work is made available to the public.[54]

The controversial aspect arises in Article 10(3), which states:

> Any substantial change, evaluated qualitatively or quantitatively, to the contents of a database, including any substantial change resulting from the accumulation of successive additions, deletions or alterations, which would result in the database being considered to be a substantial new investment, evaluated qualitatively or quantitatively, shall qualify the database resulting from that investment for its own term of protection.

From one perspective, it can be argued that the clause gives rise to a perpetual term of protection for the same database product. A new term of protection arises whenever the database shows a 'substantial change' which, in turn, must be sufficient enough to be considered a 'substantial new investment'. Note that the European Court's *British Horseracing* decision now demands a much higher standard of 'substantial' (see below).[55]

A slightly worrying aspect is that the above provision equates 'substantial change' with accumulated small or insubstantial changes. Any proprietor can argue that the addition of minuscule amounts of data on a daily basis, as is the case with many dynamic and regularly updated on-line services, represents a substantial qualitative change and investment when viewed on an accumulated basis. Moreover, the 'accumulated small changes' principle does not merely cover additions, deletions or alterations, but also the act of verification.[56] Therefore, it appears that a fresh term of protection can be triggered for the *whole* database, irrespective of the fact that the pre-existing (and possibly public domain) data or materials in the collection have not been changed or amended, but merely verified, albeit in a 'substantial' manner.

Defences

The limitations under the law are only addressed to the 'lawful user'. There are no general exceptions in relation to the use of the database by 'unlawful' users, leading to the rather interesting proposition that the rights holder may be able to prohibit virtually *all* activities by such users by merely defining the notion of a lawful user. Moreover, the rights under the database law appear to extend to the whole or a substantial or even an insubstantial part of the data-base.[57] This surprising state of affairs whereby the exclusions leave very little scope for a general third party is further heightened by the fact that the Directive is silent as to the meaning of 'lawful user'. The absence of any defi-nition has led to various definitions of the 'lawful user' in member states' laws.[58] Surely, the term should be interpreted to extend not only to purchasers or to licensees of the database, but also to persons who have, through circum-stances, acquired access to the database, for example, beneficiaries of gifts or citizens borrowing and/or utilising databases in a public library.[59]

The lawful user, in turn, can do any of the following acts, but only in rela-tion to a database which is made available to the public:

(a) extract or re-utilise *insubstantial* parts of any database which has been made available to the public – note, however that where the lawful user is only authorised to use a part of the database, he only can extract or re-utilise an insubstantial part of that portion;[60]

(b) extract *substantial parts of a non-electronic* database only for private purposes;[61]

(c) extract substantial parts of any database only for the purposes of illustra-tion for teaching or scientific research 'as long as the source is indicated and to the extent justified by the non-commercial purpose to be achieved';[62]

(d) extract and/or re-utilise substantial parts of any database for the purposes of public security or an administrative or judicial procedure.[63]

There are no realistic exceptions for educational and scientific uses, or indeed any other 'fair' or 'private' uses. There is no general private use exception for electronic databases except that the lawful user may make use of insubstantial parts of the database. Moreover, the lawful user cannot distribute or make available a non-electronic database to other persons within the family circle, even though there may be no accompanying element of profit/commerce or market harm to the database proprietor.

The exception for 'teaching or scientific research' is similarly narrow in that a prime disqualification for such uses is the necessary 'non-commercial purpose' aspect.[64] In many universities today all over the world, the current ethos is to encourage active private-public partnership and collaboration between academe and industry. This, coupled with the reality of fee-paying students, makes the demarcation between commercial and non-commercial teaching and research impossible.

In any event, the lawful user's rights to extract or re-utilise the database according to the above-stated circumstances are endangered by the wide qualification to all the stated exceptions:

> A lawful user of a database which is made available to the public in whatever manner may not perform acts which conflict with normal exploitation of the database or unreasonably prejudice the legitimate interests of the maker of the database.[65]

The wording emulates the Berne/TRIPS three-step test. Under this provision, a proprietor can argue that any act of the lawful user which affects a potential or related market amounts to prejudicing the legitimate interests of the proprietor, especially if there is a potential loss of remuneration or licensing income. Furthermore, recital 42 very clearly states that parasitical or competing uses are not the only concern of the Directive; instead, the rights of the database proprietor go further in curtailing 'any user who, through his acts, causes significant detriment, evaluated qualitatively or quantitatively, to the investment'.

Much reliance will have to be placed either on the court's forbearance or the goodwill of both the publishing industry and the rights management organisations in not automatically including every conceivable utilisation of a database in the licensing fee structure. After all, the terms 'normal exploitation' and 'legitimate interests' point to the fact that substantiality has everything to do with the perceived market harm from the perspective of the rights owner, as opposed to that of the user.

Is the EU database right in crisis?

Several concerns can be noted as one studies the EU regime. First, the database right regulates and controls not only the activities of the parasitic free-riding competitor, but also the activities of information Samaritans, and individual users. Second, the EU database right has monopolistic effects which are inherent in any proprietary system, especially with low thresholds of protection coupled with potentially long terms of protection. Third, the EU database law expressly places a statutory duty on a user of a protected database to actively ensure that no actual or potential market harm occurs. Moreover, the EU database right is not tailored to the nature of the use (for example, reasonable use, non-profit educational, scientific, research use). Instead the law sets out narrow limitations which are only granted to the 'lawful user'.

Thus, a scientific researcher coming across an electronic database in a public institution may not automatically qualify for any usage rights under the EC Database Directive unless he qualifies as a lawful user or the institutional access qualifies as public lending; even if he qualifies as a lawful user, he is under an explicit duty to act conscientiously in ensuring his insubstantial takings do not hurt the database maker's interests or potential markets. Once again, while the right is appreciated when viewed through the eyes of producers battling against misappropriation activities of competing entities, the rationale and logic of the potential permanency of database protection is slightly jarring from the perspective of academic or scientific communities accessing knowledge.

Moreover, in December 2005 the European Commission issued an evaluation of the Database Directive which concluded, among other things, that the economic impact of the database right was 'unproven', and that the empirical evidence 'cast doubts' on whether *sui generis* database protection is necessary for a thriving database industry. This finding was despite the considerable strong submissions from the European publishing industry that the database right was *crucial* to the continued success of their activities.[66]

Another concern is the European Court of Justice's 2004 decisions which have curtailed extensively the availability and scope of the database right.[67] The four cases concerned single-source databases of sports information in the areas of football and horseracing. Under the European database law, the right is only granted to databases which are a product of 'substantial investment'. The Court held that 'investment' refers to the resources used to seek out, collect and verify existing independent materials, and present them in a database, rather than the resources used to create the materials which make up the contents of the database. Thus, in one decision, the European Court of Justice found that the finding and collecting of the data which make up a football fixture list require no particular effort on the part of the professional leagues. Obtaining the contents of a football fixture list requires no investment independent of that required to create the data contained in the list.

Therefore, if the database is a reasonable and unavoidable by-product of the company's main commercial activity, it will be difficult to convince courts that a distinctively different investment has been expended to make the database. Furthermore, the Court's rather confusing judgment decrees that database protection cannot be granted if investment was directed towards the creation of the contents, as opposed to the creation of the database. This may prove to be a difficult hurdle to pass in relation to factual databases or on-line contents databases or archives. This will also prove a difficult hurdle if the contents of the database have only one source. According to the Commission Report, the judgment would not affect industries like 'publishers of directories, listings or maps', as long as they do not 'create' their own data but obtain these data from others.[68]

NOTES

1. The European Commission initially proposed a Directive on the protection of inventions by utility model in 1997. An amended version was produced in 1999. In 2001, the Commission carried out a consultation on the possibility of a unitary utility model regime.
2. Suthersanen, U., 'Incremental Inventions in Europe: A Legal and Economic Appraisal of Second Tier Patents', *Journal of Business Law*, July, 319–43, 2001.
3. For examples, see Suthersanen, U., G. Dutfield and K.B. Chow (eds), *Innovation without Patents: Harnessing the Creative Spirit in a Diverse World*, Cheltenham, UK and Northampton, MA, US: Edward Elgar, 2007.
4. See Articles 2(1) and 4(C)(1), Paris Convention (Stockholm revision). The period of priority for applications for utility models is 12 months.
5. Article 1(2), Paris Convention.
6. Articles 4(E)(1) and 4(E)(2), Paris Convention.
7. Pistorius, R., and J. van Wijk, *The Exploitation of Plant Genetic Information: Political Strategies in Crop Development*, Wallingford and New York: CABI Publishing, 1999.
8. Fowler, C., *Unnatural Selection: Technology, Politics, and Plant Evolution*, Yverdon: Gordon and Breach, 1994.
9. As of October 2007, the Union has 65 members including the European Community.
10. Fikkert, K.A., 'Netherlands – Judgement on Essentially Derived Varieties (EDVs) in the First Instance', *Plant Variety Protection*, 99, 9–10, 2005.
11. UPOV, 1991, Article 14.
12. Gervais, D., *The TRIPS Agreement: Drafting History and Analysis* – 2nd ed., London: Sweet & Maxwell, 1998, at 188.
13. Council Regulation (EEC) No. 2081/92 of 14 July 1992. The Regulation does not cover wines and spirits.
14. For some interesting articles on the system as it operates in France, see L. Bérard, M. Cegarra, K. Djama, S. Louafi, P. Marchenay, B. Roussel and F. Verdeaux (eds), *Biodiversity and Local Ecological Knowledge in France*, Paris: CIRAD/IDDRI/IFB/INRA, 2005.
15. Most of the information presented here comes from the website of the Stilton Cheesemakers' Association (http://www.stiltoncheese.com/).
16. Most of the information presented here comes from the website of the Harris Tweed Authority (http://www.harristweed.org/).
17. Similarly, 'blue denim' is a corruption of 'bleu de Nîmes'. This south of France origin of the cloth used to make jeans is of course no longer well known. Pickstone, J.V., *Ways of Knowing: A New History of Science, Technology and Medicine,* Manchester: Manchester University Press, 2000, 20.
18. Klein, S.H. and N.C. Norton, 'The Role of Trade Mark Use in US Infringement, Unfair Competition and Dilution Proceedings', in J. Phillips and I. Simon (eds), *Trade Mark Use*, Oxford: Oxford University Press, 2005, at 329–40.
19. WTO, 'European Communities – Protection of Trademarks and Geographical Indications for Agricultural Products and Foodstuffs. Complaint by the United States. Report of the Panel' [WTO document WT/DS174/R, 2005].

20. Moran, W., 'Rural Space as Intellectual Property', *Political Geography*, 12(3), 263–77, 1993.
21. For a useful analysis of the WTO negotiations concerning geographical indications, see Rangnekar, D., 'Geographical Indications: A Review of Proposals at the TRIPS Council: Extending Article 23 to Products Other than Wines and Spirits', ICTSD-UNCTAD Issue Paper No. 4, Geneva: ICTSD-UNCTAD, 2003.
22. Febvre, L. and H.-J. Martin, *The Coming of the Book: The Impact of Printing 1450–1800*, London and New York: Verso, 1976, at 21.
23. Mumby, F.A., *Publishing and Bookselling: A History from the Earliest Times to the Present Day* (4th ed.), London: Jonathan Cape, 1956, at 86–8.
24. Law of 11 June 1837.
25. Berne Convention for the Protection of Literary and Artistic Works (Paris version, 1971).
26. Dutfield, G. and U. Suthersanen, 'DNA Music: Intellectual Property and the Law of Unintended Consequences', *Science Studies*, 18(1), 5–29, 2005, at 21–3.
27. Recitals 7, 8, 10 and 12, European Parliament and Council Directive on Legal Protection of Databases, 96/9/EC, 11 March 1996; Statement of A.J. Pincus, General Counsel, US Department of Commerce before the Subcommittee on Courts and Intellectual Property of the House Committee on the Judiciary, 18 March 1999, http://www.house.gov/judiciary/106-ct18.htm (11 September 2000). For an optimistic account of why databases are economically good for developing countries, see Braunstein, Y., 'Economic Impact of Database Protection in Developing Countries and Countries in Transition', Study for WIPO Standing Committee on Copyright and Related Rights, 7th session, Geneva, 13–17 May, 2002, available at http://www.wipo.int/documents/en/meetings/2002/sccr/pdf/sccr7_2.pdf.
28. EC Directive 96/9/EC; chapter II deals only with database copyright.
29. Article 3, EC Directive 96/9/EC.
30. Article 5, EC Directive 96/9/EC.
31. Article 10(1)(I), Dutch Author's Right Law 1912; *Nederlandse Omroep Stichting v. NV Holdingmaatschappij de Telegraaf*, [2000] ECDR 129.
32. Article 49, Swedish Author's Right Law 1960; *EMAP Business Communications Ltd. v. Planit Media AB*, [2000] ECDR 93.
33. *Waterlow Publishers Ltd v. Rose* (1995) FSR 207, CA; *Football League Ltd v. Littlewoods Pools Ltd.*, [1959] 1 Ch. 637; *Ladbroke (Football) Ltd. v. William Hill (Football) Ltd.*, [1964] 1 All ER 465, HL.
34. See the French decision of *Ed. Législatives v. T. Erhmann*, TGI, 28 December 1998, (1999) 183 RIDA 256 where copyright protection was granted to an electronic database comprising several hundred collective agreements on a CD-ROM on the grounds that there was an original thematic presentation of the data which reflected the creative contribution of the author.
35. *Feist Publications v. Rural Telephone Service Co.*, (1991) 499 US 340, at pp. 345, 359–60.
36. Section 101, US Copyright Act 1976.
37. US Copyright Office, *Report on Legal Protection for Databases*, 1997, at 3–7, http://lcweb.loc.gov/copyright/reports; and also see Pollack, M., 'The Right to Know? Delimiting Database Protection at the Juncture of the Commerce Clause, the Intellectual Property Clause and the First Amendment', *Cardozo Arts and Entertainment Law Journal*, 17, 47, 1999, at 51–2.
38. *Feist Publications v. Rural Telephone Service Co.*, (1991) 499 US 340, at 345–6.
39. WIPO Basic Proposal for the Substantive Provisions of the Treaty on Intellectual Property in respect of Databases, Diplomatic Conference, Geneva, 2–20 December 1996, Doc. CRNR/DC/6 (30 August 1996) (WIPO Proposal).
40. Article 11, EC Directive 96/9/EC.
41. However, the US did, on the basis of the reciprocity provision of the Database Directive, place the EU on the Priority Watch List in its 1998 Special 301 review.
42. US Patent and Trademark Office Report, Department of Commerce: Washington, July 1998, available at http://www.uspto.gov/web/offices/dcom/olia/dbconf/dbase498.htm.
43. EC Green Paper on Copyright and Related Rights in the Information Society, COM(95) 382 final, Brussels, 19/07/1995, at 13–15, 32.
44. Recital 39, EC Directive 96/9/EC.

45. US Constitution, Article 1, § 8, cl. 8.

46. See *Feist*, (1991) 499 US at 348–50, 362–4.

47. The various bills are as follows: Consumer Access to Information Act of 2004, HR 3872, 108th Cong. (2004); Database and Collections of Information Misappropriation Act, HR 3261, 108th Cong. (2003); Collections of Information Antipiracy Act, HR 354, 106th Cong. (1999); Consumer and Investor Access to Information Act, HR 1858, 106th Cong. (1999); Collections of Information Antipiracy Act, HR 2652, 105th Cong. (1998); Database Investment and Intellectual Property Antipiracy Act of 1996 HR 3531, 104th Cong. (1996). For a comparative review of the US bills and the EU Directive, see Suthersanen, U., 'A Comparative Review of Database Protection in the European Union and United States', in F. Dessemontet and R. Gani (eds), *Creative Ideas for Intellectual Property*, Lausanne: CEDIDAC, 2002, at 49–89.

48. Article 7(2)(a), EC Directive 96/9/EC; similar to Article 2(ii), WIPO Proposal.

49. Article 7(2)(b), EC Directive 96/9/EC.

50. Recitals 33 and 43, EC Directive 96/9/EC, emphasising that every on-line service, or a material copy of the contents of such service, is in fact subject to authorisation of either the copyright or database right holder.

51. Recitals 45 and 46, EC Directive 96/9/EC.

52. Recital 44, EC Directive 96/9/EC.

53. Recital 42, EC Directive 96/9/EC.

54. Articles 10(1), (2), EC Directive 96/9/EC.

55. C-203/02 (*The British Horseracing Board Ltd. and Others v. William Hill Organisation Ltd*).

56. Recital 55, EC Directive 96/9/EC.

57. Article 7(5), EC Directive 96/9/EC – the right to stop such endemic utilisation extends to insubstantial parts of the database.

58. Chalton, S., 'The Copyright and Rights in Databases Regulation 1997: Some Outstanding Issues on Implementation of the Database Directive', *European Intellectual Property Review*, 178, 1998; Vanovermeine, V., 'The Concept of the Lawful User in the Database Directive', IIC, 31, 63, 2000 (with discussion on the Belgian implementation of the Directive); Also see the early Commission attempt to define the lawful user as a person 'having acquired a right to use the database', Explanatory Memorandum to Initial Proposal for a Council Directive on the Legal Protection of Databases, 1992 OJ C156/4.

59. See Vanovermeine *op. cit.*, at 78.

60. Article 8(1), Database Directive.

61. *Ibid.*, Article 9(a).

62. *Ibid.*, Article 9(b)

63. *Ibid.*, Article 9(c).

64. Also, see recitals 50 and 51, Database Directive.

65. Article 8(2), Database Directive.

66. Commission of the European Communities, 'DG Internal Market and Services Working Paper: First evaluation of Directive 96/9/EC on the Legal Protection of Databases', 12 December 2005, Brussels.

67. Cases C-46/02 (*Fixtures Marketing Ltd. v. Oy Veikkaus Ab*); C-203/02 (*The British Horseracing Board Ltd. and Others v. William Hill Organisation Ltd.*); C-338/02 (*Fixtures Marketing Ltd v. AB Svenska Spel*) and C-444/02 (*Fixtures Marketing Ltd. v. Organismos prognostikon agonon podosfairou AE – 'OPAP'*).

68. Commission of the European Communities, 'DG Internal Market and Services Working Paper', *op. cit.*, at p. 15.

PART III

Themes and threads

9. International human rights and intellectual property

The relationship between intellectual property and human rights is an intriguing one, raising many interesting questions for policy-makers. For example, can there be a true and proper scope of intellectual property rights unless the provisions are grounded in fundamental freedoms and rights? The relationship is also complicated and controversial. Paradoxically, there are people within the ranks of both supporters and critics of intellectual property who would like to see the future debate on intellectual property rights reframed as a human rights issue.[1] Others on both sides of the fence would prefer that human rights talk be kept out of it. Clearly, given the contradictory viewpoints, not all the reasons for framing intellectual property as a human rights issue can be valid, and it is possible that none of them are. One must also wonder, in this context, whether the parameters of the debate inevitably shift radically depending on whether we are focusing on international or national intellectual property and human rights laws.

Both classical and modern rights theories state that the existence and exercise of some rights presuppose the existence of other rights. Rights of freedom, for example, should be accompanied by welfare rights, whereas the right to education aids the exercise of a right of freedom of speech.[2] It has been further argued that the rights created through the enactment of intellectual property laws are instrumental rights, and such rights, including copyright, should serve the interests and needs that citizens identify through the language of human rights as being fundamental, for example, access to health and access to education.

Seen in this light, it is possible to argue that international intellectual property instruments like TRIPS, while supporting the legitimate rights of some people, may be doing so at the cost of eroding internationally accepted 'über-values' such as education, economic development and health.

This chapter explores the idea of human rights, considers human rights norms relating to creative individuals, and discusses the relationship between contemporary international human rights rules and intellectual property rights.

THE NATURE OF HUMAN RIGHTS

International laws recognise that there is a relevant nexus between international human rights instruments and intellectual property policies and laws, despite the recent stance taken by the United Nations Commission on Human Rights in the form, *inter alia,* of its Resolution 2000/7, which is discussed below.[3] Newer international intellectual property rights instruments, such as the TRIPS Agreement and the WIPO copyright treaties, do recognise that some balance is required between intellectual property rights and social and economic welfare, public health and nutrition. International law and policy-making should, as a matter of course, be reframed from a human rights perspective. Sometimes, however, this re-contextualisation brings forth further dilemmas. How should we balance the need to reward authors and inventors, with the need to ensure dissemination of technological, scientific, health and educational goods? How should governments balance the economic need to exploit a country's genetic and informational resources, against the rights of indigenous groups to control their knowledge and cultural resources? Should certain types of usage be outside the domain of intellectual property law, or should the author/inventor as a matter of human right, be allowed to participate in all types of economic exploitation?

We adopt the view that the primary ethos is to *try* to achieve the optimal balance between public and private interests and needs: all human rights and freedoms are a compromise between different stakeholders and a perfect balance is probably unattainable. However, we argue that the human rights perspective should, at the end of the day, prevail over the economic perspective. We acknowledge that this is a paradox: rights for authors and inventors are recognised human rights, and as such, co-exist on an equal footing with rights of citizens to free speech or to access essential medicines. The stance we take is that intellectual property rights, if *applied* properly, should and can promote a communitarian and humanitarian society.

This is no less true for property rights more generally. Early Enlightenment theories claimed that property rights emanated from the *natural* rights of man. The Lockean justification for property rights is very much embedded in man's property right in his own person, and in the products of his labour. Far from being a firm supporter of absolute private property centred on an individual, though, Locke's philosophy on rights and property has a rather socialist bent in that he typifies property rights as being a social good, arising from the law of nature, or man's natural right to the fruits of his labour, a right which is so powerful that even sovereigns and governments are powerless against it. One can even discern the fundamentals of a human rights framework in the following passage in the *Second Treatise*:

> The state of nature has a law of nature to govern it, which obliges every one; and reason, which is that law, teaches all mankind who will but consult it that, being all equal and independent, no one ought to harm another in his life, health, liberty or possessions . . .[4]

A more recent authority who supports the notion that good government and successful societies are based on freedom and respect for human rights is Nobel laureate economist Amartya Sen:

> . . . we also have to understand the remarkable empirical connection that links freedoms of different kinds with one another. Political freedoms (in the form of free speech and elections) help to promote economic security. Social opportunities (in the form of education and health facilities) facilitate economic participation. Economic facilities (in the form of opportunities for participation in trade and production) can help generate personal abundance as well as public resources for social facilities. Freedoms of different kinds can strengthen one another.[5]

What are 'human rights'? According to one definition, they are 'a set of claims and entitlements to human dignity, which the existing international regime assumes will be provided (or threatened) by the state'.[6]

The 1948 Universal Declaration of Human Rights (UDHR) offers a broader notion based around an ethical rights-based society which focuses on the 'just distribution of material and non-material advantages'. The Declaration thus seeks to guarantee everyone a dignified livelihood with opportunities for personal attainment.[7] Human rights are not merely concerned with fighting for liberation from unjust regimes; rather they concern also the myriad everyday struggles to maintain a balance between the material and moral well-being of different individuals and groups within a society.

This more holistic approach, which is further reflected in the two legally binding 1966 covenants, the International Covenant on Economic, Social and Cultural Rights (the ICESCR), and the International Covenant on Civil and Political Rights (the ICCPR), can be employed to support the following typology of human rights falling within three 'generations':

(i) Classical (individual) civil and political rights This category is the traditional bastion of rights which guarantees the rights of the private individual such as the right to life, liberty and human dignity. Sometimes also included are rights of political participation and democratic governance. Some European courts have emphasised that the rights to human dignity and personal development constitute the basis for moral rights under copyright law (see Chapter 4); moreover, this right has been important to limit the extent of patent protection on biotechnological material (see Chapter 13).

(ii)   Newer (individual) social, economic, and cultural human rights   The second generation of rights obliges public authorities to take active measures to provide for the community by granting individual rights to property, food, health care, labour and education. This set of human rights reflects the current discourse as to how intellectual property rights can affect access to knowledge and essential medicines. The debate is not new: in 1769, Mr Justice Yates argued against a perpetual or indefinite copyright stating that it would lead to anti-competitive practices, excessive pricing, and would further go against the 'natural rights of mankind in the exercise of their trade and calling', as it would restrain the natural right to labour of printers and booksellers.[8]

(iii)   Third generation (collective) human rights   This new category secures collective rights, which include rights to membership in a cultural or indigenous community, access to a healthy environment, and rights to development or self-determination.[9] The third generation of rights has much relevance today in the claims for protection of traditional knowledge, and for protection against excessive exploitation of indigenous knowledge by ethno-bioprospecting (see Chapter 14).

THE RIGHTS OF AUTHORS AND INVENTORS IN HUMAN RIGHTS LAW

There are nine core international human rights instruments, but the three most important intellectual property-related documents are the Universal Declaration of Human Rights 1948, the ICESCR 1966 and the ICCPR 1966, which together form part of the International Bill of Human Rights,[10] and can be viewed as the constitutional-like basis of human rights norms. The analysis of all these instruments is useful here, since they can be employed to bind states to design an intellectual property rights system that strikes a balance between promoting general public interests in areas of health, culture and education, whilst protecting the property rights of authors and inventors.

The Universal Declaration of Human Rights

The UDHR was adopted and proclaimed by the General Assembly of the United Nations in 1948. Although not intended to be a legally binding document, it is nevertheless an astounding document as it offers a universal moral code to 'every individual and every organ of society'[11] and was born due to the 'disregard and contempt for human rights'[12] which had resulted in the Second World War.

The primary 'intellectual property' provision is Article 27, UDHR. On the one hand, the provision prescribes rights for '*moral and material interests resulting from any scientific, literary or artistic production*' (emphasis added).[13] This is further complemented elsewhere in the Declaration by a provision which declares that everyone has the 'right to own property alone as well as in association with others', and that no one should be 'arbitrarily deprived' of his property.[14] A further basis which adopts the position that personal property is central to individual dignity is Article 12, UDHR which provides protection against interference with 'privacy, family, home or correspondence' and against attacks upon 'honour and reputation'. This may be viewed as a further basis for certain types of specific rights which exist within the broader intellectual property framework, such as an action for breach of confidence, trade secrets, moral rights, and even personality rights.

The 1966 International Covenants

Nearly 20 years later, two covenants were adopted to make the UDHR freedoms binding as a matter of international treaty law. The ICCPR does not offer a positive basis for the protection of intellectual property rights, but it does guarantee the protection of moral rights indirectly by insisting that there be no unlawful attacks on an individual's honour and reputation.[15] Further indirect guarantees for property and reputational rights can be found in the provision dealing with freedom of expression. Everyone is guaranteed the right to freedom of expression, which includes the right to receive and impart information and ideas; this right, nevertheless, is conditional on respecting the rights or reputations of others which are prescribed by law and are necessary.[16]

The ICESCR recognises at a general level that a nation's social and economic development is realised by improving methods of production, conservation and distribution of resources through technical and scientific knowledge and by developing efficient systems so as to achieve efficient development and utilisation of resources.[17] On a specific level, the ICESCR guarantees (or appears to guarantee) the protection of intellectual property as a human right for all creators.

Article 15, ICESCR, reads as follows:

1. The States Parties to the present Covenant recognize the right of everyone:
   a. To take part in cultural life;
   b. To enjoy the benefits of scientific progress and its applications;
   c. To benefit from *the protection of the moral and material interests* resulting from any scientific, literary or artistic production of which he is the author.
2. The steps to be taken by the States Parties to the present Covenant to achieve the full realization of this right shall include those necessary for the conservation, the development and the diffusion of *science and culture*.

3. The States Parties to the present Covenant undertake to respect the freedom indispensable for *scientific research and creative activity*.
4. The States Parties to the present Covenant recognize the benefits to be derived from the encouragement and development of international contacts and co-operation in the *scientific and cultural fields* (emphasis added).

Article 15 identifies a need to balance the protection of both public and private interests in intellectual property. The traditional interpretation of Article 15 is that it promotes access to scientific and cultural goods, whilst guaranteeing the protection of those 'authors' (including inventors, designers, etc.) of scientific and cultural goods, without specifying the modalities of such protection.[18] This reading of the law allows one to regard intellectual property rights as human rights. This view is further reinforced in national and regional jurisprudence. Indeed, in a recent ground-breaking decision, the European Court of Human Rights held that intellectual property 'undeniably attracted the protection of Article 1 of Protocol No. 1' of the European Convention on Human Rights. Furthermore, this protection extends also to trade mark registration.[19]

Article 15, ICESCR also recognizes the right of everyone to take part in cultural life and to enjoy the benefits of scientific progress and its applications. The delicate balance between the commercial and cultural needs of authors and of society can perhaps be achieved if national or regional intellectual property laws respect the communitarian needs mentioned in paragraphs 2, 3 and 4 of the provision, that is, conservation, development, diffusion, freedom and cooperation. Taking these two aspects of Article 15 together, ICESCR could be said to bind states to design intellectual property systems that strike a balance between promoting cultural and public interest needs in accessing knowledge as easily as possible whilst simultaneously benefiting the authors and inventors who create, produce and disseminate such knowledge.

The 2005 General Comment on Article 15(1)(c), ICESCR

A surprising *volte face* in respect of the issue of whether intellectual property rights are human rights can be seen in the 2005 General Comment on the interpretation of Article 15(1)(c) that was adopted by the UN Committee on Economic, Social and Cultural Rights.[20] First, although it is acknowledged within the General Comment that Article 15(1)(c) guarantees *some* sort of protection, the Comment nevertheless concludes that Article 15, ICESCR cannot be interpreted as guaranteeing intellectual property rights or as elevating intellectual property to the human rights stratosphere.[21] Instead, it states that human rights in this context does not 'necessarily reflect the level and means of protection found in present copyright, patent and other intellectual property regimes'. In other words, Article 15(1)(c) can be satisfied by other means.[22] This has never really been a controversial point and historically protection for authors and inventors has always been satisfied by a variety of mixed legal regimes including liability rule regimes[23] and criminal laws.

The interpretation is surprising as this does not necessarily reflect the accepted national conventions and norms in many countries where intellectual property rights have a strong deontological and constitutional basis, often based on fundamental human rights principles. The problem is that there is an over-emphasis on corporate ownership of intellectual property rights, and an under-emphasis on the natural human rights which vest in individual creators, and the need for creators (and not producers) to be concretely recognised as influential stakeholders in today's knowledge market. The following paragraph from the General Comment describes but could be construed as endorsing this inherent bias within the whole General Comment:[24]

> Whereas the human right to benefit from the protection of the moral and material interests resulting from one's scientific, literary and artistic productions safeguards the personal link between authors and their creations and between peoples, communities, or other groups and their collective cultural heritage, as well as their basic material interests which are necessary to enable authors to enjoy an adequate standard of living, *intellectual property regimes primarily protect business and corporate interests and investments* (emphasis added).[25]

Moreover, the Comment is confusing in that its definition of 'authors' clearly leaves out inventors, whilst emphasising 'writers and artists', and yet includes the 'creator'; its definition of 'scientific productions' includes

> creations of the human mind, that is to 'scientific productions', such as scientific publications and innovations, including knowledge, innovations and practices of indigenous and local communities.[26]

The notion of knowledge and innovation is incredibly broad, and yet there appears to be a conscious effort to exclude the concept of 'invention', which is the dominant subject matter of international and national patent law. And yet, surely, inventors are authors of scientific innovations and are entitled to authorial rights? Indeed, the General Comment appears to discriminate between different types of individual creators, be they individual inventors who are employed within a multinational corporation, or indigenous communities. Of course, when one further reads the General Comment, one notices that the drafters do realise that Article 15(1)(c) extends to inventions and inventors, as reference is often made to patent law. Nevertheless, we point this out as one example of the confusing stance and language within the General Comment.

A more constructive interpretation of Article 15(1)(c) would not, we submit, have so resolutely denied human rights status to individual human beings who create. From the conventional Anglo-American and common law perspective, intellectual property rights are viewed primarily as an economic or legal tool embodied in the rights to 'ownership' with concepts such as 'exclusive use', 'monopoly' and the like attached to inventions and creative works. Yet, the notion of 'moral and material interests' encourages one to go further than the traditional bifurcated approach within intellectual property law of economic rights versus societal needs. Indeed, the more conventional civil law perspective has always been that the protection of authors and inventors are both economic *and* cultural issues, with pecuniary and humanistic elements imbibed in both sets of laws protecting works and inventions. This was perhaps a lost opportunity for the drafters of the General Comment to invite nations and legislators to consider the natural humanistic social and economic rights and obligations which exist within the entire intellectual property regime, especially in relation to the phrase 'moral and material interests'.

There is an inextricable link between the author and his work that is part of the higher hierarchy of rights. The General Comment, in fact, recognises this link when it states that

> The protection of the 'moral interests' of authors was one of the main concerns of the drafters of article 27, paragraph 2, of the Universal Declaration of Human Rights . . . The Committee *stresses the importance of recognizing the value* of scientific, literary and artistic productions as expressions of the personality of their creator, and notes that protection of moral interests can be found, although to a varying extent, in most States, regardless of the legal system in force (emphasis added).[27]

Most civil law countries do have provisions which espouse the notion that some benefit-sharing must occur, especially where the invention or work is of benefit to the employer-owner of the patent. Nevertheless, many common law countries ignore this human right of creators, or offer weak recognition, for example, US law which does not afford strong moral rights to authors of literary or musical works, for instance under its federal intellectual property laws. Another area where international guidance would have been welcomed is in relation to creations made by an employee, where the universal rule appears to be that the employer is the owner of the intellectual property right. The General Comment further recognises that intellectual property rights are linked, due to their economic dimension, to other human rights including rights to the opportunity to gain one's living by work which one freely chooses,[28] to adequate remuneration,[29] and to the human right to an adequate standard of living.[30]

We submit that the proper interpretation of Article 15(1)(c) implies an agreement by the international community that a '*right*' to intellectual property is a human right, which is vested in *individual creators*. Moreover, rather than curtail intellectual property rights, perhaps the correct view is that most intellectual property laws are still in the early stages, and have yet to be properly aligned to ensure compulsory benefit-sharing safeguards for the individual creators, that intellectual property rights are inherently rights regarding the protection of:

1.   human dignity, in that 'moral interests' allow copyright and patent laws to recognise that authors and inventors have the moral right of attribution; and
2.   authors' and inventors' rights to remuneration, in that 'material interests' include the economic right to exploit a work or invention, and the social right as an author or inventor to equitable remuneration and/or employee benefits.[31]

Furthermore, all other provisions within intellectual property law must be subjected to 1 and 2 above.

Surely, such a stance within international human rights law would signal the need for countries, *and* the WTO, to interpret national, regional and supranational intellectual property laws within such a human rights framework.

HUMAN RIGHTS IN INTERNATIONAL INTELLECTUAL PROPERTY LAW

The Berne Convention and Human Rights

Further muted international legal support for the proposition that copyright is a human right lies in the Solemn Declaration adopted in the 1986 Centenary Assembly of the Berne Union, where member states declared, *inter alia*, the following:

> … that copyright is based on human rights and justice and that authors, as creators
> of beauty, entertainment and learning, deserve that their rights in their creation be
> recognized and effectively protected both in their own country and in all other countries of their world;[32]

It is worth noting that this is the only international intellectual property treaty that makes reference to human rights, even if the form adopted (that is, a solemn declaration) is legally ambiguous.

Conversely, it is argued that intellectual property cannot possibly be a form of human rights as this would be counter to the social and ethical aims of international human rights law. This line of argument notes that human rights obligations under most of the international documents advocate reward for the creative acts of individuals, whereas most national intellectual property laws are framed and justified as economic instruments which serve market, and coincidentally, public interests. Intellectual property rights may also be *one* way, though not necessarily the best way, of fulfilling obligations to reward individual authors and inventors. Examples of the latter are authors' moral rights and indigenous peoples' rights over their ancestral knowledge.

Moreover, although inventors and authors are the named creators, most intellectual property-protected works are owned by corporations, who are not necessarily entitled to *human* rights. Indeed, many argue that intellectual property rights should, on this basis, be recognised as 'intellectual monopoly privileges',[33] rather than as human rights.[34] It is, thus, understandable that there is much scepticism about a human rights-based intellectual property framework from those fully aware that most of the rights are vested in multinational corporations. A further argument is that *some* intellectual property rights exclude too many important actors, and thus, paradoxically, violate human rights norms where there is a clear cause-and-effect relationship between pricing, access and property rights. Examples include patent laws which result in a denial of access to affordable health care and/or essential drugs; intellectual property laws which protect seeds of staple crops and may negatively impact on the livelihoods of farming communities too poor to buy them; and copyright laws which deny access to vital textbooks in developing countries with low public education budgets.

TRIPS and Human Rights

It used to be that international trade law and international human rights law rarely interacted, but rather co-existed within what is an extremely broad international framework of legal and regulatory norms. This changed with the entry into force of the Agreement Establishing the World Trade Organization. Intellectual property has played a large part in forcing a re-evaluation of the relationship between these two pillars of international law. One trigger for this re-evaluation has been the public reaction to the HIV/AIDs epidemic crisis in South Africa, a story which cast this social problem from the developing countries' perspective against the backdrop of globalisation and a TRIPS Agreement which made it mandatory for all WTO countries to include patent protection for pharmaceutical products (see Chapter 13).

Articles 7 and 8
If one argues that the TRIPS Agreement overrides the mandate of members to implement national legislation as they see fit, the question then is whether the

TRIPS Agreement must be interpreted and implemented in light of international human rights norms. Traditionally, some WTO members have instituted and maintained the balancing act between property rights of individuals and corporations on the one hand, and societal rights of access to technological and cultural innovations, access to public health and educational facilities. This has been done either through limiting property rights or mandating compulsory licences to government authorities. This autonomy is also in line with the Declaration on the Right to Development, which was adopted by the United Nations General Assembly by Resolution 41/128 of 4 December 1986:

> States have the right and the duty to formulate appropriate national development policies that aim at the constant improvement of the well-being of the entire population and of all individuals, on the basis of their active, free and meaningful participation in development and in the fair distribution of the benefits resulting therefrom.[35]

One argument is that Articles 7 and 8 of the Agreement set out a human rights mandate. Indeed, these two provisions neatly provide all the relevant linkages between human rights and intellectual property rights, including public health, nutrition, environment, innovation and development. A generous and uncontroversial interpretation of these two provisions is that a balance must be struck between the 'public' and 'private' interests of producers, users and society.[36] Moreover, the provisions mirror some of the same objectives as international human rights legislation, especially the ICESCR.[37] Thus, Articles 7 and 8 should perhaps be seen as placing cultural, educational, health, free speech and development considerations on a par with, if not above, intellectual property rights.

Article 7 sets out the objectives of the TRIPS Agreement by clarifying that intellectual property rights are not an end in themselves. Instead, intellectual property protection and enforcement

> should contribute to the promotion of technological innovation and to the transfer and dissemination of technology, to the mutual advantage of producers and users of technological knowledge and in a manner conducive to social and economic welfare, and to a balance of rights and obligations.

Article 8 reminds us that members can tailor their national regimes to 'protect public health and nutrition, and to promote the public interest in sectors of vital importance to their socio-economic and technological development'. Such measures can also include laws which prevent market abuse or restraint of international transfer of technology. Moreover, Article 8, read with Article 40 on anti-competitive measures, should be implemented by countries to prevent the abuse of intellectual property rights so as to ensure a more equitable and just market.

Two points should be noted. First, there are no equivalent provisions in other international intellectual property instruments such as the Paris Convention or the Berne Convention, as such overriding principles and objectives are usually to be found in national laws. The presence of these provisions clearly indicates the shift from national to international governance of intellectual property rights. Second, the fact that these provisions have been interpreted differently by members reflects, not surprisingly, the inherent tension in contemporary intellectual property policy-making.[38]

A correlated issue is whether the principles set out in Articles 7 and 8 are expressed in terms of exceptions to the rule, rather than as the guiding principles in themselves. As stated in one report:

> A human rights approach, on the other hand, would explicitly place the promotion and protection of human rights, in particular those in ICESCR, at the heart of the objectives of intellectual property protection, rather than only as permitted exceptions that are subordinated to the other provisions of the Agreement.[39]

This tension culminated in the interpretation of these provisions by the Doha Ministerial Declaration on the TRIPS Agreement and Public Health where the issue was whether Article 8 allows countries to take whatever steps they need, irrespective of the TRIPS Agreement (for example, can countries override patent protection in order to make or import generic medicines?). Indeed, should Articles 7 and 8 be interpreted in light of Article XX, GATT 1994, which overrides trade rules in order to protect human life or health?[40]

The Doha Declaration clarified the ambit of both Articles 7 and 8 by stating that these provisions may be of more importance in interpreting the Agreement than other provisions, including the Preamble (which is biased towards rights owners).[41] Moreover, human rights considerations are clearly to be part and parcel of the interpretative matrix within the TRIPS Agreement, as the Declaration clearly states that

> the Agreement can and should be interpreted and implemented in a manner supportive of the WTO Members' right to protect public health and, in particular, to promote access to medicines for all.[42]

PRIMACY OF HUMAN RIGHTS LAW OVER ECONOMIC LAW

Out of the 149 members of WTO that have undertaken to implement the minimum standards of intellectual property protection in the TRIPS Agreement, 111 have ratified ICESCR. WTO members thus have a double duty to implement the minimum standards of the TRIPS Agreement bearing in mind their human rights obligations. How do countries proceed to implement this theoretical position in a practical manner? Can we, and should we, interpret the TRIPS Agreement as safeguarding only trade interests? Or should the TRIPS Agreement be read in light of the importance of upholding the needs and interests of all market actors, including corporations and individual human beings? Such an interpretation would naturally include human rights interests.

In the past decade, resolutions and reports produced by the UN Commission on Human Rights in the area of intellectual property rights and trade have all been in agreement on one point: that there is a need for law makers to take international human rights into account in international economic policy formulation, and indeed, emphasising the primacy of the former over the latter. In all these resolutions and reports, there is no suggestion, of course, that intellectual property rights *per se* conflict with human rights, but rather that the problems lie in the implementation of the TRIPS Agreement. The implication is that there must be a concerted attempt to interpret TRIPS as if human rights norms and considerations were part of the drafting process.

What do these reports and resolutions specifically state? Resolution 2000/7 on intellectual property and human rights concluded

> . . . that since the implementation of the TRIPS Agreement does not adequately reflect the fundamental nature and indivisibility of all human rights, including the right of everyone to enjoy the benefits of scientific progress and its applications, the right to health, the right to food and the right to self-determination, there are apparent conflicts between the intellectual property rights regime embodied in the TRIPS Agreement, on the one hand, and international human rights law, on the other . . .[43]

The Resolution set out the following areas of actual or potential conflicts between human rights and intellectual property rights:

- impediments resulting from the application of intellectual property rights to the transfer of technology to developing countries;
- the consequences of plant variety rights and the patenting of genetically modified organisms for the enjoyment of the basic right to food;
- the reduction of control by communities (especially indigenous communities) over their own genetic and natural resources and cultural values, leading to accusations of 'biopiracy';
- restrictions on access to patented pharmaceuticals and the implications for the enjoyment of a basic right to health.[44]

Resolution 2001/21, adopted the following year, confirmed this stance, recommending an analysis into:

- whether the patent 'as a legal instrument' was compatible with the promotion and protection of human rights; and
- the impact of the TRIPS Agreement on the rights of indigenous peoples.[45]

We have investigated and analysed such issues throughout this book. Our critique highlights the difficulty faced by the legislator in drawing up a set of rules in relation to human rights vis-à-vis intellectual property law. Part of this problem lies in the fact that the rights discussed can be viewed as being there for the benefit of individuals *and* the community as a whole. The query is not whether courts should adopt a more human-rights approach, but what such an approach entails? How do international and national legislators and courts interpret esoteric phrases such as 'to take part in cultural life', or 'to enjoy the benefits of scientific progress'?

According to the 2001 Report of the High Commissioner,[46] governments should be reminded of the primacy of human rights obligations over economic policies and agreements. This report identifies that intellectual property rights contained in TRIPS 'might be a means of operationalizing article 15' of the ICESCR as long as the grant and exercise of those rights promotes and protects human rights.[47] This corresponds to the view of some jurists that there is no conflict between a universally recognised human right and a commitment ensuing from an international trade agreement since 'the trade regime recognizes that human rights are fundamental and prior to free trade itself'.[48] A human rights approach would strike the public-private balance by setting international human rights laws above international economic laws, thereby promoting and protecting human rights, rather than ensuring protection of economic investment.[49]

Subsequent chapters will consider human rights implications in the specific context of the subject matter covered in those chapters, except for freedom of expression, which is discussed here.

FREEDOM OF EXPRESSION

The Preamble to the Universal Declaration of Human Rights states that 'freedom of speech and belief and freedom from fear and want has been proclaimed as the highest aspiration of the common people'. The ICCPR guarantees the right to freedom of expression, which includes the right to receive and impart information and ideas. The right is curtailed by Article 19(2), ICCPR which sets out that the right to freedom of expression and information is conditional on respecting the 'rights or reputations of others', and on protecting 'the national security or public order (*ordre public*), or of public health or morals'. The phrase 'rights or reputations of others' can, and does, refer to copyright and trade mark protection.

The European Convention on Human Rights mirrors much of the Universal Declaration, though it goes further in providing for the establishment of the European Court of Human Rights. Hence, the jurisprudence emanating from the European Court offers some guidelines as to national implementation of global human rights norms. Below is a brief précis of case law from this court, showing a lenient approach to usage of property works for human rights cases especially in relation to media reporting.

Freedom of Expression and the Public Interest[50]

The correlation between factual expressions, freedom of expression and the public interest is important where the media uses intellectual property-protected works to convey a news story. In particular, the dilemma arises from the use of copyright law to capture authentic versions of text or images and to forbid the employment of such texts/images in the course of news-reporting activities.

In the British decision of *Hyde Park Residences v. Yelland*, the lower court allowed media use of photographs of Princess Diana and Dodi Fayed just before their deaths. The court was of the view that copyright protection should be restricted as these particular photographs were carriers of information conveying the facts about the visit by both deceased parties to the Villa Windsor the day before their fatal accident rather than photographs conveying intrinsic beauty or artistic content. The trial judge's view echoed what was to become the *raison d'etre* for the global Access to Knowledge campaign (see Chapter 12). This is that the public interest clearly applied in the context of 'communication of what is essentially information – information clothed in copyright'.[51] The UK Court of Appeals rejected this approach holding that there was no excuse for using copyright-protected photographs when the information conveyed by the photographs could have been conveyed in words, rather than images.

It is clear that photographs are, in fact, one of the most convincing and credible means of reporting to the public. One only has to consider the famous examples of the My Lai massacre and the Kennedy assassination, to realise that words cannot describe or substitute for the visually conveyed 'idea' underlying a photograph.[52] Moreover, according to European Court of Human Rights jurisprudence, courts should not substitute their judgements as to what is the best manner for reporting a particular news item.

Thus, in *Fressoz and Roire v. France*,[53] the Court was unambiguous in its view that the taking of the form or expression of the work may be allowed if journalists need some credibility in order to authenticate their reports. The Court observed:

> In essence, [the right to freedom of expression] leaves it for journalists to decide whether or not it is necessary to reproduce such documents to ensure credibility. It protects journalists' right to divulge information on issues of general interest

provided that they are acting in good faith and on an accurate factual basis and provide 'reliable and precise' information in accordance with the ethics of journalism.[54]

The Court was far more forthright and explicit as to the right of freedom of expression in *News Verlags GmbH & Cokg v. Austria*.[55] The essential message of the Court is that under certain circumstances, property rights must be set aside to allow free speech usage. The Court held that freedom of expression protects the freedom in choosing the form as well as the substance of the ideas and information to be conveyed.[56] Moreover, the Court emphasised that the important issue was whether any interference with the human right of freedom of expression was 'necessary in a democratic society', which is to say that free speech rights can only be interfered with if there is a *pressing social need* for the measure taken.

There is, undoubtedly, a major flaw in intellectual property law in that existing exceptions and limitations are not governed by coherent international rules but are *ad hoc* home-grown provisions which tend to assume that intellectual property laws are compatible with international human rights norms. A second difficulty is that national courts tend to treat a defendant's claims based on human rights as an attempt by the defendant to invoke a defence to an infringement of an intellectual property right. This is a wrong approach as any counter-argument based on human rights calls for a balancing exercise between two competing and equal sets of positive rights.

Culture Jamming and Constitutional Health in South Africa

A key function of a trade mark is to convey information about a product or service. In a few instances, this function takes on an extra dimension as some trade marks evolve into cultural, scientific and quality icons. In such cases, can the trade mark be used without permission from the intellectual property owner under the guise of 'cultural' or 'free speech' rights?

In *Laugh It Off v. South African Breweries International*[57] the applicant, Laugh It Off (LIO), produced T-shirts that parodied the Carling Black Label trade mark. The trade mark states:

America's lusty, lively beer
Carling
Black Label
Beer
Brewed in South Africa

LIO substituted the original advertising phrase of the mark with their own words:

Africa's lusty, lively exploitation since 1652
White
Black Labour
Guilt
No regard given worldwide

The respondent South African Breweries (SAB), which happens to be the world's second largest brewery, sued for trade mark infringement.[58] SAB argued that LIO was operating a commercial undertaking with the aim of making money and thus did not have the freedom of expression as its main purpose. In the court of first instance SAB was successful in restraining LIO from using its trade mark. LIO unsuccessfully appealed to the Supreme Court of Appeal, which held that the constitutional right to freedom of expression did not include parody because it fed off the reputation of the trade mark in order to sell the T-shirts. The final appeal was to the South African Constitutional Court, which reversed the decision and held for LIO.

LIO's arguments were based on the provision for freedom of expression in section 16 of the South African Constitution which states that everyone has the right to freedom of expression, which includes:

- freedom of the press and other media;
- freedom to receive or impart information or ideas;
- freedom of artistic creativity; and
- academic freedom and freedom of scientific research.

LIO argued that its actions should be seen as a form of corporate attack called 'culture jamming' which uses parodies to provide social comments on brands, and attacks the use of intellectual property laws by large corporations to stifle freedom of expression and thought. Moreover, LIO asserted that the right to freedom of expression protects the right to communicate these messages and SAB can only prevent them from using the trade mark if they can prove that they will suffer economic harm as a result of the parody. LIO defined its use of SAB's trade mark as 'ideological jujitsu'.[59]

In a fascinating decision, the South African Constitutional Court held that intellectual property rights do not enjoy equality with other rights in the Constitution. The Court expressed difficulty in guaranteeing the right to freedom of expression as enshrined in the South African Constitution while protecting intellectual property rights, and concluded that trade mark infringement can be justified on the grounds of freedom of expression. The Court further stated that in a society dominated by brands, there must be scope for criticism, and that corporations should not use trade mark law indiscriminately to stifle public debate. The concluding remark is noteworthy:

This brings me to the second consideration of special constitutional import. The Constitution cannot oblige the dour to laugh. It can, however, prevent the cheerless from snuffing out the laughter of the blithe spirits among us. . . . And I can see no reason in principle why a joke against the government can be tolerated, but one at the expense of what used to be called Big Business, cannot. . . . A society that takes itself too seriously risks bottling up its tensions and treating every example of irreverence as a threat to its existence. Humour is one of the great solvents of democracy. It permits the ambiguities and contradictions of public life to be articulated in nonviolent forms. It promotes diversity. It enables a multitude of discontents to be expressed in a myriad of spontaneous ways. It is an elixir of constitutional health.[60]

NOTES

1. See UN Economic and Social Council, Commission on Human Rights, Sub-Commission on the Promotion and Protection of Human Rights, 'Intellectual Property Rights and Human Rights: Report of the Secretary General'. 14 June 2001 [Document E/CN.4/Sub.2/2001/12].
2. Drahos, P., 'Intellectual Property and Human Rights', *Intellectual Property Quarterly*, 3, 349–71, 1999, at 367.
3. UN Commission on Human Rights, Sub-Commission on the Promotion and Protection of Human Rights, 'Intellectual Property Rights and Human Rights', Resolution 2000/7, 17 August 2000, para. 1 [Document E/CN.4/Sub.2/2000/2000/7].
4. In McPherson, C.B. (ed.), *John Locke Second Treatise of Government,* Indianapolis, IN and Cambridge, UK: Hackett Publishing Company, 1980, chapter II, section 6.
5. Sen, A., *Development as Freedom*, New York: Knopf, 1999, at 3–4, 10–11.
6. Brysk, A., 'Transnational Threats and Opportunities', in A. Brysk (ed.), *Globalization and Human Rights*, Berkeley, CA: University of California Press, 2002, at 1.
7. George, S., 'Globalizing Rights?' in M. Gibney (ed.), *Globalizing Rights: Oxford Amnesty Lectures*, Oxford: Oxford University Press, 2003, at 17–18.
8. *Millar v. Taylor*, (1769) 4 Burr 2303 at 2391–2, 2393–4.
9. Brysk, *op. cit.*, at 3.
10. The two further instruments in the International Bill are the Optional Protocol to the International Covenant on Civil and Political Rights, and Second Optional Protocol to the International Covenant on Civil and Political Rights, aiming at the abolition of the death penalty.
11. Opening paragraph of Proclamation, UDHR. See generally, Morsink, J., *The Universal Declaration of Human Rights: Origins, Drafting and Intent*, Philadelphia, PA: University of Pennsylvania Press, 1999, especially chapter 2.
12. Second Preamble, UDHR.
13. Article 27(2), UDHR. Similar prescriptions are echoed in Article 13.2, American Declaration of the Rights and Duties of Man of 1948; Article 14.1(c), of the Additional Protocol to the American Convention on Human Rights in the Area of Economic, Social and Cultural Rights of 1988 ('Protocol of San Salvador').
14. Article 17(2), UDHR. Similar prescriptions are repeated in Article 21, American Convention on Human Rights, Article XXIII of the American Declaration on the Rights and Duties of Man; and Protocol No. 1 of the European Convention for the Protection of Human Rights and Fundamental Freedoms, 20 March 1952 (ECHR).
15. Article 17, ICCPR.
16. Article 19(2), ICCPR.
17. Article 11.2, ICESCR.
18. The drafting history of this provision shows that one original intention was that the provision should guarantee a moral right to the scientist and the artist, against plagiarism, theft,

mutilation and unwarranted use. See Green, M., 'Drafting History of the Article 15(1)(c) of the International Covenant', at pp. 7–8 [UN Document E/C.12/2000/15 (Oct. 9, 2000)].

19.	See *Anheuser-Busch Inc. v. Portugal*, European Court of Human Rights, Grand Chamber, No. 73049/01, 11 January 2007.

20.	UN Economic and Social Council (OHCHR on Economic, Social and Cultural Rights), Committee on Economic, Social and Cultural Rights, *General Comment No. 17 (2005)*, 35th session, Geneva, 7–25 November 2005 (hereinafter referred to as the General Comment).

21.	General Comments are highly regarded analytical statements on the interpretation of various provisions of the ICESCR. Their aim is to assist states in fulfilling their human rights obligations under the Covenant – see http://www.ohchr.org/english/bodies/cescr/workingmethods.htm.

22.	Para. 10, General Comment.

23.	For example, the United States and United Kingdom maintained in the past that they satisfied their obligations under Article 6*bis*, Berne Convention, despite the absence of clear moral rights language under their respective national copyright laws. Both countries maintained, until the mid-1980s, that they provided such protection under different statutory and common law causes of actions such as passing off, unfair competition, injurious falsehood and defamation. See *Terry Gilliam v American Broadcasting Companies*, 538 F.2d 14 (2nd Cir., 1976); *Alan Clark v. Associated Newspapers Ltd.*, (1998) RPC 261, and Griffiths, J., 'Misattribution and Misrepresentation – The Claim for Reverse Passing Off as "Paternity" Right', *Intellectual Property Quarterly*, 1, 34, 2006.

24.	Admittedly, one could perhaps counter that the General Comment is merely acknowledging the existence of such a bias and not endorsing it. Nonetheless, we would argue that such a bias should more explicitly at least be questioned.

25.	Para. 2, General Comment.

26.	Paras. 7 and 8, General Comment.

27.	Paras. 13–14, General Comment.

28.	Article 6.1, ICESCR.

29.	Article 7(a), ICESCR.

30.	Article 11.1, ICESCR.

31.	According to Article 4*ter* of the Paris Convention, 'The inventor shall have the right to be mentioned as such in the patent'. Similarly, Article 62, European Patent Convention grants an inventor 'the right, vis-à-vis the applicant for or proprietor of a European patent, to be mentioned . . .'.

32.	The declaration is reprinted in whole in 'Cérémonies du Centième Anniversaire de la Convention de Berne', *Copyright*, 22, 367–75, 1986.

33.	Tansey, G., *TRIPS with Everything: Intellectual Property in the Farming World*, Southwell: Food Ethics Council, 2002.

34.	Raghavan, C., *Recolonization. GATT, the Uruguay Round & the Third World*, London and Penang: Zed Books/Third World Network, 1990, at 115–6. Submission of Quaker United Nations Office/Friends World Committee Consultation, in UN Commission on Human Rights, Sub-commission on the Promotion and Protection of Human Rights, 'Economic, Social and Cultural Rights: Intellectual Property Rights and Human Rights: Report of the Secretary-General Addendum', 3 July 2001 [Document E/CN.4/Sub.2/2001/12/Add.1].

35.	Article 2(4), Declaration on the Right to Development. Also see Article 1(2), ICESCR, and Article 1(2), UDHR.

36.	UNCTAD-ICTSD, *Resource Book on TRIPS and Development*, Cambridge, UK: Cambridge University Press, 2005, at 126, 128.

37.	The WTO is not a 'self-contained' legal regime but is part of the international community of legal norms – see WTO, 'United States – Import Prohibition on Certain Shrimp and Shrimp Products', AB-1998-4, 12 October 1998. [Document WT/DS58/AB/R].

38.	UNCTAD-ICTSD, *op. cit.*, at 119.

39.	UN Economic and Social Council, Commission on Human Rights, Sub-commission on the Promotion and Protection of Human Rights (Report of the High Commissioner), 'The Impact of the Agreement on Trade-Related Aspects of Intellectual Property Rights on Human Rights: Report of the High Commissioner', 27 June 2001 [Document

E/CN.4/Sub.2/2001/13], citing Chapman, A., 'Approaching Intellectual Property as a Human Right: Obligations Related to Article 15 (1) (c)', para. 33. [Document E/C.12/2000/12].

40. GATT Article XX concerns general exceptions. The most relevant part of the Article is as follows:

> Subject to the requirement that such measures are not applied in a manner which would constitute a means of arbitrary or unjustifiable discrimination between countries where the same conditions prevail, or a disguised restriction on international trade, nothing in this Agreement shall be construed to prevent the adoption or enforcement by any contracting party of measures:
> (*a*) necessary to protect public morals;
> (*b*) necessary to protect human, animal or plant life or health;

41. Paragraph 5(a), Doha Declaration on the TRIPS Agreement and Public Health, WT/MIN (01)/DEC/W/2 of 14 November 2001.
42. Paragraph 4 begins with the words 'We agree', and can be viewed as a 'very close approximation of an interpretation', UNCTAD-ICTSD, *op. cit.*, at 131.
43. Commission on Human Rights, 2000, *op. cit.*, para. 2.
44. *Ibid.,* preamble.
45. UN Commission on Human Rights, Sub-commission on the Promotion and Protection of Human Rights, 'Intellectual Property Rights and Human Rights', Resolution 2001/21, 16 August 2001 [Document E/CN.4/Sub.2/Res/2001/21]. In 2003, the Office of the High Commissioner for Human Rights prepared a paper for the 5th WTO Ministerial Conference which highlighted the right to health, the availability of pharmaceuticals, the protection of economic, social and cultural rights in areas such as health, education, the protection of the environment, the rights of indigenous people over their traditional knowledge, and the grant of intellectual property rights over genetic resources. OHCHR, 'Human Rights and Trade'. Paper for the 5th WTO Ministerial Conference, Cancún, Mexico, 10–14 September 2003, 6–16.
46. Economic and Social Council, 2001, *op. cit.* [Document E/CN.4/Sub.2/2001/13]
47. Paragraph 15. This point should be contrasted with the 2005 General Comment, discussed above.
48. Resolution 2000/7 17, para. 3. Petersmann, E.U., 'The WTO Constitution and Human Rights', *Journal of International Economic Law*, 3, 19, 2000; Howse, R. and M. Mutua, 'Protecting Human Rights in a Global Economy: Challenges for the World Trade Organization', International Centre for Human Rights and Democratic Development, 2000, available at http://www.dd-rd.ca/site/publications/index.php?subsection=catalogue&lang=en&id=1271&print= true&show_all =true.
49. Article 5, ICESCR.
50. For an excellent review and analysis of the jurisprudence in this area, see Barendt, E., 'Copyright and Free Speech Theory', in J. Griffiths and U. Suthersanen (eds), *Free Speech and Copyright*, Oxford: Oxford University Press, 2005, at 11–34.
51. [1999] RPC 655 (Ch.D), 671.
52. *Time, Inc. v Bernard Geis Associates*, 293 F. Supp. 130 (SDNY, 1968). For an argument from the US perspective as to why photographs in relation to newsworthy events should be granted First Amendment treatment as opposed to all other copyright works, see Nimmer, M.B., 'Does Copyright Abridge the First Amendment Guarantees of Free Speech and Press?' *UCLA Law Review*, 17, 1180, 1970, at 1197–200.
53. (1999) 5 BHRC 654, para. 54. The Ashdown court cited the decision with approval, although *Fressoz v. France* was not concerned with copyright law as such but revolved around unlawful use of tax documents.
54. *Ibid.*
55. [2002] ECDR 21; see also case comment by Simon, I., 'Picture Perfect', *European Intellectual Property Review*, 368, 2002.

56. (1994) 19 EHRR 1, where the court considered a conviction of a journalist for aiding and abetting the making of insulting remarks by the persons he interviewed for a TV programme in violation of Article 10. In *Jersild v. Denmark*, the European Court of Human Rights held that Article 10(1) ECHR protects not only the substance of the ideas and information, but also the form in which they are conveyed.

57. *Laugh It Off Promotions CC v. South African Breweries (Finance) B.V. t/a Sabmark International,* CCT42/04, 29 August 2005.

58. The relevant provisions were section 34(1)(c), South African Trade Marks Act and section 16 of the South African Constitution. Section 34(1)(c) is virtually identical to Article 5(2) of the European Directive (89/104 of December 1988).

59. For more on Laugh It Off and culture jamming, see the South African Creative Commons site at http://za.creativecommons.org/blog/archives/2005/03/18/an-open-invitation-to-culture-jamming-with-laugh-it-off/

60. Paragraphs 107–9.

10. Information technologies and the internet

OPPORTUNITIES AND CHALLENGES

This chapter looks at the nexus between technology, especially digital technology, and intellectual property policy from a contemporary historical perspective. New technologies, for all their benefits for society and business, can upset the established patterns of production, distribution and consumption of goods. We need technology-friendly intellectual property policies. But designing such policies is far from easy. On the one hand, new technologies are helping the commercial, creative and cultural industries by opening up new streams of revenue from licensing and exploitation. E-commerce has made brand managers realise that trade marks, which were hitherto geographically limited to national markets, could now become global marks. This is all good for business, but the public can undoubtedly gain a great deal too. On the other hand, we see the confusion of European policy-makers with respect to computer software; infringement of copyright works in the digital environment seems impossible to stop; and there is frequent misappropriation of trade marks and their unauthorised use as domain names or meta tags. Such dilemmas are not new, dating at least as far back as when reprography and tape recording became cheap and easy, making the copyright laws seem obsolete to critics of the time. However, with the advent of the internet, the cacophonous discourse on the effects of technology on intellectual property rights has escalated many-fold.

In short, the twin phenomena of digitisation and the internet present several formidable challenges and opportunities to both creators and users of intellectual property. Here is a summary of the balance sheet as it stands.[1]

Risks for Owners

- *Perfect copies* – all protected content in the networked environment is in a digital form, and each new generation of software and hardware technology makes it easier to make perfect mass copies of such works.
- *Distribution* – the distribution of digital works undermines the ability of creators and rights owners to derive profits from their works, which may

in some circumstances lead to the stifling of creativity as the rewards and incentives for producing works disappear.

Opportunities for Intellectual Property Owners

- *Price diminution* – technology has led to the reduction of costs of printing and distributing books to consumers, which in turn has led to lower book prices. This has surely quelled the average consumer's enthusiasm in developed countries for photocopying whole books as opposed to purchasing them lawfully (at least for reasonably priced fictional books as opposed to extremely expensive medical and law textbooks); the same is occurring for video rental as retail stores like *Amazon* offer highly competitive pricing which has somewhat stopped the average consumer from either taping programmes from the television or from friends/shops.
- *New income sources* – the introduction of works, especially music and films, in improved digital formats raises a new source of income as the average consumer replaces his existing collection of works with these digital versions; this is especially true when one considers that the new storage mediums have very high storage capacity which permits the industry to convince the consumer, who has already viewed the film in the theatre, to purchase the 'uncut' or the 'director's cut' versions of the DVD.

Consumer Demands

- *Lower costs of products* – books and music can be distributed in an electronic format directly from the creator/producer to the consumer, and several well-known authors are toying with this phenomenon. Middlemen or retailers could be eliminated. Distribution costs would fall. Moreover, where authors and composers can distribute their own works over the internet without the assistance of publishers, the costs of such works will fall.
- *Cheaper and wider distribution* – the current formulae for the sale of consumer products is dictated by the retailer or the producer. For example, students must purchase an entire book rather than just the chapters or pages that they wish to study – though as discussed below, Googleprint may change this model. Teenagers had to purchase entire CD albums or singles rather than the two or three songs which they really wished to hear, but now new technologies and consumer demands have forced industry to offer a more demand-based distribution network, which does decrease transaction costs, especially in relation to search and consume transaction costs of global consumer goods.

- *Knowledge accessibility* – moreover, with the advent of digital libraries, difficult to obtain works and information could be readily accessed at a fraction of the current cost.
- *Cultural diversity and preservation* – global music and film production and distribution is controlled by a small group of producers/distributors who dictate the tastes of many consumers according to market demands. Usually, the music or films made by fringe artists or by artists from many countries do not reach a much wider audience. The internet does increase the opportunities available to new artists that appeal to 'niche' markets. In the field of fine art, indigenous craft and artefacts, for example, numerous museums and art galleries have digitised their collections and made them available for viewing on the internet.[2] One such site, Artnet,[3] allows users to access works by over 16,000 artists and in over 1,300 art galleries.

The primary cry of the twentieth century has been for a broader copyright regime due to the challenges posed by technologies such as the reprographic, digital and compression technologies. The current problems did not arise from any single revolutionary invention but rather are due to the convergence of different technological developments: networked computers, digital file compression, increased computing power, the semiconductor chip leading to personal computing (not to mention affordable PCs), increased telephony coverage and, most important, higher communication speed.

How do we deal with the dilemma of technologies that simultaneously expand and encroach upon a copyright holder's space? Theoretically, we should not worry as the advent of each new technological breakthrough appears to encourage new theories and justifications within the sphere of intellectual property law such as the need for new categories of rights, or for private copying levies or for either removing or expanding free usage of works for certain purposes, or the need to look elsewhere to solve problems such as competition law or new business models.

Politically and legally, however, the technology cases discussed below do cause concern because current international, US and EU copyright laws and policies all tend towards widening the scope of copyright protection, without the necessary corresponding safeguards for technological innovation. Technological protection measures and digital rights management are now core concepts within the copyright laws of major developed countries. However, these measures do not solve anything unless the corollary areas of concern are also tackled. These include the lack of transparency in the collection and distribution of royalties (this is an issue in all copyright industries), the threat posed by non-innovative and non-competitive business models for buying singles through digital musical sites, and the failure to offer consumers an entertainment-technology industries solution which offers a seamless means of paying reasonable prices for a comprehensive range of music.

It may well be true that we will need legislation to expand intellectual property laws in the impending post-digital era. But whether or not that is the case, most important of all is legislation, by way of either intellectual property, competition or contract laws, which forces a competitive market structure on the intellectual property industries.

FROM PRINTING TO PHOTOCOPYING

Mass Consumption of Books

It has been said that:

> Copyright was technology's child from the start. There was no need for copyright before the printing press. But as movable type brought literature within the reach of everyone, and as the preferences of a few royal, aristocratic or simply wealthy patrons were supplanted by the accumulated demands of mass consumers, a legal mechanism was needed to connect consumers to authors and publishers commercially. Copyright was the answer.[4]

This is not a totally accurate portrayal of the commercial and legal relationship between authors and publishers. The economic problems of mass production of books, mass consumption and book piracy were felt as far back as the Roman Empire, and were certainly one reason for the rise of the guilds' monopolies.[5] Technology was not, and is not, responsible for mass consumerism and the problems of controlling distribution. Rather, it may be more accurate to state that technology exacerbates existing problems inherent in attempting to balance the varied interests of authors, publishers and consumers.

In the immediate post-Gutenberg period, for instance, it was not only printing technology which caused mass production and consumption, but also the establishment of merchant cities throughout Europe and the concomitant expansion of a new middle class which saw the secularisation of the arts, including literature and music. This, in turn, ushered in the public consumer and the then equivalent of the publishing company or the recording company – the entrepreneurial bookseller (stationer) or music publisher.[6] Economic interests were protected by controlling not so much the manufacture as the distribution of goods. Copyright is merely one of the modern legal answers to this dilemma; other legal solutions can include, as we saw in Chapter 8, the new European database right, misappropriation, unfair competition or tort law, criminal law and even trading standards regulations. These legal tactics do not preclude other more market-based tools to control piracy such as pricing wars to ward off the imitator.[7]

Nevertheless, it is true that since the Gutenberg press, technological changes in the world of book publishing mean that the scale of 'mass' in mass consumption and mass piracy periodically expands.

Take, for example, the case history of photocopying in libraries. Prior to reprographic technology, copyright owners had had to tolerate unauthorised hand transcriptions of written works despite these being clear acts of infringement. This was largely due to the cost and sheer inconvenience of enforcing the rights, and also to the relative lack of economic harm arising from an activity that took place mostly in libraries rather than in bookshops. Even when photocopy technology became available, publishers were at first quite unconcerned about library copying. Indeed, the United States National Association of Book Publishers entered into a Gentlemen's Agreement with the American Council of Learned Societies and the US Social Science Research Council, whereby duplication

> for profit or as a substitute for purchase of a protected work was forbidden, but single photocopies in lieu of loan or in place of manual transcription and solely for the purpose of research were explicitly recognised as fair use.[8]

With the introduction of the low cost photocopying machine into libraries, offices and schools, though, it was no longer feasible to condone copying of books in libraries, especially with the possibility of libraries creating competing markets.

Controlling Photocopying

Fair use/fair dealing

Where the United States was concerned, by the 1970s, photocopying technology had enabled enough libraries to become secondary producers of intellectual property goods and to deflect the initial purchase from the copyright owner. *Williams & Wilkins Co., v. United States*[9] represented a landmark decision in this area where the plaintiff publishers sued the National Library of Medicine, claiming that the mass reproduction and distribution of the firm's medical journals was an infringement of copyright in the journals. The majority court held that this amounted to fair use due to the fact that such copying had been accepted since the 1935 Gentlemen's Agreement (see above). The court refused to accept the proposition that where there is a marked increase in volume, a use which was hitherto accepted as 'fair use' changed to 'unfair use'.[10]

The fair use solution, however, may be outmoded as the modern digital photocopier machine is part scanner, part printer with the ability to send scanned documents via email, or make them available on the local area network, and also sometimes has a built-in fax machine. Indeed, the reprography problem was dealt with in other alternative ways in most countries. First, courts could condone reprographic copying as an act of fair use as is the approach of the US courts in relation to domestic copyright law. Second, countries could condone certain amounts of reprographic copying as an act of fair dealing for private study or research, or for educational purposes, subject to licensing or levy schemes. Thus, in the United Kingdom,[11] Australia and Canada, most mass reprographic copying is considered to be beyond the fair dealing or educational exceptions and thus libraries, universities and businesses must enter into voluntary blanket licences with the relevant collecting societies.[12]

The private copying levy

The private copying levy is the favoured method in most civil law European Union countries, and has also been introduced into Canadian copyright law.[13] The levy approach has also been imposed on all EU member states by the EC InfoSoc Directive which allows all copying that is 'private and for ends that are neither directly nor indirectly commercial', on the condition that right holders must receive 'fair compensation', with the implication being that levies are to be imposed on copying, scanning and recording equipment.[14]

DIGITAL LIBRARIES

Evolution or Demise of the Traditional Library?

A recent report from British library associations states that the inter-library loan, which was the bane of the reprographic era, has dropped from its height of over 1.3 million requests in 1997 to over 380,000 in 2001. This drop in inter-library loans has been accompanied by a fall in the number of visitors to libraries. Why? A 2006 report stated that internet access was now available in 97 per cent of all public libraries in the United Kingdom. The report continues to state that

> increased availability of electronic resources, particularly at locations remote to the library buildings, is thought to have contributed to a 10 percent fall in the number of visits to library premises over the last five years.[15]

Technology has always changed the nature and role of libraries. Printing transformed and expanded the ancient libraries. In the 1950s and 1960s, vast amounts of knowledge were suddenly made available via microfilm and microfiche. The only thing that is different with the current era of digitisation and internet is that it has democratised scholarship on a global scale. As the above statistics on library visitors confirm, the ownership of personal computers with internet access and powerful search engines has made libraries almost redundant – unless libraries take on the role of university presses and make their collections of dissertations, working papers, archives and newspapers available and accessible to everyone on the planet.

Digital libraries, thus, challenge the old order of copyright which operates neatly in a bifurcated world of scholarly libraries and commercial publishing. If the photocopier created new competing markets domestically, digitisation and the internet created new competing markets on a global scale. The ability to scan works onto computers and networks changes the way in which knowledge resources are managed and accessed.

One major digital library project, which commenced in 2005, is the Google Library Project. The project involves several of the largest libraries in the world including those of Harvard, Oxford and Stanford Universities, and aims to increase internet access to all these libraries' holdings.[16] It is a laudable and magnificent project, which aims to increase our access to the world's most prestigious and largest academic libraries. The other publicised venture is that between Microsoft and the British Library, whereby the former has redeveloped the famous 'Turning the Pages' software in order to reunite two of Leonardo da Vinci's notebooks as an on-line experience. However, the British Library–Microsoft venture highlights a criticism that has been levelled at these collaborations between public or scholarly libraries and commercial organisations. The first notebook, the Codex Arundel, belongs to the British Library, whereas the second one, the Codex Leicester, belongs to the founder of Microsoft, Bill Gates. The problem is that you can only access Codex Leicester as long as you are using Vista, the latest operating system from Microsoft.[17]

This is a perennial problem in relation to intellectual property goods: public interest merely dictates access to essential intellectual property goods, but does not necessarily provide the funds to give such access a practical effect. Consequently, we often find ourselves having to share the exploitation of our common heritage with those best able to do so, often corporations having particular interests that are not always in complete alignment with those of the general public.

Digital Libraries versus Copyright Law

What is a 'public domain' work?

The above-mentioned network of libraries and Google has declared that the project will be confined to out-of-copyright works, and will give on-line readers the ability to read and print out such books, many of which are neglected or forgotten. The Oxford–Google Digitisation Agreement in relation to the scanning and creation of these digital books offers a vague definition of 'public domain' materials: printed books for which the copyright has expired, and adds that these would principally be books published before 1885.[18] Moreover, all out-of-copyright works which Google scans will also be sent to libraries, thus assisting such libraries in their various functions. As the Harvard Library states:

> Libraries are unique in their charge not only to acquire, organize, and disseminate information, but also to preserve it for future generations. The presence of these digital copies can help to ensure that the intellectual content of these works – many of which are aging and fragile – would remain available in cases of unforeseen decay or catastrophic situations such as fire.[19]

Notwithstanding these universal benefits, the project does highlight the current difficulties within copyright law. The Google Library Project envisions the complete scan of the full text of the books into Google's search database. Users will be able to browse the full text of public domain materials. The legal issue is simple: who will vouchsafe that the books being scanned are actually in the public domain?

When does the term of protection end?

The minimum term of protection is the life of the author plus 50 years thereafter under international copyright law. However, there is no ceiling on the maximum term of protection, and the rules vary from country to country. Thus, Japan has a copyright term of life plus 50 years, Indian copyright law protects its works for a term of life plus 60 years, the United States, European Union and Australia have copyright terms of life plus 70 years, while Mexico has a term of protection of life plus 100 years.

Moreover, there are anomalies and idiosyncrasies within each nation's laws which either extend protection indefinitely, or refuse protection absolutely. Consider moral rights, for example. Such rights are perpetual in some countries such as France and Egypt, in which case literary and artistic works are never truly in the public domain.[20] Thus, in 2005, the French Supreme Court confirmed that the unauthorised sequel to Victor Hugo's work *Les Misérables* would be allowed on principle, but even then, such sequels must respect the moral rights of the deceased Victor Hugo by showing no disregard towards the title of the work and its integrity.[21]

National idiosyncrasies: common law copyright and Crown copyright

Other exceptions relate to unpublished works, neighbouring rights, anonymous works, and works which fall within the transitional provisions. Some works do not fall within copyright protection at all in some jurisdictions, but do so in others. To take an example: statutes, laws and court decisions are not protected under German or United States copyright laws, but British Crown copyright protects most works produced by the British government, the King James Bible and the Book of Common Prayer.[22] As for UK judgments, it depends where the decision originates from: House of Lords judgments are subject to Parliamentary copyright but other appellate and high court judges act independently and cannot be considered to be Crown 'servants'. The official position is that judgments can be reproduced without charge or restriction but that Crown copyright (or Parliamentary copyright) protection is maintained to ensure recognition of official status.[23] More quixotic is the decision which held that sound recordings of performances made in England during the 1930s were protected under New York State common-law copyright until 2067, despite protection having expired in these recordings throughout the world, including under US federal copyright law.[24]

The Advantages and Future of Digital Libraries

We sought to highlight above the considerable legal difficulties that will be faced by authors, publishing houses and corporations (like Google and Microsoft) who wish to create digital libraries.[25] On the other hand, these difficulties appear pretty insignificant and bureaucratic if one believes that the future of electronic libraries is to become 'a universal archive that will contain not only all books and articles but all documents anywhere—the basis for a total history of the human race'.[26] The relevant Wikipedia entry sets out the advantages of digital libraries, which include:

- easy access to books, archives and images
- low cost as no payment for staff, book maintenance, rent, and additional books; though digital libraries incur costs in relation to software development and technical staff
- no physical boundary, and multiple accesses allowing same resources to be used at the same time by a number of users all over the globe
- information retrieval system which enables one to search the entire collection with any search term
- preservation and conservation as an exact copy of the original can be made any number of times without any degradation in quality
- space as traditional libraries are limited by storage space
- networking as digital libraries can provide a seamlessly integrated and shared resource.

In order to realise such a future, we will need to resolve the legal problems as highlighted above. Perhaps the best approach is to adopt a cocktail approach which amalgamates the various tried and tested methods around the world including fair use/fair dealing, blanket licensing and private copying levies. Such an approach marries the more European compromise approach of allowing author participation in all forms of exploitation, with the more Anglo-American approach of encouraging and rewarding the entrepreneurial investments of Google et al.

CAPTURING IMAGES AND SOUNDS

Mechanical Creations

Eighteenth- and nineteenth-century music industries generated their income through the control of the sale of music sheets and subscription concerts. There was no real concern as to controlling performances as long as they remained within private aristocratic or wealthy homes. Mass music-making at home eventually came about with the rise of income of the middle classes and the increased sales of domestic pianos. The mass possession of pianos led to a growing pirate music publishing industry and the sale by street hawkers of pirated printed songs. The invention of the Aeolian machine or the pianola resulted in the inevitable calls for laws to prevent 'mechanically produced music'.[27]

The nineteenth century saw further successful and commercial inventions in the field of mechanical sciences which profoundly affected the existing world of imagery and sound: Talbot's calotype process, the Daguerre photographic inventions, Scott's phonoautograph, Edison's phonograph process, Berliner's gramophone, all of which, in some ways, spurred the Lumière brothers' film recording techniques. The result was the birth of the photograph, sound recording and film industries, which eventually led to a re-evaluation of the international copyright system as conceived in the nineteenth century comprising mainly authors' rights to a bifurcated legal regime consisting of authors' rights and neighbouring/related rights.

New technologies have the ability to transform existing works and generate new markets and income streams. Authors of existing works clamour for extended protection against the perceived unauthorised exploitation of these new derivate forms of their works by 'pirates'. Thus, the technological pirates of the late nineteenth and twentieth century were sound recording and film producers who lobbied hard against authors' pressure for rights to control these derivative works. By 1908, international copyright law settled the matter and authors' rights were expanded to include the exclusive right to authorise use of works in both sound recordings and films.[28]

The second dilemma is whether new manifestations of existing works or new products of new technologies are worthy subject matter of protection. The nineteenth-century French history of the legal battle to protect photographs as artistic creations is illustrative in showing that a new intellectual property is born every time the law makes the leap from the machine-dictated act to the 'creative' act. The first reaction of the French courts was that photographs were not to be viewed as paintings. The authored work, on the one hand, was 'imbued with something of the human soul', whereas the photograph was a completely soulless machine-produced work.[29] A marked change in legal attitudes came with the commercialisation of photographs and the appearance of a new market stakeholder – the professional photographer.[30] Two elements had to be found before copyright law would extend protection to photographs: the creative subject or author, and the work, that is, a production that was more than mere plagiarism of nature. Unsurprisingly, it can be difficult to discern the exact scope of protection for photographs, for the artistic feeling and character of the photograph lies in the photographer's selection of angle, lighting, order and arrangement.[31]

The above reasoning can be extrapolated to all later technologies that were subsequently considered copyrightable. Films, for instance, were first considered to be soulless, financially dictated productions, but were later re-labelled as works of high creativity.[32] Accordingly, the Berne Convention of 1886 has been amended several times to keep pace with these technological developments and to give authors the right to prevent exploitation of their works through these new mediums.[33]

Personal Copying Machines

At issue in *Sony Corp. v. Universal Studios, Inc.*[34] was the fact that Sony's Betamax home videotape recorders were in widespread usage amongst television viewers who were employing them to record programmes for later viewing, known as time-shifting. The plaintiffs claimed that the use of the Sony recorders by private individuals in their homes for their own private use constituted copyright infringement of the works. They further claimed that the defendant Sony, as the manufacturer and seller of the recorders and Betamax tapes, was liable as a contributory infringer.

The Supreme Court concluded that Sony was not liable for contributory infringement. In doing so, it noted that Sony supplied equipment that was generally capable of copying copyright works, or non-copyright works.[35] Indeed, the product need merely be capable of substantial non-infringing uses.[36] Moreover, the Supreme Court had refused to hold the manufacturers and retailers of videotape recorders liable for contributory infringement despite evidence that such machines could be and were used to infringe plaintiffs' copyright-protected television shows.[37] Although Sony may have had general knowledge that its VCR would be used for the unauthorised copying of protected works, and although it had advertised the VCR for just such a purpose, this was insufficient. The Supreme Court was of the express opinion that such generalised knowledge was insufficient to impose liability for vicarious or contributory infringement.[38]

The Supreme Court also went further and emphasised the two different justifications for copyright protection: reward for the authorial labour and creativity, and stimulation of general creative activity and access to products of such activity. The Supreme Court then held that the reward aspect of copyright law was a secondary consideration. Instead, the ultimate aim of copyright law is the achievement of a *public purpose*: to stimulate creative activity for the general public good and to ensure public access to the products of such activity.[39]

Digital Copying Machines

In more recent times, the MP3 player phenomenon causes similar issues as the video and tape cassette machines did in the 1980s. In *Recording Industry Association of America, Inc. v. Diamond Multimedia Systems Inc.*[40] at issue was the liability of a user of the Rio player. These were portable, hand-held playing devices which were capable of receiving, storing, and re-playing MP3 files; moreover, the files were transferred to the Rio player from a compact disc to the hard drive of a personal computer. In *obiter*, the Court held that the Rio player merely makes copies in order to render portable, or 'space-shift', those files that already reside on a user's hard drive. Placing reliance on the *Sony* decision, the Court opined that such copying of files is paradigmatic non-commercial personal use which is entirely consistent with the purposes of the copyright law.[41]

Thus, the impact of the *Sony* decision is far-reaching in that it clearly puts technological progress before copyright interests. Indeed, without it, lawful purchasers of copyright works such as broadcasts, cable services, music or films would not now be able to shift, for the sake of convenience and portability, their lawful purchases from one place-time-medium dimension (such as scheduled TV programming, CDs or DVDs) to another place-time-medium dimension (such as an MP3 player, an iPod or a TiVo).

P2P NETWORKS AND THE MARKET

Technological Convergence

File-sharing, digital technology and the internet did not threaten intellectual property rights owners until several of the following factors converged. First, we had to wait for the arrival of the affordable small personal computer. The evolution of computers from room-sized mainframe computers in the 1960s, to minicomputers in the 1970s, to microcomputers (or personal computers) in the 1980s, was accompanied by IBM's policy of using a non-proprietary operating system. Other vital components which explain the increased global consumption of digital computing is the invention of the silicon-based integrated circuit.

A second important factor was the rise of the internet from its humble beginnings in the US Defense Department's ARPANET, which developed the '*internet*work' concept. Consequently, this was taken up by the civilian computer-science subculture of the 1960s. Even then three more notable events had to come into play. These were the invention of the World Wide Web and of electronic mail, and the privatisation and commercialisation of the internet in the 1990s.[42]

Third, all this would have been to no avail without sophisticated technological support and infrastructure including wireless hot points, internet cafes, extensive cable telephony which moved within 15 years from low speed modems to high speed modems to accessible and cheap broadband, compression software coupled with increasing storage capabilities. And finally, we now live in an internet-friendly society, in a world of DVD players, iPods, i-Phones, webcasts, interactive streaming, and designer-made virtual avatars.[43]

Peer-to-peer Networks

Peer-to-peer (P2P) systems usually lack dedicated, centralised infrastructures. Instead, they depend on the voluntary participation of peers to contribute resources out of which the infrastructure is constructed. In a P2P distribution network, the information available for access does not reside on a central server or one computer; rather, each computer makes information available to every other computer in the network. At any given moment, the network consists of other users of similar or the same software who are on-line at that time. The key element in a P2P network is the software which provides a method of cataloguing and indexing all the available information and files so that users may access and download them. There are three different methods of indexing. The first is as a centralized indexing system, maintaining a list of available files on one or more centralised servers. The second is as a decentralised indexing system, in which each computer maintains a list of files available on that computer only. The third is as a 'supernode' system, in which a select number of computers act as indexing servers, and which was developed by Kazaa BV, a Dutch company.[44]

Important factors in considering the technology are that the servers do not create, copy, store or make available any of the sound, text or image files on its servers (whether transient or otherwise). Neither are the contents of the files routed or transmitted through the P2P network or servers. The contents of all files are held at all times on the users' computers.

First Generation P2P: Napster

Much has been written on the major file-sharing cases and their impact, and only the main findings of the courts are discussed below.[45] Napster was sued in 1999 by several major recording companies who claimed that Napster's P2P file-sharing technology made it contributorily and vicariously liable for its users' alleged copyright infringement. The courts did not accept the defences raised by Napster, especially its attempt to come within the *Sony-Betamax* defence. Although the Napster program was capable of non-infringing uses, the courts held that the Napster program had unacceptably harmed the sound recording industry's market, especially in relation to sales within college markets. The primary issue was whether file-sharing causes market harm to the property owner. The courts were unimpressed with a report alleging that P2P file-sharing stimulates more CD sales than it displaces. Instead, it accepted the evidence that the Napster network created market barriers to the sound recording industry entering into the market for the digital downloading of music.

As the appellate court emphasised, the

> lack of harm to an established market cannot deprive the copyright holder of the right to develop alternative markets for the works . . . Having digital downloads available for free on the Napster system necessarily harms the copyright holders' attempts to charge for the same downloads.[46]

Moreover, it was concluded that Napster had both actual and constructive knowledge that its users exchanged copyright music.

Second Generation – Grokster, Kazaa, Sharman

The Napster model was replaced by newer and faster file-sharing technology such as Kazaa.[47] In the recent United States *Grokster* decision, the defendants were manufacturers and distributors freely of two P2P software applications, Grokster and Morpheus. The plaintiffs comprised a majority of the film and sound recording industry in the United States.[48]

The Court of Appeal held for the software manufacturers, relying on the *Sony* doctrine. According to the doctrine, once it is proven that a product is *capable* of substantial non-infringing uses, the remaining issue is whether the defendants have reasonable knowledge of infringing activities yet fail to act on that knowledge to prevent infringement. The district court and the Court of Appeal held that no control was possible under the decentralised, Gnutella-type network or the quasi-decentralised, supernode, Kazaa-type network since no central index is maintained; even if the defendants 'closed their doors and deactivated all computers within their control, users of their products could continue sharing files with little or no interruption'.[49]

On appeal to the Supreme Court, the majority opinion was that *Sony* was misapplied by the Court of Appeal, and that the defendants were liable for secondary infringements. The Supreme Court transplanted the common law rule of inducement of infringement into US copyright law:

> [O]ne who distributes a device with the object of promoting its use to infringe copyright, as shown by clear expression or other affirmative steps taken to foster infringement, is liable for the resulting acts of infringement by third parties. We are, of course, mindful of the need to keep from trenching on regular commerce or discouraging the development of technologies with lawful and unlawful potential. Accordingly, just as *Sony* did not find intentional inducement despite the knowledge of the VCR manufacturer that its device could be used to infringe, mere knowledge of infringing potential or of actual infringing uses would not be enough here to subject a distributor to liability. Nor would ordinary acts incident to product distribution, such as offering customers technical support or product updates, support liability in themselves. The inducement rule, instead, premises liability on purposeful, culpable expression and conduct, and thus does nothing to compromise legitimate commerce or discourage innovation having a lawful promise. (Citations omitted)[50]

The issue was tackled in a slightly different manner by the Australian courts. In *Universal Music Australia v. Sharman License Holdings*,[51] the Australian Federal Court held that Sharman had authorised the infringement of copyright by users of its file-sharing software. It further held that Sharman's warnings to users were ineffective, that it could have adopted technical measures to curtail infringement, and that it had encouraged users to increase their file-sharing. The holding basically confirms the growing view of the courts that it is acceptable to prohibit the distribution of a technological product on the grounds that after its sale it is capable of being used by its purchaser to infringe copyright, even though it may also have non-infringing uses.

The decision is also interesting as it is based on the Australian notion of 'authorisation'. Under the copyright statute, copyright will be infringed where a person, who is not the owner or licensee, authorises the doing in Australia of any act comprised in the copyright. In doing so, the statute requires the court to take into account the following non-exhaustive list of factors:

- the extent (if any) of the person's power to prevent the doing of the act concerned;

- the nature of any relationship existing between the person and the person who did the act concerned;
- whether the person took any other reasonable steps to prevent or avoid the doing of the act, including whether the person complied with any relevant industry codes of practice.[52]

The court held, despite Sharman's arguments, that the company 'was in a position, through keyword filtering or gold file flood filtering, to prevent or restrict users' access to identified copyright works; in that sense, Sharman could control users' copyright infringing activities'.[53] The injunction provided that the continuation of the Kazaa system would not be regarded as a violation of the injunction if the software was modified to implement filtering technology to a standard agreed between the parties or approved by the court. The order is instructive in how the courts do try to find a balance between property and technology:

> I have had to bear in mind the possibility that, even with the best will in the world, the respondents probably cannot totally prevent copyright infringement by users. I am anxious not to make an order which the respondents are not able to obey, except at the unacceptable cost of preventing the sharing even of files which do not infringe the applicants' copyright. There needs to be an opportunity for the relevant respondents to modify the Kazaa system in a targeted way, so as to protect the applicants' copyright interests (as far as possible) but without unnecessarily intruding on others' freedom of speech and communication.

In contrast, the Federal Court of Canada in *BMG Canada Inc v. John Doe*[54] held that uploading music files onto P2P networks did not necessarily constitute copyright infringement. The plaintiffs, the Canadian Recording Industry Association, brought a motion seeking pre-action discovery from five ISPs alleged to have illegally traded in music downloaded from the internet. Both the Federal Court of Canada and the Federal Court of Appeal refused to allow the intellectual property owners to obtain subscriber information of allegedly infringing ISP customers. Instead, it held that the plaintiffs needed to satisfy a range of criteria which included: establishing a *prima facie* case of infringement of copyright by the defendants, and proving that the public interest in disclosure outweighed the importance of the right to privacy.

A similar decision was handed down by the Tribunal de Grande Instance de Paris which held that file-sharing through a P2P network is legal as all users have a private copying exception to copyright which exists under French law. Compensation to copyright owners is obtained not by denying file sharing but through levies imposed on blank media and copying machines.[55] However, this stance may have changed dramatically after the August 2006 adoption of the controversial French law which makes software providers criminally liable where they knowingly publish, make available to or communicate to the general public in any form whatsoever, software obviously intended to provide unauthorised access to protected works or objects; or knowingly encourage, including through advertisements, the use of such software.[56] In Belgium, the courts have gone further and imposed liability on internet service providers, making the latter responsible for copyright infringements committed by unauthorised file-sharing of electronic music files using P2P software via Tiscali's services.[57] The court further rejected the 'mere conduit' defence which is available under EU law to offer some protection to ISPs.[58]

Is File-sharing all Bad?

It is tempting to view these judgments as disincentives to new types of technologies or business models. It is true that the individual users of P2P systems indulge in infringing activities by making available, downloading and generally trafficking in digital versions of music, films and texts. However, should the producers of the technology which enables such activity be punished? Is not the ultimate aim of copyright law the achievement of a public purpose rather than reward or a fair return for labour invested in the work?[59]

Sharing activities are important in achieving public policy aims. Benkler's study of large-scale sharing activities leads him to conclude that sharing enables market models through which excess capacity of private goods can be cleared.[60] He points out, for example, that many users take part in file-sharing for social reasons as well as for personal gains such as the SETI@home[61] (where 5.3 million users from 226 countries allow their idle computers to be used for analysis of radio astronomy signals as part of the search for extraterrestrial intelligence) and Genome@home[62] projects (a project dedicated to modelling new artificial genes that can create artificial proteins). The reason that peer-to-peer architecture is scientifically important is that this type of architecture makes efficient use of growing distributed processing and storage capacity of networked computers. Altruistic P2P sharing activities enable special-purpose virtual supercomputers to exist. This is vital in certain public resource computing projects that would otherwise not be feasible.

Legal Solutions for Creative Industries in the Digital Environment

What general legal approaches are being employed to deal with copyright infringement in the digital environment? The first of these is to control unlawful mass reproduction whilst still allowing for certain types of uses on public policy grounds such as private use or educational use. US copyright law, for example, has a flexible fair use provision, whereas the UK copyright law has strictly defined fair dealing and educational provisions. This form of control is usually exercised in tandem with intricate blanket licensing schemes which monitor the premises and environment in which the copying occurs. Thus, most universities, libraries, businesses and commercial organisations undertake blanket licences which are administered by national collecting societies. The European civil law countries tend to rely more on private copying levy schemes which may be, as we see below, the ultimate solution to the digital/internet problem.

The second legal solution is to focus on the means or devices or apparatus or even the premises which enable individual users to commit mass infringing activities. We return to the old solution of levy systems whereby rights holders identify and charge users. The rationale of a copying levy is heavily reliant on placing the fault or blame not only on the actual copier but also on the manufacturer or supplier or importer of the copying device or equipment which includes photocopying machines, tape recorders, file-sharing software, copying equipment such as scanners, and even the computer. Alongside these mechanisms, international copyright law has also sought to help intellectual property owners by prioritising rights management.

DIGITAL RIGHTS MANAGEMENT[63]

The two 1996 WIPO Internet Treaties introduced a new regulatory landscape for the governance of copyright and related rights, especially in the digital and internet context. The Treaties envisage intellectual property owners locking up digital versions of works by employing technological protection measures.[64] The provisions dictate that contracting parties provide adequate legal protection and effective remedies against the circumvention of the effective technological measures that authors or other copyright owners (such as performers and sound recording companies) use *in connection* with the exercise of their rights and that restrict acts which they have not authorised and that are not permitted by law.[65]

General Concerns on Freedom of Competition

The new provisions on technological protection measures (TPMs) allow copyright owners to limit reproduction or communication of a locked copyright work, sometimes even to the extent of stopping third parties accessing works which have been digitally locked up (either by encoding, scrambling, encryption or other tools). Is this a new 'right of access'? Copyright has traditionally been concerned with acts of copying and misappropriation, and rights of access are not part of this tradition. Can these technological measures prevent access to those who have a legitimate right to use a technologically protected work? Can this new 'right' be abused to digitally lock up non-copyright works, especially compilations or databases of public domain materials?[66]

Of particular concern with the new provision on TPMs is that, if unchecked, they may overprotect works by being employed to work against other copyright principles such as the private copying, fair use or fair dealing defences. Thus, TPMs may not only prevent copying or downloading of copyright works, but they can also prevent access to works which are excepted under general copyright principles.

For example, the TPMs provisions, as implemented in some countries, expose a lawful purchaser of a digital product to both civil and criminal sanctions if such a lawful purchaser circumvents a technological lock to access forbidden material on the digital product. This is so even when the product comprises the following types of material or data:

- pure data or ideas, either wholly or substantially;
- those materials or data which are not subject to copyright protection under certain jurisdictions. These may include laws, government reports and court judgments (specific exceptions which are allowed under the Berne Convention and the TRIPS Agreement);
- materials which have fallen out of copyright protection;
- educational or historical documents which may be used in normal circumstances under a fair use or fair dealing or educational or a public interest defence.

We can take the scenario one step further. The TPMs provision, as implemented in some countries, can also be used to prevent a lawful purchaser from copying any part of the digital product even where the lawful purchaser of the physical product wishes to copy insubstantial parts of the work (which is a non-infringing act under copyright law), or where the user has a valid defence for copying parts of the work (for example, educational or library or archival usage).

Finally, the TPMs can be used by rights holders to allow a lawful purchaser of the digital product to access (and maybe to copy) the product but limits the number of times this may be done. There are a variety of permutations which allow the rights holders to wield the TPMs as a Damocles sword over traditional copyright principles. The question then is: should we be allowing provisions on TPMs to override traditional copyright defences? This relegation of copyright principles to the second division is already being accepted by courts in some jurisdictions, though surprisingly it is being pushed back in others.[67]

The US and EU Approaches

In the US, domestic legislation appears to be relatively clear and balanced. The federal copyright law protects DRMs under its Digital Millennium Copyright Act (DMCA) 1998, but more importantly, the Act has a specific mandatory provision in section 1201(f) for reverse engineering for the purpose of inter-operability between software components – these are similar to the EU's Computer Program Directive.[68] Moreover, the courts appear to be somewhat cautious in allowing the DMCA to create monopolies by tying in protected works to manufactured goods.[69]

Within the EU context, Article 6(4) of the InfoSoc Directive sets out the TPM rules which work within another internal balance.[70] Thus, on the one hand, the Directive provides for a right to fair compensation to intellectual property owners for reprographic reproduction, private copying, and for repro-duction of broadcast programmes by certain public institutions; the term 'fair compensation' is a thinly veiled reference to the private copying levy schemes which operate in most European civil law systems.[71] Thus, the TPM rules oper-ate within this European legal framework in most of the member states, save the United Kingdom and Ireland. Collecting societies are pressed to take into account, when collecting the private copying levy, the presence or absence of technical protection measures and rights management information.[72]

This has raised difficulties in many European civil law countries as the private copying levy appears to presume that every citizen has a 'right to copy', since compensation is built into the levy system. If that is so, TPMs upset this user and consumer 'right' as it curtails their ability to exercise an excepted use. Moreover, the TPM rules prohibit the manufacture and sale of anti-circumvention devices. There has been no decision from the European Court of Justice in this area, though the various national courts have delivered judgments which seek to reconcile the intellectual property owners' rights with societal interests.

A related concern is that TPMs can be employed to stop the progress of technology by allowing rights holders to sue manufacturers and suppliers of decryption and decoding hardware and software tools. Are there adequate checks and balances to ensure that encryption and other related technological research and study are not stifled? This issue arose in France in relation to the effect of TPMs on the private copying exception.

In 2006, the French Supreme Court in the *Mulholland Drive* case held that copyright owners could assert their TPMs against users. In doing so it reversed the Court of Appeal's ruling that the TPMs unduly restricted the private copy-ing exception under French copyright law. According to the Supreme Court, though, private copying was not an absolute right for consumers, only an exception to an author's rights – an exception which, as all exceptions under French law, should be strictly construed.[73]

Indeed, the problem of TPMs has proved so difficult that the French legis-lature tackled it by providing for the establishment of the 'Authority for the

Regulations of Technical Measures' (*Autorité de régulation des mesures techniques*). This body was duly created in 2007 with the objective of ensuring the interoperability of all DRM systems and allowing private copies.[74] The attempt to regulate and limit (and even neutralise) DRMs caused a furore and led to an unexpected statement by Steve Jobs, the Apple CEO:

> Imagine a world where every online store sells DRM-free music encoded in open licensable formats. In such a world, any player can play music purchased from any store, and any store can sell music which is playable on all players. This is clearly the best alternative for consumers, and Apple would embrace it in a heartbeat . . . Every iPod ever made will play this DRM-free music. Though the big four music companies require that all their music sold online be protected with DRMs, these same music companies continue to sell billions of CDs a year which contain completely unprotected music . . . Much of the concern over DRM systems has arisen in European countries. Perhaps those unhappy with the current situation should redirect their energies towards persuading the music companies to sell their music DRM-free.[75]

Both EMI and Apple now release TPM-free music for Apple's iTunes service.

CONTROLLING MARKETS AND STANDARDS

The 'war' between copyright and technology is also one between two giant industrial sectors competing for market space and power. Is the scope of copyright protection being extended so as to prevent new streams of goods and services? The concern is that the legislator and some courts are heeding the industry's chant that large-scale file-sharing compromises private property rights. However, such sharing, as we indicated above, may also enable new downstream or secondary products and services, thus generating another revenue stream for the economy as a whole.

Moreover, today's technologies are being developed so as to be network-enabled, with built-in communication functions to connect to other software, computers and servers in order to facilitate both collaboration between creators of works and the dissemination of that information to audiences worldwide. Such technology wares provide the basic infrastructure for local networks and the internet.

And indeed, this is the argument in the brief of the Business Software Alliance, submitted for the Supreme Court's review of the *Grokster* decision in March 2005. The brief emphasises the view that technologies which enable users to exchange information, especially peer-to-peer technology, are a critical component of future product innovation.[76] Shifting liability to Grokster has an impact on technology producers. Imagine corporations such as Adobe, Apple, Autodesk, Borland, Dell, Hewlett Packard, IBM, Intel, Microsoft and others who, as creators of software products, are subject to significant piracy but who also have significant interest in the parameters of secondary infringement liability rules. As their brief indicates in the Grokster trial, manufacturers of software and hardware technologies need to ensure that copyright protection and secondary liability rules do not impede or hamper technological innovation and product development.

The particular concern of technology developers and manufacturers relates to general purpose and multi-use technologies and products.[77] In a sense, the potentially infringing technologies of earlier periods were easier to control – photocopier machines had specific uses as did video-cassette recorders. The computer or the file-sharing software or the latest mobile phone, on the other hand, is capable of many uses including uploading, downloading and copying. As the *Sony-Betamax* case noted, even single-use technologies and products are capable of both infringing and non-infringing activities. Courts cannot second-guess what a new product is capable of – who could have envisaged the shape of mobile telephony today with downloadable tunes and photo-messaging?

Interoperability

In the *Microsoft*[78] decision, the European Commission held Microsoft's refusal to supply to its competitors 'interoperability information' as constituting anti-competitive behaviour. Interoperable information is the software code information required by competing software applications firms in order to interface with another program or operating system. Competitors would not be allowed to use the information, at least under European software law, to manufacture competing operating systems such as a substitute for Microsoft's XP software but they are allowed to develop secondary application products such as media players or word processors. However, this would also allow the competing firms to develop products in competition with Microsoft's own application products.

This refusal to license intellectual property rights was part of Microsoft's larger strategy – its practice of bundling its personal computers with its own proprietary digital media player, Windows Media Player (WMP). WMP is on over 90 per cent of all Windows machines, with the result that media streams are now encoded in the Windows Media format. Nevertheless, WMP standards do not merely reflect music platforms but also Digital Rights Management control and the nature of operating systems on downstream markets, that is, mobile phones or television. Thus, by using its intellectual property rights and refusing licences on its protocols, Microsoft is betting that when digital media are delivered to other platforms beyond the PC, there will not be effective competition in the player market since all content will be in Microsoft's proprietary WMP format.

Why? Because content created on PC platforms would be tied to the WMP format, the *de facto* standard. Ayres and Nalebuff suggest a further reason why firms employ every possible tactic to dominate and control the complementary downstream market. In their view, Microsoft bundles products and then uses intellectual property rights to deny licences of access to such products so as to prevent secondary markets becoming 'entry point(s)' into Microsoft's operating system software. Media players can, the authors assert, morph into operating systems for mobile phones, TV set-top boxes, and handheld devices.[79]

ICT Patents and Standards

A further reason for exercising caution in allowing intellectual property rights to control the downstream market is that this extension can be used to develop a *de facto* standard – the war between the entertainment industries and the ICT sector can develop into a battle of standards. Intellectual property rights can and do hamper international and national standard-setting exercises. Standard-setting is when investors agree to invest in a particular technology as the *de facto* standard in the marketplace. Intellectual property owners who show up towards the latter stages of the standard-setting process, when the investment has been committed, can demand high royalties which may be out of proportion to the actual inventive contribution they have made or to the market value of the invention.

The International Organization for Standardization (ISO) defines a formal standard as 'a document, established by consensus that provides rules, guidelines or characteristics for activities or their results'. A standard, therefore, is generally a set of characteristics or qualities that describes features of a product, process, service, interface or material. The existence of standards makes it possible to develop compatible or interoperable products by competing firms. In particular, the global information and communications technology (ICT) sector requires compatible and harmonised standards to be fully effective, especially in relation to the internet, semiconductors, telecommunications, computer hardware and computer software. These technologies are often heavily patented with more than 100 patents involved in an average ICT product.

Moreover, due to the interrelated nature of these technologies, and the ways in which they interact, new innovation within the different ICT sectors requires a number of different components which may be covered by different patents. If one firm in the market dominates through the creation of a *de facto* standard, or alternatively secures a patent which covers key aspects of the preferred standard, it can exert substantial leverage and even threaten to block the standard-setting process.[80] As Lemley notes:

Therein lies the basic problem. In the pharmaceutical industry or the medical device field or the traditional mechanical field, you might have a patent on your invention or maybe you have had to combine a couple of different patents. In IT, you regularly have to combine 50, 100, even 1,000, or – as Intel lawyers, themselves, say with respect to their own core microprocessor – 10,000 different patent rights together into one product. You've got to clear all those rights or do something about them in order to get your product to market.[81]

How then should we balance the legitimate rights of intellectual property owners to receive reasonable compensation against the interests of those seeking harmonisation by implementing international standards? Lemley sets out ten different legal and business tactics that can be adopted by standard-setting organisations in order to soften the impact of intellectual property owners in this area, including revising the law on injunctions and damages; none of his remedies includes, however, enlisting the help of competition (antitrust) law.[82]

Within the international arena, the area is governed by the WTO Agreement on Technical Barriers to Trade (TBT).[83] The primary tenet of this Agreement is that countries have the right to adopt the standards they consider appropriate for human, animal or plant life or health, for the protection of the environment or to meet other consumer interests. However, in order to prevent too much diversity, the Agreement encourages countries to use international standards where these are appropriate. Currently, the TBT Agreement is silent on the issue of intellectual property rights in international standard-setting. Similarly, TRIPS does not address standards issues. So, perhaps one recommendation is that intellectual property rights should be integrated into the TBT Agreement framework.

DOMAIN NAMES AND VIRTUAL WORLDS

Domain Names

To obtain a domain name, an individual or entity files an application with a private organisation, such as Network Solutions in the United States or Nominet in the United Kingdom. There is no accepted international legal treaty on domain names though domain name disputes are currently within the jurisdiction of the WIPO Dispute Resolution Process. It has been held, at least under UK law, that no one can register and use a domain name which is identical or similar to someone else's trade mark, as such an act constitutes trade mark infringement, fraud and passing off.[84] However, this is solely a UK-based solution, and is of no assistance when one is faced with an international domain name dispute.

The cheaper and more effective manner of settling such disputes is to employ the ICANN process. ICANN was established as a result of the US legislative decision to have little governmental intervention in the management of internet resources. Part of this initiative called for the privatisation of the Domain Name System (DNS).[85] In 1999, the Internet Corporation for Assigned Names and Numbers (ICANN) Board adopted a set of Rules for the Uniform Domain Name Dispute Resolution Policy ('the ICANN Rules') setting out the procedures and other requirements for each stage of the dispute resolution administrative procedure. The procedure is administered by the WIPO Arbitration and Mediation Center (WIPO Center).

The Uniform Domain Name Policy

The Uniform Domain Name Dispute Resolution Policy ('the ICANN Policy') sets out the legal framework for the resolution of disputes between a domain name registrant and a third party (that is, a party other than the registrar) over the abusive registration and use of an internet domain name in several top level domains (TLDs). Any person or company in the world can file a domain name complaint concerning an alleged domain name infringement using the ICANN Administrative Procedure. The main advantage of the Administrative Procedure is that it typically provides a faster and cheaper way to resolve a dispute regarding the registration and use of an internet domain name than going to court. In addition, the procedures are considerably more informal than litigation. It is also international in scope, providing a single mechanism for resolving a domain name dispute regardless of where the registrar or the domain name holder or the complainant is located.

The Administrative Procedure is only available for disputes concerning an alleged abusive registration of a domain name; that is, those which meet the following criteria:

(a)   the domain name registered by the domain name registrant is identical or confusingly similar to a trade mark or service mark in which the complainant (the person or entity bringing the complaint) has rights;

(b)   the domain name registrant has no rights or legitimate interests in respect of the domain name in question; and

(c)   the domain name has been registered and is being used in bad faith.

Circumstances which are evidence that a domain name has been registered and is being used in bad faith include circumstances indicating that the domain name was registered or acquired primarily for the purpose of selling, renting or otherwise transferring the domain name registration to the complainant who is the owner of the trade mark or service mark or to a competitor of that complainant, for valuable consideration in excess of the domain name registrant's out-of-pocket costs directly related to the domain name.

Thus, in *Winterson v. Hogarth*[86] the respondent, Hogarth, registered the domain name writerdomains.com, for his personal web page, which was to be devoted to the world's favourite writers including the British authoress Jeanette Winterson. Hogarth additionally registered the domain names jeanettewinterson.com, jeanettewinterson.net and jeanettewinterson.org. It was clear that Hogarth was indulging in what is known as 'cybersquatting' as he was willing to sell the domain names registered for 3 per cent of each writer's gross book sales. Winterson filed a complaint with the WIPO Center, which held that the domain names had been registered in bad faith and should be transferred to the complainant. The Uniform Domain Name Dispute Resolution Policy's requirement that 'the respondent's domain name is identical or confusingly similar to a trade mark or service mark in which the complainant has rights' was not limited to those situations in which the complainant's trade or service mark was a registered right and thus included those situations in which the complainant enjoyed an unregistered trade mark in her own name.

Digital and Virtual Mimicry

What if a website looks similar to that of a well-known retailer or corporation such as Amazon or Google or BBC? Can digital mimicry of a site be an infringement of intellectual property? This is similar to the on-going battle played out between brand leaders and supermarkets against the latters' look-alike products which manage to skilfully avoid copyright and trade mark infringement but nevertheless produce very similar packaging to that of the brand leader.

Under many national trade mark laws, there is nothing to prevent parties from creating a web page that merely 'looks like' that of Amazon or Yahoo, as long as there is no appropriation of copyright text, artistic images (which could be copyright or trade mark protected), logos, graphic icons or artwork, etc. The line between acceptable and unacceptable taking can be very thin. For example, a multicoloured banner may be considered to be protectable, or it may be considered that such a banal or commonplace combination of colours cannot possibly come within copyright or trade mark protection.

However, this may soon change as virtual worlds become popular. The notion of a virtual world is not new. The entire internet, after all, is largely devoted to sharing, socialising and playing. In 2003, however, the 'Second Life' concept was launched.[87] In Second Life, users are slightly different in that they enjoy almost complete freedom to modify the world however they choose, they can own virtual 'real property' within the world, and users can retain the intellectual property rights to anything they create in the Second Life world. There is, therefore, much potential for intellectual property disputes especially in the area of brand names and trade marks.

The 'Second Life' world is not a trivial phenomenon. Statistics indicate that in 2006, the value of transactions between players exceeded US$100,000 in real-world money.[88] Moreover, real-world brand owners such as Nike, IBM, Sony BMG and Reebok have stores or advertising presence within the virtual world. Of course, many brands have no 'authorised' presence and virtual people (or avatars) sport 'illegally traded' branded items including virtual iPod players.

The main issue, as noted by one commentator, is whether 'a real-world mark owner [can] enforce its rights against an in-world user producing knock off products?'[89] Conversely, can an in-world brand or mark be protected under real-world trade mark or common law protection? There are no definite answers, though the legal situation in relation to domain names and look-alike websites indicates that not all infringing virtual activity escapes legal liability in the real world.

COMPUTER PROGRAMS

Copyright Protection

Computer programs are primarily protected under copyright law. They have been accepted as 'literary works', both in the international and European legal arena.[90] As such, the law on literary works will ordinarily apply. In an attempt to deal with the more difficult aspects of copyright protection of computer programs, the EU introduced a harmonised Directive on computer programs[91] with several special provisions.

Subject matter of protection

There is no definition of computer programs under EC law, though the term includes preparatory design material leading to the development of a computer program provided that the nature of the preparatory work is such that a computer program can result from it at a later stage.[92] This would presumably include product specifications, flowcharts and diagrams. Under EU law, protection will be granted to a computer program which is original in the sense that it is the author's own intellectual creation – no further criteria as to the qualitative or aesthetic merit of the program will be applied.[93]

Ideas and expressions

The EU Directive clearly stipulates that copyright protection will only extend to the expression of a computer program, and that ideas and principles which underlie any element of the computer program, including its interfaces, will be excluded from protection.[94] In the case of computer programs, the difficulty in demarcating ideas from expression is heightened by the fact that many programs operate under the same technical or functional constraints. Under such circumstances, two programs may be identical due to the fact that there is only one way of expressing an idea, which is to say that the idea has merged with the expression. In such an event, it may be decided that the computer program cannot enjoy copyright protection.[95]

Scope of protection

Infringement usually occurs if it can be shown that the whole or a substantial part of the program has been copied. One difficulty lies in determining the scope of copyright protection especially in relation to whether a program has been unlawfully reproduced. For example, if a person is given a diskette containing a computer program, what is that person allowed to do under copyright law? Does the mere use (that is, loading or running) of a computer program constitute infringement? The answer appears to be yes as the act of reproduction is defined as including

> the permanent or temporary reproduction of a computer program by any means and in any form, in part or in whole. Insofar as loading, displaying, running, transmission or storage of the computer program necessitate such reproduction, such acts shall be subject to authorization by the rightholder;[96]

Even the temporary reproduction of the computer program onto the offender's RAM or on his hard drive may be held infringing, if it is done without the copyright owner's consent. However, where a person is a lawful user of the program, there are certain permitted acts (see below).

A further difficulty is as to what is meant by substantial copying. In the case of written or printed literary works, this is a matter of comparing the two works, and judging whether there is a similarity of expression between the two. However, in the case of computer programs, the courts have to face issues such as non-literal copying, where the exact program code is not copied but the end-result is that the offending program creates the same overall organisation, structure, user interface and screen display as the protected program. The offending program will have the same 'look and feel' or 'structure, sequence and organisation' as the protected program.

The EC directive on computer programs is silent on this issue, and the situation must be examined country by country.

In one British decision, the court issued the following guidelines as to how the question of substantial copying should be dealt with:

(a) First, a literal comparison between programs is difficult as programs can be written in different computer languages which bear no literal similarity. Thus, non-literal elements such as structure, arrangement, menus, formats, etc. should be considered.

(b) Secondly, one should compare the protected program with the offending program to see whether there are any similarities between the two works. If so, were such similarities due to copying?

(c) Finally, if some elements have been copied, are such elements a substantial part of the protected program or an insubstantial part of the protected program.[97]

However, a subsequent decision rejected these guidelines and held that the question of substantial copying in relation to computer programs was to be answered by the simple expedient of judging the degree of over-borrowing by the defendant of the skill, labour and judgement which went into the copyright work. In considering reproduction, one should not only compare the literal similarities between the protected program and the allegedly infringing program, but also the 'program structure' and the 'design features' of the programs.[98]

General exceptions

In general, the copyright provisions which permit a person to do certain acts in relation to a copyright work will apply equally to computer programs. In addition, the EC software directive accords the lawful user of a computer program the following additional privileges:

(a) doing anything which is necessary for the use of the computer program in accordance with its intended purpose, including for error correction;

(b) making of a back-up copy by a person having a right to use the computer program;

(c) having the right to observe, study or test the functioning of the program in order to determine the ideas and principles which underlie any element of the program if it is done while performing any of the acts of loading, displaying, running, transmitting or storing the program which a lawful user is entitled to do.[99]

However, it should be noted that if the lawful purchaser of a copy of a computer software has the right to copy or adapt the work in connection with his normal use of the work, he may lose this right if he transfers the purchased copy to a third party. In such instances, barring any contractual obligations to the contrary which may have been imposed by the copyright owner, the transferee will be allowed to do any act which the original purchaser was entitled to do – conversely, the original purchaser will no longer be entitled to do such acts after the transfer.

Decompilation

One major issue in respect of copyright protection of computer programs is that of interoperability. A common goal of most application software programs is to interface successfully with another program or operating system so as to be compatible with the other program or system. Decompilation of the other program or system is a vital procedure in order to obtain interface details such as the source code. A second objective of decompilation however may also be for the decompiler to create a new competing program, to the detriment of the copyright owner of the first program. Any process of decompilation would ordinarily result in infringement. In order to address this problem, the European Union member states, including the United Kingdom, have introduced a specific decompilation defence.

Under this defence, it is not an infringement for a lawful user to convert a computer program which is expressed in a low level language into a version expressed in a higher level language or to copy it while doing so. However, this is only allowed if the following conditions are fulfilled:

- it must be necessary to decompile the program to obtain the necessary information to create an independent program which can operate or interface with the decompiled program or with another program;
- the information obtained from decompilation must not be used for any other purpose;
- decompilation is not allowed if the information is readily available elsewhere to the user;
- the decompiler must not supply the information to any other person to whom it is not necessary to supply it in order to accomplish the decompilation;
- the decompiler must not use the information to create a program which is substantially similar in its expression to the decompiled program.[100]

US Patent Law and Policy

The software patents issue is a thorny one, especially for European Union legislators, and for US–Europe trade relations. The issue is clearly this: software is patentable in the US, whereas it is not clear to what extent it is patentable under the European Patent Convention. The crux of the matter is not whether software is patentable or not, but rather should software be patentable subject matter?

Arguably, the best exposé of this thorny problem is the Manifesto by Samuelson, Reichman, Kapor and Davis, which still remains relevant in understanding the nature of computer programs.[101] The Manifesto teaches us that the salient features of computer programs are as follows: (a) programs are both texts and behavioural patterns; (b) innovation in software is incremental and cumulative in character; (c) a *sui generis* market-oriented protection regime would offer innovators an artificial market lead-time sufficient to protect against market failure, as well as provide incentives to disclose their innovations to the public. Thus, the Manifesto eschews patent law as a means to protect computer programs.

Whilst this is an understandable position under the European patent law, it is an unrealistic proposition in the US where patent law has apparently surpassed copyright law as the primary protection regime.[102]

The US patent statute adopts four categories of subject matter which are susceptible to patent protection – processes, machines, articles of manufacture, and compositions of matter.[103] The US courts, nevertheless, discard this categorisation in the case of computer programs. The test set down in the *State Street Bank* decision is that to qualify as patentable, the subject matter must show a 'practical utility', that is a 'useful, concrete and tangible result'.[104] The Court of Appeals tried to explain this concept thus:

> the transformation of data, representing discrete dollar amounts, by a machine through a series of mathematical calculations into a final share price, constitutes a practical application of a mathematical algorithm, formula, or calculation, because it produces 'a useful, concrete and tangible result' – a final share price momentarily fixed for recording and reporting purposes and even accepted and relied upon by regulatory authorities and in subsequent trades.[105]

European Patent Law on Software

Nearly every treatise and judgment in the last 20 years declares that European patent law does not protect 'computer programs'. In February 2002, the European Commission drafted a directive on the patentability of computer-implemented inventions[106] (CII) which basically sought to clarify this position by stating the following principles of law that while computer programs as such cannot constitute patentable inventions, nevertheless computer-implemented inventions can constitute patentable inventions as long as they are novel, inventive and make a technical contribution. Considerable delays and controversy ensued as the proposed directive was heavily amended. The directive was finally rejected by the Parliament at its second reading on 6 July 2005. The European Commission has confirmed it will not draw up another version of the CII directive.

Legally speaking, the rejected CII directive is an attempt to clarify the issue of 'software patents'. The European Patent Convention takes a more limiting approach by requiring that inventions be 'susceptible of industrial application',[107] and also providing a list of expressly excluded categories of subject matter including computer programs; however, computer programs are only excluded 'as such'.[108]

The goal of the rejected directive was to provide legal certainty to potential patentees by resolving the legal ambiguities concerning the ambit of Article 52, EPC – that is, what exactly is the difference between 'computer programs as such' and 'computer-implemented inventions' (CII)? Related to the objective of legal certainty within Europe was the need to harmonise the current divergent approaches to the issue of CII patenting between the national patent offices vis-à-vis the European Patent Office.

It is undeniable that there is divergence between the German and British approaches. The UK Intellectual Property Office confirmed in the recent decision of *Franks's Application* that although UK law was governed by the EPC, in cases of conflict on the interpretation of the EPC, the UK Intellectual Property Office would follow British rather than EPO jurisprudence. There are views that the UK patent regime is the most liberalised regime in relation to CII patents compared to the German Patent Office which applies Article 52 strictly. The German office only issues patents for CII if the invention is part of a physical device. This divergence stems not so much from the differing national attitudes but rather from the wording of the EPC.

However, it is this case law that lies at the heart of the debate and has led to an almost surreal linguistic debate between the supporters and detractors of software patenting. On the one hand, the written law is clear and no patent protection can be granted to computer programs. On the other hand, however, for the past 20 years the EPC has interpreted the law so as to grant patent protection to 'computer-implemented inventions' as long as such inventions showed technical effect or technical contribution.[109]

Does the European software industry need clarification in this area? Do CII patents stifle future innovation and creativity especially with respect to open or free source software? Do they create patent thickets and patent trolls (companies such as Acacia which acquire and license patented software and thus derive licensing incomes but do not actually develop software)?[110] Looking to the US, is there evidence that any of the 200,000 software patents issued in the US have been used to sue future innovators? Or do companies such as Microsoft employ patents as a defensive mechanism, whilst using the longer (and surprisingly robust) copyright law as an offensive mechanism?

Perhaps the CII directive fiasco serves as a salutary lesson for future lobbyists and policy-makers that at the end of the day, what matters more is good policy rather than semantic *cul-de-sacs*. Indeed, it is surprising how little debate there was on these key policy points:

- Do we need dual protection under both patent and copyright laws considering that international copyright law was specifically amended by TRIPS to include computer programs?
- Are software patents in the interest of the EU's industrial economy, and if patents for software (and business methods) are thought to be essential

to our regional well-being, why are we not deleting them from the list of excluded subject matter within Article 52? Historically, this list of exclusions was put into the draft Convention merely to ensure harmonisation in the 1970s with the Patent Cooperation Treaty. Is not Article 52 a fictional provision, at odds with current technological developments?[111]

- Do we need clarification, either from the EPO or in the future Community Patent Convention, of technical contribution? One should note that all policy and legal attempts to clarify or legislate in relation to software patents and Article 52 may also extend to the other prohibitions within Article 52 (the patenting of mental steps, discoveries and business methods).

There was always, from the beginning of the rejected directive's life, little 'official' evidence and consultative documents from European stakeholders (electronics companies, local government authorities, patent attorney and agents and software developers) to show what improvements or developments such stakeholders saw as being vital to build a competitive and innovative society. Indeed, it would have been more fruitful had the discussions concentrated, not on whether certain fields of technologies should be patented, but on the quality of the patent system in relation to criteria of patentability, and on the accessibility of the system in terms of cost and priority.

NOTES

1. Also see Fisher III, W.W., *Promises to Keep: Technology, Law and the Future of Entertainment*, Stanford: Stanford University Press, 2004, at 18–37.
2. Museum Computer Network (at http://www.mcn.edu/resources/sitesonline.htm) and Virtual Library Museums Pages (at http://vlmp.museophile.com/).
3. Artnet (at http://www.artnet.com/).
4. Goldstein, P., *Copyright's Highway: From Gutenberg to the Celestial Jukebox*, Stanford: Stanford University Press, 2003, at 21.
5. See discussion on copyright history in Chapter 4.
6. Sanjek, R., *American Popular Music and its Business: The First Four Hundred Years. Volume 1: The Beginning to 1790*, New York: Oxford University Press, 1988, Volume 1, at 37–8.
7. Breyer, S., 'The Uneasy Case for Copyright: A Study in Copyright for Books, Photocopies and Computer Programs', *Harvard Law Review*, 84, 281, 1970.
8. Adelstein, R. and S. Peretz, 'The Competition of Technologies in Markets for Ideas: Copyright and Fair Use in Evolutionary Perspective', *International Review of Law and Economics*, 5, 209, 1985.
9. 487 F.2d 1345 (Court of Claims) (affirmed 420 US 376, (S. Ct., 1975). The Supreme Court affirmed the decision on review.
10. For a historical review of the position taken in other countries during this period, see G. Kolle, 'Reprography and Copyright Law: A Comparative Law Study concerning the Role of Copyright Law', IIC, 6, 382, 1975; and Cornish, J. and D. Llewelyn, *Intellectual*

Property: Patents, Copyright, Trade Marks and Allied Marks, 5th ed., London: Sweet & Maxwell, 2003, at 507–17 (United Kingdom solution to the reprography problem, involving owner concessions, voluntary licensing schemes and statutory provisions).

11. For examples of very limited educational and library exceptions, see sections 29, 38–43 UK Copyright, Designs and Patents Act 1988.

12. For the UK position, see Suthersanen, U., 'Copyright and Educational Policies', *Oxford Journal of Legal Studies*, 23, 585, 2003. For the Canadian position, see *CCH Canadian Ltd. v. Law Society of Upper Canada*, [2004] 1 SCR 339. For the Australian position, see *University of New South Wales v. Moorhouse* [1975] HCA 26.

13. Sections 79–88, Canadian Copyright Act 1997, which allows some types of copying of musical works, performances and sound recordings for the private use of the person. The provisions also confer a right to remuneration on authors, performers and makers which is to be collected from 'manufacturers and importers of blank audio recording media'.

14. InfoSoc Directive, Article 5(2)(b), together with 5(3)(a) allowing reproduction for non-commercial teaching and scientific research. See also Suthersanen, U., 'Technology, Time and Market Forces', in M. Pugatch, *The Intellectual Property Debate: Perspectives from Law, Economics and Political Economy*, Cheltenham, UK and Northampton, MA, US: Edward Elgar, 230–67, 2006, at 243–4.

15. Creaser, C., S. Maynard and S. White, *LISU Annual Library Statistics 2006*, LISU, 2006, at 4.

16. The other partners are: Cornell, Princeton, the University of California, the University of Wisconsin–Madison, the University of Michigan, the University of Virginia, the University of Texas at Austin, the New York Public Library, the University Library of Lausanne, Ghent University Library, Keio University Library, the Bavarian State Library, the University Complutense of Madrid and the National Library of Catalonia.

17. Other older and more philanthropic projects include the Project Perseus and Project Gutenberg.

18. At http://www.bodley.ox.ac.uk/google/.

19. At http://hul.harvard.edu/hgproject/index.html.

20. The moral right, on the author's death, is transmitted to the author's heirs – Article L. 121-1, French Intellectual Property Code 1992; Chapter III, 2002 Law no. 82/2002 on Intellectual Property (Egypt).

21. *Société Plon and another v. P. Hugo and the Société des Gens de Lettres*, Court of Cassation (1st civil chamber), 30 January 2007; [2007] 4 ECDR 205.

22. Article 5, German Copyright Law 1965, as amended; section 105, US Copyright Act 1976. The US policy dates back to *Wheaton v. Peters*, 33 US (8 Pet) 591, 668 (1834). For UK Crown copyright, see section 163, Copyright, Designs and Patents Act 1988.

23. *Crown Copyright in the Digital Age – Green Paper on Crown Copyright*, 1998, available at http://www.opsi.gov.uk/advice/crown-copyright/crown-copyright-in-the-information-age.pdf.

24. *Capitol Records, Inc. v. Naxos of America, Inc.*, 45 NY3d 5540 (NY2005).

25. The validity of Google's project is pending the outcome of *Author's Guild v. Google Inc.*, No. 05cv8136 (SDNY), complaint (Dkt. 1, 20 September 2005); *McGraw-Hill Cos, Pearson Education Inc., Penguin Group Inc. Simon & Schuster Inc. and John Wiley & Sons*, United States District Court for the Southern District of New York, Docket No. 2005 CV 08881, filed 19 October 2005. See also Band, J., 'The Google Print Library Project: A Copyright Analysis', at http://www.policybandwidth.com/doc/googleprint.pdf.

26. Grafton, A., 'Future Reading: Digitization and its Discontents', *The New Yorker*, 5 November 2007.

27. Bonham-Carter, V., *Authors by Profession*, Volume 1, London: The Society of Authors and Bodley Head, 1978, at 214–15; and Suthersanen, U., 'Collectivism of Copyright: The Future of Rights Management in the European Union', in E. Barendt and A. Firth (eds), *Oxford Yearbook of Copyright and Media Law*, Oxford: Oxford University Press, Volume 5, 15–42, 2000, at 15.

28. Article 9(3), Berne Convention recognising that sound and visual recordings came within the right of reproduction.

29. Edelman, B., *Ownership of the Image*, London: Routledge & Kegan Paul, 1979, at 44; Gaines, J., *Contested Culture: The Image, the Voice, the Law*, Chapel Hill: The University of North Carolina Press, 1991, at 46.

30. Edelman describes this journey: 'In order to "intellectually" appropriate what belongs to everyone, I must not reproduce it, for then I shall do not more than expose what belongs to everyone, but I must produce it', Edelman, at 47. The French courts were among the first to recognise photographs as copyright works. The US Supreme Court soon followed by decreeing photographs as writings in *Burrow-Giles v. Sarony* (111 US 53, 1884).

31. *Baumen v. Fussell* (1978) RPC 485

32. Edelman, *op. cit.,* 44–67. The US recognised films as copyright works in *Edison v. Lubin* (122 F. 240 1903).

33. The revisions were Berlin (1908) incorporating photography, film, and sound recording; Rome (1928), adding broadcasting rights to the author; and Brussels (1948), adding television. Note however that these merely dealt with the author's rights – broadcasters and sound recording producers drafted a separate convention – the Rome Convention 1960.

34. 464 US 417 (S. Ct. 1984). For an interesting analysis of this decision, see Fisher, *op. cit.,* at 70–5.

35. 464 US 417 (S. Ct. 1984), at 436–7.

36. *Ibid.,* at 442.

37. *Sony,* 464 US 417 (S. Ct. 1984), at 439.

38. *Sony,* 464 US 417, at 434–42. A similar stance is adopted by the United Kingdom House of Lords in *C.B.S. Inc. v. Ames Records & Tapes Ltd.* [1982] Ch. 91 and *C.B.S. Songs Ltd. & Ors v. Amstrad Consumer Electronics Plc. & Anor,* [1988] AC 1013. In the latter, the court held that a manufacturer may have conferred on the purchaser the power to copy 'but did not grant or purport to grant the right to copy'. For a full discussion of these cases and their impact, see Suthersanen, 'Technology, Time and Market Forces', *op. cit.*

39. 464 US 417 (S. Ct. 1984) at 429–32.

40. 29 F.Supp.2d 624 (C.D. Cal. 1998), 180 F.3d 1072 (9th Cir. 1999).

41. *Ibid.,* at 1079.

42. *Ibid.,* at 248, 252.

43. Fisher, *op. cit.,* at 13–18.

44. *A&M Records, Inc. v. Napster, Inc.*, 293 F.3d 1004, 1011–13 (9th Cir. 2001); *In Re Aimster Copyright Litigation, Appeal of John Deep,* 334 F.3d 642, 646–7 (7th Cir. 2003); *Metro-Goldwyn-Mayer Studios, Inc. v. Grokster Ltd.,* 380 F.3d 1154, 1158–60 (9th Cir. 2004).

45. See Suthersanen, U., 'Napster, DVD and All That: Developing a Coherent Copyright Grid for Internet Entertainment', in E. Barendt and A. Firth (eds), *Oxford Yearbook of Copyright and Media Law,* Volume 6, Oxford: Oxford University Press, 2002, 207–50.

46. *Napster,* 239 F.3d 1004 (9th Cir. 2001), at 1017.

47. Other P2P networks include Gnutella, eDonkey, WinMX and BitTorrent.

48. *Metro-Goldwyn-Mayer Studios, Inc. et al. v. Grokster, Ltd., Streamcast Networks Inc. et al* 259 F. Supp. 2d 1029 (C.D. Cal. 2003), at 1041; 380 F.3d 1154 (C.A. 9 (Cal.), 2004); 125 S. Ct. 2764 (S. Ct, 2005).

49. *Metro-Goldwyn-Mayer Studios, Inc.* 259 F. Supp. 2d 1029 (C.D. Cal. 2003), at 1041.

50. It is worth reading Justice Breyer's intriguing concurring opinion whereby he appears to have painstakingly proven that, had it not been for the inducement issue, the facts relating to this decision were indeed very similar to the Sony facts. Breyer also emphasised the significant future market for non-infringing uses of Grokster-type peer-to-peer software, citing Robert Merges' work in 'A New Dynamism in the Public Domain', *University of Chicago Law Review,* 71, 183, 2004. See also *Metro-Goldwyn-Mayer Studios, Inc. and ors,* 125 S. Ct. 2764 (S. Ct, 2005), at 2789–91.

51. *Universal Music Australia Pty Ltd v. Sharman License Holdings Ltd* (2005) 65 IPR 289.

52. Section 101(1), Australian Copyright Act 1968 (Cth).

53. (2005) 65 IPR 289 at 387.

54. [2004] FC 488 aff'd 2005 FCA 193.

55. *Société Civile des Producteurs Phonographiques v. Anthony G,* 31éme chambre/2, le 8 Décembre 2005.

56. *Loi sur le Droit d'Auteur et les Droits Voisins dans la Société de l'Information* introducing Article L.335-2, I.P. Code. For the position in the other EU Member States, see Daly, M., 'Life after Grokster: Analysis of US and European Approaches to File-sharing', *European Intellectual Property Review*, 29(8), 319, 2007, at 320–3.

57. *SCRL Societe Belge des Auteurs, Compositeurs et Editeurs v. SA Scarlet (formerly known as Tiscali)*, Tribunal de Première Instance de Bruxelles, 29 June 2007, [2007] *European Copyright and Design Reports*, 19. For a Dutch perspective, see *Vereniging Buma, Stichting Stemra v KaZaA BV*, Supreme Court of the Netherlands, The Hague, 19 December 2003, [2004] ECDR 16.

58. Article 12, Directive 2000/31 of 8 June 2000 on electronic commerce.

59. See for instance, the evidence of Liebowitz, S., 'Will MP3 Downloads Annihilate the Record Industry? The Evidence So Far' (June 2003), http:// www.utdallas.edu/liebowit/ intprop/records.pdf; and Oberholzer, F. and K. Strumpf, 'The Effect of File Sharing on Record Sales: An Empirical Analysis' (March 2004), www.unc.edu/cigar/papers/ FileSharing_March 2004.pdf.

60. Benkler, Y., 'Sharing Nicely: On Shareable Goods and the Emergence of Sharing as a Modality of Economic Production', *Yale Law Journal*, 114, 273–358, 2004, at 281. Note also his discussion of the much vaunted open source phenomenon as exemplified by the GNU-Linux open operating systems, or the intriguingly altruistic 'Distributed Proofreaders' service which proofreads voluntarily e-texts posted on Project Gutenberg – Benkler, Y., 'Coase's Penguin, or, Linux and the Nature of the Firm', *Yale Law Journal*, 112, 369, 2002, at 398.

61. http://setiathome.ssl.berkeley.edu/.

62. http://www.stanford.edu/group/pandegroup/genome/.

63. It should be noted that the terminology can be confusing. DRMs or digital rights management are sometimes used confusingly to refer solely to technological protection measures (TPMs) – see for example, the Wikipedia entry on this subject which is solely devoted to TPMs and access controls. Sometimes, however, DRMs refer to both TPMs and rights management information provisions. The OECD Working Party on the Information Economy describes DRM as three key procedures: (a) the encryption of content to keep it unavailable to unauthorised users; (b) the establishment of a licence system for controlling who can access the content and what can be done with it in specific circumstances; and (c) the authentication of the identity of the user, a required step for accessing the different usage rights awarded by the licence, DSTI/ICCP/IE(2004)12/FINAL, 8 June 2005.

64. Article 11, WIPO Copyright Treaty and Article 18, WIPO Performances and Phonograms Treaty.

65. For a full account, see Ficsor, M., *The Law of Copyright and the Internet*, Oxford: Oxford University Press, 2002, chapter 11.

66. For examples of technological measures employed by the copyright owners, and how they may obstruct the exercise of such legitimate rights, see Dutfield, G. and U. Suthersanen, 'The Innovation Dilemma: Intellectual Property and the Historical Legacy of Cumulative Creativity', *Intellectual Property Quarterly*, 379–421, 2004, at 399.

67. For the US approach, see *Lexmark International v. Static Control Components Inc.*, 387 F.3d 522 (2004), holding that the *Lexmark* court ruled that circumventing a printer's scheme to prevent the use of third-party toner cartridges did not violate the DMCA.

68. Article 6, Council Directive 91/250 of 14 May 1991 on the legal protection of computer programs.

69. See *Chamberlain Group, Inc v. Skylink Technologies, Inc.* 381 F.3d 1178 (Fed. Cir. 2004); *Lexmark Int'l, Inc. v. Static Control Components, Inc.* 387 F.3d 522 (6th Cir. 2004); *cf. Davidson & Associates v. Jung*, 422 F.3d 630 (8th Cir. 2005) (*Blizzard v. BnetD*). See also Burk, D.L., 'Legal and Technical Standards in Digital Rights Management Technology', *Fordham Law Review*, 537, 2005. For a comparative North American perspective on whether the levy system in Canada will prove useful, and how it fares against the TPMs system under the DMCA, see Debeer, J., 'Locks & Levies', *Denver University Law Review*, 84(1), 143, 2006.

70. Directive 2001/29 of the European Parliament and of the Council on the harmonisation of certain aspects of copyright and related rights in the information society.
71. *Ibid.*, Articles 5(2)(a), (b), (e).
72. *Ibid.*, Articles 6–7.
73. *P v. Universal Pictures Video France*, Cass. Civ. 1ère, 28 February 2006; more intriguing was the French Supreme Court's application of the 'three-step' test under Article 5(5), InfoSoc Directive, which derives from Article 9(2), Berne Convention and Article 13, TRIPS Agreement. See also Maxwell, W. and J. Massaloux, 'French Copyright Law Reform: French Supreme Court Upholds Legality of DVD Anti-copy Measures', *Entertainment Law Review*, 17(5), 2006, 145.
74. Décret n° 2007-510 du 4 avril 2007 relatif à l'Autorité de régulation des mesures techniques instituée par l'article L. 331-17 du code de la propriété intellectuelle, available at http://www.legifrance.gouv.fr/WAspad/UnTexteDeJorf?numjo=MCCB0700270D.
75. Jobs, S., 'Thoughts on Music', at http://www.apple.com/hotnews/thoughtsonmusic/.
76. *Metro-Goldwyn-Mayer Studios Inc., et al. v. Grokster, Ltd., et al.*, No. 04-480, 24 January 2005, On Writ of Certiorari to the United States Court of Appeals for the Ninth Circuit, Brief of the Business Software Alliance as Amicus Curiae Supporting Petitioners, available at Westlaw, 2005 WL 166590.
77. *Ibid.*
78. *Microsoft* case COMP/C-3/37.792. Another very interesting facet to the case was the issue of Microsoft bundling its Media Player to the Windows operating system. See Ayres, I. and B. Nalebuff, 'Going Soft on Microsoft? The EU's Antitrust Case and Remedy', *The Economists' Voice*, 2(2), Article 4, 2005, at http://www.bepress.com/ev.
79. Ayres and Nalebuff, *op. cit.*
80. Lemley, M., 'Ten Things to Do about Patent Holdup of Standards (And One Not to)', *Boston College Law Review*, 48, 149, 2007, at 150–1.
81. *Ibid.*
82. *Ibid.*
83. Part of Annex 1A, Multilateral Agreements on Trade in Goods, WTO Agreement.
84. *British Telecommunications Plc. v. One In A Million Ltd.* [1999] FSR 1.
85. See Bill Clinton and Al Gore's 'Global Framework for eCommerce', Washington, 1 July 1997, at http://www.ecommerce.gov.
86. Administrative Panel Decision No. D2000-0235, WIPO Arbitration and Mediation Center, 22 May 2000, reported in [2000] ETMR 783.
87. http://secondlife.com/whatis/.
88. Varas, C., 'Virtual Protection: Applying Trade Mark Law within Virtual Worlds Such as Second Life', *Entertainment Law Review*, 19(1), 5, 2008.
89. *Ibid.*
90. Article 10(1), TRIPS Agreement; Article 4, WIPO Copyright Treaty.
91. Council Directive of 14 May 1991 on the legal protection of computer programs, 91/250/EEC; OJ 1991 L122/42.
92. *Ibid.*, recital 7.
93. *Ibid.*, Article 1(3), recital 8.
94. *Ibid.*, Article 1(2), recital 13.
95. For a very current discussion of this issue, see *Nova Productions Ltd. v. Mazooma Games Ltd. and Others Same v. Bell Fruit Games Ltd.*, [2007] EWCA Civ. 219.
96. *Ibid.*, Article 4(a).
97. *John Richardson Computers Ltd. v. Flanders*, (1993) FSR 497. The test is a variation of the 'abstraction, filtration, comparison' test applied in the United States, see *Computer Associates v. Altai*, 23 USPQ 2d 1241 (2nd Cir., 1992).
98. *Ibcos v. Barclay* (1994) FSR 725; see also *Nova Productions Ltd v. Mazooma Games Ltd and Others Same v. Bell Fruit Games Ltd*, [2007] EWCA Civ. 219.
99. *Ibid.*, Article 5.
100. *Ibid.*, section 50(B).
101. Samuelson, P., J.H. Reichman, M. Kapor and R. Davis, 'A Manifesto Concerning the Legal Protection of Computer Programs', *Columbia Law Review*, 94, 2308, 1994.

102. Plotkin, R., 'Software Patentability and Practical Utility: What's the Use?' *International Review of Law, Computers & Technology*, 19(1), 23, 2005, at 25.
103. 35 USC § 101.
104. *State Street Bank & Trust Co. v. Signature Financial Group, Inc.*, 149 F.3d 1368, 1375 (Fed. Cir. 1998). This test allows courts to exclude things such as abstract ideas, laws of nature, and natural phenomena – *Diamond v. Diehr*, 450 US 175, 185 (1981).
105. *State Street Bank*, 149 F.3d 1368, 1373 (Fed. Cir. 1998).
106. Proposal for a Directive of the European Parliament and of the Council on the patentability of computer-implemented inventions, COD/2002/0047.
107. Article 52(1) EPC.
108. Article 52(2), (3), EPC.
109. See decisions T208/84 *Vicom*, T26/86 *Koch,* and T115/85 IBM.
110. Note Ronald Mann's view that patent thickets are a fiction – 'Do Patents Facilitate Financing in the Software Industry?', available at The University of Texas Law and Economics Working Paper No. 022, March 2005: http://ssrn.com/abstract=510103.
111. Pila, J., 'Dispute over the Meaning of "Invention" in Article 52(2) EPC – The Patentability of computer-implemented Inventions in Europe', IIC, 36, 173, 2005.

11. Intellectual property and development

WHAT IS DEVELOPMENT?

'Development' is a term whose meaning is contested by social scientists and international development experts and organisations. Nowadays, it is common to speak of 'economic development', which focuses on a country's measurable economic performance relative to that of other countries; of 'human development', which supplements economic development by incorporating social welfare considerations; and of 'sustainable development', which takes into account the environment as well.

In 2000, the United Nations Millennium Summit was held at which UN member states agreed on a set of goals and targets for achieving development. The eight goals are now known as the Millennium Development Goals (MDGs), and are as follows:

1. Eradicate extreme poverty and hunger
2. Achieve universal primary education
3. Promote gender equality and empower women
4. Reduce child mortality
5. Improve maternal health
6. Combat HIV/AIDS, malaria and other diseases
7. Ensure environmental sustainability
8. Develop a global partnership for development

Given the existence of Goal 7, the version of development that best captures the intent of the MDGs is sustainable development. It is especially noteworthy that several multilateral environmental agreements contain provisions on technology transfer,[1] which is undeniably an intellectual property-related issue.

INTERNATIONAL DIPLOMACY ON INTELLECTUAL PROPERTY AND DEVELOPMENT

The first official attempt to challenge the international intellectual property regime for failing to meet the development needs of poor countries was made in 1961, when the government of Brazil submitted a draft resolution co-sponsored by Bolivia to a committee of the United Nations General Assembly. The draft put forward various concerns including that 'access to . . . knowledge and experience in science and technology is often limited by patents and similar arrangements designed to protect the right of ownership and exploitation of investors of new processes, techniques and products'. In view of the perceived economically detrimental impacts of patents on underdeveloped countries, Brazil put forward a request that the United Nations Secretary-General prepare a report containing:

(a) a survey of patent legislation in selected developed and underdeveloped countries, with primary emphasis on the treatment given to foreign patents;
(b) a study of the effects of royalties paid for the use of patents in the balance of payments of underdeveloped countries;
(c) a preliminary analysis of the characteristics of the domestic legislation of underdeveloped countries in the light of economic development objectives;
(d) an indication of the possibility of revising legislation in accordance with the principles of international law, with a view to permitting the rapid absorption of new products and techniques to accelerate the rate of economic development;
(e) a recommendation on the advisability of holding an international conference with the aim of adjusting the existing patent conventions to the needs of developing countries.

The resolution also made the suggestion that United Nations 'Member States, especially the under-developed countries, in the granting of patents and in the elaboration or revision of their patent laws, should take into consideration the needs and peculiarities of their economies as well as the rights of the patent-holders, with a view to eliminating the distortions to which the patent system may give rise, to encouraging the productive incorporation of the new products and techniques into the national economy, and to improving its productivity levels, without interfering with the rights of industrial property, as recognized by international law'.

The International Bureau and the International Chamber of Commerce (ICC) were alarmed by the tone of the draft and the fact that Brazil was seeking to shift deliberations on patent standard-setting to the United Nations General Assembly. In response, they lobbied for a radical change of tone.[2] This move was successful and Resolution 1713(XVI), entitled 'The role of patents in the transfer of technology to under-developed countries', was much more satisfactory from the point of view of both the ICC and BIRPI. It shifted the terms of reference of the requested Secretary-General's report in a less patent-hostile direction.[3] And thanks also to BIRPI's direct involvement in drafting it, the 1964 report's[4] conclusions were far less critical than the Brazilians would presumably have wished for.

Nonetheless, discontent with the status quo in intellectual property rules, especially patents, persisted, and the United Nations system provided spaces for such discontent to be aired. At the first meeting of the United Nations Conference on Trade and Development (UNCTAD), a Resolution was adopted recommending, *inter alia*, that:

- Developed countries should encourage the holders of patented and unpatented technology to facilitate the transfer of licenses, know-how, technical documentation, and new technology in general to developing countries, including the financing of the procurement of licenses and related technology on favourable terms.
- Additional facilities for information on, and for the transfer of, technical documentation and know-how should be organized within the framework of the United Nations in consultation with the appropriate international organizations.[5]

In the same year, the Economic and Social Council of the United Nations adopted a Resolution which reaffirmed that 'access to knowledge and experience in the field of applied science and technology would facilitate the continued development of industrialization and international economic relations'.[6]

In 1974, the United Nations General Assembly adopted two documents, the Declaration on the Establishment of a New International Economic Order (NIEO) and the Programme of Action on the Establishment of a New International Economic Order. Neither dealt explicitly with intellectual property, but they both covered technology transfer in ways that implied dissatisfaction with the international intellectual property regime for failing to contribute in this regard. According to the Declaration, one of the principles upon which the NIEO should be founded are: 'giving to the developing countries access to the achievements of modern science and technology, and promoting the transfer of technology and the creation of indigenous technology for the benefit of the developing countries in forms and in accordance with procedures which are suited to their economies'. With respect to transfer of technology, the Programme of Action stated that:

All efforts should be made:

(a)   To formulate an international code of conduct for the transfer of technology corresponding to needs and conditions prevalent in developing countries;

(b)   To give access on improved terms to modern technology and to adapt that technology, as appropriate, to specific economic, social and ecological conditions and varying stages of development in developing countries;

(c)   To expand significantly the assistance from developed to developing countries in research and development programmes and in the creation of suitable indigenous technology;

(d)   To adapt commercial practices governing transfer of technology to the requirements of the developing countries and to prevent abuse of the rights of sellers;

(e)   To promote international co-operation in research and development in exploration and exploitation, conservation and the legitimate utilization of natural resources and all sources of energy.

(f)   In taking the above measures, the special needs of the least developed and land-locked countries should be borne in mind.

The idea for a code of conduct for technology transfer led to negotiations on a draft International Code of Conduct on Transfer of Technology. These talks were conducted under the aegis of UNCTAD. Despite ten years of deliberations, no final agreement could be reached.[7]

A similar lack of consensus arose in the early 1980s from efforts by a grouping of developing countries (the Group of 77) at WIPO to revise the Paris Convention. Among other things, they sought preferential treatment for developing countries and additional measures to require foreign patent holders to work their patents in countries granting them. The failure of the Diplomatic Conference on the Revision of the Paris Convention had much to do with opposition to such measures from many of the developed countries but was due also to differences among the developing countries themselves.[8]

Discontent with international intellectual property rules, and especially TRIPS, persists among developing countries. A number of reports have been published which have either claimed that TRIPS and current trends in international intellectual property rule-making are harmful for development, or suggested that some aspects of them may be. Among these are the UNDP Human Development Reports of 1999,[9] 2000,[10] 2001,[11] the UNDP publication, *Making Global Trade Work for People*[12] – which was especially critical – and the World Bank's *Global Economic Prospects and the Developing Countries 2002*,[13] which was more cautious.

Perhaps the most thorough and well-publicised study on the intellectual property–development nexus was produced by the Commission on Intellectual Property Rights (CIPR).[14] This UK government-sponsored body, convened to investigate concerns such as those expressed in the above reports, was headed by Professor John Barton of Stanford University, and comprised widely respected authorities on intellectual property from developed and developing countries with varied backgrounds and expertise. It was mandated to look at how intellectual property rights might work better for poor people and developing countries by providing balanced, evidence-based policy recommendations. Published in 2002, the document contained some quite far-reaching recommendations directed at the global intellectual property system including the institutions within it (such as the WTO and WIPO), national intellectual property policy-making, and covering the following six areas: intellectual property and development; health; agriculture and genetic resources; traditional knowledge, access and benefit-sharing and geographical indications; copyright, software and the internet; and patent reform.

Overall, the Commission expressed serious doubts that the international intellectual property regime in its present form, and current processes to further strengthen intellectual property protection, are in the interests of the poor. It also considered that TRIPS imposes onerous costs on most developing countries. The report made a strong case that a one-size-fits-all approach to intellectual property protection simply does not work, especially when the required levels of protection are as high as they are today and are likely to become in the near future (which is even higher).

The Commissioners presented strong evidence for their critical stance with respect to the international intellectual property regime, but at the same time avoided the error of treating developing countries as homogeneous. Rather they argued that due to their different scientific and technological capacities and social and economic structures, an optimal intellectual property system is bound to vary widely from one country to another. For example, developing countries that have relatively advanced scientific and technological capacities like India and China may well benefit from high levels of intellectual property protection in some areas, whereas many other countries are likely not to do so.

In the present decade, criticisms have been made not just of the multilateral intellectual property agreements, but of the intergovernmental organisations responsible for administering them and under whose auspices negotiations on international intellectual property rule-making take place. In particular, WIPO has come under heavy criticism for giving priority to the interests and demands of private intellectual property owners, legal practitioners for whom the owners are clients, and developed countries governments over those of developing countries and those organisations that believe the international rules are unbalanced in favour of intellectual property owners and are bad for development.[15] WIPO's favouritism towards the first group of stakeholders is manifested in several ways including the provision of technical assistance to developing countries, which is believed by some to deliberately overlook the flexibilities of TRIPS and other multilateral intellectual property agreements, and promote what are effectively TRIPS plus standards.

Increasingly, developing countries are much better able to acquire alternative sources of technical expertise and documentation. It is partly for this reason that they have enhanced their capacity to put forward substantial and technically sound counter-proposals at the WTO and WIPO relating to such matters as public health, technology transfer, development, traditional knowledge and the compatibility between TRIPS and the provisions of the Convention on Biological Diversity concerning benefit-sharing and protection of traditional knowledge. And through improved negotiating strategies they have upheld their freedom to provide generic versions of patented essential medicines to the poor, delayed moves to harmonise international patent law, and moderated some recent copyright treaties.

The alternative expertise has come from certain NGOs and in some cases private individuals including academics acting as consultants. Very useful and high quality documentation has been produced by some of these NGOs and individuals. Organisations publishing rigorous technical materials include the Quaker United Nations Office, the South Centre and the International Centre for Trade and Sustainable Development (ICTSD), the latter working in collaboration with UNCTAD.

Two important proposals that have arisen are to draft an Access to Knowledge (A2K) Treaty and for WIPO to address the development-related interests of developing countries by establishing a Development Agenda. The A2K proposal is dealt with elsewhere in this book (Chapter 12). It suffices here to remind readers that concern about limitations on access to knowledge resulting from the overprotection of intellectual property had been expressed in Brazil's draft resolution of 1961. It is interesting to see how developing countries and their supporters – and NGOs in the developed world – have returned to an issue first expressed in public by the Brazilian government over four decades ago.

As for the Development Agenda proposal, this was initially mooted by the governments of Brazil and Argentina. These countries submitted a document to WIPO which was circulated and discussed at its General Assembly which took place in 2004.[16] The initiative of these countries was so well received by several other developing countries that they united to form a 14-country-strong grouping called the Friends of Development,[17] which produced a follow-up submission to WIPO. This latter document elaborated on the first one and responded to some developed countries, especially the United States, that were opposed to any comprehensive initiative to explicitly incorporate development concerns into the mandate and activities of WIPO.[18] The four issues covered in the second submission were: (i) WIPO's mandate and governance; (ii) norm-setting; (iii) technical cooperation; and (iv) transfer of technology.

With regard to WIPO's mandate, the Friends of Development noted that as a UN agency, WIPO should be guided by the UN's development goals including the MDGs. Moreover, development concerns should be incorporated into all of WIPO's work. Indeed, the Development Agenda is partially premised along the UN mandate to WIPO to be responsible for promoting creative intellectual activity and for facilitating the transfer of technology related to industrial property to the developing countries in order to accelerate economic, social and cultural development, subject to the competence and responsibilities of the United Nations and its organs, particularly the United Nations Conference on Trade and Development, the United Nations Development Programme and the United Nations Industrial Development Organization, as well as of the United Nations Educational, Scientific and Cultural Organization and of other agencies within the United Nations system.[19]

As to pro-development intellectual property norm-setting, the document offered some principles and guidelines to make negotiations more inclusive and pro-development. These include:

(a) undertaking independent, evidence-based 'Development Impact Assessment' (DIA) to consider the possible implications of each norm-setting initiative for core sustainable development indicators;
(b) incorporating provisions recognizing the difference between developed and developing WIPO member states in all norm-setting initiatives;
(c) holding public hearings prior to the initiation of any discussion towards norm-setting in WIPO, with the broad participation of different stakeholders, including other intergovernmental organisations, academia, consumer groups, and other civil society organisations.

For more developmentally sensitive technical assistance, the Friends of Development suggested the following principles and guidelines:

(a) development-focused technical assistance fulfilling national and broader development goals including the MDGs and taking into account differing levels of development;
(b) comprehensive and coherent assistance programmes that enable countries to take advantage of the in-built flexibilities provided in different intellectual property agreements;
(c) an integrated approach that includes coverage of competition law and policy in order to deal with abuses of IPRs and restraints on trade and technology transfer and dissemination;
(d) neutral, unbiased and non-discriminatory;
(e) tailor-made and demand-driven in order to accommodate levels of development, the specific needs and problems of individual societies, and the needs of the various local stakeholders, not just the intellectual property offices and right holders;
(f) independence of providers;
(g) continuous evaluation as to effectiveness;
(h) transparency.

Turning finally to technology transfer, the document suggested a range of supportive measures for adoption by industrialised countries and at the multilateral level. Such supportive measures might include:

- technical and financial assistance for improving the ability of countries to absorb technology;
- fiscal benefits to firms transferring technologies to developing countries of the same type;
- the same tax advantages for R&D performed abroad as for R&D done at home;
- fiscal incentives to encourage enterprises to train scientific, engineering and management graduates from developing countries;
- public resources could be used to support research into the technology development and technology transfer needs of developing countries;
- grant programmes could be established for research into technologies that would be of greatest productivity for the purpose of meeting priority social needs of developing countries;
- grant programmes to support proposals that meaningfully involve research teams in developing countries, in partnership with research groups in donor countries;
- universities should be encouraged to recruit and train students from developing countries in science, technology, and management;
- special trust funds for the training of scientific and technical personnel, for facilitating the transfer of technologies that are particularly sensitive for the provision of public goods, and for encouraging research in developing countries.

At the multilateral level, suggestions by the Friends of Development included:

- the establishment of a special fee on applications through the Patent Cooperation Treaty, the revenues of which would be earmarked for the promotion of R&D activities in developing and least developed countries;
- a multilateral agreement where signatories would place in the public domain, or find other means of sharing at modest cost, the results of largely publicly funded research. The idea is to set out a mechanism for increasing the international flow of technical information, especially to developing countries, through expansion of the public domain in scientific and technological information, safeguarding, in particular, the public nature of information that is publicly developed and funded without unduly restricting private rights in commercial technologies.

After considerable debate, the submission of a vast range of proposals and counter-proposals by numerous governments, and a certain amount of resistance, even from WIPO, members of the organisation agreed in September 2007 to formally adopt the Development Agenda by establishing a new Committee on Development and Intellectual Property. The Committee is charged with overseeing the implementation of 45 proposals about which consensus was reached.[20]

NOTES

1. These include the Convention on Biological Diversity, the Convention to Combat Desertification in those Countries Experiencing Serious Drought and/or Desertification, Particularly in Africa, the Framework Convention on Climate Change, and the Montreal Protocol on Substances that Deplete the Ozone Layer.
2. See International Chamber of Commerce Commission on the International Protection of Industrial Property, Summary Record, *Industrial Property*, 1st year no. 1, 38–40, 1962.
3. Menescal, A.K., 'Those behind the TRIPS Agreement: The Influence of the ICC and the AIPPI on International Intellectual Property Decisions', *Intellectual Property Quarterly*, 2, 155–82, 2005, at 172. See also Penrose, E., 'International Patenting and the Less-developed Countries', *The Economic Journal*, 83(331), 768–86, 1973.
4. United Nations Secretary General. 'The Role of Patents in the Transfer of Technology for Developing Countries', 1964 [Document E/3681].
5. In Ladas, S., *Patents, Trademarks, and Related Rights: National and International Protection*, Cambridge, MA: Harvard University Press, 1975, at 174.
6. *Ibid.*
7. Patel, S.J., P. Roffe and A. Yusuf (eds) *International Technology Transfer: The Origins and Aftermath of the United Nations Negotiations on a Draft Code of Conduct*, The Hague, Boston and London: Kluwer Law International; Sell, S.K., *Power and Ideas: North-South Politics of Intellectual Property and Antitrust*, Suny Series in Global Politics, Albany: State University of New York Press, 1998, 79–106.
8. Sell, *op. cit.*, 107–40.
9. UNDP, *Human Development Report 1999*, New York and Oxford: UNDP and Oxford University Press, at 67–76.
10. UNDP, *Human Development Report 2000*, at 84.
11. UNDP, *Human Development Report 2001*, at 97–109.
12. UNDP, *Making Global Trade Work for People*, London: Earthscan, 2003, at 203–34.
13. The World Bank, *Global Economic Prospects and the Developing Countries 2002: Making Trade Work for the World's Poor*, Washington DC: The World Bank, 2001, at 129–50.
14. http://www.iprcommission.org.
15. Musungu, F.S. and G. Dutfield, 'Multilateral Agreement and a TRIPS Plus World: The World Intellectual Property Organization', TRIPS Issues paper no. 3, QUNO-QIAP, 2003.
16. WIPO, 'Proposal by Argentina and Brazil for the Establishment of a Development Agenda for WIPO. Note prepared by the Secretariat', 2004 [Document WO/GA/31/11].
17. The Friends of Development are Argentina, Bolivia, Brazil, Cuba, Dominican Republic, Ecuador, Egypt, Iran, Kenya, Peru, Sierra Leone, South Africa, Tanzania and Venezuela.
18. WIPO, 'Proposal to Establish a Development Agenda for the World Intellectual Property Organization (WIPO): An Elaboration of Issues Raised in Document WO/GA/31/11. Submission by the Group of Friends of Development', 2005 [Document IIM/1/4].
19. Article 1, Agreement between the United Nations and the World Intellectual Property Organization, 1974. This was, interestingly, never part of WIPO's own constitutional mandate. See Articles 3 and 4, Convention Establishing the World Intellectual Property

Organization (as amended in 1979), which states two objectives and its function. One of the objectives is to promote the protection 'of intellectual property throughout the world through cooperation', and the Preamble to the Convention notes that one rationale for setting up the WIPO is to 'to encourage creative activity' by the promotion of the protection of intellectual property throughout the world. There is, however, no mention within the Convention of 'transfer of technology' or encouragement of social, economic or cultural development.

20.   WIPO, 'Report of the Provisional Committee on Proposals Related to a WIPO Development Agenda', 2007 [WIPO Document A/43/13 Rev.].

12. Education, culture and knowledge

The advent of the internet coupled with the increasing availability of individual computing power has expanded access to and usage of informational products, especially cultural, scientific and academic works. However, the downside has been that far-reaching provisions have been introduced into international and national intellectual property laws (especially copyright law) which curtail access to such products, and may even have tipped the balance towards the intellectual property owners and away from the general public. There is, thus, a growing realisation of the potential impact of current intellectual property laws on cultural and educational policies.

Can countries, especially developing countries, take advantage of the flexibilities provided in existing international treaties to establish strong and reliable exceptions for the cultural, research, educational and scientific usage of protected intellectual property material? Should countries develop a more positive rights approach so that educational and developmental needs can be met? Will NGO-initiated international ventures such as the proposed Treaty on Access to Knowledge or the WIPO Development Agenda promote intellectual property policies that prioritise the educational and knowledge needs of the general public, especially in developing countries? What measures, if any, are available under international intellectual property law that can enhance rather than undermine educational usage?

As we saw, information technology provides both opportunities and threats for the copyright industries that include the publishing industry, the main supplier of educational content. It sometimes appears, though, that these industries would prefer to emphasise the threats when lobbying governments to reform the law to accommodate technological changes. It has been argued that technological developments make it difficult for both authors and publishers to control the dissemination and use of works, and to enforce their exclusive rights. Technological developments, however, enable the digitisation of copyright works and now facilitate access to many works which hitherto may have been denied to many consumers.

Technology can be further employed to assist rights owners in tracking their works, in collecting and distributing monies payable to authors, and in allowing enhancements to the educational sector such as easier clearance for the use of both paper and electronic material, bibliographic material in journals which will include not only ISBN numbers, names of publishers, but also the names of the authors of individual articles, on-line sale of extracts or individual chapters of books, or journal articles rather than whole books or whole series of titles, and offer a site licence for certain books or chapters to be placed on-line on closed or locked university websites.[1]

Users, in both developed and developing countries, perceive a new age of information goods which has little or no relationship with the previous world of copyright and access in relation to analogue materials. It has been argued that the attendant problems discussed above are primarily concerns for the North or developed countries. Developing countries, on the other hand, are more concerned with pricing of software and books, and mass reprography. Moreover, it may be that the latter nations are still mostly at the analogue stage, demanding physical copies of educational goods, and tape and video reproductions of entertainment goods. This is probably an oversimplification, though, since there is a wide divergence in conditions within the developing world. Digital usage has increased in most areas, as has internet usage. One study reveals that the majority of users in the world originate from North America, Asia and the European Union regions, with little increase in the number of users in Africa due to the lack of telecommunications infrastructure in this region.[2] Other cost-benefit analyses may show differing results. Putting aside the internet revolution, there is definitely a high global demand for affordable hardware and software in all countries, which in turn is linked to a demand for digital educational goods.

The increased availability and attraction of digital works, as well as public domain and public commons projects and organisations such as Open Source, IP Justice, the Electronic Frontier Foundation, the Global Internet Liberation Campaign, the Digital Divide Network, the Digital Libraries project by Google and Microsoft, the Adelphi Charter, the BBC Creative Archive, and the Creative Commons licence project, have merely highlighted the growing public interest need for a review of the balance which copyright law has hitherto attempted to achieve vis-à-vis access and learning.

As access to the internet becomes more globalised, concerns about access and fair use have grown. For developing countries with heavy reliance on foreign materials, the new international copyright law arena appears hostile in relation to attempts to harness resources at zero or little cost. This in turn is viewed as being a threat to the educational and developmental needs and rights of citizens of such countries.

Public education systems in many developing countries are dependent upon foreign publications. The pricing of books, journals and on-line databases is an important consideration. This is especially true of academic and educational works, as opposed to fictional or populist works. Educational and research materials cover a much wider range of goods such as electronic databases comprising digital journals and teaching and research software.[3] However, the cost of academic journals is an issue not only in developing countries but also in developed countries with established publishing industries like the UK.[4]

One reason for concern is that the market for academic journals, especially in certain areas like medicine and science, is controlled by very few publishers who use their copyright and database right to extract high rents. Economists have always argued that intellectual property protection should be limited in such circumstances where the rights holder gains an excessive control over a specific product market or where the consumer is left with no alternative competing substitute product. Consider the following scenario: if one publishing house manages to capture and control a disproportionately large number of journal titles in several disciplines, an increase in the subscription price will not necessarily cause the user to switch to another publisher unless there is a meaningful substitute. The more extreme scenario arises where the publishing house in question is the sole source of certain types of information, for example, industry statistics or case reports which are used in official citations. For example, some law reviews in the UK, and several courts in the US, require citations to specific publishers' reports of court decisions.[5]

It is all too probable, therefore, that consumers can get locked into certain suppliers due to the unavailability of affordable informational resources. This is problematic for public schools and universities who cannot afford imported copyright-protected texts. The problem is further exacerbated by the fact that many developed countries refuse to accept international exhaustion principles. These principles were accepted in Australia and New Zealand due to the heavy costs of importation of foreign books, and the fact that copyright law was being used to prevent competitive importation and sale of legitimate books.[6] Such educational users may have no alternative but to allow the copying of texts by students, schools and colleges without payment or authorisation. This creates a difficult dilemma for developing countries: should they clamp down on copyright infringers but allow textbook prices to be prohibitively high for schools, most students and higher education institutions? Or should they allow mass copying but risk being placed on the US Watch List or being threatened with trade sanctions by copyright exporter countries?

THE HUMAN RIGHT TO EDUCATION

The human right to education implicitly carries much larger public welfare and communitarian elements than compulsory elementary education alone. It is said that it 'epitomizes the indivisibility and interdependence of all human rights'.[7] After all, it is not just the individual but also society which has an interest in having an educated society and citizenry.[8] Moreover, international human rights discourse recognises that education is an indispensable means of realising other human rights. It empowers the poor, women and children from exploitative and hazardous labour, it protects the environment, and is a financial investment for States.[9] The right to education can also be considered as both a civil right and a political right, as it is also directed at the 'full development of the human personality and the sense of its dignity'.[10]

The gist of the education components as found in Article 26 of the Universal Declaration of Human Rights (UDHR) and Articles 13–14 of the International Covenant on Economic, Social and Cultural Rights (ICESCR), is as follows:

- education shall be directed to the full development of the human personality and the sense of its dignity;
- to secure *compulsory*, *free* primary education;
- to ensure secondary education is made generally available and accessible to all, especially by the progressive introduction of *free* education;
- to ensure higher education is made equally accessible to all, on the basis of capacity, in particular by the progressive introduction of *free* education;
- fundamental education shall be encouraged or intensified.

The issues are as follows. First, should intellectual property rights be subject to the right of education? And if so, how should this subjugation of intellectual property rights be implemented?

The 1999 General Comment No. 13 on the right to education[11] states that part of the aim of the provision is to make states set up an adequate infrastructure to facilitate the proper functioning of educational institutions. Accordingly, factors to be taken into account include (i) teaching materials; (ii) library facilities; (iii) computer facilities and (iv) information technology.

Thus, it seems inevitable that the educational needs of individuals should be taken into account within the international intellectual property framework. Yet there is a dearth of provisions sanctioning *free* educational usage of materials within most intellectual property laws, and especially within the international copyright system.

COPYRIGHT AND EDUCATION IN INTERNATIONAL AND NATIONAL LAW

Since the adoption of the UDHR, no fewer than 24 treaties and agreements have either been revised or introduced and all of them have had the uniform effect of strengthening international intellectual property protection.[12] In contrast, the only treaty which appeared to lower intellectual property standards and to prioritise the needs of developing and intellectual property importing countries was the UNESCO-governed Universal Copyright Convention 1971 (UCC).

In the years following decolonisation, a large number of newly independent states, especially within Asia and Africa, came into existence. These countries were unhappy with the copyright norms as established under the Berne Convention with its inherent bias towards rights owners and developed countries. Developing countries were particularly concerned as to the need to provide for free or cheap educational usage of copyright-protected materials. A national priority in most newly independent states was the building of schools and hospitals, accompanied by a national policy allowing free or low cost availability of books (especially scientific and technical books) and medicine. The national government in India, for instance, took the position that

> the high production costs of scientific and technical books standing in the way of their dissemination in developing countries could be substantially reduced if the advanced countries would freely allow their books to be reprinted and translated by underdeveloped countries.[13]

The UCC was popular with developing countries as it had fewer mandatory requirements and lower thresholds of protection. For instance, countries could introduce any limitation or exception as long as these provisions did 'not conflict with the spirit and provisions of this Convention', and if the state gave a 'reasonable degree of effective protection to each of the rights' to which exception was made.[14] This is a much more flexible form of general limitation clause than the Berne/TRIPS three-step test we discussed earlier. The Convention was also perceived as being more developing country friendly with its extensive restrictions on the right of translation; thus, for example the Convention declared that if there was no translation of a work into the local language of a country after seven years from the publication of a work, then any national person could obtain a non-exclusive compulsory licence to translate the work, subject to certain formalities.[15] Even the compulsory duration of protection was (and still is) shorter than the Berne Convention – countries have to grant a term of protection of not less than life plus 25 years; however, where a country computed duration of protection from the first publication of the work (such as the United States prior to its 1976 Copyright Act), then the term of protection had only to be at least 25 years from first publication or registration.

The UCC was revised in Paris in 1971, at the same time as the Berne Convention revision, with the two meetings being held one after the other. The general tenor of the two meetings was clear – developing countries wanted clear concessions for educational usage of copyright materials. This key issue had already been raised in the 1967 Stockholm Protocol to the Berne Convention and had been heavily resisted by authors' organisations, publishers, and other rights holders in the developed world. The view of these stakeholders can be summarised in an opinion issued by ALAI, that 'the Protocol constitutes a sacrifice of the rights of authors in developed countries and jeopardizes the best interests of authors in developing countries'.[16]

Nevertheless, one may view the 1971 revisions to both Conventions as a harmonisation of international copyright law in the sense that the concessions towards developing countries recognised within the UCC were transferred to the Berne Convention. In theory at least, the educational use is now an acknowledged exception to international copyright protection.[17]

The Berne Convention and Education

Article 10(2)
Article 10(2), Berne Convention (which is now part of the TRIPS Agreement) provides authorisation to developing countries to permit reproductions for educational purposes:

> It shall be a matter for legislation in the countries of the Union, and for special agreements existing or to be concluded between them, to permit the utilization, to the extent justified by the purpose, of literary or artistic works by way of illustration in publications, broadcasts or sound or visual recordings for *teaching*, provided such utilization is compatible with fair practice.

However, the wording within the provision is ambiguous. For example, is there a limit on the amount that may be copied from any given work? What do the words 'to the extent justified by the purpose' mean? It is arguable that there is no necessity to copy a whole work in order to convey the information required for the teaching purpose. On the other hand, the phrase does not preclude copying the whole of a work in appropriate circumstances. Ricketson suggests that Article 10(2) also permits the preparation for teaching purposes of compilations anthologising all or parts of a variety of works.[18] The term 'provided such utilization is compatible with fair practice' also suggests that one has to refer back to the three-step test.

The 1971 Berne Appendix
The 1971 Paris Act of the Berne Convention contains an Appendix, now part of the TRIPS Agreement, which allows compulsory licensing in relation to mass reproduction and translation of works for educational purposes. These provisions were to be the post-colonial solution to the 'international crisis of

copyright' in the 1960s and 1970s. A euphemistic view of the 1971 Appendix is that it acts as an incentive to authors and publishers, and is a bargaining tool for developing countries to enable a degree of practical cooperation with the possibility of establishing an affordable book supply system.[19] Nevertheless, it is highly doubtful that the Berne Appendix did anything to give practical effect to the notion that the educational needs of people in developing countries should have priority over intellectual property rights. Specifically, the Appendix provides that, subject to compensation to the copyright owner, there is a possibility of granting non-exclusive and non-transferable compulsory licensing in respect of (i) translation for the purpose of teaching, scholarship or research, and (ii) reproduction for use in connection with systematic instructional activities, of works protected under the Convention.[20] In reality, the Appendix is limited in the following manner. First, it is so highly detailed and complicated that it exceeds the original Berne Act in length.[21] Second, although the Appendix does permit the invocation of a compulsory licence of works if voluntary negotiations over translations and reproduction rights are not successful, the provisions are extremely complex.[22] Third, the Appendix only extends to translation and reproduction rights, and does not apply to broadcasting or other communication rights – hence on-line transmission of works does not come within the exceptions. Fourth, the Appendix contains no provisions for free educational use or for any reduction in duration of copyright.

How many countries have actually taken advantage of the Berne Convention Appendix provisions? The general consensus is that no more than nine developing countries have adopted the options. Indeed, despite the anxieties regarding access to copyright works for educational purposes, the copyright laws in most developing countries reflect the international standard of protection without much divergence. Yet the Berne Appendix 1971 is probably the only generally accepted bulk access tool in international copyright law.

Other International Treaties

With the advent of digital technology and the internet, and with the growing economic needs of developing countries in the area of health, there has been increasing demand for the lowering of intellectual property protection. During the 1990s, for example, copyright holders and managers argued successfully that international copyright laws had to be revised to accommodate 'new technologies' and for WIPO to incorporate a 'digital agenda'. The resulting two 1996 WIPO Internet Treaties provide an additional layer of protection for copyright rights holders in the face of the new digital technologies.

Can countries, especially developing countries, take advantage of the wide flexibilities provided in the latter WIPO treaties, the Berne Appendix and in

TRIPS to establish and defend strong exceptions for the research, educational and scientific usage of copyright material? Or do we need yet another treaty – such as the proposed Access to Knowledge Treaty – discussed below?

National Laws and Education Exceptions

National copyright law has always sought to strike a balance between the rights of the owners and the rights of users by allowing – within certain limits – unauthorised reproduction or communication of protected works. This is called private use in EU and other civil law jurisdictions, or fair use in the United States, and fair dealing in the UK and other commonwealth jurisdictions.

One solution for developing countries is to refuse to pay for any educational usage of copyright material by relying on the exceptions within national copyright laws. Section 107 of the US Copyright Act, for example, sets out the scope of the fair use exception:

> Notwithstanding the provisions of sections 106 and 106A, use by reproduction in copies or phonorecords or by any other means specified by that section, for purposes such as criticism, comment, news reporting, *teaching (including multiple copies for classroom use), scholarship, or research*, is not an infringement of copyright (emphasis added).

It is clear that non-commercial use, especially by educational institutions, will be given much more latitude in making use of copyrighted materials than commercial use of the same materials.[23] But how much more? As discussed above, strengthened international copyright law means that the concept of fair use, as set out in US copyright law, may have become more restricted. Under international copyright law, it may be argued that such a no-payment copyright policy in relation to educational works falls foul of the three-step test set out in TRIPS (see Chapter 4). All exceptions must comply with this test, and the foremost rule is that exceptions to copyright protection can only be granted in 'special circumstances'. Usage for educational purposes may be too widespread to count as a special circumstance.

Second, the fair dealing or fair use defence is usually limited to the person actually engaged in study or research, and does not extend to the person or firm facilitating these activities for others. Thus, copy shops or university libraries with photocopying machines which enable such educational usage cannot avail themselves of such defences.[24] The reservation of the defence for a private individual, however, does not take into account the commonplace and economically dictated practice of multiple copying within educational institutions and copy shops caused by the high ratio of students to library resources, and the widened selection of reading material today as opposed to 30 years ago.

Developing Countries' Experiences of Collective Management[25]

It is clear that public policy favours access to works for educational usage, and this is true both in developing and developed countries. In the latter countries, a balance has been reached by allowing complete reliance on the private use/fair dealing exceptions but only in conjunction with some sort of payment of a licensing fee. Works are freely available for educational copying but local collecting societies, representing authors and/or publishers, negotiate with user groups and collect a fee. There are three types of fees: (i) compulsory license fees; (ii) voluntary collective licencing fees; and (iii) equipment levies.

Collecting societies or rights management organisations have become an essential practical and economic ingredient within the copyright regime. If educational usage is to be compensated for, the most common approach is for a collective agreement between the rights owners and the main users of the works, that is, the relevant government authorities in charge of schools and universities. A blanket licence obliterates the need to determine whether the usage in question is inside or outside the fair use or fair dealing exceptions. For a user, it is more expedient to be directed to one entity which manages the rights in relation to a specific category of work, thus saving him from incurring transaction costs in terms of search and negotiation in obtaining licences from different authors in respect of different works. Collective management and blanket licensing are the common means by which reprographic copying in the educational sector is controlled.

The burden of administration and proof, however, should be placed on rights owners rather than users. That there is a high transactional cost involved in collective management is clear from the evidence tendered by Denise Nicholson, Copyright Services Librarian at the University of the Witwatersrand in South Africa, to the UK Commission on Intellectual Property Rights. She highlighted the following problems which are likely to be experienced by other universities not only in the developing world, but also in the developed world:[26]

(i)   getting copyright clearance imposes a heavy administrative burden;
(ii)   obtaining permission directly from publishers for works excluded from or not mandated to the collecting society is time-consuming, expensive (payable in foreign currency) and difficult;
(iii)   in respect of translation, in some developing countries many languages may be spoken, and permission normally has to be sought for all translations;
(iv)   public domain material such as government documents are not easily accessible and must often be reproduced from published versions of the documents which involves having to get copyright clearance and paying high copyright fees;
(v)   obtaining permission to transfer print into other formats, e.g. onto CDs, websites, etc. creates problems as publishers are reluctant to give permission,

or they charge exorbitant fees; medical lecturers, for example, wishing to use anatomical diagrams from websites or wanting to scan them into other formats, cannot do this without going through the whole process of getting permission, which is often not given or is levied with high copyright costs. In many instances, rural medical personnel do not have access to computers, etc. and their only source of information is programmes prepared and provided by medical institutions and academic teaching hospitals;

(vi)   using material from multimedia or online resources for educational and other programmes creates problems as users do not always know where to obtain permission as often no response is received or strict conditions are applied and high levies are charged for use of the material;

(vii)   copyright fees for electronic databases are usually incorporated in the subscription fee; however, each database has its own contract and conditions as to what can and cannot be copied, which makes it difficult for users and library staff to know how to respond.

The above evidence testifies to the further problems which will ensue when the international community adopts *sui generis* protection of databases as has been the case within the EU. Where publishers release digital versions of journals as part of a larger database, the user may have to contend with the database right which is independent of copyright. This right will inevitably reside with the publisher, and the author will not necessarily have an implied licence with which to use the work.[27] The alternative licensing programme is the continental European levy system where a 'tax' is placed on all copying machines (including scanners) and accessories (such as blank tapes, paper and diskettes). This is the system in place in most European countries. This would have the effect of directly targeting, and taxing, the manufacturers of such devices as opposed to placing the whole burden of usage of materials on educational users.

ACCESS TO CULTURE AND SCIENCE

There are various provisions in the current International Bill of Human Rights (see Chapter 9), and in other treaties which propose that benefits of culture and science should be promoted and shared by all.

Human Rights Law

As discussed above, Article 15(1), ICESCR recognises the right of creators to claim protection for their works. This recognition is cocooned, nevertheless, in a bundle of communitarian rights – to take part in cultural life, to enjoy the benefits of scientific progress and its applications, to enable the conservation, the development and the diffusion of science and culture, and to respect the freedom indispensable for scientific research and creative activity.

Although 'intellectual property' is accepted as a valid subject matter under international human rights, the drafting history of the UDHR indicates that the impulse behind property rights did not stem from the Western notion of possessive individualism, but rather from a more communitarian root.[28] Thus, the guarantee of intellectual property protection under both the UDHR and ICESCR is dependent on how committed is humanity to the more communitarian interests entailed by participation in the cultural life of the community, enjoyment of the arts, and in sharing in scientific advancements and their benefits. Article 27(1) guarantees the usage rights of society by stressing communitarian values with the pronouncement that everyone has the right *'freely to participate in the cultural life of the community, to enjoy the arts and to share in scientific advancement and its benefits'* (emphasis added).[29] We discuss this balance below in relation to culture and intellectual property rights. This is complemented by the further communitarian provision for freedom of opinion and expression, which includes the 'right to receive and impart information and ideas' – this is discussed below in relation to freedom of expression.[30]

According to Morsink's account of the drafting history of Article 27, UDHR, there was no disagreement in relation to the notion that everyone has a right, including those who did not participate in creating them, to enjoy the benefits of artistic and scientific advancements.[31] A similar account is offered by Green in relation to the drafting history of Article 15(a), ICESCR which guarantees certain cultural and scientific rights.[32] One delegate in an early drafting session declared that the right of everyone to enjoy the benefits of science

> implied the dissemination of basic scientific knowledge, especially knowledge best calculated to enlighten men's minds and combat prejudices, coordinated efforts on the part of States, in conjunction with the competent specialized agencies, to raise standards of living, and a wider dissemination of culture through the processes and apparatus created by science.[33]

Yet, this enlightened vision is continuously frustrated in practice by the dearth of guidelines as to how this vision is to be implemented in practice. Indeed, as Green concludes in her paper, the drafters of the ICESCR did not envisage

> an AIDS epidemic reigning in one part of the world while the drugs that could help are largely owned in another, to scientifically engineered non-reproducing crops, to scientists 'bio-prospecting' for traditional knowledge whose ownership does not fit into existing patent definitions.[34]

Once again, it boils down to how we grant intellectual property owners their full property rights whilst enabling individuals to exercise their right to access scientific and cultural outputs. Two instruments are worth noting briefly in their attempts to address this issue.

The UNESCO Convention on the Protection and Promotion of the Diversity of Cultural Expressions

The UNESCO Convention on the Protection and Promotion of the Diversity of Cultural Expressions 2005 ('Cultural Diversity Convention') entered into force on 18 March 2007 and adopts the approach that intellectual property rights should be subservient to demands concerning culture and development. The ultimate objectives of the Convention are set out in Article 1, and include the reaffirmation of the sovereign rights of states to elaborate cultural policies with a view both 'to protect and promote the diversity of cultural expressions' and 'to create the conditions for cultures to flourish and to freely interact in a mutually beneficial manner'.[35]

There is some vague recognition that cultural diversity and expressions may have to be promoted and disseminated via market mechanisms under the principle of 'complementarity of economic and cultural aspects of development'.[36] The Cultural Diversity Convention adopts the approach that 'cultural activities, goods and services' are products of creativity which are different from other global goods and services; the definition of 'cultural expressions' is expansive and includes wine or cheese or *foie gras* – traditionally protected as geographical indications.[37] This capacious definition brings the Convention in direct competition with TRIPS.

Although not an international human rights instrument in the strict, technical sense, the Cultural Diversity Convention has eight guiding principles which do explicitly espouse several human rights principles. The pertinent sections within the Convention are:

- . . . importance of traditional knowledge as a source of intangible and material wealth, and in particular the knowledge systems of indigenous peoples (Preamble)
- . . . freedom to create, disseminate and distribute their traditional cultural expressions and to have access thereto, so as to benefit them for their own development (Preamble)
- Recognizing the importance of intellectual property rights in sustaining those involved in cultural creativity (Preamble)
- . . . cultural activities, goods and services have both an economic and a cultural nature . . . must therefore not be treated as solely having commercial value' (Preamble)
- Cultural diversity can be protected and promoted only if human rights and fundamental freedoms, such as freedom of expression, information and communication . . . (Article 2.1)
- Equitable access to . . . cultural expressions . . . and access of cultures to the means of expressions and dissemination (Article 2.7)

- 'Cultural expressions' are those *expressions that result from the creativity* of individuals, groups and societies, and that have cultural content (Article 4.3)
- . . . cultural policies and measures . . . may include . . . measures aimed at *nurturing and supporting artists and others involved in the creation* of cultural expressions (Articles 6.1 and 6.2(g), emphasis added)
- . . . protection, promotion and maintenance of cultural diversity are an essential requirement for sustainable development for the benefit of present and future generations (Article 2.6)
- . . . encourages individuals and social groups . . . to create, produce, disseminate, distribute and have access to their own cultural expressions . . . including indigenous peoples (Article 7)

In contrast to intellectual property treaties, this Convention embraces a holistic perspective of intellectual property lawmaking whereby intellectual property rights are treated strictly as the means to several ends. Moreover, as one can foretell from the language of the Convention, part of its objective is to showcase several alternative ways whereby some balance can be achieved between competing, though not necessarily conflicting, rights and goals, including intellectual property rights, human rights, cultural diversity, development and indigenous peoples' rights. Two of the mechanisms discussed within the Cultural Diversity Convention are noteworthy and may possibly be effective in the future. These are benefit-sharing and the setting up of the International Fund for Cultural Diversity.[38]

However, it is clear from the Cultural Diversity Convention that intellectual property is not emphasised at all (it is mentioned once in the Preamble), especially when compared to the other human rights which are referred to such as freedom of expression, information and communication, and freedom of thought.

THE PROPOSED ACCESS TO KNOWLEDGE (A2K) TREATY

The proposal for a Treaty on Access to Knowledge coincided with the Development Agenda movement (discussed below), and was promulgated by an international cohort of academics, civil society groups and other NGOs representing teachers, researchers and librarians. The stated aim of the treaty is to protect and enhance access to knowledge, and to facilitate the transfer of technology to developing countries. Although not explicit, it is clear that the instrument is premised on the idea of a system of governance of knowledge that places intellectual property as the exception to the general rule that knowledge is accessible to all. Indeed, the A2K Treaty's goal is to 'enhance participation in cultural, civic and educational affairs, and sharing of the benefits of scientific advancement'. This of course reflects the language of the ICESCR and UDHR. The proposed Treaty provisions focus, *inter alia*, on 'expanding and enhancing the knowledge commons'; measures to promote open standards; control of anti-competitive practices; and technology transfer.[39]

The major part of the proposed draft however emphasises limitations and exceptions within patent and copyright laws, most of which are mandatory. For example, the following educational uses are excepted from the scope of copyright:

- use of relevant excerpts, selections and quotations for purposes of explanation and illustration in connection with not-for-profit teaching and scholarship;
- use of relevant excerpts, selections and quotations for purposes of criticism and comment, including but not limited to parody;
- use of works, by educational institutions, as secondary readings by enrolled students;
- use of works, by educational institutions, as primary instructional materials, if those materials are not made readily available by right-holders at a reasonable price; provided that in case of such use the right-holder shall be entitled to equitable remuneration.[40]

More controversial perhaps are allowances for libraries or archives to 'migrate content to a new format', to allow usage of works for 'legitimate reverse-engineering', and to allow libraries, archivists or educational institutions 'to make copies of works that are protected by copyright but which are not currently the subject of commercial exploitation, for purposes of preservation, education or research'.[41] All these provisions undoubtedly seek to legitimise the digitisation of books and seek to liberalise the Berne Appendix. Perhaps the final sting for rights holders is the following presumption, which would emasculate the Berne/TRIPS three-step test:

> It shall be presumed that these uses constitute special cases that do not conflict with a normal exploitation of the work and do not unreasonably prejudice the legitimate interests of the right-holder . . . In determining whether applying any limitation or exception to exclusive rights to a particular use of a work would conflict with its normal exploitation or unreasonably prejudices the legitimate interests of the right holder, the extent to which the use benefits the larger public interest shall be taken into account . . . parties to this treaty also shall implement a general exception to copyright law, applicable in special cases where the social, cultural, educational or other developmental benefit of a use outweigh the costs imposed by it on private parties.[42]

A recent report by the British Academy[43] argues that copyright is impeding scholarship in social sciences and the humanities and that the existing copyright exceptions are not clear enough. Suggested strategies by the Academy

report are the same as one reads in almost every other report on intellectual
property rights and knowledge and education:

- educating authors about their interests;
- clarifying copyright law to make clear that the use of copyright material in the normal course of scholarly research in universities and other
  public research institutions is covered by the exemptions;
- preventing from using legal or technological measures to circumvent
  copyright exemptions;
- monitoring digital databases to ensure access for the purposes of scholarship.

Like the Access to Knowledge Treaty initiative, the British Academy report
promotes a balance which has long been overdue in the governance of intellectual property. The proposals of the Treaty and in the report are not so very
revolutionary,[44] consistent as they are with a more liberal and teleological
interpretation of the extant international intellectual property treaties,[45] and
the relevant provisions of the UDHR and ICESCR.

Finally, it may be of interest to many to note that one of the first clarion
calls for 'access to knowledge' and the 'public domain' was not made by
today's civil society organisations or activist academics, but by Fidel Castro in
1967 where he noted (quite correctly) that historically 'intellectual creators
have generally been poorly paid and many have suffered hunger', adding:

> And our country, de facto, adopted the decision to also abolish intellectual property.
> (applause) What does this mean? We think that technical knowledge should be the
> patrimony of all mankind. We feel that what man's intelligence has created should
> be the patrimony of all mankind. Who pays Cervantes his royalties for intellectual
> property? Who pays Shakespeare? Who pays the ones who invented the alphabet,
> those who invented numerals, arithmetic, mathematics? All mankind has benefited
> in one way or another. All mankind in one way or another uses the creations of
> man's intelligence throughout history . . . Everybody feels he has the right to enjoy
> all the creations of past generations. How is it possible to want to deny man today,
> hundreds of thousands of human beings, not hundreds of thousands, I am wrong,
> hundreds of millions, billions of human beings who now live in poverty, in under-
> development – how is it possible to want to block the access to technology for
> billions of human beings, a technology that they need for such basic things as nour-
> ishment, such as life itself.[46]

NOTES

1. Koskinen-Olsson, T. and D. Gervais, 'Electronic Commerce and Copyright: A Key Role for
   WIPO', in *WIPO Advisory Committee on Management of Copyright and Related Rights in
   Global Information Networks*, Geneva, WIPO, 1999, Document ACMC/2/1.

2. A May 2002 report stated that the countries with the highest level of internet penetration were located primarily on the European continent: Sweden (64.6%), Denmark (60.3%), Netherlands (58.07%), United Kingdom (56.88%) and Norway (54.4%); in the Asian region: Hong Kong (59.58%); and in North America: United States (59.22%) and Canada (52.79%). See Nua Internet Surveys, at http://www.nua.com/surveys. Moreover, in Africa, if the more developed South African and North African markets are excluded, the average user figure in 2002 was one in 250 African internet users as opposed to one in two North American/European internet users.

3. Some of the text in this section is from the 2003 UNCTAD-ICTSD report: 'Intellectual Property Rights: Implications for Development', of which G. Dutfield was lead author. The report is available from http://www.iprsonline.org/unctadictsd/policyDpaper.htm.

4. *Universities UK (formerly Committee of Vice-Chancellors and Principals of the Universities of the United Kingdom) v. Copyright Licensing Agency Limited, and Design and Artists Copyright Society Ltd*, Copyright Tribunal Case Nos. CT 71/00, 72/00, 73/00, 74/00 and 75/01, unreported. The decision can be accessed at http://www.patent.gov.uk/copy/tribunal/triabissued.htm; Suthersanen, U., 'Copyright and Educational Policies: A Stakeholder Analysis', *Oxford Journal of Legal Studies*, 23(4), 585–609, 2003.

5. *Matthew Bender & Co. v. West Publishing Co.*, 158 F.3d 693 (2nd Cir. 1998).

6. Vautier, K., 'The Economics of Parallel Imports', in C. Heath and A. Kamperman Sanders (eds), *Industrial Property in the Bio-medical Age*, The Hague: Kluwer Law International, 2003, 185–218.

7. Committee on Economic, Social and Cultural Rights, 20th session, *General Comment No. 11 on the Plans of Action for Primary Education* (Article 14), E/C.12/1999/4, 10 May 1999.

8. Morsink, J., *The Universal Declaration of Human Rights: Origins, Drafting and Intent*, Philadelphia, PA: University of Pennsylvania Press, 1999, at 212–15, explaining that the drafting of Article 26, UDHR was influenced by the many delegates who emphasised the link between education and civic training.

9. Committee on Economic, Social and Cultural Rights, 21st session, *General Comment No. 13 on the right to education* (Article 13), General E/C.12/1999/10, 8 December 1999.

10. Morsink, *op. cit.*, at 212–15; and Article 13, ICESCR.

11. CESCR, *General Comment No. 13, op. cit.*

12. The current list is available on the WIPO website – see http://www.wipo.int/treaties/en/.

13. Johnson, C.F., 'The Origins of the Stockholm Protocol', *Bulletin of the Copyright Society of the USA*, 18, 91, 1970.

14. Article IV*bis*(2), Universal Copyright Convention; *cf.* Article 9(2), Berne Convention and Articles 13 and 30, TRIPS Agreement.

15. Article 5, Universal Copyright Convention.

16. General Assembly of ALAI, 23 April 1968, Paris, reproduced in *Copyright*, 189, 1968. For a full account of the Stockholm Protocol and its aftermath, see Ricketson, S. and J. Ginsburg, *International Copyright and Neighbouring Rights: The Berne Convention and Beyond*, Oxford: Oxford University Press, chapter 14.

17. These concessions are to be found in the Appendix to the Berne Convention, and within Articles V*bis*, V*ter* and V*quarter*, Universal Copyright Convention (that is, compulsory licences for the translation and reproduction of works in developing countries).

18. Ricketson, S., *The Berne Convention for the Protection of Literary and Artistic Works*, London: Queen Mary College Centre for Commercial Law Studies, 1987, at 499.

19. Such as the International Student Edition versions of many textbooks which are available in Asia but not North America or Europe.

20. WIPO, *Intellectual Property Reading Material*, Geneva: WIPO, 1998, at 260–1.

21. Ricketson and Ginsburg, *op. cit.*, detail the provisions in great length, see 930–56.

22. Correa, C.M., *Intellectual Property Rights, the WTO and Developing Countries: The TRIPS Agreement and Policy Options*, London, New York and Penang: Zed Books and Third World Network, 2000.

23. *Basic Books, Inc. v. Kinko's Graphics Corp.*, 758 F. Supp. 1522 (SDNY 1991).

24. Under US law, see *American Geophysical Union v. Texaco, Inc.*, 60 F.3d 913 (2nd Cir. 1995); for UK law, see *Sillitoe & ors v. McGraw-Hill Book Co. (UK) Ltd.*, [1983] FSR 545

(Ch.D.); for Australia, see *University of New South Wales v Moorhouse & Anor*, [1976] RPC 151 (High Court, A'lia).

25. This section is summarised from Suthersanen, U., 'Collectivism of Copyright: The Future of Rights Management in the European Union', in E. Barendt and A. Firth (eds), *Oxford Yearbook of Copyright and Media Law*, Volume 5, Oxford: Oxford University Press, 15–42, 2000; and Story, A., *Study on Intellectual Property Rights, the Internet, and Copyright*, London: Commission on Intellectual Property Rights, 2002.

26. Quoted verbatim from Story's study for CIPR, see above.

27. Directive 96/9/EC of the European Parliament and of the Council of 11 March 1996 on the legal protection of databases.

28. Morsink, *op. cit.*, at 139

29. The suggestion of the communitarian ethos in Article 27(1) is further substantiated by Article 1 of UNESCO's Declaration of Principles of International Co-operation.

30. Articles 27, 19, UDHR.

31. Morsink, *op. cit.*, at 219.

32. Green, M., 'Drafting History of the Article 15(1)(c) of the International Covenant', at 7–8 [UN Document E/C.12/2000/15 (9 October 2000)].

33. *Ibid.*, at 7.

34. *Ibid.*, at 13–14.

35. Article 1, UNESCO Cultural Diversity Convention.

36. Article 2, UNESCO Cultural Diversity Convention.

37. Khachaturian, A., 'The New Cultural Diversity Convention and its Implications on the WTO International Trade Regime: A Critical Comparative Analysis', *Texas International Law Journal*, 42, 191, 2006, at 194.

38. Articles 2.6, 13

39. For the latest version, see http://www.cptech.org/a2k/a2k_treaty_may9.pdf.

40. Article 3-1, Proposed Treaty on Access to Knowledge, 9 May 2005 draft.

41. *Ibid.*

42. A similar ethos is clear in the Treaty's treatment of inventions. There is a lengthy list of exclusions including computer programs and business methods.

43. The British Academy, 'Copyright and Research in the Humanities and Social Sciences', 2006. Downloadable from http://www.britac.ac.uk/reports/copyright/.

44. Preamble, WIPO Copyright Treaty 1996.

45. Suthersanen, U. 'The Future of Copyright Reform in Developing Countries: Teleological Interpretation, Localized Globalism and the "Public Interest" Rule', available at http://www.iprsonline.org/unctadictsd/bellagio/Bellagio2005/Suthersanen_final.pdf.

46. 'Castro Delivers Speech at Guane Ceremony', Havana Domestic Television and Radio Services, April 1967, with an English translation available at http://info.lanic.utexas.edu/la/cb/cuba/castro/1967/19670430, and cited in Story, A., C. Darch and D. Halbert (eds), 'The Copy/South Dossier: Issues in the Economics, Politics, and Ideology of Copyright in the Global South', May 2006, available at https://www.kent.ac.uk/law/copysouthfiles/dossier.htm.

13. Biology, life and health

PATENTING LIFE AND BIOTECHNOLOGY[1]

The assumption that inventions are essentially mechanical devices and that patents are therefore intended to protect machines is a deep-seated one. But this has never really been accurate. Admittedly, the patenting of living things and the constituent parts of life-forms was not at all common until well into the twentieth century. Until the modern biotechnology era began in the United States in the 1970s, of the four million US patents issued since 1790, only 70 had protected 'mixtures or compounds that included microorganisms in unmodified form'.[2] Only Pasteur's anomalous yeast culture product patent granted in 1873 exclusively covered living organisms. The 'product of nature' doctrine had since the 1880s apparently precluded the patenting of any further life forms. Even so, the United States was the first country where the patentability of natural substances was considered by the courts and found in some cases to be possible.

A good example is a 1911 case concerning two patents relating to a glandular extractive product in the form of purified adrenaline, and for this compound in a solution with salt and a preservative. Parke Davis accused H.K. Mulford of infringing its patents. The latter company defended itself on a number of grounds, one of which was that the inventions were mere products of nature and that this made the patents invalid. The judge ruled in favour of Parke Davis.[3]

Three early pharmaceutical breakthroughs that turned out to be patentable despite their being new types of subject were insulin, vitamin B12 and the antibiotic streptomycin. In the early 1920s, US, UK and Canadian patents were filed by the University of Toronto for isolated and purified insulin and the extractive process was granted and assigned to the University of Toronto. In December 1947, scientists at Merck isolated a naturally occurring substance called cyanocobalamin. This substance, christened vitamin B12 by the scientists who had isolated it, was protected by two US patents issued in 1951 and 1955. Although the product claims of the latter patent were invalidated by a district court in 1957, they were reinstated on appeal. Both patents were the subject of another court case in 1967. The court upheld the first patent entirely.[4] Although five of the 12 claims in the second patent were invalidated, the principle that a 'composition of matter' consisting of a purified form of a natural product could be patented subject to passing the tests of non-obviousness and utility was not called into question.

In 1948, Merck was granted a patent for crystalline salts of the antibiotic, streptomycin, and for a process for preparing them. Streptomycin, the second antibiotic to come onto the market after penicillin and the first drug to be effective against tuberculosis, was discovered by Selman Waksman of Rutgers University. The streptomycin patent was in itself an important new regulatory development since it clarified to the industry that the new antibiotics were patentable despite being 'products of nature'.

As for plants, patents were from time to time granted in the decades either side of the Second World War. After the war, some European countries for a brief period allowed plants to be patented. But between the adoption of the UPOV Convention in 1961 and the advent of the new biotechnologies, plants were clearly excluded in Europe for the obvious reasons that there was a *sui generis* intellectual property system for plant varieties, and that possibilities to transform plants through new gene technologies did not exist.

As for micro-organisms, in 1975 the German Federal Supreme Court affirmed their patentability. In 1980, in a much higher profile decision, the US Supreme Court ruled by a narrow majority in *Diamond v. Chakrabarty* that a man-made oil-eating bacterium produced by Anand Chakrabarty, an employee of General Electric, could be classed as a 'composition of matter' or a 'manufacture', and therefore be treated as a patentable invention. According to the majority opinion, the US legislature (that is, Congress) 'recognized that the relevant distinction was not between living and inanimate things, but between products of nature, whether living or not, and human-made inventions'.

Initially, the Patent and Trademark Office rejected the claims directed to the bacterium itself on the grounds that it was a product of nature. On appeal, the patent rejection was overturned. This was consistent with an earlier decision of the Court of Customs and Patent Appeals at which Judge Rich had made the following statement when delivering the majority opinion:[5] 'we think the fact that microorganisms, as distinguished from chemical compounds, are alive is a distinction without legal significance'. He also opined that micro-organisms 'are much more akin to inanimate chemical compositions such as reactants, reagents, and catalysts than they are to horses and honeybees or raspberries and roses'. And so, when the same court ruled jointly on the patentability of the Chakrabarty micro-organism and a similar patent application by Bergy that was assigned to Upjohn, Rich applied the same logic, finding in favour of Chakrabarty's application.

There is no question that this 'life as chemistry' conceptualisation is a powerful one. Indeed, it is now implicitly recognised by other patent offices, including the European Patent Office.[6] By treating micro-organisms as natural chemical substances into which a useful new characteristic has been introduced and thereby rendered unnatural, they are assumed to be patentable in accordance with long-established practice with respect to chemical products that allows a natural chemical to be the basis for an invention as long as it is modified by adding something to it (such as a gene), subtracting something from it (that is, purifying it), mixing it with something else to create a new or synergistic effect, or structurally modifying it so that it differs in an identifiable manner from what it was before.

Since then the US has gone tumbling down what many critics would consider a slippery slope, pulling the rest of the world at least part of the way with it. In a 1985 patent appeals case, the Patent and Trademark Office affirmed the patentability of plants, seeds and plant tissue cultures. By 1988 over 40 patents on crop plants had already been issued. By the end of September 2001, there were more than 1,800 US patents with claims to plants, seeds, or plant parts or tissues. Nonetheless, the 1985 decision did not permanently settle the question of whether or not plants are patentable. In December 2001, the Supreme Court finally confirmed the legality of patents on plants. The opportunity to do so arose because lawyers representing a company called J.E.M. Ag Supply, which was being sued by Pioneer Hi-Bred for patent infringement, requested the court to determine whether plant-related patents are invalid because of the existence of two intellectual property laws designed specifically to protect plants: the 1930 Plant Patent Act and the 1970 Plant Variety Protection Act. By a six–two majority, the Supreme Court rejected J.E.M. Ag Supply's argument and upheld Pioneer's patents.[7]

In 1987, the PTO Board produced another ground-breaking ruling (in *ex parte* Allen) concerning a patent application on polyploid oysters. Although the patent was rejected, the ruling established that multicellular organisms were patentable. A year later the first ever animal patent was granted for 'a transgenic nonhuman mammal' containing an activated oncogene sequence. The patent is commonly referred to as the oncomouse patent, since it describes a mouse into which a gene has been introduced which induces increased susceptibility to cancer.

Europe has tended to follow the trends pioneered by the US, albeit with some important differences. In 1988 the European Patent Office granted the first patent on a plant. The European oncomouse patent, about which much more will be said below, was also granted after initially being rejected. In the late 1980s, the European Commission decided to draft a directive on the legal protection of biotechnological inventions. The European Commission was motivated by concerns about the legal uncertainties which, it was felt, could be prejudicial to the future of biotechnology in Europe, and fears that some European countries might respond to mounting controversy by banning patents on living organisms and genes. However, it was only in 1998 that the Directive on the Legal Protection of Biotechnological Inventions was finally adopted.

The situation in Europe with respect to the patenting of plant-related inventions has been plagued by legal uncertainties, due to the difficult wording of European patent legislation in the face of rapidly changing scientific and business possibilities, concerns about the moral implications of the new biotechnologies, and the ambivalence about biotechnological innovation among citizens and some of the governments.

The 1973 European Patent Convention (EPC) states in Article 53(b) that patents shall not be granted in respect of 'plant or animal varieties or essentially biological processes for the production of plants or animals'. This did not settle matters completely. Although from 1988, the European Patent Office (EPO) began to grant patents on plants, in 1995, the EPO Technical Board of Appeal in *Greenpeace v. Plant Genetic Systems* ruled on an appeal against the upholding of a plant-related patent and determined that a claim for plant cells contained in a plant is unpatentable since it does not exclude plant varieties from its scope, and also that 'plant cells as such cannot be considered to fall under the definition of plant or of plant variety'.[8] This implied that transgenic plants *per se* were unpatentable because of the plant variety exclusion. Consequently, for the next four years, the EPO stopped accepting claims on plants *per se*. However, in December 1999, the EPO Enlarged Board of Appeal decided that, while 'plant varieties containing genes introduced into an ancestral plant by recombinant gene technology are excluded from patentability', 'a claim wherein specific plant varieties are not individually claimed is not excluded from patentability under Article 53(b), EPC even though it may embrace plant varieties'.[9]

According to Article 3(2) of the Directive on the Legal Protection of Biotechnological Inventions, 'biological material which is isolated from its natural environment or produced by means of a technical process may be the subject of an invention even if it previously occurred in nature'. As with the Convention, animal and plant varieties and essentially biological processes for the production of plants and animals are excepted. Article 2.2 clarifies that 'a process for the production of plants or animals is essentially biological if it consists entirely of natural phenomena such as crossing or selection'. This definition has been accepted by the EPO.

Patenting Genes and DNA Sequences

One of the most controversial areas of patenting is that of genes and other DNA sequences. DNA sequences started being claimed in the early 1980s. By the end of the century this number had increased enormously. 'In 2000 over

355,000 sequences were published in patents, a 5000 per cent increase over 1990'.[10]

The view of many if not most businesses and patent practitioners is that DNA is a chemical, no more nor less. As such, it should be possible to claim a disclosed DNA sequence in the same way as a newly characterised chemical can be claimed for all known and yet to be discovered uses. At first glance, this DNA-as-a-chemical view seems rather persuasive. But surely DNA is a product of nature and merely describing its composition and naming a function, or at best editing out the non-protein coding nucleotides and cloning it, cannot turn the discovery of a work of nature into a human invention?

In response to arguments that full product patent protection of DNA sequences is undesirable, France and Germany have opted, in the case of human sequences, for so-called 'purpose-bound protection' according to which DNA can only be claimed in respect of a specified use. Let us suppose there is a gene that codes for proteins A, B and C. The company that finds the gene discovers only that it codes for A and patents it on that basis. In the United Kingdom and the United States, that company can control use of the gene for any application or function subsequently discovered while the patent remains in force. But in Germany and France, another company that discovers the gene's role in producing proteins B and C can independently patent the gene in relation to those functions (but only those functions).

So what is the appropriate position to adopt: full product protection or purpose-bound protection? The only honest answer is the underwhelming one of 'it's difficult to say for sure'. Nonetheless, the purpose-bound approach makes much sense whether or not it makes much difference in actual practice.

Certainly, supporters of the French and German positions could deploy some persuasive scientific and economic arguments. Scientifically speaking, the state of the art in molecular biology is whizzing forward. If the recent past is even a halfway decent guide to the near future, much of what we assume to be true today will seem pathetically misguided in a few years. Scientists now believe that as much as 98.5 per cent of human deoxyribonucleic acid (DNA) is non protein-encoding even though much of it is still transcribed into ribonucleic acid (RNA) for reasons that we hardly understand (but probably will in the coming years). Until recently, this 98.5 per cent was dismissed as 'junk DNA'.

In brief, each gene contains within its DNA the instructions for the synthesis of one or more proteins. Just as proteins consist of chains of amino acids, each gene may be sub-divided into units called codons that comprise three nucleotide bases and code for – by way of a closely related chemical, the aforementioned RNA – the preparation of a particular amino acid. These amino acids are then combined in a specified way to form the required protein, that is, the one 'expressed' by the gene. However, RNA appears to perform many functions unrelated to protein manufacture. The conundrum is that 'either the human genome . . . is replete with useless transcription, or these nonprotein-coding RNAs fulfil some unexpected function'.[11] Apparently, 'these RNAs may be transmitting a level of information that is crucial, particularly to development, and that plays a pivotal role in evolution'.[12]

The widespread assumption till recently, and one evidently shared by many patent applicants, agents and examiners, that genes operate independently and perform single functions, is now demonstrably false. Indeed, the 'gene' itself is beginning to look like a rather shaky concept. A scientist at the Karolinska Institute in Sweden admitted that 'we tend not to talk about "genes" anymore; we just refer to any segment that is transcribed to RNA as a "transcriptional unit" '.[13] Admittedly, it has been known for some time that a gene can produce more than one protein, for example by means of a process called 'alternative splicing' in which coding sections of the gene are selectively deleted. But it is now more apparent than ever that genomes consist largely of multiple intersecting 'mini-ecosystems' forming one larger one (that is, the genome itself). They are definitely not single collections of separately functioning 'Lego bricks' (that is, the individual genes) that can be combined and recombined precisely, predictably and with no possibility of unintended consequences.[14]

Consequently, one can argue on sound scientific grounds that treating genes as patentable inventions on the basis of a single disclosed function or discovery such as that it codes for a particular protein, or that it is associated with a disease, is a rather generous interpretation of the 'inventor's' relatively modest addition to the state of the art. This is not to say that such discoveries are necessarily easy or inexpensive to attain and undeserving of any reward. The point is that there may well be much more to be discovered about the gene of both scientific and commercial interest, and such future discoveries may well be a whole lot more important.

Such a practice may also be anti-innovation. First, broad patent protection – and patents in new technological fields tend to be excessively broad – can stifle innovation in new industries, especially those operating in fields like molecular biology where the learning curve is particularly steep. Broad protection potentially hinders opportunities for follow-on researchers to carry out further investigations on genes and find out much more interesting things about them, including how they interact with other parts of the genome and with what effects, and their relationship to particular diseases.

Second, a disproportionately large quantity of patents is being granted in relation to the number of commercial products based upon them. This is because of the enormous quantity of patents on genes and gene fragments that are basically research tools. Of course, companies file such patents because the rules allow them to do so. But their patenting decisions are dictated also by the fragmented nature of the genomics innovation chain and by small companies' desperate need for finance. For new biotech firms that provide genetic information to the drug development corporations, what they sell are to them final products but to their customers further down the chain are mere research tools. In order to protect these 'products' – and to secure funding to produce further ones – the biotech firms have a strong incentive to privatise their information through patents. But since the development of future commercial products such as therapeutic proteins or genetic diagnostic tests often requires the use of multiple research tools, such as gene fragments, many of which are patented, companies and public sector researchers intending to develop such products will need to acquire licences from other patent holders. In doing so, they will incur large, and possibly prohibitive, transaction costs. In a now well-known article in *Science*, Heller and Eisenberg warn of an emerging intellectual property problem in the USA in the field of biomedical research which they call the 'tragedy of the anticommons'.[15] What they refer to is a situation in which the increased patenting of pre-market, or 'upstream' research, 'may be stifling life-saving innovations further downstream in the course of research and product development'.

It is worth noting here that the US patent system has until recently been rather permissive in terms of applying the non-obviousness and utility criteria with the result that inventions patented in the US were too obvious to be patentable in Europe. Indeed, a recent study in *Science* found that of 74 US human gene patents examined by researchers, 73 per cent of them contained one or more claims considered to be 'problematic'.[16] However, the situation has been corrected to some extent.

This is not just academic. Gene patenting can be a life or death issue.[17] Patents on genes linked to particular diseases tend to claim a range of applications including diagnostic tests, and owners can be quite aggressive in enforcing their rights even though the validity of such patents is often considered to be questionable. Even non-commercial entities like public sector hospitals may be the target of companies demanding royalties. It was recently reported, for example, that 'after the gene for the iron overload condition haemochromatosis was patented, 30 per cent of labs surveyed stopped testing for the disease-causing gene variant, or developing such tests'.[18]

However, just as it is difficult to prove that extending the coverage of the patent system to cover DNA sequences as protectable subject matter guarantees there will be more investment in public health-improving research and development than there would be otherwise, proving the opposite is just as difficult. In addition to the example just given, the well-publicised patenting by Myriad Genetics relating to and covering two genes (BRCA1 and BRCA2) linked to a certain proportion of breast cancer cases and the aggressive assertion of these patents by the company lend plausibility to the view that DNA patenting is bad for public health research.[19] Human Genome Sciences' patenting of the CCR5 receptor gene that was subsequently discovered by other scientists to have a link to HIV infection raises serious doubts about the wisdom of allowing genes to be patented when very little is known about them.[20] Nonetheless, the use of a limited number of examples such as these does not prove beyond doubt that DNA patenting is necessarily *per se* a bad thing. But while empirical studies have been published that find little evidence to support the view that there would be more and better public health-oriented research without DNA patenting,[21] one should not rely too much on such findings. It is very difficult to estimate the size of the 'chilling effect' of patents on such research, which anecdotal evidence suggests may be substantial. Furthermore, reliable empirical evidence exists to support the claim that the aggressive assertion of DNA patent rights is unduly restricting the availability of diagnostic tests for patients in hospitals and other public service institutions.[22] This is sometimes the case even when testing by others does not require access to information disclosed in a patent.[23]

Of course concerns about DNA patenting are not confined to their effects on research. To the extent that patents are legal monopolies that can in some cases create market monopolies, they are bound to affect the prices of health products protected by patents including in developing countries. While the relationship between DNA patents and the prices of drugs, vaccines, diagnostic kits and other health products in the developed and developing worlds is often a complex one, to the extent that patents restrict competition it seems implausible, as is sometimes claimed, that patents can have no effect on prices.

The question is what to do? One could simply exclude DNA sequences from patentability. But would this necessarily be good for innovation or for society? In such a case, business will probably resort to copyright or trade secrecy. Since legal and technological measures provided under current copyright and trade secrecy laws lock up information much more securely than under patent law, the cure could become more harmful than the disease.

Inventing Animals: The Case of the Oncomouse

Aside from patenting a human being, the most radical subject-matter for a patent would appear to be an animal. Let us now turn to the first animal patent, the oncomouse. One of the reasons why the oncomouse case is interesting is that patent-granting offices and courts in three important jurisdictions have been called on to assess the patentability of the oncomouse but have failed to come up with the same conclusions. This not only raises the question of how far patent law *should* go but also how far the harmonisation of patent standards in biotechnology *can* go.

The oncomouse patent saga begins in June 1985, when Harvard University filed a patent application for 'transgenic non-human mammals', naming as inventors Philip Leder and Timothy A. Stewart. The patent was granted in April 1988. The primary claim covers the following:

> A transgenic non-human mammal all of whose germ cells and somatic cells contain a recombinant activated oncogene sequence introduced into said mammal, or an ancestor of said animal, at an embryonic stage.

Three things are interesting here. The first is the obvious fact that a living organism is being claimed as an invention. The second is that the patent describes the successful introduction of oncogenes into mice and yet it claims not only mice but all transgenic non-human mammals transformed through the same process. The third is that the scope of the patent includes not just animals with activated oncogenes, of which an increasing number are being discovered, but also their ancestors into which the oncogenes were initially introduced by the inventors. In other words, the patent owners have rights to all future generations of mice that inherit the oncogenes up to the expiry date of the patent.

The first interesting feature, that for the first time, an animal has been claimed as a patentable invention, raises the question of whether this is consistent with well-established patent doctrines. While no US courts were called on to answer this question, the decision of the Supreme Court in *Diamond v. Chakrabarty* suggests that the Court may have answered in the affirmative. Indeed, the ruling in *ex parte* Allen, mentioned above, relied in part on the Chakrabarty decision (as for that matter did the Court in *J.E.M. Ag Supply v. Pioneer*).

As for the second feature of the US oncomouse patent, this appears to claim too much, since for all anybody knows, the use of the technique to transform other animals may prove to be far more difficult and may require unobvious modifications to the technique. This is a problem of excessive patent breadth that is not limited to the life sciences, but is nonetheless very important and will be considered further below.

Turning to the third feature, this situation is clearly problematic. One of the ways in which the patent system seeks to balance the interests of owners and the public is through the concept of exhaustion of rights (or the first sale doctrine in the United States). Once a patent-protected product is sold by the owner or the licensee, his or her rights over that product are usually exhausted, unless there is a contract of sale imposing conditions on buyers. When it comes to patents on life forms, the rights are not exhausted when the 'product' is sold but extend to the progeny whether or not the progeny is directly 'manufactured' by the 'inventors'. In this sense, we are making a concession to the patent owner in order to make the patent monopoly meaningful. It is not necessarily wrong to do this. After all, the public may benefit from the use of transgenic animals. In the oncomouse case, their use in cancer research could be of tremendous benefit to society (though this may not be the case at all given that assertion of the patent has allegedly inhibited research elsewhere).[24] Nonetheless, the patent – though not necessarily patents claiming higher life forms *per se* – reflects a clear departure from conventional patent practice.

Treatment in Canada of the patentability of the oncomouse patent application by the Canadian Supreme Court is fascinating for two reasons. First, it considered at far greater depth than did the US Supreme Court in *Diamond v. Chakrabarty* the scientific and technical character of the claimed invention. Second, faced with similar statutory language, namely the terms 'manufacture' and 'composition of matter',[25] the Court came up with a very different interpretation to its US counterpart.

Upon examination, the Canadian Patent Office allowed the process claims but rejected the product claims, and this was confirmed on appeal. Eventually the case made its way to the Supreme Court, which in 2002 ruled that the terms 'manufacture' and 'composition of manufacture' in the Patent Act were insufficiently broad to encompass higher life forms within their scope. In doing so, and in contrast to its United States counterpart (but perhaps consistently with Judge Rich), the Canadian Supreme Court (i) rejected the applicability of the above two terms to higher life forms, and (ii) drew a distinction between higher life forms, which were not patentable, and lower life forms, which were. Accordingly, the Court took 'manufacture' 'to denote a non-living mechanistic product or process, not a higher life form'. It denied that the body of a mouse could be considered as a 'composition'. Furthermore, ' "matter" captures only one aspect of a higher life form, generally regarded as possessing qualities and characteristics that transcend the particular genetic material of which it is composed'. Setting aside the Federal Court of Appeals' ruling in 2000 that the oncomouse *is* a composition of matter, the Supreme Court was drawn to conclude that:

> Since patenting higher life forms would involve a radical departure from the traditional patent regime, and since the patentability of such life forms is a highly contentious matter that raises a number of extremely complex issues, clear and unequivocal legislation is required for higher life forms to be patentable. The current Act does not clearly indicate that higher life forms are patentable.

With respect to the distinction between higher and lower life forms, the Court had the following to say:

> If the line between lower and higher life forms is indefensible and arbitrary, so too is the line between human beings and other higher life forms. It is now accepted in Canada that lower life forms are patentable but this does not necessarily lead to the conclusion that higher life forms are patentable, at least in part for the reasons that it is easier to conceptualize a lower life form as a 'composition of matter' or 'manufacture' than it is to conceptualize a higher life form in these terms.

Patentable micro-organisms are formed in such large numbers that any measurable quantity will possess uniform properties and characteristics. The same cannot be said for plants and animals. It is far easier to analogize a micro-organism to a chemical compound or another inanimate object than it is to analogize an animal to an inanimate object. Moreover, several important features possessed by animals distinguish them from both micro-organisms and plants and remove them even further from being considered a 'composition of matter' or a 'manufacture'. Given the complexity of the issues involved, it is not the task of the Court to situate the line between higher and lower life forms. Also, the specific exception for plants and animals in trade agreements demonstrates that a distinction between higher and lower life forms is widely accepted as valid.

In all probability, like the Court, most people would consider it somewhat easier to think of a lower life form in these terms than a plant or an animal. Nonetheless, contrary to the US Supreme Court, we would suggest that the fact of micro-organisms being alive and chemical compounds not *is* significant. This is not only because members of the public are likely to have difficulties in conceptualising living things as inventions, but because they can reproduce out of the control of the patent owners. Normally, as indicated earlier, once a patent-protected product is sold by the owner or the licensee, his or her rights over that product are usually exhausted. So allowing patent claims to cover organisms not directly 'manufactured' by the inventors or by anybody else who could be identified as a patent infringer is a generous concession that may or may not be in the public interest.

The dissenting judges had the following response to the point of whether a human-transformed higher life form is any less a composition of matter than a lower life form:

> The oncomouse is patentable subject matter. The extraordinary scientific achievement of altering every single cell in the body of an animal which does not in this altered form exist in nature, by human modification of the genetic material of which it is composed, is an inventive 'composition of matter' within the meaning of s. 2 of the Patent Act.

Justice Binnie, speaking for the minority went on to point out that to find a fertilised, genetically altered oncomouse egg to be patentable, as the majority did, but not the resulting mouse growing from that egg, was unsupported by the statute.

In doing so, the minority confronts us with a vital question: if the transformation of a single-cell organism constitutes an invention, why should a collection of transformed cells forming a multicellular organism be treated any differently? To answer this question it would be important, among other factors, to take account of the extent to which current processes to genetically transform micro-organisms are more predictable and controllable than those to transform multicellular organisms.

Politically, what is interesting to note here is that industry used to find the distinction drawn in the Supreme Court decision between higher and lower life forms to be convenient but does not any more. The 1963 Strasbourg Convention, from which the relevant parts of the European Convention and TRIPS borrowed language, stated that 'parties were not required to grant patents in respect of . . . (b) plant or animal varieties or essentially biological processes for the production of plants or animals; *this provision does not apply to microbiological processes and the products thereof*' (emphasis added). The singling out of microbiological processes and products was made at the urging of a pro-industry lawyers' association, which pointed out that micro-organisms were commonly used in well-established industrial activities such as brewing and baking.

In Europe, the oncomouse patent story is a long one, and appears only in 2004 to have reached a final conclusion. During prosecution of the patent application, the Examining Division objected to the broad scope of the product claims, which extended to 'transgenic non-human eukaryotic animals' despite, as with the US patent, only disclosing the insertion of the oncogenes in mice. In response, the applicants narrowed the claims to 'non-human mammalian animals'.

Nonetheless, while the Canadian Patent Office rejected the product claims alone, the European Patent Office in July 1989 rejected the patent entirely on two grounds. The first was that in claiming animals that were new on the basis of the introduction of oncogenes, the patent was to all intents and purposes claiming animal 'varieties'. According to Article 53(b) of the European Patent Convention (EPC), animal varieties are not patentable.

The second was insufficiency of disclosure, which was not satisfied by the narrowed-down product claims. According to Article 83 of the EPC, 'the European patent application must disclose the invention in a manner sufficiently clear and complete for it to be carried out by a person skilled in the art'. The Examining Division's reasons for rejecting the patent on the grounds of insufficient disclosure were as follows:

> The claims as they presently stand refer to non-human mammalian animals, i.e. not only to mice or more generally to rodents but to any kind of mammals such as anthropoid apes or elephants, all of which have a highly different number of genes and differently developed immune systems.

The Examining Division added that:

> Mr Philip Leder, one of the inventors of the present case, declared . . . before the United States Patent and Trademark Office how surprising it was to obtain positive results on the mouse and reasons are given why he thought that he might have failed. This clearly shows that the success with the transgenic mouse cannot be reasonably extrapolated to all mammals.[26]

On appeal, the Technical Board of Appeal (TBA) decided in October 1990 that animals *per se* were not excluded from patentability under Article 53(b) EPC. It followed that since claims to genetically modified animals, mammals or any other taxonomic groups higher than that of species were not animal varieties, the oncomouse patent could not therefore be rejected on such grounds. In addition, the TBA pointed out that animals produced by microbiological processes would not fall under the exception anyway. It therefore requested that the Examining Division reconsider its interpretation. The TBA also denied that the disclosure was insufficient. Furthermore, in light of the many objections to the patent from animal welfare, religious and environmental organisations on the basis of Article 53(a) of the EPC, according to which patents 'in respect of inventions the publication or exploitation of which would be contrary to ordre public or morality'[27] would not be granted, the TBA came up with a so-called balancing test which it requested the EPO Examining Division to apply. According to the test, the examiners were required by the TBA to conduct 'a careful weighing up of the suffering of animals and possible risks to the environment on the one hand, and the invention's usefulness to mankind on the other'.[28] In October 1992, the grant of European Patent 169,672 was formally announced.

But the story did not end there. Further oppositions to the patent were filed during the 1990s and led in 2001 to the EPO's Opposition Division's response of restricting the product-related scope of the patent from 'non-human mammalian animals' to 'transgenic rodents'. In 2003, an interlocutory decision of the EPO's Opposition Division held the patent to be valid on the basis of the reduced scope but also affirmed that EPC rule 23d(d),[29] which requires that patents not be granted for 'processes for modifying the genetic identity of animals which are likely to cause them suffering without any substantial medical benefit to man or animal, and also animals resulting from such processes', is applicable for drawing the appropriate scope of a patent such as the oncomouse one.

In July 2004, the TBA was again required to assess the validity of the patent. The TBA's application of both the balancing test it had formulated in 1990 and rule 23d(d) resulted in a finding that the patent was valid but only on the basis of claims confined to 'transgenic mouse',[30] thereby vindicating the Examining Division's objections 15 years earlier to the patent's over-broad scope!

The differing treatment of the oncomouse patents in these three jurisdictions suggests that without a clear understanding of why we have patent systems in the first place and what they are meant to achieve, it may not be easy to argue conclusively that patenting life departs from the basic tenets of patent law *and* should not therefore be allowed. However, one clear point of divergence from conventional patent norms is that since living things have a tendency to reproduce by themselves, or at least with willing partners, in granting patents on life forms we are being very generous to the owners when we allow them to claim ancestors and progeny. But in our view, to know whether this is right or wrong we need to consider what we, that is to say, the public, gets out of the bargain so simply expressed by Lord Mansfield over 200 years ago (see Chapter 5).

HEALTH

The relationship between intellectual property and public health has attracted controversy in both the developed and the developing worlds. However, the debate has, for understandable reasons, been most heated in areas like Africa where millions of people suffer and die from diseases for which medicines exist that could vastly improve and prolong their lives. As a recent report puts it:

> Many of the diseases and health conditions that account for a large part of the disease burden in low- and middle-income countries are far less common in high-income countries. These burdens are primarily associated with infectious diseases, reproductive health, and childhood illnesses. Just eight diseases and conditions account for 29 percent of all deaths in low- and middle-income countries: TB, HIV/AIDS, diarrheal diseases, vaccine-preventable diseases of childhood, malaria, respiratory infections, maternal conditions, and neonatal deaths. Approximately 17.6 million people in low- and middle-income countries die each year from communicable diseases and maternal and neonatal conditions. Both the occurrence of and the death rates from such diseases and conditions are far lower in all high-income countries.[31]

High-profile pandemics like HIV/AIDS understandably attract considerable attention. Millions of people have died of this terrible disease – 2.6 million in 2003 and 2.8 million in 2005, of which Sub-Saharan Africa contributed 1.9 million and 2.0 million respectively.[32] But as the above quote makes clear there are a whole host of diseases that have particularly devastating impacts on the poor.

The obvious reason why treatment access is such a problem is poverty. People do not have the money to buy the drugs, and governments, even those that are not corrupt or otherwise woefully dysfunctional, lack the resources and infrastructure to get them to those who need them but cannot afford them. The pharmaceutical industry certainly prefers to blame poverty and poor governance, and rejects arguments that patent rights allow them to set high prices that keep them out of the reach of the poor.[33] Up to a point, the industry is right. But to suggest this is a sufficient explanation is to be disingenuous.

High drug prices are not of course the only factor limiting patients' access to them. Access even to very cheap drugs tends to be inadequate too. Poor people often live far away from clinics and hospitals. Also, many countries are short of medical practitioners trained to prescribe drugs to patients in the appropriate combinations and dosages. Nonetheless, high prices obviously have a profound impact on the ability of cash-strapped governments and other health-care-providing organisations to deliver drugs to the poor. National pharmaceutical markets are often highly regulated, and companies are not always free to set prices entirely as they wish. Patent monopolies place the companies holding them in a strong bargaining position for as long as they can keep out the generic competition which potentially could drive prices downwards towards the marginal cost of making the drug in question.

Do Patents Kill?

The pharmaceutical industry is frequently criticised in relation to its research priorities. Specifically, critics point out that the industry invests heavily in developing treatments for relatively trivial ailments rather than life-threatening ones, drugs for chronic health problems that do not cure patients but that need to be taken continually for many years, and ones that address the diet-related health concerns of the 'worried well' in affluent societies but not those of the under-nourished.[34] Relatively little is spent on diseases that disproportionately affect the poor, such as malaria and tuberculosis, and public and non-profit sector research efforts are insufficient to make up for the lack of interest in neglected diseases.[35] Thus, while 95 per cent of active TB cases occur in developing countries, no new drugs for the disease have been developed since 1967.[36] And the World Health Organization has estimated that only 4.3 per cent of pharmaceutical research and development expenditure is aimed at those health problems mainly concerning low and middle income countries.[37]

   In addition, many of the 'new' products that come on the market are variants of, or slight improvements upon, existing rather than radically novel drugs.[38] A further criticism of the industry is that it is guilty of so-called 'disease mongering', defined by Moynihan and Henry as 'the selling of sickness that widens the boundaries of illness and grows the markets for those who sell and deliver treatments'.[39] In an economic sense, prioritising research in these ways is perfectly rational, whether or not it is entirely admirable.

   It is rather difficult to say whether patents are directly responsible for this lack of interest in addressing the needs of the poor. With or without patents, the pursuit of profit and shareholder value is in any case bound to encourage pharmaceutical research to be aimed at areas where most money can be made. But this does not let patents completely off the hook. One could argue that if patents are meant to serve the public interest then they should do more to encourage research where public needs are greatest.

But let us say no more about this particular issue, important as it is. The most heated attacks on the industry at the international level concern the lack of access to *existing* life-saving medicines for the poor in developing countries, and this issue and its solutions are the focus of this chapter insofar as intellectual property is treated as part of the problem. This debate was triggered by the HIV/AIDS crisis, and coincided with the research-based pharmaceutical industry's success in securing changes to international rules on intellectual property by means of the TRIPS Agreement that were intended to eliminate or delay price-lowering competition from generic producers.[40] It did not take long for individuals and NGOs to link the two, that is, lack of treatment access and intellectual property rules.

The extent to which patents affect the prices of drugs varies and it is not enough to say that drugs will always be expensive where they are patented and cheap where they are not. Nonetheless, to the extent that patents restrict competition they are likely to have the effect of keeping prices artificially high, and also of making it more difficult for countries to respond speedily to health crises where drugs do exist but cannot be accessed either because they are expensive or because they are not sufficiently available in that particular market.

The advantage of high prices for industry in poor country markets is not self-evident. However it may be very rational economically in that the wealthy sick will be willing to pay whatever the drug costs, while pricing the drug at levels the poor could afford would not generate as much overall revenue. This is because the rich would be paying so much less than they could be made to pay and many poor people could still not pay for it even at a lowered price. There is another possible reason why patent-holding companies are reluctant to drop drug prices in developing countries to marginal cost or just above it. Trebilcock and Howse suggest that drug companies have a 'strategic desire . . . not to reveal, by such pricing, just how low their marginal costs actually were; this information could be used by large purchasers of medicines – governments or private health insurers – to bargain down the price of medicines in rich, developed countries. Hence, drug companies have been prepared in some instances to give away medicines to poor countries, rather than price them at marginal cost – and have presented this behaviour as "charitable"'.[41] Of course, giving away drugs to the poor is to be welcomed whether or not the motivations are altruistic!

Research-based pharmaceutical companies and associations representing them have been highly effective in recruiting some governments to support their international commercial interests.[42] The US government in particular has been very willing to offer political support for the intellectual property interests of pharmaceutical companies. Indeed, as we saw earlier in this book, the TRIPS Agreement was in large part a consequence of aggressive lobbying of the US government by a grouping of corporations[43] that were intent on eliminating copyright piracy, the unauthorised use of trade marks, and unwelcome competition from generic drug firms able to take advantage of patent regimes excluding drugs from protection.[44]

The US, in particular, has openly expressed its displeasure when developing country governments have brought in measures to prioritise public health in ways that limit the full enjoyment of the intellectual property rights of US businesses, such as through compulsory licensing and parallel importation, or even where they just indicated they were seriously considering doing so. This is extraordinary. For one thing, governments have human rights obligations to put the lives of their citizens before the commercial interests of foreign companies. The basis for this view is the existence of Article 12 of the International Covenant on Economic, Social and Cultural Rights,[45] which states that:

> The States Parties to the present Covenant recognize the right of everyone to the enjoyment of the highest attainable standard of physical and mental health.
> The steps to be taken by the States Parties to the present Covenant to achieve the full realization of this right shall include those necessary for:
> (a) the provision for the reduction of the stillbirth-rate and of infant mortality and for the healthy development of the child;
> (b) the improvement of all aspects of environmental and industrial hygiene;
> (c) the prevention, treatment and control of epidemic, endemic, occupational and other diseases;
> (d) the creation of conditions which would assure to all medical service and medical attention in the event of sickness.

Furthermore, as we saw in Chapter 5, public interest safeguards go back to the very beginnings of patent law so such practices are entirely consistent with five centuries of intellectual property regulating. These particular measures are also consistent with present international law.

One might also add that expressions of outrage in this context are hypocritical given the behavior of the US government in the Cipro case. In 2001, mail infected with anthrax spores killed a number of unfortunate individuals. Consequently, the government decided to stockpile vast quantities of Bayer's ciprofloxacin (Cipro), which it considered to be the most effective drug for anthrax. Tommy Thompson, then Secretary of Health and Human Services, threatened Bayer that if they did not halve the price he would simply acquire the drug from other sources. At one stage he even raised the possibility of asking Congress to pass legislation exempting the government from compensating Bayer for ignoring its patent.[46] Thompson successfully negotiated a large discount. Since then, the US government has been pressuring developing country governments not to issue compulsory licences to generic drug producers.

Correa provides more evidence to suggest that the condemnation of developing country governments' threatening of compulsory licensing is an instance of what one might call 'selective indignation':

> in the case of the acquisition of shares of Rugby-Darby Group Companies by Dow Chemical Co, the Federal Trade Commission required Dow to license formulations, patents, trade secrets, technology, know-how, specifications, processes, quality control data, the Drug Master File, and all information relating to the FDA approvals to potential entrants into the dicyclomine market.[47]

It should be emphasised that the FTC's decision had nothing to do with saving lives but about competition policy. In addition, one finds that the use of compulsory licensing by developing countries to safeguard public health gets referred to, misleadingly by critics and journalists, as 'breaking patents', as if the patents are being revoked or ignored, as Thompson had suggested might be done in the Cipro case. Brazil is frequently condemned for being tough negotiators with drug companies in demanding that prices be drastically reduced and for threatening to grant compulsory licences if they are not. Such licensed patents of course remain in force and can still be enforced against other infringing parties. In addition, the owners are legally entitled to compensation.

Developing countries have found themselves being attacked merely for interpreting TRIPS in ways that differed from those of powerful firms and governments yet are nonetheless legal. South Africa came under extremely heavy pressure both diplomatically and in the courts when it passed amendments to its Medicine and Related Substances Control Act concerning, among other matters, parallel importation and compulsory licensing. The US government repeatedly demanded that the law be repealed, and in 1998, the Pharmaceutical Manufacturers Association of South Africa and 39 pharmaceutical corporations initiated legal proceedings against the national government to have the legislation overturned. In early 2001, the case was dropped in the face of severe national and international condemnation that only the companies involved appeared not to have expected, and probably in the realisation that they would have lost anyway.[48]

It is not just patents. New drugs in the industrialised countries must undergo extensive clinical trials and other tests to demonstrate efficacy and safety. Data arising from these trials and tests must be submitted to a government regulatory office before marketing of drugs can be approved. Some countries, especially developing countries, may not require such data but merely approve a drug on the basis that it has been approved by a reliable authority such as the US's Food and Drug Administration (FDA).

Amassing the data can be hugely expensive in both time and money. Since patents on new therapeutic substances have to be filed at the drug discovery phase prior to the development period, by the time the product reaches the market the patent may well have less than half of its 20-year term left to run. And once patents on drugs expire in Europe and the US, it does not usually take long for much cheaper generic versions to enter those markets.[49]

In the US and Europe, the law promotes the early entry of generic competitors by requiring firms only to demonstrate that their version of the soon to go off-patent drug is a safe and effective equivalent rather than to repeat the clinical trials performed earlier. To have to do so would not only entail unnecessary expense, but would constitute unethical behaviour towards those patients involved in these additional trials who are given placebos. In practice, then, authorisation to market the drug is given on the basis of proof of equivalence *and* by reference to the clinical trial data submitted by the maker of the original drug (see Chapter 5).

TRIPS Article 39.3 provides for the protection of test data in respect of pharmaceutical and agricultural chemical products that utilise new chemical entities. It must be protected against 'unfair commercial use'. Disclosure of such data is prohibited but may be allowed if necessary to protect the public or if legal protection measures against unfair commercial use are already in place. In justifying such provisions, Article 39.1 refers to Article 10*bis* of the Paris Convention, according to which 'any act of competition contrary to honest practices in industrial or commercial matters constitutes an act of unfair competition'.

How countries may give effect to Article 39.3 is a matter of quite heated debate. This is hardly surprising given the vagueness of the language and the economic and social welfare stakes involved. Some of them have extended a period of exclusivity – typically at least five years – to the originator of the data during which drug regulators may not use the data to determine whether to approve the marketing of purportedly equivalent products. Alternatively, the provision can be interpreted as not prohibiting regulators from doing this but merely as preventing generic producers from being able to acquire the data through dishonest commercial practices.[50]

Developing countries are being pressured to emulate the developed countries by implementing Article 39.3 in their national laws in the form of a limited period of data exclusivity. Frequently data exclusivity provisions crop up in bilateral and regional free trade agreements where the United States is one of the parties. In some cases, they are bound to become a barrier to the market entry of generic drugs.

Consider two recent free trade agreements, the 2004 US-Chile FTA and the 2005 US-Dominican Republic-Central America FTA (US-DR-CAFTA). The US-Chile FTA provides that generic companies are prohibited from marketing a new chemical entity-based drug on the basis of undisclosed clinical trial data submitted to the government as a condition of its approval. This prohibition is for at least five years after the approval date. Conceivably, this could hold up the marketing of some generic drugs until some years after the expiry of any patent on the drug.

The US-DR-CAFTA differs somewhat, for example, in recognising that some countries may approve a new drug on the basis of its prior approval in another country (for instance, the US) without the company having to submit clinical trial data in those countries too. But as with the US-Chile FTA, the prohibition on marketing the generic version is for at least five years from the date of approval of the original pharmaceutical product.

Such a provision applies even in cases where a generic firm is seeking to enter the national market before the original manufacturer, who may not be genuinely interested in supplying this particular market. Clearly, these requirements have the potential to stall the introduction of generics in cases where the patent has already expired *or where there was no patent in the first place*, and are not balanced by any language affirming the right of countries to respond to public health crises as they see fit.[51] Not only that, but data exclusivity requirements are bound to make it harder for governments to grant compulsory licences. Indeed, this is almost certainly one of the reasons for having these requirements in FTAs.

These provisions in FTAs are testament to the influence of the pharmaceutical industry in Washington. But by insisting on respect for their patent and rights throughout the world in such an aggressive manner, the research-based pharmaceutical industry has paid a heavy price. While it was busy asserting its economic interests, others were able to portray the industry as ruthless, over-remunerated and uncaring.

Patents do not of course kill; neither is the TRIPS Agreement so inflexible as to prevent countries from dealing with public health crises. But by imposing FTA provisions that are inimical to public health in developing countries and promoting interpretations of TRIPS in ways that suit the interest of 'big pharma', anti-intellectual property sentiments among ministries of health, developing country diplomats, poor patients and health workers are very understandable and to a large extent justified.

Giving TRIPS a (Healthy) Human Face

Article 31 sets out a list of conditions on unauthorised use by the government, or by government-approved third parties, of a patent's subject matter. Normally, before using the invention, the proposed user is required, under clause (b), to make 'efforts to obtain authorization from the right holder on reasonable commercial terms and conditions'. Such efforts should not have 'been successful within a reasonable period of time'. However, and this is extremely important in the present context, 'this requirement may be waived by a Member in the case of a national emergency or other circumstances of extreme urgency or in cases of public non-commercial use'. For reasons that will become clear, it is important to note, as clause (f) states, that 'any such use shall be authorized predominantly for the supply of the domestic market of the Member authorizing such use'. However, as clause (k) states in part, all of these conditions may be set aside 'where such use is permitted to remedy a practice determined after judicial or administrative process to be anti-competitive. The need to correct anti-competitive practices may be taken into account in determining the amount of remuneration in such cases.' This allows for the possibility of fast-tracking compulsory licensing procedures as long as use of the patent made by the owning company can be deemed anti-competitive.[52] According to clause (h), 'the right holder shall be paid adequate remuneration in the circumstances of each case, taking into account the economic value of the authorization'.

It must be said that compulsory licensing, while a potentially useful mechanism to enhance access, is not a panacea.[53] In cases where prior authorisation from the patent owner is required (as is normally the case), negotiations can be complicated and take a long time to conclude. Second, the patent specification may not provide sufficient information to enable copying of the drug. In fact, with some drugs, the most efficient manufacturing process is protected by a separate patent, which may even be owned by a different company, or it may involve know-how that is protected under trade secrecy law. Third, many countries may lack chemists who can do the copying, and licensees may not necessarily be able profitably to sell the drug at a much lower price than that of the patent-holding firm. Fourth, data exclusivity provisions may render a compulsory licence worthless if a licence to copy the invention is not accompanied by freedom to use the data so that approval can be given for the generic drug to be made available to the public. This may be one of the reasons why data exclusivity provisions crop up so often in FTAs.

However, the very possibility of compulsory licensing tends to strengthen the bargaining position of governments, even if it is rarely used. It has worked for Brazil in its negotiations with companies to lower the prices of anti-AIDS drugs and also for the USA when in 2001 it requested Bayer to lower the price of Cipro, considered to be the best treatment for anthrax.

In 2001, the Doha Ministerial Conference of the WTO adopted the Declaration on the TRIPS Agreement and Public Health, incorporating very similar language to that proposed initially by the developing countries. The Declaration consists of seven paragraphs. The Declaration allows least-developed countries to delay implementation of patent protection for pharmaceutical products and legal protection of undisclosed test data submitted as a condition of approving the marketing of pharmaceuticals until 1 January 2016.[54] Perhaps the most important paragraph is the fifth, which clarifies the freedoms all WTO members have with respect to compulsory licensing, their determination of what constitutes a national emergency or other circumstances of extreme urgency, and exhaustion of rights. Thus, the Declaration reaffirms the right to use to the full the provisions in TRIPS allowing each member 'to grant compulsory licenses and the freedom to determine the grounds upon which such licenses are granted'. The Declaration explicitly mentions that public health crises 'relating to HIV/AIDS, tuberculosis, malaria and other epidemics, can represent a national emergency or other circumstances of extreme urgency'. Moreover, WTO members are free to establish their own regime for exhaustion of intellectual property rights. This is important because it means that, if national laws indicate that patent rights over drugs are exhausted by their first legitimate sale anywhere in the world,[55] countries can then import drugs legally purchased in countries where they are sold at a lower price. Understandably, such freedom is anathema to the industry. The persistence of parallel importation freedom helps to explain why companies are so reluctant to be open about the prices they charge for the same drugs in different countries.

One matter the Declaration left unresolved concerns the predicament of countries that cannot manufacture drugs themselves. Since TRIPS stipulates under Article 31(f) that unauthorised use of a patent shall be, as we mentioned, 'predominantly for the supply of the domestic market', awarding a licence to an overseas manufacturer would conflict with TRIPS since the use would be to supply a foreign market. This is an important issue because many poor countries lack the capacity to manufacture life-saving drugs such as HIV/AIDS treatments, and would therefore need to import them from countries like India, an important international supplier of relatively cheap generic drugs. To make the situation even more difficult, India was required by TRIPS to introduce product patents on drugs from 1 January 2005 and subsequently complied. Normally patents prevent not just the unauthorised sale of protected products but also their manufacture.[56] Therefore, even if a poor country granted a compulsory licence to a generic firm in India or in any other foreign country, if the drug were protected by a patent in the generic firm's country too, the licensee would not actually be able to make the drug unless the government of India also granted a compulsory licence, something that it would not be allowed to do on account of Article 31(f).

Paragraph Six of the Declaration recognised that 'WTO Members with insufficient or no manufacturing capacities in the pharmaceutical sector could face difficulties in making effective use of compulsory licensing under the TRIPS Agreement', and instructed the TRIPS Council 'to find an expeditious solution to this problem and to report to the General Council before the end of

2002'. No solution was reached within this deadline, and it was only in August 2003 that one was agreed, the 30 August Decision.[57]

The most important part of the 30 August Decision is Paragraph 2, which provides the terms under which a WTO member may export a pharmaceutical product under a compulsory licence to a country with no or insufficient manufacturing capacity on the basis of a waiver of the condition in Article 31(f). These terms are fairly detailed in part because the pharmaceutical industry was concerned that drugs manufactured under the waiver might be diverted to other markets.

'Eligible importing Members' of the WTO who may take advantage of the system are all least-developed countries or any other country that notifies the TRIPS Council of its intention to do so. According to the Decision, an eligible exporter's normal obligations under Article 31(f) may be waived in order for a domestic producer to manufacture and export the requested pharmaceutical to an eligible importer under the grant by itself of a compulsory licence. For this to be permitted, the importing country must make a notification to the TRIPS Council that:[58]

(i)   specifies the names and expected quantities of the product(s) needed;

(ii)   confirms that the eligible importing Member in question, other than a least-developed country Member, has established that it has insufficient or no manufacturing capacities in the pharmaceutical sector for the product(s) in question . . .; and

(iii) confirms that, where a pharmaceutical product is patented in its territory, it has granted or intends to grant a compulsory licence in accordance with Article 31 of the TRIPS Agreement and the provisions of this Decision.

The exporter is required to notify the TRIPS Council and provide full details of the compulsory licence, which is required to contain certain conditions. In practice, this at least should not be particularly onerous.

Patent holders whose inventions are subject to a compulsory licence are normally entitled to remuneration. On this issue, Paragraph 3 places the obligation to remunerate the owner on the exporter who in calculating the amount must take 'into account the economic value to the *importing Member* of the use that has been authorized in the exporting Member'.[59] As for the compulsory license granted for the same products by the importer, the obligation to remunerate is waived, leaving this requirement to the exporter.

All of this requires, of course, the existence of a generic company both willing and able to make the drug to supply this particular market. Since generic companies are just as much in the business of making a profit as the research-based ones, it is not self-evident that such a company will always be found. One important consideration here is the size of the market and the possibility of economies of scale. Since 23 developed countries stated in a footnote to the

Decision that they would not use the system as eligible importers, one may reasonably wonder whether there is sufficient incentive for many generic firms to produce a pharmaceutical to supply only one or a few developing countries with low populations. However, the Decision recognises this may be a problem, since in the case of a developing or least-developed (LDC) importer being a party to a regional trade agreement at least half of whose members are LDCs, the pharmaceutical can be exported to those other party countries, albeit without prejudice to the territorial nature of the patent rights.[60] It is mentioned in the Decision that regional patent systems are a good thing in this respect since a compulsory licence would have effect in all countries in which the regional patent is valid.

On 6 December 2005, a more permanent solution was found when the WTO members agreed to amend TRIPS by adopting a Protocol that supplements TRIPS with the insertion of an Article 31*bis* and an annex, which follow very closely the text of the earlier Decision.[61] The Protocol is yet to be implemented.

Will the Amendment Make a Difference?

Disappointingly, only 13 WTO Member States plus the European Union have formally accepted the amendment to date. These include the United States, Switzerland, India and the Philippines. And no developing or least-developed countries have come forward to take advantage of the 30 August Decision waiver or 6 December Amendment. This suggests that cross-boundary compulsory licensing procedures may still be too complex. It may also be the case that generic firms outside of India, which has only just introduced a product patent regime, may not be very interested in the rigmarole of negotiating with both domestic patent-owning firms and foreign governments *and* in such a public way. As for developing country governments, since the notification must be made, it is very possible that many of them fear trade retaliation, particularly from the United States, which is so hostile to 'breaking patents' when it is done abroad.

However, in July 2007, Rwanda informed the WTO of its intention to import some anti-AIDS medicines from Canada. Strictly speaking, as an LDC, Rwanda is not required to do this. In its submission to the TRIPS Council,[62] the Rwandan government indicated its desire to import '260,000 packs of TriAvir, a fixed-dose combination of Zidovudine, Lamivudine and Nevirapine manufactured in Canada by Apotex, Inc.'. As a combination of drugs, Apotex needs to agree terms with two companies to make TriAvir, Boehringer Ingelheim and GlaxoSmithKline. While both companies have expressed willingness to cooperate it remains to be seen how long it will take for a final agreement to be struck.[63] In other cases, companies will be much less forthcoming, especially for countries that are larger than Rwanda and have sufficient numbers of wealthy people to make it feasible to enter the market.

So far we do not have sufficient evidence to justify enthusiasm or pessimism about this 'solution'. But some scepticism is warranted for two reasons. The first is the low uptake so far. It would be useful to investigate the reasons for this. The second is that while the Amendment reflects a genuine attempt, albeit an imperfect one, to improve access, the intellectual property chapters of recent Free Trade Agreements seem to reflect a *deliberate* attempt to undermine anything that the international community can achieve multilaterally. That is an avoidable tragedy.

An Alternative to Patents? The Medical Research and Development Treaty[64]

In 2005, a coalition of NGOs, public heath experts, economists and legal scholars proposed a Medical Research and Development Treaty. The proposed Treaty would establish a new legal framework to promote research and development for pharmaceuticals and other medical treatments that functions as an *alternative* to patents and the alleged monopoly drug pricing patents engender. The Treaty's basic premise is that patent (and other intellectual property) protection restricts access to essential medicines, involves wasteful marketing exercises, and channels investment away from neglected diseases into more 'profitable' diseases offering more promising returns. As a means of implementing human rights, the Treaty is intriguingly focused on the economics of the entire operation: it proposes that relevant health-related goals be achieved by setting minimum financial obligations for qualifying research and development based upon each nation's gross domestic product. Such 'qualifying research projects' can be funded through a system of tradable credits.

NOTES

1. For a more detailed history of patenting in the life sciences, see Dutfield, G., *Intellectual Property Rights and the Life Science Industries: A Twentieth Century History*, Aldershot: Ashgate.
2. Kevles, D.J., 'Ananda Chakrabarty Wins a Patent: Biotechnology, Law, and Society, 1972–1980', *Historical Studies in the Physical and Biological Sciences*, 25(1), 111–135, 1994, at 111.
3. *Parke Davis and Co. v. H.K. Mulford and Co.*, 189 Fed. 95 (SDNY 1911), affirmed, 196 Fed. 496 (2nd Cir. 1912).
4. *Merck and Co., Inc. v. Chase Chemical Company et al.* (1967) USPQ 155, 152.
5. *In re Bergy – Application of Malcolm E. Bergy*, SPQ, 195, 344, 346, 1977.
6. 'DNA is Not "Life", but a Chemical Substance which Carries Genetic Information', *Howard Florey/Relaxin*, EPOR 1995, 541, at 551.
7. *J.E.M. Ag Supply, Inc. v. Pioneer Hi-Bred Int'l., Inc.*, 534 US 124 (2001).

8.   *Greenpeace v. Plant Genetic Systems NV* [1995] OJEPO 545.
9.   EPO Decision G 01/98 – http://www.european-patent-office.org/dg3/biblio/g980001ex1.htm.
10. Stokes, G., 'Patenting of Genetic Sequences: On the Up and Up', *IP Matters*, April 2001 (http://www.derwent.com/ipmatters/2001_01/genetics.html).
11. Mattick, J.S., 'The Hidden Genetic Program of Complex Organisms', *Scientific American*, 291(4), 30–7, 2004, at 32.
12. *Ibid.*, at 32–3.
13. Quoted in Gibbs, W.W., 'The Unseen Genome: Gems Among the Junk', *Scientific American*, 289(5), 26–33, 2003, at 29.
14. Some of the text is drawn from the following article: Dutfield, G. and U. Suthersanen, 'DNA Music: Intellectual Property and the Law of Unintended Consequences', *Science Studies*, 18(1), 5–29, 2005, at 21–3. See also Krimsky, S., 'Risk Assessment and Regulation of Bioengineered Food Products', *International Journal of Biotechnology*, 2(1/2/3), 231–8, 2000.
15. Heller, M.A. and R.S. Eisenberg, 'Can Patents Deter Innovation? The Anticommons in Biomedical Research', *Science*, 280: 698–701, 1998.
16. Paradise, J., L. Andrews and T. Holbrook, T., 'Patents on Human Genes: An Analysis of Scope and Claims', *Science*, 307, 1566–7, 2005.
17. See Montgomery, D., 'Human Gene Patent Plan Could Hit Tests to Cure Fatal Diseases', *The Scotsman*, 24 April 2001, 5; Anand, G., 'HIV Patent Holder is Slowing Spread of Fast AIDS Test', *Wall Street Journal Europe*, 20 December 2001, 1, 11.
18. Kleiner, K., 'Bad for your Health: Are Gene Patents Stopping Patients Getting the Latest Tests?', *New Scientist*, 23 March 2002, 6.
19. See Aldhous, P., 'Patent Battle Could Hold up Tests for Cancer Gene', *New Scientist*, 149, 8, 1996; Brown, P. and K. Kleiner, 'Patent Row Splits Breast Cancer Researchers', *New Scientist*, 143, 4, 1994; Ernhofer, K., 'Who Really Owns Your Genes?', *Christian Science Monitor*, 27 February 2003; Henley, J., 'Cancer Unit Fights US Gene Patent', *The Guardian*, 8 September 2001; Krimsky, S., *Science in the Private Interest: Has the Lure of Profits Corrupted Biomedical Research?* Lanham: Rowman & Littlefield, 2003, at 67–8; Meek, J., 'US Firm May Double Cost of UK Cancer Checks', *The Guardian*, 17 January 2000.
20. See Nuffield Council on Bioethics, 'The Ethics of Patenting DNA: A Discussion Paper', London: Nuffield Council on Bioethics, 2002, at 39–42.
21. National Academies of Science, Board on Science, Technology, and Economic Policy (STEP), and Committee on Science, Technology, and Law (STL), *Reaping the Benefits of Genomic and Proteomic Research: Intellectual Property Rights, Innovation, and Public Health*, Washington, DC: NAS, 2005; Howlett, M.J. and A.F. Christie, 'An Analysis of the Approach of the European, Japanese and United States Patent Offices to Patenting Partial DNA Sequences (ESTs)', University of Melbourne Faculty of Law Legal Studies Research Paper No. 82, 2004.
22. Merz J.F., A.G. Kriss, D.G. Leonard and M.K. Cho, 'Diagnostic Testing Fails the Test', *Nature*, 415(6872), 577–9, 2002.
23. Dutfield, *op. cit.*, at 168; Meek, *op. cit.*
24. Jaffe, S., 'Ongoing Battle over Transgenic Mice', *The Scientist*, 18(14), 46, 2004.
25. In the Patent Act, 'invention' is defined as 'any new and useful art, process, machine, manufacture or composition of matter, or any new and useful improvement in any art, process, machine, manufacture or composition of matter'.
26. Decision of the Examining Division dated 14 July 1989, OJEPO (1989) volume 12, pp 451–61.
27. In 2000, the contracting states agree to strike out the words 'publication or' from the Convention text, and this and other amendments agreed at the time have now entered into force.
28. Decision of Technical Board of Appeal 3.3.2 dated 3 October 1990. T 19/90 – 3.3.2 OJEPO 13, 476–91, 1990.
29. This is the updated version of the TBA's balancing test referred to earlier.
30. T 0315/03 – 3.3.8.

31. Jamison, D.T. *et al.*, 'Cost-effective Strategies for the Excess Burden of Disease in Developing Countries', in Jamison, D.T., J.G. Breman, A.R. Measham, G. Alleyne, M. Claeson, D.B. Evans, P. Jha, A. Mills and P. Musgrove (eds.), *Priorities in Health*, New York: World Bank and Oxford University Press, 2006, at 59.

32. Joint United Nations Programme on HIV/AIDS (UNAIDS), *2006 Report on the Global AIDS Epidemic*, Geneva, 2006, at 13.

33. 'Concerning access, patents are not the issue but the overwhelming poverty of individuals, absence of state healthcare financing, lack of medical personnel, transport and distribution infrastructure plus supply chain charges which can make affordable originator or generic products unaffordable. In many countries, medicines are unaffordable from whatever source, price or patent status.' Statement by Trevor Jones, former Director-General of the Association of the British Pharmaceutical Industry, as published in the annex to the World Health Organization report: 'Public Health, Innovation and Intellectual Property Rights. Report of the Commission on Intellectual Property Rights, Innovation and Public Health', 2006.

34. Weintraub, A., 'Are Pharmas Addicted to Lifestyle Drugs?' *BusinessWeek*, 15 June 2007; Gilbert, D., T. Walley and D. New, 'Lifestyle Medicines', *British Medical Journal*, 321, 1341–4, 2000.

35. See Médicins Sans Frontières (MSF) and Drugs for Neglected Diseases (DND) Working Group, 'Fatal Imbalance: The Crisis in Research and Development for Drugs for Neglected Diseases', Geneva: MSF and DND Working Group, 2001.

36. Orbinski, J., 'Health, Equity, and Trade: A Failure in Global Governance', in G.P. Sampson (ed.), *The Role of the World Trade Organization in Global Governance*, Tokyo: United Nations University, 2001, 230–1.

37. WHO, 'Investing in Health Research and Development: Report of the ad hoc Committee on Health Research Relating to Future Intervention Options', Geneva: WHO, 1996.

38. For two critical perspectives on this issue and the industry more generally, see Angell, M., *The Truth about the Drug Companies: How They Deceive Us and What to Do about It*, New York: Random House, 2004; Goozner, M., *The $800 Million Pill: The Truth Behind the Cost of New Drugs*, Berkeley, Los Angeles and London: University of California Press, 2004.

39. Payer, L., *Disease-Mongers: How Doctors, Drug Companies, and Insurers Are Making You Feel Sick*, New York: John Wiley, 1992. Moynihan, R. and D. Henry, 'The Fight against Disease Mongering: Generating Knowledge for Action', *PLoS Medicine*, 3(4), 2006. See also, Moynihan, R. and A. Cassels, *Selling Sickness: How the World's Biggest Pharmaceutical Companies are Turning us all into Patients*, Vancouver: Greystone Books, 2005.

40. Sell, S.K., *Private Power, Public Law: The Globalization of Intellectual Property Rights*, Cambridge, UK: Cambridge University Press, 2003.

41. Trebilcock, M.J. and R. Howse, *The Regulation of International Trade* (3rd ed.), London: Routledge, 2005, 430.

42. This is particularly well evidenced by the annual Special 301 Reports of the Office of the United States Trade Representative.

43. Drahos, P., 'Global Property Rights in Information: The Story of TRIPS at the GATT', *Prometheus*, 13(1), 6–19, 1995; Matthews, D., *Globalising Intellectual Property Rights: The TRIPS Agreement*, London: Routledge, 2002; Sell, *op cit*.

44. Dutfield, G., '"To Copy is to Steal": TRIPS, (Un)free Trade Agreements & the New Intellectual Property Fundamentalism', *Journal of Information Law & Technology*, 1, 2006.

45. It should be noted that the access to essential medicines issue implicates several other international human rights standards: the right to life, the right to the benefits of scientific progress, the rights to education, to work, and to an adequate standard of living. See UN Millennium Project Task Force on HIV/AIDS, Malaria, TB, and Access to Essential Medicines, Working Group on Access to Essential Medicines, *Prescription for Healthy Development: Increasing Access to Medicines*, London: Earthscan, 2005, at 33–4.

46. Bradsher, K., 'Bayer Agrees to Charge Government a Lower Price for Anthrax Medicine', *New York Times*, 25 October, 2001.

47. Correa, C.M., 'Protecting Test Data for Pharmaceutical and Agrochemical Products under

Free Trade Agreements', in P. Roffe, G. Tansey and D. Vivas-Eugui, *Negotiating Health: Intellectual Property and Access to Medicines*, London: Earthscan, 81–96, 2006, at 91.

48. According to a key World Bank publication of the time, 'while it may be a heavy dose of regulation, South Africa's law is probably consistent with TRIPS', The World Bank, *Global Economic Prospects and the Developing Countries 2002: Making Trade Work for the World's Poor*, Washington DC: The World Bank, 2001, 138.

49. But having made this point, drug companies can be very creative and aggressive in using legal means to prevent generic producers from entering the market even when the patents protecting the drug have expired. See Dutfield, G., *Intellectual Property Rights and the Life Science Industries: A Twentieth Century History*, Aldershot: Ashgate, 2003, 109–11.

50. UNCTAD-ICTSD, *Resource Book on TRIPS and Development*, Cambridge, UK: Cambridge University Press, 2005, at 531.

51. For more detailed explanations of the data protection-related problems with US-DR-CAFTA and other FTAs, see Abbott, F., 'The Doha Declaration on the TRIPS Agreement and Public Health and the Contradictory Trend in Bilateral and Regional Free Trade Agreements', Occasional Paper no. 14, Geneva: Quaker United Nations Office, 2004.

52. Curiously this clause is rarely discussed in debates on access to medicines. The reason may be that many developing countries have deficient competition regulations.

53. Scherer, F.M. and J. Watal, 'The Economics of TRIPS Option for Access to Medicines', in B. Granville (ed.) *The Economics of Essential Medicines*, London: Royal Institute of International Affairs, 32–56, 2002, at 37–8.

54. In November 2005, the TRIPS Council extended the deadline for LDCs to fully implementing TRIPS by a further seven and a half years to 1 July 2013.

55. This is known as 'international exhaustion'. It may be contrasted with 'national exhaustion' according to which rights are exhausted only in the case of first sale in that country. With national exhaustion regimes, parallel importation is not permitted.

56. See Article 28, TRIPS.

57. WTO, 'Implementation of Paragraph 6 of the Doha Declaration on the TRIPS Agreement and Public Health: Decision of 30 August 2003" [Document WT/L/540].

58. Paragraph 2(a).

59. Emphasis added.

60. Paragraph 6(i).

61. WTO, 'Amendment of the TRIPS Agreement: Decision of 6 December 2005' [Document WT/L/641].

62. WTO, 'Notification under Paragraph 2(A) of the Decision of 30 August 2003 on the Implementation of Paragraph 6 of the Doha Declaration on the TRIPS Agreement and Public Health', 2007 [Document IP/N/9/RWA/1].

63. See South Centre and CIEL, 'Rwanda and Canada: Leading the Implementation of the August 2003 Decision for Import/Export of Pharmaceuticals Produced Under Compulsory License', *Intellectual Property Quarterly Update*, 3rd Quarter, 1–9, 2007.

64. For the full background and text of the proposed treaty, see http://www.cptech.org/working-drafts/rndtreaty.html.

14. Traditional knowledge: an emerging right?[1]

WHY IT SHOULD (OR SHOULD NOT) BE PROTECTED

The Role of Knowledge in Traditional Societies

It is common to say that while the modern economy is knowledge-based, earlier and present-day traditional societies are purely resource-based. But it is not that simple. Knowledge, technology and resources are the basis of all economies including those of traditional societies. Traditional knowledge provides the underpinning for successful ways of subsisting in what are often hostile natural environments. Indeed, there is growing recognition that traditional knowledge, technologies and cultural expressions are not just old, obsolete and maladaptive; they can be highly evolutionary, adaptive, creative and even novel. Moreover, as a body of knowledge, customs, beliefs and cultural works and expressions handed down from generation to generation, tradition forms the 'glue' that strengthens social cohesiveness and cultural identity.

Few if any human societies are totally isolated or self-sufficient in all respects. People in traditional societies not only consume knowledge-based and other goods that are produced locally, whether by themselves or their neighbours; they give them, receive them, share them, own them and *exchange* them with others including from different societies.

Benefiting from trade depends not only on the availability of legal rights that are enforceable beyond the locality, but also on the ability of traditional communities to take advantage of national and international law including property and access rights relating to land, natural resources and intellectual property. It also depends on specific capacity-building measures to address problems of lack of information and production and marketing weaknesses. Indeed, capacity building is absolutely vital.

Traditional proprietary systems relating to scarce tangibles such as land, resources and goods, and to valuable intangibles like certain knowledge and cultural expressions, are often highly complex and varied. Generalisations should be made with extreme caution. However, it appears frequently to be the case that knowledge and resources are communally held. While individuals and families may hold lands, resources or knowledge for their own use, ownership is often subject to customary law and practice and based on the collective consent of the community.

Nonetheless, the idea that traditional property rights are always collective or communal in nature while Western notions of property are inherently individualist is an inaccurate cliché. While this may appear to contradict what we have just stated, specialised knowledge may be held exclusively by males, females, certain lineage groups, or ritual or society specialists (such as shamans) to which they have rights of varying levels of exclusivity. But in many cases, this does not necessarily give that group the right to privatise what may be more widely considered to be the communal heritage.

In short, customary laws regulating access and use of local knowledge, resources, cultural products and locally produced manufactured goods do exist. But what can be done when these spread beyond the control of the local administrative or juridical institutions, either through trade or misappropriation, and are commercialised without the consent of the providing communities or any benefits flowing back to them? Probably very little, at least in the present situation. This problem is what an international traditional knowledge regime should be able to respond to.

Justifying Traditional Knowledge Protection and the Need for Consensus and Clear Objectives

Why legally protect traditional knowledge? Many advocates of traditional knowledge protection will consider this to be hardly worth asking. But it is far from self-evident that just because some traditional knowledge has commercial value in the local and wider economy, it should therefore be protected. A popular view is that traditional knowledge should be protected because pharmaceutical corporations and bioprospectors are misappropriating it and making huge profits. It follows that if corporate 'biopiracy' were not taking place on a sufficient scale to require a legal response, there would be no reason to protect traditional knowledge at all. But if it turns out that corporate copying of traditional knowledge is less common than commonly believed, should we simply abandon efforts to give legal expression to the demands and concerns of traditional knowledge holders and their communities relating to extra-community use of their knowledge?

In fact, there are various other reasons to protect traditional knowledge than that corporations find it worthwhile to copy it and yet rarely have to compensate the knowledge holders. This chapter reviews various justifications for protecting traditional knowledge and finds that there are several plausible reasons to do so. Those countries which seek legal solutions to the lack of traditional knowledge protection should ideally seek a consensus on what the objective or objectives should be. The same applies to national legal protection. Without clear objectives, laws and policies to protect traditional knowledge are unlikely to be effective. There are various plausible reasons to protect traditional knowledge. The text that follows covers some of the most contentious of these.

To improve the lives of traditional knowledge holders and communities

Great as its wider economic potential may be, traditional knowledge is valuable first and foremost to indigenous and local communities that depend on traditional knowledge for their health, livelihoods and general well-being. Thus, a traditional knowledge regime that encouraged the conservation and continued use of traditional knowledge relating to health and food production could potentially improve the lives of millions of people.

According to the World Health Organization, up to 80 per cent of the world's population depends on traditional medicine for its primary health needs.[2] While the high cost of pharmaceuticals is a factor in this, for many ailments traditional medicine is preferred, even by many urban populations.

Traditional low-input agricultural systems, based on extensive and applied knowledge about natural processes and local ecosystems, have successfully enabled millions of people to subsist for thousands of years in some of the most hostile environments. However, many traditional knowledge-based agricultural systems have fallen into decline. This situation does not necessarily mean that people are abandoning them because they are obsolete. Factors in this decline include the spread of market economies, commercialisation of agriculture with the introduction of export crops and Green Revolution technologies, all-too-prevalent assumptions that Western techniques and methods such as high-input monocultural agriculture are superior to local ones like intercropping, and the imposition of inappropriate laws and regulations by governments. The results are likely to be increasing impoverishment rather than the opposite.

Despite this, the original agricultural systems are intact in many parts of the world and continue to be the basis of much innovation. For example, in some parts of the world farming communities continue effectively to manage agricultural genetic diversity, experiment on-farm with traditional *and modern* crop varieties and to produce their own varieties whose performance may be better than those provided by extension services.[3]

To benefit national economies

Some traditional medicines are used as inputs in biomedical research, suggesting that they may constitute a source of income not just as drugs in themselves but as the sources of chemical substances forming the basis of new pharmaceuticals. Indeed, traditional communities have already been responsible for the discovery, development and preservation of a tremendous range of medicinal plants, health-giving herbal formulations, agricultural and forest products, and handicrafts that are traded internationally and generate considerable economic value – but not for those communities. However, policies that enable traditional communities and provider countries to capture more of the value while at the same time encouraging commercially oriented natural product research are generally lacking.

Traditional knowledge is also used as an input into modern industries such as pharmaceuticals, botanical medicines, cosmetics and toiletries, agriculture and biological pesticides. In most cases, firms based in developed countries that can harness advanced scientific, technological and marketing capabilities capture virtually all the value added. This situation needs to be addressed so that traditional knowledge holders, their communities and developing countries can capture much more value. However, one should not overestimate the industrial demand for *in situ* genetic resources and associated traditional knowledge. While enhanced abilities to screen huge quantities of natural products and analyse and manipulate their DNA structures might suggest that bioprospecting will become more popular, it seems more likely that advances in biotechnology and new drug discovery approaches will, in the long term, reduce industrial interest in natural product research for food, agriculture and health, as well as associated traditional knowledge.[4]

If we just consider pharmaceuticals, while many companies invest in natural product research, such an approach competes with others such as combinatorial chemistry, rational drug design, genomics,[5] proteomics[6] and RNA interference[7] that many in the industry consider to be more promising.[8] Moreover, many of these firms maintain large 'compound libraries' and often see no reason to prospect for more compounds. Nevertheless, as long as it remains extremely difficult for therapeutic molecules to be designed and manufactured from scratch without using existing chemical structures as initial leads, many firms will continue to screen natural compounds. Even the new combinatorial chemistry techniques need to work on existing lead structures, which will originate from natural or mineral sources, to generate the large compound libraries firms use in their screening programmes.[9] So, combinatorial chemistry does not necessarily conflict with natural product research. Even so, interest in genetic resources does not necessarily indicate interest in traditional knowledge. Many firms claim to have no interest at all in traditional knowledge.

Although his research focuses mainly on India, Gupta's list of technological fields, in which traditional societies can be highly innovative and contribute substantially to local and national economies, is surely of wider relevance. These fields are as follows: (i) crop protection; (ii) crop production; (iii) animal husbandry; (iv) grain storage; (v) pisciculture: (vi) poultry; (vii) leather industry; (viii) soil and water conservation; (ix) forest conservation; (x) farm implements; (xi) organic farming; (xii) local varieties of seeds; (xiii) informal institutions (common property resources); and (xiv) ecological indicators.[10]

In 1999 the Indian government established a National Innovation Foundation. The NIF's goals are as follows:[11]

1. to help India become an inventive and creative society and a global leader in sustainable technologies;
2. to ensure evolution and diffusion of green grassroots innovations in a time-bound and mission-oriented manner;
3. to support scouting, spawning, sustaining and scaling up of grassroots green innovations and link innovation, enterprises and investments;
4. to strengthen research and development linkages between excellence in formal and informal knowledge systems and create a knowledge network;
5. to promote wider social awareness and possible commercial and non-commercial applications of innovations.

No other government has made such a significant official commitment to harnessing traditional technologies for sustainable development. Given that many traditional societies are rich sources of innovation in the above-mentioned technological fields among others, India's initiative merits investigation by policy-makers and development agencies elsewhere in the world.

In short, it seems that protecting traditional knowledge has the potential to improve the performance of many developing-country economies by enabling greater commercial use of their biological wealth and increasing exports of traditional knowledge-related products. At the same time, it is important not to overestimate traditional knowledge's economic potential.

So far we have neglected traditional cultural expressions in the discussion. In fact, traditional cultural expressions may be very promising sources of wealth not just for communities but also for national economies. For example, trade in handicrafts is substantial. According to Fowler, 'artisan handicrafts represent an estimated US$30 billion world market. In addition, handicraft production and sales represent a substantial percentage of gross domestic product (GDP) for some countries'.[12]

However, continued production and further development of traditional handicrafts and artworks are threatened sometimes by the disappearance of traditional skills. Another serious problem is copying and mass production by outsiders, who thereby deprive artisans of a source of income. Copyright infringement tends to be a major problem. And even where copyright legislation is in place, collection and distribution of royalties amongst the key parties (that is, composers, performers, publishers and the recording companies) is difficult without an efficient, transparent and *fully* accountable collective management structure that seeks primarily to benefit local musicians rather than international ones.[13] Indeed, while a weak copyright system may on balance benefit some nations by decreasing the rate of imported intellectual property goods in certain areas such as software and educational products, such a policy may also undermine those industries which a developing nation may wish to nurture. The local music industries in Mali and South Africa have complained that they suffer heavily from losses and damages due to copyright infringement.[14]

To prevent 'biopiracy'

The vast majority of countries formally recognise that cross-border exchange of genetic resources and traditional knowledge should be carried out in compliance with the principles of the Convention on Biological Diversity (CBD). For a number of reasons, intellectual property rights, particularly patents but also plant variety protection, have become central to discussions on this matter. These reasons relate to the following:

1. the conviction – widely held among developing countries and NGOs – that biodiversity and associated traditional knowledge have tremendous economic potential;
2. the fact that patent claims in various countries may incorporate biological and genetic material including life forms within their scope;
3. the belief, also shared by developing countries and NGOs, that this feature of the patent system enables corporations to misappropriate genetic resources and associated traditional knowledge or at least to unfairly free-ride on them;[15]
4. the ability of modern intellectual property law to protection the innovations produced by industries based mainly in the developed world and its *in*ability to protect adequately those in which the developing countries are relatively well-endowed;
5. the perception that as a consequence of reasons 2–4, the unequal distributions and concentrations of patent ownership and the unequal share of benefits obtained from industrial use of biogenetic resources are closely related.

'Biopiracy' has emerged as a term to describe the ways that corporations from the developed world free-ride on the genetic resources and traditional knowledge and technologies of the developing countries. While these and other corporations complain about 'intellectual piracy' perpetrated by people in developing countries, the latter group of nations counters that their biological, scientific and cultural assets are being 'pirated' by these same businesses. Intellectual piracy is a political term, and as such is inaccurate and deliberately so. The assumption behind it is that the copying and selling of pharmaceuticals, music CDs and films anywhere in the world is intellectual piracy irrespective of whether the works in question had patent or copyright protection under domestic laws. After all, if drugs cannot be patented in a certain country, copying them by local companies for the domestic market and/or overseas markets where the drugs in question are also not patented is hardly piracy in the legal sense of the word.

Similarly, biopiracy is an imprecise term, and there are good reasons to keep it so, at least in the international arena. But such 'strategic vagueness' is not a helpful approach for those working on legal solutions in such forms as national laws, regulations or international conventions.

Let us start by elucidating, as far as we can, the actual meaning of the word. To start with the obvious, 'biopiracy' is a compound word consisting of 'bio', which is short for 'biological', and 'piracy'. According to the *Concise Oxford Dictionary*, 'piracy' means the following: (1) the practice or an act of robbery of ships at sea; (2) a similar practice or act in other forms, especially hijacking; and (3) the infringement of copyright.

Apart from the use of 'piracy' for rhetorical effect, the word does not seem to be applicable to the kinds of act referred to as biopiracy. But let us now turn to the verb 'to pirate'. The two definitions given are: (1) appropriate or reproduce (the work or ideas etc. of another) without permission for one's own benefit; and (2) plunder.

These definitions seem to be more appropriate since inherent in the biopiracy rhetoric are misappropriation and theft. In essence, 'biopirates' are those individuals and companies accused of one or both of the following acts: (i) the misappropriation of genetic resources and/or traditional knowledge through the patent system; and (ii) the unauthorised collection for commercial ends of genetic resources and/or traditional knowledge. But since biopiracy is not just a matter of law but is also one of morality and of fairness, we need to acknowledge that where the line should be drawn between an act of biopiracy and a legitimate practice may not always be easy to draw. The difficulty in drawing the line is compounded by the vagueness in the way the term is applied.

To illustrate this point, a wide range of acts listed below have been considered as acts of biopiracy of traditional knowledge.

Collection and use:

- the unauthorised use of common traditional knowledge;
- the unauthorised use of traditional knowledge only found among one indigenous group;
- the unauthorised use of traditional knowledge acquired by deception or failure to fully disclosure the commercial motive behind the acquisition;

- the unauthorised use of traditional knowledge acquired on the basis of a transaction deemed to be exploitative;
- the unauthorised use of traditional knowledge acquired on the basis of a conviction that all such transactions are inherently exploitative ('all bioprospecting is biopiracy');
- the commercial use of traditional knowledge on the basis of a literature search.

Patenting:

- the patent claims traditional knowledge in the form in which it was acquired;
- the patent covers a refinement of the traditional knowledge;
- patent covers an invention based on traditional knowledge *and* other modern/traditional knowledge.

It is by no means clear how much biopiracy actually goes on. Apart from lack of information, the answer depends on how one differentiates between legitimate and unfair exploitation. The distinction is not always obvious. The answer also depends on whether resources are considered to be wild and unowned or domesticated and owned. A common view among critics of conventional business practice is that most companies do not recognise that they may have a moral obligation to compensate communities providing genetic material for their intellectual contribution, *even when* such material is assumed to be 'wild'. Often genetic resources considered 'gifts of nature' are in fact the results of many generations of selective crop breeding and landscape management. Essentially the argument is that failing to recognise and compensate for the past and present intellectual contributions of traditional communities is a form of intellectual piracy.

The likely response from industry is that this is not piracy since the present generation may have done little to develop or conserve these resources. The argument might continue that this is, at worst, a policy failure, and that measures – outside the intellectual property system – could be put in place to ensure that traditional communities are rewarded.

As for the patent-related version of 'biopiracy', there is little doubt that companies are in an advantageous position in the sense that, while a useful characteristic of a plant or animal may be well-known to a traditional community, without being able to describe the phenomenon in the language of chemistry or molecular biology, the community cannot obtain a patent even if it could afford to do so.[16] While it is unlikely that a company could then obtain a patent simply by describing the mode of action or the active compound,[17] it could claim a synthetic version of the compound or even a purified extract. In the absence of a contract or specific regulation, the company would have no requirement to compensate the communities concerned.

The whole point of this discussion is not to deny the existence of biopiracy, but to show that the lack of clarity is becoming counterproductive. The problem with the 'biopiracy' rhetoric and the 'strategic vagueness' behind its usage is that if you cannot agree on what it is, you cannot measure it. Neither can you agree on what should be done about it. One extreme view is that all bioprospecting is biopiracy. If so, the answer is to ban access outright. If biopiracy is merely an irritation, then such a ban need not be enforced too rigorously, since legal enforcement of higher-stakes areas of the law would have to take priority. If biopiracy causes demonstrable economic or cultural harm, the country should invest in enforcing the ban. On the other hand, if the problem is that provider countries or communities are unable to negotiate beneficial agreements, the answer may be to improve the provision of legal and technical assistance. If the problem is that the patent system legitimises or encourages misappropriation, then we may need to improve the standards of examination, ban patents on life forms and natural, or even modified, compounds, or incorporate a disclosure of origin requirement. In sum, how you define biopiracy goes a long way towards determining what you should do about it.

Objections to Protecting Traditional Knowledge

Objections to traditional knowledge are not necessarily motivated by bad faith and deserve a considered response.[18] Three commonly expressed objections are as follows: first, that at a time when the public domain is threatened by ever more comprehensive intellectual property protection we should not be creating new rights or extending existing ones that will further accelerate the enclosure of the public domain. The second is that biopiracy claims are exaggerated or even mythical. Since biopiracy is therefore not a genuine threat to traditional knowledge holders and their communities, there is no need for a traditional knowledge protection regime. Third, if commercial users have to pay to access or use knowledge that has hitherto been freely available they will simply not use it and no benefits will be generated to be shared with the traditional knowledge holders and their communities.

Traditional knowledge and the public domain

To some critics, the creation of a traditional knowledge regime would represent the removal from the public domain of a very large body of practical knowledge about the biosphere including solutions to health, agricultural and environmental problems affecting many people. Since the existence of a large public domain is good for everybody such removal, it is argued, would be a bad thing. Undoubtedly, some of the more extreme claims for traditional knowledge protection to some extent justify this concern. But one may counter such a view on the following three grounds.

(i) Traditional knowledge holders and communities have their own regimes to regulate access and use of knowledge   Many traditional societies have their own custom-based 'intellectual property' systems, which are sometimes quite complex. Customary rules governing access to and use of knowledge do not necessarily differ all that widely from Western intellectual property formulations, but in the vast majority of cases they almost certainly do. Nonetheless, there is a tendency to treat such rules with disrespect or to ignore them as if they do not exist. However, knowledge thought to be part of the public domain may in some cases turn out under customary law to remain subject to the legal claims of individuals and communities. Even if one disregards customary law, the unauthorised dissemination or use of certain publicly available traditional knowledge could sometimes be challenged on the basis of concepts existing in the Western legal system, such as copyright, breach of confidence and misappropriation. Accordingly and in consequence, nothing is being taken from the public domain that should be there, but only what should not be.

(ii) Recognising existing rights, not creating new ones   Demands for traditional knowledge protection are not necessarily seeking the creation of new rights but the wider recognition and enforceability of those which already exist, basically those custom-based knowledge regulatory regimes referred to above. Accordingly, a traditional knowledge protection regime would merely translate and codify existing rights, thereby making them enforceable in national courts and possibly across international borders as well. In this sense, traditional knowledge protection would neither add to nor subtract from the public domain, but would merely help to clarify what is and what is not in it.

(iii) Not everything in the public domain should be in the public domain   The public domain is being promoted in opposition to privatisation as part of a debate about intellectual property rights, a discussion that does not easily accommodate the specific interests and claims of non-Western societies. Why is this the case? Disclosed traditional knowledge has from the distant past to the present been treated as belonging to nobody. Consequently, many indigenous peoples' representatives are concerned that pro-public domain rhetoric, sympathetic as many of them are about the sentiments behind it, may inadvertently threaten their rights. Indeed, the public domain concept is problematic from the perspective of many traditional societies in which traditional knowledge holders or others, such as tribal elders, have permanent responsibilities concerning the use of such knowledge, irrespective of whether it is

secret, is known to just a few people, or is known to thousands of people throughout the world.[19] Custodianship responsibilities do not necessarily cease to exist just because the knowledge has been placed in the so-called public domain. There is no doubt that a tremendous amount of traditional knowledge has been disclosed and disseminated over the years without the authorisation of the holders.

'There's no such thing as biopiracy . . .'

Despite the emotional tone of the debate, as shown above, 'biopiracy' is used in various ways. To some extent this invites cynicism. If we cannot agree on what biopiracy is, and if so much of the evidence put forward to justify concern is anecdotal in nature, it is hardly surprising that some people have countered that fears over biopiracy are exaggerated. Whether they are right to do so or not, it should be beyond debate that more reliable and accurate information is necessary, and terminology should be better defined if we really want to achieve practical and effective solutions. Fortunately, several countries have taken the initiative of documenting cases of biopiracy and presenting them for debate in international forums. Perhaps the most notable initiative is that of Peru, which has established a National Anti-Biopiracy Commission and whose work has been reported on at the WIPO IGC.[20]

Nonetheless, one should make clear that if there is such thing as intellectual property piracy then there is certainly such a thing as biopiracy. If unauthorised access, use, ownership claiming and commercialisation of traditional knowledge conflicts with the customary laws of the source communities, then biopiracy is occurring as far as those communities are concerned whether or not 'biopiracy' is the word the communities themselves would use to describe such acts. And if genetic resources are being accessed, used, 'owned' and commercialised in ways that conflict with international law, particularly the CBD, and the laws of provider countries, then we should be able to accept that this is biopiracy too.

The disincentive effect

Industry commonly expresses the view that ethno-bioprospecting, and natural product research more generally, are scientifically and commercially unproven drug discovery strategies in the present era however effective they may been in the past. While nature used, before the emergence of synthetic chemistry, to provide all of the drugs on the market and traditional knowledge much of the inspiration, most pharmaceutical companies purport to have little if any interest in the 'jungle pharmacy'. If they have to comply with complex traditional knowledge protection regimes and benefit-sharing, their scepticism about traditional knowledge and bioprospecting could well increase further and alternative drug discovery strategies may look even more promising. Again, evidence for such admittedly plausible assertions is lacking, and we should certainly not accept them as given. Indeed, the statistical evidence produced so far to support such a view is not at all credible, making it hard to know whether concerns are genuine or are groundless scaremongering.[21]

TRADITIONAL KNOWLEDGE AND INTERNATIONAL DIPLOMACY: THE CURRENT STATE OF PLAY

The Convention on Biological Diversity

The Convention on Biological Diversity (CBD), which entered into force in 1993,[22] has as its three objectives 'the conservation of biological diversity, the sustainable use of its components and the fair and equitable sharing of the benefits arising out of the utilization of genetic resources'. As should be well known to many readers of this chapter, Article 8(j) requires parties to

> respect, preserve and maintain knowledge, innovations and practices of indigenous and local communities embodying traditional lifestyles relevant for the conservation and sustainable use of biological diversity and promote their wider application with the approval and involvement of the holders of such knowledge, innovations and practices and encourage the equitable sharing of the benefits arising from the utilization of such knowledge, innovations and practices.

The international negotiations on the CBD that deal with legal solutions to traditional knowledge protection have considered, *inter alia*, the following: (i) national and international *sui generis* regimes; (ii) legally and non-legally binding instruments and agreements including contracts, guidelines and codes of conduct; (iii) specific protection measures such as traditional knowledge databases and disclosure of origin of genetic resources and associated traditional knowledge in patent applications; (iv) principles such as prior informed consent and respect for customary law; and (v) the incorporation of traditional knowledge protection provisions in the International Regime on Access and Benefit Sharing that is currently being negotiated (see below).

To review implementation of the CBD, the Conference of the Parties meets biannually. Intellectual property rights are most frequently discussed in deliberations on such topics as access to genetic resources, benefit-sharing, and the knowledge innovations and practices of indigenous and local communities.

At the Sixth Meeting of the Conference of the Parties (COP-6), which took place in The Hague in 2002, the Bonn Guidelines on Access to Genetic Resources and Fair and Equitable Sharing of the Benefits Arising out of their Utilization were officially adopted.[23] The Guidelines, which are intended to be used when developing and drafting legislative, administrative or policy measures on access and benefit-sharing and contracts, have a number of provisions relating to intellectual property. Parties with genetic resource users under their jurisdiction are invited to consider adopting 'measures to encourage the disclosure of the country of origin of the genetic resources and of the origin of traditional knowledge, innovations and practices of indigenous and local communities in applications for intellectual property rights'.[24] As means to implement the CBD provision that benefit-sharing be upon mutually agreed terms, two elements to be considered as guiding parameters in contracts and as basic requirements for mutually agreed terms are (i) that 'provision for the use of intellectual property rights include joint research, obligation to implement rights on inventions obtained and to provide licences by common consent', and (ii) 'the possibility of joint ownership of intellectual property rights according to the degree of contribution'.[25] COP Decision VI/24, to which the Bonn Guidelines were annexed, also called for further information gathering and analysis regarding several matters including:

- role of customary laws and practices in relation to the protection of genetic resources and traditional knowledge, innovations and practices, and their relationship with intellectual property rights;
- efficacy of country of origin and prior informed consent disclosures in assisting the examination of intellectual property rights application and the re-examination of intellectual property rights granted;
- feasibility of an internationally recognized certification of origin system as evidence of prior informed consent and mutually agreed terms;
- role of oral evidence of prior art in the examination, granting and maintenance of intellectual property rights.

In addition, the Decision invited WIPO, which as we will see is actively engaged in these same issues,

to prepare a technical study, and to report its findings to the Conference of the Parties at its seventh meeting, on methods consistent with obligations in treaties administered by the World Intellectual Property Organization for requiring the disclosure within patent applications of, *inter alia*:

(a) Genetic resources utilized in the development of the claimed inventions;
(b) The country of origin of genetic resources utilized in the claimed inventions;
(c) Associated traditional knowledge, innovations and practices utilized in the development of the claimed inventions;
(d) The source of associated traditional knowledge, innovations and practices; and
(e) Evidence of prior informed consent.

Since then, a subsequent COP Decision (VII/7) requested WIPO and UNCTAD to analyse issues relating to the implementation of disclosure or origin. Specifically, these issues were as follows:

- options for model provisions on proposed disclosure requirements;
- practical options for intellectual property application procedures with regard to the triggers of disclosure requirements;
- options for incentive measures for applicants;
- identification of the implications for the functioning of disclosure requirements in various WIPO-administered treaties; and
- intellectual property-related issues raised by proposed international certificates of origin/source/legal provenance.

Both WIPO[26] and UNCTAD[27] have subsequently produced substantial documents on disclosure of origin.

In a separate COP-6 Decision on Article 8 (j) and related provisions, the COP invited

> Parties and Governments, with the approval and involvement of indigenous and local communities representatives, to develop and implement strategies to protect traditional knowledge, innovations and practices based on a combination of appropriate approaches, respecting customary laws and practices, including the use of existing intellectual property mechanisms, *sui generis* systems, customary law, the use of contractual arrangements, registers of traditional knowledge, and guidelines and codes of practice.

It also requested 'the Ad Hoc Open-ended Inter-Sessional Working Group on Article 8(j) and Related Provisions of the Convention on Biological Diversity[28] to address the issue of *sui generis* systems for the protection of traditional knowledge'.

The Seventh Meeting of the COP (COP-7), which took place in Kuala Lumpur in 2004, adopted Decision VII/16 on 'Article 8(j) and Related Provisions'. Section H of the Decision was on the development of elements of *sui generis* systems for the protection of traditional knowledge, innovations and practices. Drawing on the work of the Working Group on Article 8(j), its annex offered the following list of potential elements.

1. Statement of purpose, objectives and scope.
2. Clarity with regard to ownership of traditional knowledge associated with biological and genetic resources.
3. Set of relevant definitions.
4. Recognition of elements of customary law relevant to the conservation and sustainable use of biological diversity with respect to: (i) customary rights in indigenous/traditional/local knowledge; (ii) customary rights regarding biological resources; and (iii) customary procedures governing access to and consent to use traditional knowledge, biological and genetic resources.
5. A process and set of requirements governing prior informed consent, mutually agreed terms and equitable sharing of benefits with respect to traditional knowledge, innovations and practices associated with genetic resources and relevant for the conservation and sustainable use of biological diversity.

6. Rights of traditional knowledge holders and conditions for the grant of rights.
7. The rights conferred.
8. A system for the registration of indigenous/local knowledge/Systems for the protection and preservation of indigenous/local knowledge.
9. The competent authority to manage relevant procedural/administrative matters with regard to the protection of traditional knowledge and benefit-sharing arrangements.
10. Provisions regarding enforcement and remedies.
11. Relationship to other laws, including international law.
12. Extra-territorial protections.

Activities relating to traditional knowledge are being carried out not just by the Working Group on Article 8(j) and Related Provisions (hereafter '8(j) Working Group'), but also by the Working Group on Access and Benefit Sharing (hereafter 'ABS Working Group'), most importantly in the context of the International Regime on Access to Genetic Resources and Benefit Sharing. Agreement that there should be such a regime was reached at the 2002 World Summit on Sustainable Development, specifically 'to negotiate within the framework of the Convention on Biological Diversity, bearing in mind the Bonn Guidelines, an international regime to promote and safeguard the fair and equitable sharing of benefits arising out of the utilization of genetic resources'. The International Regime is currently under negotiation and the Conference of the Parties is the body mandated by the United Nations General Assembly to be the principal forum to develop the regime. As indicated in COP-7 Decision VII/19 Section D, a number of elements the Working Group on Access and Benefit Sharing is required to consider are relevant to traditional knowledge protection:

(x) Measures to ensure compliance with prior informed consent of indigenous and local communities holding traditional knowledge associated with genetic resources, in accordance with Article 8(j).

(xiv) Disclosure of origin/source/legal provenance of genetic resources and associated traditional knowledge in applications for intellectual property rights.

(xv) Recognition and protection of the rights of indigenous and local communities over their traditional knowledge associated to genetic resources subject to the national legislation of the countries where these communities are located.

(xvi) Customary law and traditional cultural practices of indigenous and local communities.

(xviii) Code of ethics/code of conduct/models of prior informed consent or other instruments in order to ensure fair and equitable sharing of benefits with indigenous and local communities.

At COP-8, which took place in March 2006, two relevant decisions were adopted, Decision VIII/4 on Access and Benefit Sharing, and Decision VIII/5 on Article 8(j) and Related Provisions. Decision VIII/4 requested the ABS Working Group 'to continue the elaboration and negotiation of the international regime' and instructed it 'to complete its work at the earliest possible time before the tenth meeting of the Conference of the Parties'. COP-10 is likely to take place in 2010. This is somewhat later than many countries had been demanding.

Decision VIII/5 contains a sub-section titled 'Development of elements of *sui generis* systems for the protection of the knowledge, innovations and practices of indigenous and local communities'. Among other provisions, the subsection

> Urges Parties and Governments to develop, adopt and/or recognize national and local *sui generis* models for the protection of traditional knowledge, innovations and practices with the full and effective participation of indigenous and local communities;
> Urges Parties and Governments to report on these initiatives to adopt local and national *sui generis* models and to share experiences through the clearing-house mechanism;
> Invites Parties and Governments with transboundary distribution of some biological and genetic resources and associated traditional knowledge to consider the establishment of regional *sui generis* frameworks for the protection of traditional knowledge, innovations and practices, as appropriate, with the full and effective participation of indigenous and local communities;
> Requests the Executive Secretary to continue gathering and analysing information, in consultation with Parties, Governments, indigenous and local communities, to further develop as a priority issue, the possible elements listed in the annex to decision VII/16 H for consideration by the Ad Hoc Open-ended Inter-Sessional Working Group on Article 8(j) and Related Provisions at its fifth meeting, and further requests the Working Group on 8(j) to identify priority elements of *sui generis* systems;

The World Intellectual Property Organization

At the 25th Session of WIPO's General Assembly in 2000, the decision was taken to establish an Intergovernmental Committee on Intellectual Property and Genetic Resources, Traditional Knowledge and Folklore (IGC). In the early years, most of the IGC's work on traditional knowledge and on folklore (nowadays referred to more often as traditional cultural expressions) concentrated on defensive protection. More specifically, the Committee has been considering ways to improve the availability to patent examiners of traditional knowledge and of publications describing traditional knowledge. In addition, much discussion has covered disclosure of origin of genetic resources and/or related traditional knowledge in patent applications, as at the CBD COP meetings and the WTO.

However, positive protection is increasingly being discussed in a substantive manner. The first shift in this direction came at the third session of the IGC in June 2002, for which WIPO prepared a paper called 'Elements of a *Sui Generis* System for the Protection of Traditional Knowledge'.[29] It was given further impetus in Autumn 2003 when the WIPO General Assembly decided that the IGC's new work would focus particularly on the international dimension of the relevant issues and agreed that 'no outcome of its work is excluded, including the possible development of an international instrument or instruments'.

The IGC has drafted two sets of provisions: the Provisions for the Protection of Traditional Knowledge,[30] and the Provisions for the Protection of Traditional Cultural Expressions.[31] Both of these were presented first at the eighth session of the IGC and were further deliberated on at the ninth session, and could conceivably form the basis for international legal instruments. Unsurprisingly perhaps, both sets of draft Provisions are controversial. The ultimate outcome could be one or two treaties but that would presumably come several years down the road. Nonetheless, despite the efforts of countries that would like to see meaningful results, there still remains a strong possibility that these texts and the processes which are pushing them forward will run into the sands of stalemate and recriminations.

For several developed countries, there is little for them to gain economically from a legal regime on traditional knowledge or traditional cultural expressions. Consequently, they are not interested in participating positively in negotiations targeted at such an outcome even if they agree that the IGC continue to exist. There are exceptions to this general observation. Some European countries that wish to maintain good relations with developing country governments are willing to go much further than, say, the United States. On the other, some developing countries are becoming rather negative about the IGC. They suspect two things. First, that they can never get the international treaty on traditional knowledge that they seek through the IGC. Second, that the Committee's very existence serves as a justification for developed country opponents to actively keep the subjects of traditional knowledge and access and benefit-sharing out of negotiations on intellectual property at the WTO and other WIPO forums using the argument that these are matters exclusively for the IGC to deal with.

As for traditional knowledge holders and their representatives, they have serious concerns that WIPO's mandate to promote intellectual property conflicts with their wish to roll back intellectual property regimes they find intrusive, and that the intellectual property focus of discussion on traditional knowledge, inevitable perhaps for such an organisation, is too constraining since it reduces a highly complex issue to the technicalities of the formal intellectual property rights of patents, copyright, trade marks, trade secrets and geographical indications.

The World Trade Organization

TRIPS is silent on traditional knowledge. Nonetheless, discussions on traditional knowledge have come up, mostly at the TRIPS Council. These initially took place in the context of the review of implementation of Article 27(b). The 2001 launching of the Doha Development Agenda has made traditional knowledge and folklore as well as the relationship between TRIPS and the CBD integral to the TRIPS Council's work.

Specifically, at the fourth meeting of the WTO Ministerial Conference which took place in Doha in November 2001, a Ministerial Declaration was adopted according to which the WTO member states instructed

> the Council for TRIPS, in pursuing its work programme including under the review of Article 27.3(b), the review of the implementation of the TRIPS Agreement under Article 71.1 and the work foreseen pursuant to paragraph 12 of this Declaration, to examine, *inter alia*, the relationship between the TRIPS Agreement and the Convention on Biological Diversity, the protection of traditional knowledge and folklore, and other relevant new developments raised by Members pursuant to Article 71.1. In undertaking this work, the TRIPS Council shall be guided by the objectives and principles set out in Articles 7 and 8 of the TRIPS Agreement and shall take fully into account the development dimension.

As a contribution to this examination, Brazil, China, Cuba, Dominican Republic, Ecuador, India, Pakistan, Thailand, Venezuela, Zambia and Zimbabwe jointly submitted a paper to the Council for TRIPS in June 2002.[32] The paper, noting the relevant provisions of the Bonn Guidelines, proposed that TRIPS be amended to provide that WTO member states must require

> that an applicant for a patent relating to biological materials or to traditional knowledge shall provide, as a condition to acquiring patent rights: (i) disclosure of the source and country of origin of the biological resource and of the traditional knowledge used in the invention; (ii) evidence of prior informed consent through approval of authorities under the relevant national regimes; and (iii) evidence of fair and equitable benefit sharing under the national regime of the country of origin.

As at the CBD COP and at WIPO, disclosure of origin has been debated at some length, and several follow-up proposals have been tabled.[33] The most recent of these, in May 2006 was submitted by Brazil, Pakistan, Peru, Thailand and Tanzania.[34] Annexed to this document is text that would form an additional section of TRIPS, namely Article 29*bis* ('Disclosure of Origin of Biological Resources and/or Associated Traditional Knowledge'). The most substantial part is paragraph 2, which states as follows:

> Where the subject matter of a patent application concerns, is derived from or developed with biological resources and/or associated traditional knowledge, Members

shall require applicants to disclose the country providing the resources and/or associated traditional knowledge, from whom in the providing country they were obtained, and, as known after reasonable inquiry, the country of origin. Members shall also require that applicants provide information including evidence of compliance with the applicable legal requirements in the providing country for prior informed consent for access and fair and equitable benefit-sharing arising from the commercial or other utilization of such resources and/or associated traditional knowledge.

The WTO may not be the most appropriate venue for establishing new norms on positive traditional knowledge protection that would require the insertion of additional text in the TRIPS Agreement or the possible deletion of existing text. A modest amendment aimed at improving access to medicines involved a considerable amount of effort and it is hard to imagine the achievement of the more substantial revisions that positive traditional knowledge protection would entail. However, this is not to suggest that disclosure of origin need not be discussed at the WTO. Indeed, the TRIPS Council has a clear mandate to do so and, compared to positive traditional knowledge protection, the measures required are comparatively uncomplicated.

FROM THEORY TO PRACTICE IN LEGAL PROTECTION OF TRADITIONAL KNOWLEDGE

Possible Approaches to Traditional Knowledge Protection

Solutions to the protection of traditional knowledge in intellectual property law are being sought in the forms of 'positive protection' and 'defensive protection'. Positive protection refers to the acquisition by the traditional knowledge holders themselves of an intellectual property right such as a patent or an alternative right provided in a *sui generis* system. Defensive protection refers to provisions adopted in the law or by the regulatory authorities to prevent intellectual property right claims to knowledge, a cultural expression or a product being granted to unauthorised persons or organisations. It is important to mention here that positive protection measures may also serve to provide defensive protection and vice versa. The distinction between the two, then, is not always clear-cut.

To many countries, non-governmental organisations and others, defensive protection is necessary because the intellectual property system, and especially patents, is considered defective in certain ways and allows companies to unfairly exploit traditional knowledge. It may also be true that defensive protection may be more achievable than positive protection. This is because some of the most commonly discussed defensive protection measures are basically enhancements to or modifications of existing intellectual property rights. Effective positive protection is likely to require a completely new system whose development will require the very active and committed participation of many governments.

Positive protection

Property rights and liability rules   Entitlement theory and experience to date both suggest that extant legal systems for protecting knowledge and intellectual works tend to operate as either property regimes, liability regimes, or as combined systems containing elements of both. Perhaps a consideration of these is a good way to start.

What is the difference between property and liability regimes? A property regime vests exclusive rights in owners, of which the right to refuse, authorise and determine conditions for access to the property in question is the most fundamental. For these rights to mean anything, it must of course be possible for holders to enforce them.

A liability regime is a 'use now pay later' system according to which use is allowed without the authorisation of the rights holders. But it is not free access because ex post compensation is still required. A *sui generis* system based on such a principle has certain advantages in countries where much of the traditional knowledge is already in wide circulation but may still be subject to the claims of the original holders. Asserting a property right over knowledge is insufficient to prevent abuses when so much traditional knowledge has fallen into the public domain and can no longer be controlled by the original traditional knowledge holders. A pragmatic response is to allow the use of such knowledge but to require that its original producers or providers be compensated.[35] Interestingly, this approach has been adopted by Peru through a law passed in 2002, known as the Regime of Protection of the Collective Knowledge of Indigenous Peoples. In the case of use of public domain traditional knowledge, an indigenous group may be entitled to compensation from outside parties in the form of 0.5 per cent of the value of sales of any product developed from the knowledge. The money is paid into the Fund for the Development of Indigenous Peoples.

There are different ways the compensation payments could be handled. The government could determine the rights by law. Alternatively, a private collective management institution could be established, which would monitor use of traditional knowledge, issue licences to users, and distribute fees to right holders in proportion to the extent to which their knowledge was used by others. They could also collect and distribute royalties where commercial applications are developed by users and the licences require such benefits to go back to the holders. Such organisations exist in many countries for the benefit of musicians, performers and artists. Alternatively, in jurisdictions where traditional knowledge holders are prepared to place their trust in a state or government-created competent authority to perform the same function, a public institution could be created instead.

While such organisations have the potential to reduce transaction and enforcement costs, considerations of economic efficiency should not be the only criteria for designing an effective and appropriate *sui generis* system. Traditional knowledge holders and communities will be its principal users and beneficiaries. They will not endorse a system that fails to accommodate their world views and customs but rather imposes other norms with which they feel uncomfortable and wish to avoid. Clearly, traditional knowledge holders and communities must be partners in the development of a *sui generis* system lest it become an inappropriate and unworkable system.

Those who would oppose a liability regime may object on the ground that we should not have to pay for public domain knowledge. One may counter this view by observing that 'the public domain' is an alien concept to many indigenous groups. Just because an ethnobiologist described a community's use of a medicinal plant in an academic journal without asking permission, this does not mean that the community has abandoned its property rights in that knowledge or its interest in ensuring that the knowledge be used in a culturally appropriate manner. Seen this way, a liability regime should not be considered an alternative to a property regime but as a means to ensure that traditional knowledge holders and communities can exercise their property rights more effectively.

Whichever approach is selected – and a combination of both is probably essential – the question arises of whether rights must be claimed through registration, or whether the rights should exist in law irrespective of whether they are filed with a government agency. It seems only fair that the rights should exist regardless of whether they are declared to the government, and that these rights should not be exhausted by publication unless the holders have agreed to renounce their claims. Yet, protection and enforcement would probably become more effective with registration, and knowledge transactions would become much easier to conduct if claims over traditional knowledge were registered. Consequently, the *sui generis* system should encourage the registration of right claims but not make this a legal requirement for protection.

Finally, it must be cautioned that devising the most sophisticated and elaborate system is useless if the potential users and beneficiaries remain unaware of its existence or have more immediate concerns, such as extreme poverty, deprivation and societal breakdown caused by the insufficient recognition of their basic rights. It will also fail if it does not take their world views and customary norms into account.

A customary law-based regime?   Traditional societies may be governed by a set of formal or informal juridical and administrative institutions such as councils of the elders, spiritual leaders, chiefs, courts, and widely accepted and enforced customary norms including those relating to property rights. Indeed, according to the Four Directions Council, a Canadian indigenous peoples' organisation: 'Indigenous peoples possess their own locally-specific systems of jurisprudence with respect to the classification of different types of knowledge, proper procedures for acquiring and sharing knowledge, and the rights and responsibilities which attach to possessing knowledge, all of which are embedded uniquely in each culture and its language'.[36]

In traditional societies customs are often of major importance in regulating social and economic behaviour. Customs are established modes of behaviour within a cultural community that may have the force of law. Customary norms and rules exist in all cultures, although not all cultural communities have dedicated judicial institutions to enforce them and to resolve disputes.

How is customary law different from state law? First, generally speaking customary laws are unwritten while state law is codified or at least is founded upon a tradition of documented case law augmented by statutes. Second, for many traditional societies, customary law is not a subject for legal specialists; nor is it at all divorced from people's everyday lives. On the contrary, a customary law system may be regarded as 'a living law, a law activated and modified not by specialised practitioners but by those who in their daily lives, practice the law, living out their traditional customs in everyday contacts – and occasional confrontation with neighbours, rivals, partners, relatives'.[37] Third, customary laws tend to be unwritten.

In some countries there has been much discussion concerning recognition and the question of whether or not customary law should be codified. Whether or not to codify customary law is a genuine dilemma. It can be argued that codifying customary laws will freeze them in time and prevent them from evolving. On the other hand, integrating them into the national legal system may require in-depth understanding and analyses that only codification would make possible. Nonetheless, recognition of customary law need not require codification. Moreover, stipulating precise definitions is not desirable unless strictly necessary. After all, few patent laws provide a definition of 'invention'.

While it is important to be pragmatic, traditional communities in their dealings with industry normally have to accept that Western legal forms and instruments including patents and contracts are the basic rules of the game. Traditional knowledge holders and communities are understandably concerned that one type of intellectual property system is being universalised and prioritised to the exclusion of all others, including their counterpart customary systems. This does not seem fair. After all, if indigenous peoples in WTO member states are required to accept the existence of patents that they are economically prevented from availing themselves of and contracts that they cannot realistically enforce in the courts, why should their own knowledge-related customary regimes including property rules not be respected by others?

Securing the protection of traditional knowledge, technologies and resources according to the local regulations requires the existence of effective local governance structures and customary law, including property regimes, and respect for these structures and regimes from outsiders. This is easiest to achieve in countries where customary law systems can operate with relative freedom and where rights are enforceable. In such cases, the possibility arises for traditional rules and norms to be asserted with as much (or as little) legal effect within that country as, say, patent rights, trade marks and copyrights. But whether customary laws regulating cultural, intellectual and physical property are fully incorporated into national legal systems, are enforceable in local courts alone, or are just given some minimal recognition at the state level, the common assumption that traditional knowledge and resources are by definition part of the public domain becomes much more open to challenge than if customary law has no recognition at all. This is extremely important since so much of what traditional knowledge holders apparently want to protect is considered to be in the public domain.

Defensive Protection

A misappropriation regime?
Carlos Correa initially proposed a misappropriation regime. According to his proposal:

> National laws would be free to determine the means to prevent it, including criminal and civil remedies (such as an obligation to stop using the relevant knowledge or to pay compensation for such use) . . . as well as how to empower communities for the exercise and enforcement of their rights.[38]

He recommended that, in view of the lack of experience to date in developing such a regime, a step-by-step approach may be necessary. In the first instance, such a regime should contain three elements: documentation of traditional knowledge, proof of origin or materials, and prior informed consent.

Correa refers to two United Nations documents that implicitly support his proposal. The first of these is Decision V/16 of the CBD's Conference of the Parties, which states

> Request[ed] Parties to support the development of registers of traditional knowledge, innovations and practices of indigenous and local communities embodying traditional lifestyles relevant for the conservation and sustainable use of biological diversity through participatory programmes and consultations with indigenous and

local communities, taking into account strengthening legislation, customary practices and traditional systems of resource management, such as the protection of
traditional knowledge against unauthorized use.[39]

The second is the 'Principles and Guidelines for the Protection of the Heritage
of Indigenous Peoples', which were elaborated in 1995 by Erica-Irene Daes,
then Special Rapporteur of the UN Sub-Commission on Prevention of
Discrimination and Protection of Minorities.[40] Paragraphs 26 and 27 state the
following:

> National laws should deny to any person or corporation the right to obtain patent,
> copyright or other legal protection for any element of indigenous peoples' heritage
> without adequate documentation of the free and informed consent of the traditional
> owners to an arrangement for the sharing of ownership, control, use and benefits.
> National laws should ensure the labelling and correct attribution of indigenous
> peoples' artistic, literary and cultural works whenever they are offered for public
> display or sale. Attribution should be in the form of a trademark or an appellation
> of origin, authorized by the peoples or communities concerned.

The WIPO IGC's draft Provisions for the Protection of Traditional Knowledge
contains an article on protection against misappropriation.[41] It states as
follows:

ARTICLE 1

PROTECTION AGAINST MISAPPROPRIATION

1. Traditional knowledge shall be protected against misappropriation.
2. Any acquisition, appropriation or utilization of traditional knowledge by unfair
or illicit means constitutes an act of misappropriation. Misappropriation may also
include deriving commercial benefit from the acquisition, appropriation or utilization of traditional knowledge when the person using that knowledge knows, or is
negligent in failing to know, that it was acquired or appropriated by unfair means;
and other commercial activities contrary to honest practices that gain inequitable
benefit from traditional knowledge.
3. In particular, legal means should be provided to prevent:
    (i) acquisition of traditional knowledge by theft, bribery, coercion, fraud, tres-
pass, breach or inducement of breach of contract, breach or inducement of breach
of confidence or confidentiality, breach of fiduciary obligations or other relations of
trust, deception, misrepresentation, the provision of misleading information when
obtaining prior informed consent for access to traditional knowledge, or other unfair
or dishonest means;
    (ii) acquisition of traditional knowledge or exercising control over it in violation
of legal measures that require prior informed consent as a condition of access to the
knowledge, and use of traditional knowledge that violates terms that were mutually
agreed as a condition of prior informed consent concerning access to that knowledge;

(iii) false claims or assertions of ownership or control over traditional knowledge, including acquiring, claiming or asserting intellectual property rights over traditional knowledge-related subject matter when those intellectual property rights are not validly held in the light of that traditional knowledge and any conditions relating to its access;

(iv) if traditional knowledge has been accessed, commercial or industrial use of traditional knowledge without just and appropriate compensation to the recognized holders of the knowledge, when such use has gainful intent and confers a technological or commercial advantage on its user, and when compensation would be consistent with fairness and equity in relation to the holders of the knowledge in view of the circumstances in which the user acquired the knowledge; and

(v) wilful offensive use of traditional knowledge of particular moral or spiritual value to its holders by third parties outside the customary context, when such use clearly constitutes a mutilation, distortion or derogatory modification of that knowledge and is contrary to ordre public or morality.

4. Traditional knowledge holders should also be effectively protected against other acts of unfair competition, including acts specified in Article 10bis of the Paris Convention. This includes false or misleading representations that a product or service is produced or provided with the involvement or endorsement of traditional knowledge holders, or that the commercial exploitation of products or services benefits holders of traditional knowledge. It also includes acts of such a nature as to create confusion with a product or service of traditional knowledge holders; and false allegations in the course of trade which discredit the products or services of traditional knowledge holders.

5. The application, interpretation and enforcement of protection against misappropriation of traditional knowledge, including determination of equitable sharing and distribution of benefits, should be guided, as far as possible and appropriate, by respect for the customary practices, norms, laws and understandings of the holder of the knowledge, including the spiritual, sacred or ceremonial characteristics of the traditional origin of the knowledge.

Paragraph 1 of the following article states that:

1. The protection of traditional knowledge against misappropriation may be implemented through a range of legal measures, including: a special law on traditional knowledge; laws on intellectual property, including laws governing unfair competition and unjust enrichment; the law of contracts; the law of civil liability, including torts and liability for compensation; criminal law; laws concerning the interests of indigenous peoples; fisheries laws and environmental laws; regimes governing access and benefit-sharing; or any other law or any combination of those laws. This paragraph is subject to Article 11(1).[42]

Arguably, such a misappropriation regime could and probably should incorporate: (1) the concept of unfair competition; (2) moral rights; and (3) cultural rights. Unfair competition would deal with situations in which traditional knowledge holders engaged in commercial activities pertaining, for example, to know-how, medicinal plants, artworks or handicrafts, had their trade affected by certain unfair commercial practices committed by others.

According to Article 10*bis* of the Paris Convention for the Protection of Intellectual Property, the following acts are prohibited on the grounds of constituting unfair competition:

> 1. all acts of such a nature as to create confusion by any means whatever with the establishment, the goods, or the industrial or commercial activities, of a competitor;
> 2. false allegations in the course of trade of such a nature as to discredit the establishment, the goods, or the industrial or commercial activities, of a competitor;
> 3. indications or allegations the use of which in the course of trade is liable to mislead the public as to the nature, the manufacturing process, the characteristics, the suitability for their purpose, or the quantity, of the goods.

The TRIPS Agreement incorporates the substantive provisions of the Paris Convention by reference and explicitly mentions Article 10*bis* in the sections dealing with geographical indications and undisclosed information.[43] Specifically, WTO members must provide legal means to prevent any use of geographical indications that would constitute unfair competition. Also, members must ensure effective protection against unfair competition with respect to undisclosed information.

Norway is proposing that Article 10*bis* be used as the model for an international misappropriation regime that would go beyond just unfair competition. Accordingly, further discussion on such a regime could start off on the following bases:[44]

> 1. The members of the Paris Union for the Protection of Industrial Property and the World Intellectual Property Organization should assure nationals of member countries adequate and effective protection against misappropriation and unfair use of Traditional Knowledge (TK)
> 2. Any use of TK against honest practices in cultural, industrial or commercial matters should be considered as actions in breach of paragraph one.
> 3. TK holders should in particular be provided with effective means to ensure that:
>   (i) the principle of prior informed consent applies to access to TK, benefits arising from certain uses of TK are fair and equitably shared,
>   (ii) all acts of such a nature as to create confusion by any means whatever with the origin of the TK are repressed, and
>   (iii) all acts of such a nature that would be offensive for the holder of the TK are repressed.

Moral rights, as we have seen, are provided in Article 6*bis* of the Berne Convention. Moral rights usually consist of the right of authors to be identified as such (sometimes referred to as the right of paternity), and to object to having their works altered in ways that would prejudice their honour or reputation (the right of integrity).

It could be argued that free-riding on the knowledge, cultural works and expressions of traditional communities who are not themselves interested in commercialising them does no direct harm. Consequently, the doctrine of misappropriation does not apply to such acts. But is it really the case that there are no victims? One could reply that such behaviour infringes on certain cultural rights that these communities are entitled to enjoy. Prott identified a set of individual and collective rights that could be described as 'cultural rights', and which are supported to a greater or lesser extent by international law.[45] Of these, the following (of which only the first is an individual right) stand out in light of the present discussion:

- the right to protection of artistic, literary and scientific works;
- the right to develop a culture;
- the right to respect of cultural identity;
- the right of minority peoples to respect for identity, traditions, language and cultural heritage;
- the right of a people to its own artistic, historical, and cultural wealth;
- the right of a people not to have an alien culture imposed on it.

To the extent that unauthorised or improper use of a cultural group's artefacts and expressions imbued with cultural, spiritual or aesthetic value erodes the integrity of the culture of origin, it is reasonable to treat such uses as manifestations of a form of misappropriation that the law should arguably provide remedies for.

NOTES

1. Some of this text was published earlier in the following paper: Dutfield, G., 'Protecting Traditional Knowledge: Pathways to the Future', International Centre for Trade and Sustainable Development, Issue Paper 16, 2006.
2. WHO, IUCN and WWF, *Guidelines for Conservation of Medicinal Plants*, Gland: IUCN, 1993.
3. For example, Richards, P., 'Casting Seeds to the Four Winds: A Modest Proposal for Plant Genetic Diversity Management', in Posey, D.A. (ed.) *Cultural and Spiritual Values of Biodiversity*, Nairobi and London: UNEP and IT Publications, 1999, 315–16.
4. UNCTAD, 'Systems and National Experiences for Protecting Traditional Knowledge, Innovations and Practices. Background Note by the UNCTAD Secretariat', 2000.
5. Genomics refers to the mapping, sequencing and analysis of the full set of genes (that is, the genome) of different organisms or species. The human genome has always been the most interesting for governments and foundations, as well as for companies seeking to identify commercial applications.
6. The proteome is the 'protein complement encoded by a genome'. Ezzell, C., 'Proteins Rule', *Scientific American*, 286(4), 26–33, 2002, at 28.
7. RNA (ribonucleic acid) interference ('RNAi'), or 'gene silencing', is a method of disrupting the body's production of proteins associated with diseases and is considered to be quite promising.
8. Dutfield, G., *Intellectual Property, Biogenetic Resources and Traditional Knowledge*, London: Earthscan Publications, 2004.

9. ten Kate, K. and S.A. Laird, *The Commercial Use of Biodiversity: Access to Genetic Resources and Benefit Sharing*, London: Earthscan, 1995, at 50, 57.

10. Gupta, A.K., 'Making Indian Agriculture More Knowledge Intensive and Competitive: The case of Intellectual Property Rights', *Indian Journal of Agricultural Economics*, 54(3), 342–69, 1999.

11. http://www.nifindia.org.

12. Fowler, B.J., 'Preventing Counterfeit Craft Designs', in J.M. Finger and P. Schuler (eds), *Poor People's Knowledge: Promoting Intellectual Property in Developing Countries*, Washington, DC: The World Bank, 113–31, 2004.

13. UNCTAD-ICTSD, *Intellectual Property Rights: Implications for Development*, Geneva: UNCTAD and ICTSD, 2003.

14. Business Day (Johannesburg), 21 November 2002; *Daily News* (Harare), 14 May 2003.

15. The distinction we seek to draw between misappropriation and unfair free-riding is that with misappropriation, there must be victims as well as beneficiaries for the word to apply. However free-riding is not necessarily harmful to anybody, and there is likely to be considerable disagreement about where to draw the line between fair and unfair free-riding.

16. It may be able to if it can describe a specific formulation, even in fairly non-technical terms.

17. In some circumstances this may be allowable under the US patent system.

18. See Chen, J., 'There's No Such Thing as Biopiracy . . . and It's a Good Thing Too'. *McGeorge Law Review*, 36, 2005.

19. See Posey, D.A., 'Selling Grandma: Commodification of the Sacred Through Intellectual Property Rights', in Barkan, E. and R. Bush (eds), *Claiming the Stones/Naming the Bones: Cultural Property and the Negotiation of National and Ethnic Identity*, Los Angeles, CA: Getty Research Institute, 2002.

20. Most recently see WIPO, 'Patent System and the Fight against Biopiracy: The Peruvian Experience. Document Submitted by Peru', 2005 [Document WIPO/GRTFK/IC/ 8/12].

21. Wolfe, T.A. and B. Zycher, *Biotechnological and Pharmaceutical Research and Development Investment under a Patent-based Access and Benefit Sharing Regime*, San Francisco, CA: Pacific Research Institute, 2005. http://www.pacificresearch.org/pub/sab/health/ 2005/ABS.pdf.

22. As of December 2007, the CBD has 190 contracting parties including the European Community.

23. In Secretariat of the Convention on Biological Diversity (2002), 'Report of the Sixth Meeting of the Conference of the Parties to the Convention on Biological Diversity' [UNEP/CBD/COP/6/20].

24. Para. 16(d)(ii).

25. Para. 43(c) and (d).

26. WIPO, 'Examination of issues regarding the interrelation of access to genetic resources and disclosure requirements in intellectual property rights applications', transmitted by the General Assembly of the World Intellectual Property Organization (WIPO) to the Conference of the Parties of the Convention on Biological Diversity by the decision of the General Assembly at its 32nd Session, 26 September to 5 October 2005. This third draft of the technical study is annexed to document WO/GA/32/8.

27. See Sarnoff, J.D. and C.M. Correa, *Analysis of Options for Implementing Disclosure of Origin Requirements in Intellectual Property Applications*, Geneva and New York: United Nations, 2006.

28. This body was established by the COP in 1998.

29. WIPO, 'Elements of a *Sui Generis* System for the Protection of Traditional Knowledge', 2002 [Document WIPO/GRTKF/IC/3/8]. An updated version was prepared for the following IGC Document WIPO/GRTKF/IC/4/8.

30. WIPO, 'Provisions for the Protection of Traditional Knowledge', as revised for the eighth session of the IGC. See annex to document WIPO/GRTKF/IC/8/5, 2005 and reproduced in annex to document WIPO/GRTKF/IC/9/5, 2006.

31. WIPO, 'Provisions for the Protection of Traditional Cultural Expressions', as revised for the eighth session of the IGC. See annex to document WIPO/GRTKF/IC/8/4, 2005 and reproduced in annex to document WIPO/GRTKF/IC/9/4, 2006.

32. WTO, 'The Relationship between the TRIPS Agreement and the Convention on Biological Diversity and the Protection of Traditional Knowledge', 2003. [Document No. IP/C/W/356].

33. These are summarised and listed in WTO, 'The Relationship between the TRIPS Agreement and the Convention on Biological Diversity: Summary of Issues Raised and Points Made. Note by the Secretariat. Revision', 2006 [Document IP/C/W/368/Rev.1]. Also, see http://www.iprsonline.org/submissions/article273.htm.

34. 'Doha Work Programme – the Outstanding Implementation Issue on the Relationship between the TRIPS Agreement and the Convention on Biological Diversity. Communication from Brazil, India, Pakistan, Peru, Thailand and Tanzania', 2006 [Document WT/GC/W/564].

35. For economic analysis and a detailed blueprint for applying a compensatory liability regime to applications of traditional knowledge, see Lewis, T. and J.H. Reichman, 'Using Liability Rules to Stimulate Local Innovation in Developing Countries', in K.E. Maskus and J.H. Reichman (eds), *International Public Goods and Transfer of Technology under a Globalized Intellectual Property Regime*, Cambridge, UK: Cambridge University Press, 2005.

36. Four Directions Council, 'Forests, Indigenous Peoples and Biodiversity. Contribution of the Four Directions Council to the Secretariat of the Convention on Biological Diversity', Lethbridge: FDC, 1996.

37. Sheleff, L., *The Future of Tradition: Customary Law, Common Law and Legal Pluralism*, London and Portland: Frank Cass, 1999.

38. Correa, C.M., 'Traditional Knowledge and Intellectual Property: Issues and Options Surrounding the Protection of Traditional Knowledge', Quaker United Nations Office Discussion Paper 18, 2001.

39. Convention on Biological Diversity – Conference of the Parties, Decision V/16, 2000.

40. United Nations Economic and Social Council, Commission on Human Rights, Sub-Commission on Prevention of Discrimination and Protection of Minorities, 'Principles and Guidelines for the Protection of the Heritage of Indigenous Peoples', 1995 [Document E/CN.4/Sub.2/1995/26, annex 1].

41. As revised for the eighth session of the IGC. See annex to document WIPO/GRTKF/IC/8/5, 2005.

42. 'Eligibility for protection of traditional knowledge against acts of misappropriation should not require any formalities'.

43. Articles 22.2(b), 39.1.

44. WIPO-IGC, 'Norway: Memorandum on Documents WIPO/GRTKF/IC/9/4 and WIPO/GRTKF/IC/9/5. Document Submitted by Norway', 2006, para. 38 [Document WIPO/GRTKF/IC/9/12].

45. Prott, L.V., 'Cultural Rights as Peoples' Rights in International Law', in J. Crawford (ed.), *The Rights of Peoples*, Oxford: Clarendon Press, 93–106, 1988.

Index